The Re-Evolution of
AMERICAN
STREET GANGS

The Re-Evolution of
AMERICAN STREET GANGS

Edited by

Dale L. June
National University-Los Angeles
Los Angeles, California, USA

Mohamad Khatibloo
ASTIS Consulting
Los Angeles, California, USA

Gregorio Estevane
ASTIS Consulting
Los Angeles, California, USA

CRC Press
Taylor & Francis Group
Boca Raton London New York

CRC Press is an imprint of the
Taylor & Francis Group, an **informa** business

CRC Press
Taylor & Francis Group
6000 Broken Sound Parkway NW, Suite 300
Boca Raton, FL 33487-2742

First issued in paperback 2020

© 2016 by Taylor & Francis Group, LLC
CRC Press is an imprint of Taylor & Francis Group, an Informa business

No claim to original U.S. Government works

ISBN-13: 978-1-4398-7151-5 (hbk)
ISBN-13: 978-0-367-59817-4 (pbk)

Visit the Taylor & Francis Web site at
http://www.taylorandfrancis.com

and the CRC Press Web site at
http://www.crcpress.com

Contents

Preface

DENNIS ALVARADO
Parole Agent, retired

Gangs

Organized crime and prison gangs are mentioned in numerous articles, books, and literature. They often are referred to in newspapers and television shows and movies. Quite often, prison gangs are glamorized and romanticized as symbols of defiance, anarchy, and desperation. More often than not, prison gangs serve a cultural norm for those who are within their ranks. However, prison gangs have a devastating effect on society, and there is no question that their activities are affecting communities throughout the United States. Prison gangs have increased their reach, recruiting members from neighborhood streets, and significant numbers of organized gangs are indoctrinating thousands of youths to participate in criminal enterprises on behalf of the gangs. Contemporary gangs have influenced culture, values, and mores of American society. Contemporary clothing, language, and physical characteristics and traits are often used by professional law enforcement investigators to identify and validate street gang affiliation and prison gang membership.

There has been evidence that organized gangs have infiltrated military organizations and have spread their philosophy and gang markings throughout the United States and the world, wherever American military personnel are deployed. Central American gangs have been actively involved in cartel activities, leading to numerous killings and human trafficking to support organized crime. The American appetite for illegal narcotics has contributed to organized crime, and, in developing countries like Mexico, cartels have extended a welcome to prison gangs to participate in criminal ventures within the confines of penal institutions.

The fundamental flaw of organized society with regard to a social contract is to maintain a degree of public safety. When a society fails to protect its people and places them at risk, the outcome produced is unforgivable.

Gangs work on the fundamental approach toward commonality, and their philosophical paintings support the notion that they are going against the grain, and, therefore, it's much easier for gang members to identify common denominators that reflect family relationships and organizational acceptance based on that commonality. Gang members see themselves as a unique entity within their community, having a privilege and a right to live as they will. They have a significant value system based on entitlement or pseudorespect manifestations. Their flawed sense of morality has contributed a sense of governance that is untenable. Gang members have no respect for life nor will they ever be able to organize themselves to overcome indifference, adversity, and morality.

The following is an introduction to the California Street Terrorism Enforcement and Prevention Act—California Penal Code Sections 186.20-186.33. Further definition of street gangs and prescribed penalties can be found in Appendix C.

> The Legislature hereby finds and declares that it is the right of every person, regardless of race, color, creed, religion, national origin, gender, gender identity, gender expression, age, sexual orientation, or handicap, to be secure and protected from fear, intimidation, and physical harm caused by the activities of violent groups and individuals.
>
> It is not the intent of this chapter to interfere with the exercise of the constitutionally protected rights of freedom of expression and association. The Legislature hereby recognizes the constitutional right of every citizen to harbor and express beliefs on any lawful subject whatsoever, to lawfully associate with others who share similar beliefs, to petition lawfully constituted authority for a redress of perceived grievances, and to participate in the electoral process.
>
> The Legislature, however, further finds that the State of California is in a state of crisis, which has been caused by violent street gangs whose members threaten, terrorize, and commit a multitude of crimes against the peaceful citizens of their neighborhoods. These activities, both individually and collectively, present a clear and present danger to public order and safety and are not constitutionally protected. The Legislature finds that there are nearly 600 criminal street gangs operating in California, and that the number of gang-related murders is increasing. The Legislature also finds that in Los Angeles County alone there were 328 gang-related murders in 1986, and that gang homicides in 1987 have increased 80 percent over 1986. It is the intent of the Legislature in enacting this chapter to seek the eradication of criminal activity by street gangs by focusing upon patterns of criminal gang activity and upon the organized nature of street gangs, which together, are the chief source of terror created by street gangs. The Legislature further finds that an effective means of punishing and deterring the criminal activities of street gangs is through forfeiture of the profits, proceeds, and instrumentalities acquired, accumulated, or used by street gangs.

Acknowledgments

The editors of this book wish to acknowledge the chapter contributors who so graciously took the time and made the effort to write essays and provide information about gangs that we hope will assist scholars, sociologists, and others who are heavily involved in studying and working with gangs. Some readers of this book may believe it was targeted toward criminal justice practitioners to help them gain a better perspective on the criminal problem of gangs; others may view it as a source for sociologists to grasp more meaningful understanding of subcultures of violence; and still others, out of mere curiosity, may find a viewpoint inspiring them to seek further information. If that is the result of our efforts, we wish to thank the readers for their interest.

The idea of the book originated with Dr. Gregorio Estavane and Dr. Mohamad Khatibloo during a criminal justice faculty "skull" session at the school where we all worked. There were several reasons we wanted to create this book; among them was a belief that a book should be informative (foremost reason), interesting, and entertaining. We are confident, with the support of the contributors, that all three goals have been met.

Through the good graces of Carolyn A. Spence, senior acquisitions editor at Taylor & Francis Group, we were allowed extra time to bring it all together. Thank you again, Carolyn. Extra considerations of appreciation go to Jennifer Ahringer, project coordinator and editorial project development, for all her help keeping this book on track to finally be published, and to Robin Lloyd-Starkes, project editor, for her eagle-eyed editing and for adding authenticity and expertise with her unique understanding of Los Angeles area street gangs.

A special thanks goes to the unnamed contributors who spoke freely about their life in gangs and living in a "gang neighborhood." There was no hesitation when they were asked to tell their respective stories. We would like to name and recognize them for their willingness to share their stories, but we also realize that could perhaps be a death sentence for them because their stories divulge damaging information about gang life.

An extra special thanks goes to Yozie Garcia, a criminal justice student, having talent as an artist, who quickly accepted the challenge of designing the cover for the book.

Dale June
Gregorio Estavane
Mohamad Khatibloo

The Editors

Dale L. June has been involved in criminal justice for his entire adult life. After a career in policing and government service, he became a private investigator and personal protection specialist. He has given protective services training to law enforcement officers and private and public corporations both domestically and internationally.

June earned a master's degree from George Washington University with a major in criminal justice. He served in the US Secret Service under Presidents Nixon, Ford, Carter, and Reagan. In 2001, he became a cofounder of Henley-Putnam University (Santa Clara, California) and remained with the university as a special consultant and adjunct instructor until 2010. In 2004, he was selected to travel to Jordan as part of a team to train the security personnel for the judges in the Saddam Hussein trial. The assignment, however, was canceled by the government a week prior to departure.

This is June's 10th book, with the most recent ones being *Introduction to Executive Protection*, 2nd ed. (2008); *Terrorism and Homeland Security: Perspectives, Thoughts and Opinions* (2011); *Protection, Security, and Safeguard: Practical Approaches and Perspectives*, 2nd ed. (2012); and *What They Didn't Teach at the Academy* (2013), all published by Taylor & Francis Group/CRC Press. He also has written articles about executive protection that have appeared in security magazines in Mexico, Germany, Great Britain, and New Zealand.

In addition to his law enforcement and personal protection career, June is a longtime criminal justice, history, sociology, and psychology teacher at the college and university levels. In 2005, he was honored by the US Martial Artists Association Hall of Fame and inducted as Martial Artist of the Year. He currently trains in Wing Chun Kung Fu. His martial arts experience (judo) began as an 18-year-old soldier at military police school in the sawdust pits of Fort Gordon, Georgia. His military service was with the 110th Military Police Platoon in Stuttgart, Germany. His police service was with the cities of Redding and Sacramento, California, prior to becoming a member of the US Secret Service.

He may be contacted at djune.4mrusss@gmail.com.

Gregorio "Greg" Estevane, PI/JD, is an adjunct criminal justice professor currently at DeVry–Sherman Oaks, California and Argosy–Los Angeles universities, teaching and researching in the areas of gangs and criminal investigations as a criminal justice professor. Estevane was the 2004 chair/ dean of the School of Criminal Justice at Westwood College (Los Angeles) for five years and built that department from 200 to 600 students, building an "all-star cast" staff of 15 adjunct professors including a sitting judge, FBI agent, former Secret Service agent, district attorney investigators, city gang prosecutors, probation officers, police, defense attorneys, and others. Estevane is a Los Angeles, San Bernardino, Riverside, and San Diego County Superior Court gang expert witness/investigator panel member. He is recognized as an "expert witness on gangs," being the court-appointed "gang expert" in more than 100 criminal cases while testifying as an expert witness in trials involving murder, gangs, and cartels. He is a current licensed private investigator (PI) with 33 years of field/street experience working with gang members. He also is on multiple superior court panel boards as a criminal defense investigator, working on thousands of murder, gang, cartel, and other high-level criminal trials throughout Southern California. Estevane's bachelor's degree is from the University of California at Riverside. His juris doctorate degree (JD) was earned at Thomas Jefferson School of Law in San Diego, California.

He may be contacted at: greg@astis4u.com or www.astis4u.com.

Mohamad A. Khatibloo, PhD, is a co-founder and vice president of operations for ASTIS Consulting, a Southern California–based private investigation and gangs expert witness and death penalty mitigation firm, having affiliates across the country and worldwide, specializing in investigative and expert testimony in gang typology and terrorism issues, and related traditional investigative cases.

Dr. Khatibloo holds a bachelor's degree and a master's degree in criminal justice from Chapman University (Orange, California) and completed his doctorate in criminal justice management from James Madison University and a second PhD in psychology, specializing in criminal and deviant behavior from the University of Hertfordshire/United Kingdom.

In addition, Dr. Khatibloo has an extensive background in education, having taught professionally for nearly 13 years in both in-the-classroom and online platforms for a number of colleges and universities across the United States and in the Middle East. He has consistently earned the top one percent of faculty course evaluations in classes taught, and maintains a strong and strict academic code of ethics and integrity. Dr. Khatibloo continues to serve on the board of a local nonprofit college specializing in educating underprivileged youths in security and criminal justice courses (Southwest Vocational College). He continues to serve as an evaluator on WASC (Western Association of School and Colleges) related colleges and university advisements. He also serves as an evaluator for (ACCST) and the

Accrediting Commission of Career Schools and Colleges (ACCSC) boards in relation to US colleges and universities.

Dr. Khatibloo has extensive training in emergency management, mental health, and forensic investigations through the National Institute of Justice, as well as counterterrorism training through the Naval Postgraduate School and US Department of Homeland Security. He also has training in fraud prevention through the Association of Fraud Examiners (ACFE), and Professional Certified Investigator (PCI) status through the American Society of Industrial Security (ASIS).

He was a major contributor to *Homeland Security and Terrorism* (CRC Press, 2010). He also has publishing credits with law enforcement and Islam (CRC Press, 2013), and a new text proposal on the effects of the War on Terror in Afghanistan. Dr. Khatibloo also has publishing credits with Azad University in Tehran, Iran, on the topics of criminology and deviant behavior.

He has extensive experience in criminal justice course development with a growing number of colleges and universities. To date, Dr. Khatibloo has developed complete criminal justice course curriculum for three colleges and has contributed to curricula for five more colleges and universities. He also has cocreated a clinical program that aligns government agencies, insurance companies, law firms, US military, and others, to provide job training with the purpose of job placement for college students.

Dr Khatibloo is a codeveloper of Cross Training American Muslim Communities & Law Enforcement seminars to aid law enforcement in gaining better understanding of the various cultural groups within the Southern California region. He regularly provides seminars and training on this topic to many legal and law enforcement firms and agencies in the Southern California area, including the Los Angeles Bar Association, Riverside Public Defenders, and the Chicano Correctional Workers Association, to name a few. He continues to proudly serve as a member of the local police chiefs' roundtable on Muslim affairs.

Dr. Khatibloo is also the cofounder and executive director of a local non-profit called the Probation Education Project. He is aligning members of law enforcement, probation, and juvenile courts to promote a revolutionary education program for juveniles to help reduce the rates of recidivism.

Outside of academia, Dr. Khatibloo has more than 20 years of experience in business and corporate settings and management, private security and investigations, insurance, and operations.

He may be contacted at mohamadk@astis4u.com.

Contributors

Dennis Alvarado
Los Angeles County Parole Officer (Retired)
Los Angeles, California

Jeffrey Bledsoe
National University
Los Angeles, California

Ken Davis
Graffiti and Gangs Specialist (Retired)
Yonkers Police Department
Yonkers, New York

"Johnnie" (Last Name Withheld Due to Employment Restrictions)
Profession (Classified)
Location (Classified)

Aaron Kipnis
Private Practice Psychologist
Topanga, California

Michael S. Oden
(Formerly) Los Angeles County Probation
Department
Los Angeles, California

Robert Taylor
Los Angeles County Probation Department
Los Angeles, California

Michael Tuimavave
National University
Oceanside, California

Introduction

DALE L. JUNE

It was nearly 9:30 on a Sunday night. I was sitting in my living room working on the computer; my wife and young son were sitting on the floor watching television. Suddenly, several shots (with the telltale sound of an AK-47 assault rifle) rang out—pop! pop! pop! The shooting stopped, the sounds of running and shouting were heard, followed by the screeching of tires as a car quickly sped away.

I dialed 911 for the police while looking out my bedroom window to see if I could get a description of the car. At the same time, I saw a police car in hot pursuit (the police car was on the next block over and witnessed the car speeding away). I opened my front door to see if I could assist any possible victim. To my surprise, the top of a person's skull was lying on my doorstep. A dead young boy was in the street near the sidewalk. Later, I learned the boy was a 16-year-old recent immigrant from Mexico walking to the bus stop from his job at a nearby fast food restaurant.

The police pursued the shooter's car to a large shopping mall approximately three miles away, where the car came to a halt. As the police officers exited their car, the shooters in the suspect's car jumped out, shooting. One officer (the father of a 5-year-old boy) was killed. The suspects then jumped into their car and sped away, but were finally stopped near the airport and were arrested.

My apartment building and the entire crime scene were cordoned off, and officers began the all-night job of interviewing residents of the apartments and scouring the crime scene. They found an AK-47 in the parking lot of the grade school next door. The apartment building had been hit by 17 bullets; my own apartment was struck three times, with one bullet stopping just inside the paint of my son's bedroom.

A few months later, I was called to testify in court about the events of that night. I believed that was the end of the story. One day, a year or two after, I was relating the story in my university criminal justice class. After class, one girl came to me and said, "The shooter was my cousin." She then went on to tell the "rest of the story."

"My cousin and his friend (both gang members) were sitting around drinking when one of them said, 'Let's go for a ride.' This meant they were going to do a drive-by. They drove around until they saw the boy and began shooting for no reason. He wasn't even a gang member. My cousin is spending the rest of his life in prison."

One of my top students was a 20-year-old widow with two children. One day she and her family were stopped at a traffic light when suddenly two people ran up to the driver's side door of her car and opened fire, killing her husband, a rival gang member.

Several years ago, I was retained by a criminal defense attorney in San Diego to conduct an investigation for his clients, teenage members of a gang in Long Beach, California, charged with murder in a drive-by shooting of a 15-year-old girl at a beach in San Diego.

The victim and her friends had skipped school in Long Beach that day to party at the San Diego beach. Late in the afternoon, as they were in the parking lot preparing to leave, a car loaded with four teenage boys suddenly started moving toward them and shots were fired. The girl's boyfriend pushed her onto the back seat floor area of his car and jumped in on top of her, shielding her body with his.

The shooter's car sped away and it appeared no one had been hit. As the young people exited their cars and regrouped, they discovered that the girl had been shot in the head and was dead. A bullet had gone through the trunk and the back seat, hitting the girl.

The police gave me an opportunity to view all the evidence in the case. When they showed me the girl's blood-soaked clothing, this became one of the most difficult moments in my law enforcement and private investigative career. The victim was the same age as my second daughter, and the clothing she wore that day was similar to what my daughter wore—the same white tennis shoes, the blue jeans, the blue and white print shirt. It took a lot of self-control to hide my feelings at that moment, because I saw my daughter as the victim in that instant.

I conducted my investigation as nonpartisan as any other case and wrote my report. When I handed it to the defense attorney, I told him, "There is no way these guys can get off; the police did a good job and the evidence is irrefutable. You better work a plea bargain if you can, but I hope they fry the bastards!"

The average age of a gang member ranges from 12 to 25 (within the normal age demographics of crime in general). Such impulsive acts are indicative of the possibility that "gangsters" don't consider consequences of their act or respect the finality of death. Most likely, they never consider the possibility they will be arrested and prosecuted, spending the rest of their lives in prison, never having a chance for normal lives with wives and children, or, if they already have children, never seeing them except through unbreakable glass and steel bars. They also will be depriving their parents from ever enjoying grandchildren if they have no children when they go to prison (perhaps on death row). Perhaps, gang members are unaware or don't care about the wide ripple of victims they create when engaged in a serious gang-related crime, such as "drive-by homicide." Even in street gang drive-by killings,

Victims of a Crime

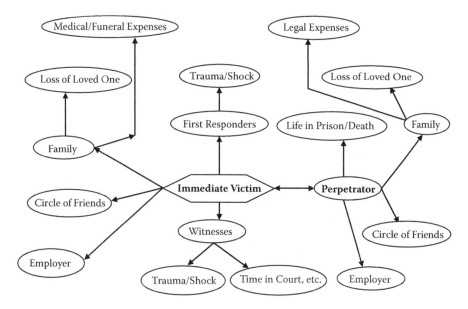

Figure I.1 Model victims of a crime.

there are always more victims than the immediate victim. Victims include the families of both the perpetrator and immediate victim, everyone in their circle of friends and relatives, witnesses, and first responders. The ripple or "butterfly" effect is in full play. The model in Figure I.1 is used to illustrate the point that there is no one single victim of a crime.

One young gang member with "slick black hair and tattoos on his neck and arms, once bragged to a parole supervisor that he aspired to land on death row for his allegiance to his gang."[1] That is exactly what he received at his sentencing after his conviction for killing a nongang-affiliated, young high-school star athlete for coincidently wearing a shirt of the color of a rival gang. The convicted killer, now 22, was 19 at the time he killed his victim, who was shot once, then again, up close in the head, execution style. Families of both the killer and the victim appeared in tears at the sentencing. One family asked for the maximum death penalty; the other asked for mercy.

The problem of gangs and gang subculture as a growing threat to the stability of neighborhoods and entire communities is seen as a major concern to American society (and, to a lesser extent, internationally). Sociologists, law enforcement, neighborhood leaders, and many community-oriented organizations have dissected, analyzed, and discussed gangs as serious crime problems, often the No. 1 local concern of a city. No university course in criminal justice would be complete without a study of gangs and the gang relationship to crimes ranging from gang graffiti splashed on walls to drug distribution to extortion and homicide (most often consummated by the reality of a drive-by shooting). Gangs often exemplify aspects of terrorism if terrorism includes holding entire neighborhoods in fear for their safety for wearing the "wrong" color, for walking in another "gang's territory," for not paying a "street tax," or "insurance" that their business won't be robbed, burglarized, or destroyed.

Guns and Gangs

Blood, guts, gore, hair, and eyeballs scattered all over the room or highway. We have become desensitized by violence and death. We see it every day on the news (street gang killings, drive-by shootings) and in entertainment (violent games and movies), war (faceless and depersonalized drones killing from the sky), and acts of terrorism (by definition, violent death) that every instance of mass killings and neighborhoods shot up in a gangland killing with toddlers and others in the line of fire seems to set new records for depravity and body count. What new madman will soon step up to take a new record number of victims? What 17-year-old gang member will become an executioner?

"Take away the guns!" becomes the cry of the day. Put up walls, and barricade our schools, homes, and communities. Turn the entire country into a prison. Take away freedoms, monitor everyone (friends, family, and neighbors spying on each other to report "suspicious behavior"), obtain injunctions making it illegal for suspected gang members to congregate on public streets (bar their freedom of assembly).

What effect would even one suicide-murdering bomber make in a crowded New York subway, nightclub, or other crowded venue? Wake up, world. It's not the instrument, but the musician who makes the music. A trumpet by itself is nothing but a piece of steel. It needs someone to blow it.

When I was in the sixth grade and learning proper English, the teacher was explaining the use of auxiliary or "helper" words, such as had, have, and has. "When using 'begun' you always need a 'helper' word because a gun always needs a helper to make it work." In cases and times like this, the gun is merely the instrument and the shooter is the "helper." It is not the gun that is sick, but the mind of the person holding it.

Let us not medicate ourselves by thinking guns are the villains; it is the warped minds of the individuals who wish to "cleanse" the world of what they perceive as "demons," or those who seek revenge for some imagined slight, offense, or cause, perhaps "invasion" or "trespassing" in territory "owned" by a rival, and, yes, for wearing a shirt or scarf of the color of an opposing gang. Desensitization of death by emphasizing it as a resolution to personal problems and as a "game" has only made the minds of those "sick individuals," those "lone wolves," those "friendless outcasts" and street gang members in society who believe they are "Zendor, ruler of the universe" plan and execute more and more heinous crimes.

In a recent police gun buyback program, thousands of guns were turned in to the police—shotguns, low caliber rifles, even a frontier musket. The people surrendering the guns were homeowners and family members. But not one gun was turned in by a gang member.

Video games and other modes of entertainment seem to become bloodier and bloodier as the makers spill more and more red to rake in the "green." We cannot pacify the world by disarming, but we can make it a better world by learning concepts of peace, love, and harmony, and teaching the finality of death.

Introduction to the material in this book can best be expressed by the ones who have lived in a gang and in a "'gang neighborhood," the ones who have been there and lived it. Chapter 1 comprises stories by the ones who have lived the lifestyle or, as the saying goes, "Walked the walk, talked the talk." These are stories told in their own words; the first from a gang member, and the second and third from young girls, though not gang members, born and raised in a gang neighborhood. The fourth story is from a young girl who began her gang or crew membership at the age of 13. The stories are reproduced here exactly as written by them. The only changes are made for spelling. Following the first-person stories is a glossary of "gangsta" words and definitions compiled by a former member who has seen and walked on the dark side.

The uniting links between all of their stories and reasons for belonging to a gang are the feeling or search of "family," a sense of belonging, to be respected, to be supported in times of need. One former gang member, however, put a lie to that linkage. "When I was recruited, I was told: 'We'll always be there for you. We'll have your back if anyone tries to mess with you.' When I got into trouble with the police, I was expected to keep my mouth shut and not rat anyone, but they turned their backs and wouldn't even give me any help."

While some might argue that gangs have been around forever and that history is replete with stories of outlaws and lawmen, today's gang problem is much different than it was a generation or more ago.

We can treat a troubled body, but a troubled spirit is up to the individual to cure.

Dale L. June

Reference

Lowery, W. 2012. "18th street to death row." *The Los Angeles Times,* November 3, p. AA1.

Gang Life 1

Contents

Gangster

By Anonymous (a gang member)[*]

Growing up on the streets of East Los Angeles, what I call home, Gage Ave., has been a tough life. I got jumped in by three guys at the age of 12. It lasted 30 seconds; I felt proud when they finished. I am from Gage Maravilla. The only reason I joined was because I saw my family in it. I loved the attention I was getting; whether it was good or bad. I have seen many shootings, stabbings, and drugs, as well as being involved in them. For the love of the gang life, I have had to kill rival gang members for disrespecting the homeboys.

One day the homies and I were hanging out at our usual spot, when a rival gang came and started shooting at us. I lost a homie that day; he was shot in the face and died instantly; I was only 14.

I have lost count of how many homies have died since. Earlier this year a homie was killed in a drive-by, his daughter was wounded in the face, and his wife is paralyzed from the waist down. He was a big drug dealer and someone told a rival gang where he was living. At the age of 17, I got my first gang-related tattoo. My entire back, chest, and arms are covered with tattoos, I dress in baggy clothes, and I'm bald; the average looking gangster.

---

[*] Contributors must remain anonymous for obvious safety reasons. The section is presented as it was written by the contributors.

I dropped out of high school after my junior year ended. I had been kicked out of six different schools for gang-affiliated fights. I was 18 and decided that studying was not for me, that drinking with the homies all day was better than being in school.

When I had kids, I distanced myself from the gang. I sell drugs to make a living, but I no longer participate in meetings or drive-bys or jumping people in, etc. I am what we gangsters call a nonactive gang member. Now at the age of 33 I have grown and learned that there is more to life than the streets. I don't want my kids to experience the life I did. I want them to go to college and be doctors, business owners, anything to keep them out of the streets. Homies don't last very long. Most of the guys I grew up with are in prison, hiding from police, still on the streets, or dead. Several times of the year I visit cemeteries to pay my respect to the homies I have lost to gang violence. Although I am not too involved with the gang, I am still a gang member; my only way out is death.

Anonymous Gang Member

The Ghetto Life

I come from what most people would call ghetto, a neighborhood
    that can be confused with the halls from hell.
But to me that's home, the place I grew up, a place I love to be in.
What most people see when they pass by is low-life thugs roaming
    the streets; what I see is "homies" struggling to survive.
Graffiti on the walls, cops call it vandalism, but in reality it's just a
    way of expression and a way to claim their territory.
Drug dealers in every other corner, but those "dealers" are
    always there when a friend is in need. No matter what the
    circumstances, their loved ones are their priority, and drugs are
    just a way to keep them on their feet.
The gangsters protect their "hood," in other words their home and
    the people who live there; their *familia*.
"Cops be acting shady" is what the homies say right after the 5.0*
    have destroyed the place where they stay at.
All they see is a bald head and right away they think that person
    is corrupted, as if that person is just waiting for someone to
    come so they can shoot them down and rob them.
Cops don't think about them having a family and wanting to take
    care of them; all they want to do is act like they are larger than
    anything and bust them 'cause they are the "enemy."
The gangsters sell the drugs, but it's just a job in their eyes.

You'll mainly see them posted on the corner waiting for a client.
They are all trying to make it one way or another; food on the
 table and a roof over their heads is all that really matters.
Things like this don't even bother me because they are all my family.
Survival of the fittest, you can say, but to me it's just another day
 in LA.

–ANONYMOUS

Growing Up in a Gang Neighborhood

By Anonymous

I grew up in a typical Mexican family; my parents were illegal immigrants up until 2010. My mom has epilepsy, and my father was strained to work from 3 a.m. to 5 p.m. every day for 15 years at a meat company located in Ontario, California, to support his family. After the September 11 event, my father was forced to quit that job due to not having "papers." He was unemployed for five months before he found a job in Rancho Cucamonga, where he was injured and had surgery, but remains injured.

My parents have not moved from our home because the economy sucks and we pay $600 for a two bedroom. I have two brothers and two sisters, and I am the youngest. I have lived my entire life in East Los Angeles, where I witness two rival gangs, Pomeroy Maravilla and Juarez Maravilla, fight for the territory I call home. My neighborhood is filled with trash on the ground, tagging on garage doors, no parking, and bald gangsters in baggy clothes and tattoos all over their body on every corner; half of my block is filled with gang members.

Walking out the door as a child was terrifying, and it still is; I never knew what to expect from the *cholos* [Latin American males] that lived three houses away from me. I was 10 when I witnessed my first murder. A classmate's brother was shot in a drive-by and sadly died in his arms; he was from Pomeroy. I was walking down the hill to the store when I heard the shots fired. I ran home and began to watch television to try and ignore what I had just seen. I knew that, if I spoke a word of what just happened, my life would be in great danger. As a young girl, I learned it is always best to remain friends with gangsters so they do not harm me or my family; I stay out of their way and they stay away from me and my loved ones! At the age of 15, a dear friend of mine, who was not gang affiliated, but his friends were, was also shot in a drive-by at a party near my home. It was unbelievable to hear about the tragedy; he passed away at the scene. Once more at the age of 20, my next-door neighbor was shot on his stairs, in front of his 2- and 3-year-old children and brother-in-law; he passed away in the ambulance on his way to hospital. It was approximately 9 p.m., my block was cordened off by law enforcement for 13 hours—nobody was allowed in or out. The family was promptly relocated by a witness protection program. I was in my room the entire time; police came to my house asking questions about the shooting and the screams, and they asked permission to go to my back yard and see if anyone was hiding there.

The police response time to get to my neighborhood that night was about eight minutes. By the time police arrive, the *cholo* had fled the scene. Once again, these *cholos* had ruined the peace that our neighborhood worked hard to obtain.

My oldest brother joined a "crew" at the age of 14. He began to drink alcohol, party in clubs, use drugs, stay out all night, dropped out of high school his sophomore year, rebelled against my mom (my father was too tired to deal with him), got into trouble with the law, and he became a drug dealer. He was in and out of jail for many years, until one day he borrowed a friend's car; the car was stolen, and my brother had a fake license. He was sentenced to one year in prison for identity theft. After his time was served, he was deported, and has been in Mexico for the past four years. His family, eight kids and wife, are left behind without a father or husband. My oldest sister got pregnant at the age of 17; she dropped out of high school at the beginning of her senior year. My parents could not believe she was pregnant and kicked her out as a form of punishment; she rarely spoke to my family. My younger brother followed in my oldest brother's footsteps. He too joined the crew, partied with my brother, drank alcohol, used drugs, dropped out of high school in his junior year, and made friends that were a bad influence.

My younger brother was 17 when he was arrested—his first time in trouble with the law. He and two friends were out late, approximately 11 p.m. "just having fun"; nevertheless, one of the guys brought a gun with him. My brother was on a pay phone talking to his girlfriend while his friends were robbing two men. It's funny, the men only had $8 and a VHS movie. This night ruined my brother's life. His friends testified in trial that my brother did not participate in the crime, but my brother was still charged along with his friends. He was sentenced to three years in prison. My brother served four years total; he got extra time for bad behavior. When he was released, he was deported and has been in Mexico for about 10 years.

My younger sister, who is a year older than me, moved out of my home at the age of 18 to live with her boyfriend and his family. She loves to party, drink alcohol, and dropped out of high school during the last semester of her senior year. Her boyfriend is a gang member and was recently stabbed on the chest by a rival gang member. He is now in deep debt with expensive hospital bills and, since my sister is their sole support, they are always broke.

One of my closest friends married a gang member; they have five kids. When he is stopped by police, the first thing they ask him is: "What's your name? Where are you from? Where are you going?" Even when his kids are with him, they ask him gang-related questions, in front of them. I wonder, will he allow his kids to follow in his path and become gang members, or will he want them to do better than him? He is unemployed, sells drugs for a living, drives without a license, and has his homies over at his house about every day. Last year, they were living with a friend of his, two weeks after they left that place that house was shot and one of his friends is now paralyzed and his 1-year-old daughter was killed. If they were still living there, I wonder would I still have a friend.

I am the first in my family to graduate high school and continue my education by attending college. I learned from the mistakes of my siblings that the only way to survive in this world is to be educated, get a good job, and move out of East Los Angeles. I was doing well, until I met who I thought was the "love of my life." He was sweet and amazing and loved me. He is a gang member from South Central Los Angeles; our relationship was going well. We started a family together. After our two sons were born, he began to choose his friends over them and me. His homies always encouraged him to ditch me and go do "missions" with them to get some extra money. One day while I waited for him to pick me up from school, I received a call from the Los Angeles Police Department letting me know he was arrested for robbing a liquor store, possession of weapons, possession of drugs, and evading an officer. He served three weeks in jail and was released on probation. About two months later, we had an argument, and he was arrested for domestic violence and criminal threats. He became very violent, and I knew I did not want my sons growing up in an environment where their lives were always at risk, and where their parents were always fighting. He was sentenced to two years in prison, but only served eight months and was deported to Mexico. As a result of his actions and subsequent deportation, he is no longer in our lives.

Growing up around gangs has taught me how to be strong emotionally and to never trust anyone. One minute everything can be calm, and the next there can be complete chaos. About half of my friends are gangsters, date gangsters, or are related to gangsters. Why people choose to take the "easy" life, I will never understand. It is because of these people that I honestly say gangs will never go away; they exist everywhere and are expanding rapidly.

Editor's Note: The following is the true story of a 20-year-old girl who attempted to return to school and earn a degree. During her second term in school, she was physically attacked by her drunken father, she was able to fight him off, but he made her move out of the house. A few days later, her father also forced the mother to get out. The girl left school after her third term. She recently emailed that she was in Mexico and "smoking a big fat blunt."

Crew

By Anonymous

I was in the sixth grade at the age of 13 when I joined a crew. What I wanted was respect from the others and the power that goes with being "a family." Three to five people "jumped" me in (beat me up and I couldn't hit back) to initiate me into the crew. Once I was jumped in, I was given a nickname (*deleted by editor for safety of the writer*). The crew was the Brown Pride Queens (BPQ).

They taught me all the basic stuff like how to use a spray can for graffiti and to throw up signs (symbols) to represent where I was from. The things they had me doing was to recruit new members into the crew (which I did) and to go tagging (writing up my crew's name and my nickname). They already had me fighting with other gang members and telling me to ditch school (getting out). I was caught ditching and tagging a few times, but I didn't give a fuck. I guess it was because I wanted to be cool like everybody or everyone else.

When I would get caught, I was sent to the dean, Ms. Zimbalist (*name changed by editor*). I was sent so many times, and that after a while, she didn't even want to see me. She had me in a daily program, but even it didn't work out. So, Ms. Zimbalist would sometimes send me back to class and call me up before lunch, so I would spend my lunch with her at her office. Sometimes she would call my mom to come and pick me up from school. But, when she would come and pick me up she would say, "*Ahora que hicistes*" (What did you do now?). I would answer her back and tell her *nada* (nothing). She would say, "*Tu nunca haces nada, como siempre*" (You never do nothing, like always). Not only had I got in trouble for ditching, but for fighting, too. My mom would tell me that she was sick and tired of me, that she always had to get out of work because of me. She would have headaches. But, I wasn't the only one that was causing her problems. My mom was the one that would always go to school for me because my dad would tell my mom that he didn't want to be dealing with me. So, there she goes. She would always tell me, if I love her, I would tell her I do. Why? She would say, "Well, it doesn't seem like [it] because I tell you something and you do the opposite." I would tell her, "Why you got to beat me down like that?" Tears would come out of me. But, then later I would kiss her, hug her, and tell her how much I love her.

School and home were my routine since my parents never let me stay in any after-school programs. So, every day I had to wake my ass up to go to school. My mom really didn't know the types of people or friends that I had or hanging out with. And she didn't even know that I was in [a] crew or that I belong[ed] in a group of people. I was failing my classes. At the beginning of school, I had good grades, but out of nowhere I just end it up doing bad. The crew we beefed it with was BPT (Brown Pride Traviesas).

I joined the crew because of the peer pressure I had. Also, because I wanted to escape from intolerable situations at home. I wanted to be "somebody" and gain respect. I wanted to experience adventures and excitement. Which I actually did. But, not only that, also because I wanted to see how it feels like being in a crew and having people that would tell me that they would always have my back. I definitely felt good for myself because I had all that. Maybe just a couple of times they had my back, but, later, they just forgot about me. So, I was on my own now. I once or maybe many other times I needed them and they wouldn't appear, so I had to find my way through. It was all a lie. I would see them the next day and I would tell them "that where were they at." They would always come up with an excuse. So, I just ignored it. But, when they needed my help, I would go and find them.

Later, in the seventh grade, they would offer me drugs and tell me that it would make me feel good. They ask me and told me, "You should try it at least once." So, I did try bud (marijuana) and some other types of drugs such as yayo (cocaine), ice (crystallized methamphetamine), c.c. (computer cleaners), and roll (ecstasy pills). I liked them all and enjoyed them; they just all made me forget about everything and made me feel good.

Later, I got out of BPQ and join[ed] another crew named EDW (Evil Down Wicked). I join EDW because I had heard that it was the deepest crew and had boys and girls in it. I was barely going to be a ninth grader and was 15 years old when I had heard about that crew. So, I had to go through the same thing. Them jumping me in. So, they did but I still had my nickname. I started hanging out with them. But, when it was my first day at school at James A. Garfield High School, I saw few of them. So, I called them up and told them "what's up?" So, they answer me back and said, "What's up, come to the spot." So, I did after I got my lunch. I seen that it was crowded where they kicked it at, really crowded. But, EDW had so many beefs with other crews. The crews that they didn't get along are called or were called DWP, WES, TSL, and UPS. They also beefed it with LIL VALLEY, which is a gang. I actually stayed by them and we beefed with LIL VALLEY because supposedly we were writing on their territory. Which we weren't. They called us up so many times. So, my brother went and told them whenever they wanted to get down as in fight that they would be posted up. So, once LIL VALLEY did call us, so all four of us went. Which were my brother (Roberto), my brother (Rigoberto), my dad (Jesus), and I. After we went they were scared of my brother, the smallest which is Rigoberto. Ever since he told them off they left us alone.

Once, after school, WES waited for us; they had so many weapons on them. We didn't know that they were going to be there; they just came out of nowhere. But, some of us also had our shanks, which is a pocket knife. There were people all over. I also seen people running to each other. I saw that one of us had been hit in the head with a metal stick. I was like OOOUUUCCCHHH. When I seen that I really didn't know what to do; I just stood there not knowing who was coming to me or not. But, later I reacted. I told myself that I had to run before they get me too. So, I did, I left. I was scared at that time. I heard sirens from the cops and everybody started running away. Days passed after the fight. And everybody was still talking about it.

Later that month I got into a fight, so I got suspended. And when I went back, I had to take one of my parents. So, I did and took my mom. The only thing that the dean Mr. *Masa el calabaza* (pumpkin head) would tell my mom is what had happen about the fight. But, Mr. *Masa el calabaza* would put things in my mom's head and tell her lies about me. I would get mad and tell my mom that it wasn't truth. He would tell me that it was and he would ask me that if I was calling him a liar in front of my mom and I told him, "Yes!" After when the conference was over, Mr. *Masa el calabaza* would give me a pass to go back to class.

Later, one of the girls that were in EDW went with me to go write on one of the buildings. So, we go during lunch and I do my thing, my job. Then, Maria* goes and does her thing and she gets caught up with a teacher that was coming out. So, the teacher calls her and takes her to the dean's office. Later, during third period Spanish class, Ms. Soboto* called me up and told me to go to the dean's office, So, while I was going into the office, I saw Maria. I was so mad because I already knew why they had called me out from class. Maria had gone rata on me (snitch). So, Mr. *Masa la calabaza* called me up. But, he had sent Maria back outside so he could talk to me. So, he asked me why had I got in her in the crew? I answered, "I didn't get her in the crew, she got herself in." So, he told me that where did I go writing and I told him I didn't write anything. I also told him that Maria was a straight out snitch and he got mad and told me that that wasn't snitching. I told him, "OK, whatever." So, he told me, "If you don't tell me that truth of what you wrote and where you wrote, we are going to call your parents." So, I answered him back and told him, "Go ahead. I ain't stopping you." So, he did and called my mom and he told her if she could come to school. So, my mom comes and asks me, "What was happening?" I told her, "Nothing is happening." Mr. *Masa el calabaza* had told my mom what had happened. So, that's when she found out that I was in crew and hanging out with the bad crowd.

She didn't look happy. So, Mr. *Masa la calabaza* told my mom that I couldn't be in James A. Garfield High School. So, he sends me to Woodrow Wilson High School. I really didn't last a semester in Garfield. Before, I left and went back to Garfield to turn in the books and I saw Maria and told her to better watch her back because she was going to get fucked up by everyone by snitching. My mom asked me, "*Otra ves con lo mismo*?"(Again, with the

---

* Names changed to protect the subjects.

same thing?). I told her "no." When we got home, she asked me since when had I been in a crew or joined one; I told her "barely." She asked me if I was stupid. I told her "no." She also told me what else I was doing besides me being in a crew; I told her nothing else. She didn't believe me, though.

My first day at Wilson wasn't good. Why? Because it was a whole week of violence. There was a stabbing and the school was locked down. Next day, there was another one; so, lock down again. After that, there was a shooting and lock down again. The ghetto birds (helicopters) were all over. It was terrible. I wanted to go back to my home school. I really didn't have friends in school. But, my mom didn't let me although I told her what had happened. I was actually getting good grades in Wilson and was on the role of honor. I was doing well because the school had me in Melas Counseling where they would drug test me. When I got home, I had showed my mom and she was really proud of me and told me that "*lla ves que si puedes*" (See, you can do it). But I didn't answer back. Two years had passed by and I went and talked to my counselor.

The teachers that I had didn't want me to leave. But, I told them that I didn't want to be there anymore. I had talked to my mom and asked her if I could go back to my own school and she said, "YES," so when I heard that YES word I was so happy. My counselor had told me to keep up the good work and to go and visit him. I answer him back and told him, "HELL NO! I ain't coming back to this school." I never did go and visit.

When I went back to my home school, they put me in tenth grade and put me with ninth graders. The classes that they assigned me I had already taken in Wilson. So, I went to go complain to my counselor and told her. So, she changed my classes and put me in the right classes. I was so happy going back and seeing my people (friends). But, most of them weren't there anymore. I had heard that most of them were locked up or had dropped out of school. I was all good in the first two weeks, but later again I started messing up. Doing the same old stuff like before. Later, when those two weeks had passed by, we "busted a mission" and broke into a school. It was six of us. We left the school really bad. We took so many computers and "slang" them to friends and other people that we knew, as in sold them.

I would also go shoplifting, but I got caught. Later I started to realize that I had to get my act together and start changing. So, I did after I started my senior year. When I got to my senior year, I was kind of messing up. Not a lot like before, but like, for example, ditching school and not doing my homework and class work, but I was in the right track. I left all the things behind me and moved on. I had realized that I didn't want to end up like most of those kids. So I had told them that I wanted to get out of the crew and that they could do anything they wanted to do with me to get me out. Well, not anything, but yeah. So, I got out.

I really wanted to be somebody as in a good way. I wanted to graduate, which I did. But I almost didn't because I had a BIG FAT "F". So, I talked to my teacher Ms. Saramondo* what I could do to bring my grade up to at least a "D". She told me, "Do me a project about animals." So, I did and I had to represent it in front of class. My counselor calls me up and told me that Ms. Saramondo had passed me and that I would be able to graduate on stage. I was crying because I never thought that I would make it through high school.

Once I was out, I really didn't know what to do. Until a friend of mine got me to go to school, East Lost Angeles College (ELAC). While I was going to school I was taking two classes, PE and math. I also was going to The Police Explorer Program. It was kind of hard, the stuff they had me doing. But, I learned a lot from them. I really enjoyed it a lot. That was when I had realized what I wanted to study for or major. I would always tell myself how much I hate school and now I love going to school. It's my life. I thank my mom for always being there for me and pushing me. Telling me, "*Echale ganas mija tu puedes*" (You can do it, daughter). Now that I seen most of my old friends, they ask me what I've been doing. I tell them, "Going to school." They tell me that's good to hear. And I tell them what they are doing, they say "Nothing." Most of my old friends already have kids. And still doing stupid stuff.

Now, I've changed and see things through my life and around me. And I also see those young kids messing up and getting into crews and gangs at a young age. I just wish I could make a difference. I go back and think the things that I used to do when I was young and I tell myself, "I can't believe that was me when I was young." But, I believe it. I had friends that belong to a gang and were forced at a young age. Many of them told me that they will always be a gang member even though they knew they wouldn't be able to get out. The only way for them to get out of the gang was either dead or locked up; those were their only two choices they had. Most of them join[ed] a gang because they wanted to have a family that will protect them from others. They want to have money and respect, which they had it all. They would say to me that when they first join[ed] a gang they felt loved by everyone in there.

When people get jumped in into a gang, most girls get "sex in." Requires members to sleep with certain members of the gang or with certain numbers of members of the gang. Most of my old friends took a long time to realize that joining a gang wasn't a good decision to make. They also realized that no one from the gang would care about them. They finally realized that it was too late to get out and start over. They would never live life happy and peaceful. They would be hiding from their predators and the cops. Gangs aren't social clubs. Gangs are members that are in big groups and have their own cliques. Gang members say that it's like an addiction for them. A gang and a crew don't have a lot in common. There are a few things they do have in common like, for example, the tagging and maybe getting people in.

---

* Name changed to protect the subject.

You people have read my story, now is time for you to GET THE FUCK OUT and get a life. I'M OUTTTIIEES OF HERE!!!

"Gangsta": Gang Slang Terms

The following list of terms was compiled by a crew member, who has been deeply entrenched in the gang culture since she was 9 years old. These are her words as she uses them:

Aight, aite, ight: All right
AR—AR 15: An automatic assault rifle
Areous: Area
Bad Bone: Don't trust him
Bail: Leave; "I'm going to bail"
Banger: Gang member
Bangin: Gang fighting or violence: being in a gang
Barrio (Varrio): Spanish for "neighborhood"
Base-head: A person who "free bases" cocain.
Be down: Loyalty; defends set during adversity
Benjamins: One-hundred dollar bills
BG: Baby gangster; very young (7–12 years old); children who are used by gangs to act as lookouts, hold drugs, guns, etc.
Biscuit: Gun
Bizzle: Bitch
Blood in: Initiation, initiated member, must shed someone's blood, may include murder as in "drive-by"
Blood out: Member leaving gang; must shed blood to get out; may mean being killed
Blunt: A cigar with most tobacco removed and replaced with marijuana and/or cocaine
Boned out: To run away; chickened out; left
Book: To run away or to leave
Bote: Jail (Spanish)
Bounce: To go somewhere; to leave; "to go bouncing;" to go to the bars or clubs
Brand: Tattoo (tatt)
Break: Run; get away
Breakdown: A shotgun
Buck: Prison-made alcohol; home brew
Bullet: One year in custody
Bumpin: To one's liking; "That song is bumpin'"

Bust a cap: To shoot a gun; "I'm gonna bust a cap in yo ass"; to shoot at someone

Bust a move: To act quickly or to perform a dance move

Bust out: To leave, to exit; "He busted out of the club"

Busted: To shoot at someone; to be arrested

Buster: A fake gang member (undercover cop)

Busters: The police

BVD: Marijuana

Bling: Expensive jewelry or other expensive material

Cap: Bullet

Carhala: Latino female "sister"

Checked in: Used by Hispanics; meaning to be initiated into a gang

Chiva: Spanish slang for heroin

Chola: Hispanic female involved in gangs

Cholo: Hispanic male involved in gangs

Chuco: Short term for "pachuco" (referring to the "zoot suiters" of the 1930s–1950s); a street gang

Clica: Spanish slang for gang

Clique: Synonymous with gang

Cop: To steal; to get

Courting in: Initiation process; fighting two or more gang members for a certain length of time (usually 15–30 seconds)

Courting out: Departing member fighting two or more gang members for a certain time limit (usually 15–60 seconds); blood out

Crew: A group of people usually associated with a gang or gang members

Crib: Home

Cuete: Gun (Spanish)

Dawg (or Dog): Friend, buddy, companion

Deuce and a half: A 25 caliber semiautomatic pistol

Dime, dime bag, dime sack: A $10 bag of illegal drugs; a 10-year prison sentence

Dime him: To inform on someone; to "drop a dime"

Divorce: To get out of a gang

Do-rag: Bandana worn to keep the "do" (hair style) in place or to keep the sweat from the eyes; usually the gang colors

Do you want to ride: Tear his ass up

Doing a jack: Committing a robbery

Double deuce: 22 caliber gun

Double OG: Second generation gang member

Down: Connected with; as in, "He's down with the set"

Down or "down for it": Willing or wanting to do something

Down for the hood: Loyalty to the neighborhood

Dressed down: Wearing gang colors

Drive-by: A planned or random shooting primarily from a car; sometimes used as an initiation for a new member

Dropping the flag: Quitting the gang

Dub: A $20 bag of illegal drugs

Dusted: Killed; high on angel dust (PCP)

Eight ball: An eight ounce bag of illegal drugs

Elbow (lb): A pound of illegal drugs

Fizzle: Can be female or fuck

Gangsta: A street gang member

Gank: To steal; "He ganked my ride"

Heat: Gun or police

Homegirl: Female friend/buddy

Homie, homeboy: Friend, buddy

Hood: Neighborhood

Ice: Crystal meth

Jakes: Police

Jet: Leave; "We gotta jet"

K: AK 47; an automatic assault rifle

Mac: Blunt (see above)

Mac: A Mac 10; an automatic weapon

Nick, nickel, nickel bag, nickel sack: A $5 bag of illegal drugs

Nigga, niggaz: One's boys; those one hangs out with

Nine, nina: 9 mm handgun

Off the hook, off the chain: Unbelievable, outrageous, wild; not being charged with a crime

Peace out: Goodbye

Piece: Gun

Pistol: A handgun

Playa: Someone who has lots of girlfriends (plays around); a person to whom much respect is due

Playa hata: One who has bad feeling toward a "playa"; no respect for a "playa"

Po-Po: Short for police

Posse: Friends, crew, gang

Pump: Shotgun

Quarter: A $25 bag of illegal drugs

Rat: An informant; to inform on someone

"Rise up foo": Rise up, fool. Bring it on; let's fight

Roll out: To leave

Roll (or roofer or ruffie): Ecstasy pills

Ruger: Gun

School Ya': To teach a lesson; to win a confrontation

Scrap: To fight

Sex in: A female's initiation into a gang; she must have sex with certain gang individuals or a specific number of gang members

Strapped up: Holding a gun; armed; carrying "heat"

'Sup: What's up; what is going on

Thug: A hard core gangster

Wanksta: Fake ass gangsta

Weed: Marijuana, buda, shwag, mota, bud, maryjane, do-do, green, fire, smoke, peace, stick, water, bluntos

Whas goin' down: What's happening; "What are we doing?"

What tha dilly yo: What is going on?; what's the deal?

Word up: Get it straight; that's right, how's it going?

Yayo, ya: Cocaine

5-0: Police (apparently from the television show *Hawaii 5-0*

8 Ball: ⅛ ounce of cocaine

4 pounda: 40 caliber gun

13 or XIII or X3: M (thirteenth letter of the alphabet); gangs of Latino heritage usually refers to Mexican Mafia (shows allegiance to gangs in Southern California)

14 or XIV of X4: N (used by Latino gangs in Northern California) (Norteño 14 or Norte 14)

18 or 18th Street: Refers to the 18th Street Gang in Los Angeles aligned with Mexican Mafia

44: A 44 caliber gun

187: Murder (California penal code section for murder); sometimes seen in graffiti

211: Robbery (California penal code section for robbery); also a Crip term meaning "blood killer" (2nd and 11th letters of the alphabet: BK)

420: Marijuana; also refers to a counterculture code for a certain time of day for "pot" smokers to light up

911: Warning! The police are coming!

Editors Note: David was a graduate student in a chemical dependency class when he wrote the following essay. It may or may not be true—he said it was true. However, it expresses those issues that relate to one concept of the thinking of a young man who turns to drugs and the gang lifestyle … all in the name of "having fun."

Isn't Life Funny?

David

Life has just got to be funny. Its paradox is just too painful not to be. I thought life was going to bring me a great education, a great family life, a wife and kids who would love me, a top-notch job with a great salary that matched my great job (with benefits and bonuses, and a lucrative retirement plan), friends who respected me, a good reputation in the community, maybe even dabble successfully in politics. I didn't think anything could stop me from success. And I wanted to have some fun, a payoff for all my hard work.

Everyone, and I do mean everyone, was doing it. No one got hurt. One day I started the fun days of college. One day I took what everyone else was taking. One day I took more and more still. After all, I was going to be somebody, somebody unique. What could happen that was so serious, so bad? I had heard the stories of those other stupid kids. I could resist any kind of challenge that came my way. I was brilliant, magna cum laude, conservative. I knew the limit. If it got too much for me, I could stop.

It was true that all my friends could take this stuff—no problem. Except I don't think it was true for me. Another day I took more, and even more, to get through school, to make my college days even more fun, to cope with my girlfriend (Bobbi), and to cope with my parents.

They were noticing something different about me. But there wasn't—no not really—there wasn't, at least not until something really funny happened. I blanked out taking my finals. I couldn't remember anything. I tried more of the juice; for the first time it didn't help. I crashed my grades and ruined my average. I thought it was pretty funny, actually; no one would believe this. I couldn't tell anyone; no one would understand, not if I became a loser. And so I took more—nothing helped—and more, but it didn't last as long. I took more and more and more. I began to fail more and more and more.

In short, it was more and more funny. I just ... I don't know ... just failed. It didn't matter because I would find out the problem and get back on track. My parents, my girlfriend, Bobbie, my friends were saying pretty funny things. Pretty soon I couldn't stomach them anymore, since they were so smart. They said strange stuff, like I was ruining my life, that I would never get anywhere. I actually laughed my head off. I couldn't take them like that. How could they say that about me?

So, I got new friends. They didn't live near me, and their gang life-style sucked, but we had the most fun I ever had. I had to go to a part of town I didn't like, but I just had to get back on track. These guys in the gang were cool. They even showed me how to have more fun. I began to see that I was wasting my life with so many "serious" concerns of life. There were so many things about life that were unpredictable. What if I died tomorrow? Would all the education, judgmental family, and friends be worth my unhappiness? I thought life would have been such a downer without the freedom to be happy. Fun did not have the same meaning for me as it did for everyone else, it seemed. I loved my life, and my new relationships would see me through any tough times.

So what was the funniest thing that ever happened to me? What was so meaningful and profoundly fun about my new life? How did that great paradox present the comedy routine of life to me? Well, it was strange; when my money ran out, so did my friends, and they left me with the rap.

As weird as this whole thing had turned out, I thought the officer was actually pretty funny when he told me I was going to jail. I told the judge it was ridiculously funny that this could happen to me. Something was wrong because I was brilliant, slated to success, would have a great wife, kids, a job, a rich future, a home where I could live my life the way I wanted to, a real life!

The judge looked at my filthy face, my "needled" arms, my bloodshot eyes, and the rap sheet. He said, "Funny, it's funny how much fun prison can be to a brilliant kid."

Violence and Youth
A Growing Relationship?

2

JEFFERY BLEDSOE
DALE L. JUNE

Contents

Introduction

My name is Jeffery Bledsoe. As I search through the library for books that will expand my understanding of violent crime among juveniles, a particular cover catches my eye. I stare at it in wonder, not totally surprised, yet bewildered at the truth that leapt from the photograph. Seated on the ground in front of a wall littered with gang graffiti are two young Latino boys. They look to be no more than 13 or 14 years old, yet their eyes are ageless, almost lifeless. The one on the left has long, straight black hair and has one knee propped up in front of him. His right arm rests on the knee and his hand is held in some contorted figure that I can only presume to be a gang sign. His face shows no emotion, his lips sealed, yet relaxed. Resting against his left shoulder is his friend, who seems to be a bit younger. The younger of the two has short dark hair, and faint black hairs paint a soft moustache on his upper lip. His face is almost expressionless, except for his eyebrows being drawn up slightly in the middle, as if in a manner of questioning. In his right hand, held across his chest and upward, is a compact semiautomatic handgun. The picture speaks to the reality of violence and youth in today's society.

While most of the population would agree that violence among juveniles is on the rise, there are those who believe otherwise. The fact that violence exists among juveniles, especially gang violence, is not a question. However, the news media would have us believe the tragedies we are witness to around us are happening more frequently and are much more severe than ever before. Are today's youths really that much worse? Are their crimes so much more frequent and more violent that we should be overly concerned? If the situation is so horrible, how much of our resources are we willing to expend to remedy the situation? Is the relationship between violent crime and youths really growing? In researching these and other questions, one can hope to have a better understanding of how extensive the problem youth gang violence truly is for our society.

The Influence of Family Life

One of the few things we know for sure about the subject of violence is that one of the greatest determining factors in a young person's behavior is his or her family life and background. We gain a great sense of this from the previous essays in Chapter 1 written by gang members and associates. Violence is in all of us; it is a part of life. Historically, violence has been a necessity for survival. "Violence is a sudden physical force causing injury, death, or destruction. It can be accidental, intentional, manmade, or a force of nature."[1] Even today, in certain situations, it is a necessary reaction. "Violence has permeated all societies throughout pre- and recorded history. By the very nature of human behavior, violence should be considered inevitable. ... Many experts in criminology, sociology, and psychology argue that all individuals have a choice as to whether to participate in criminal or violent behavior."[2]

As society progressed and cultures advanced, the need for violence slowly receded. All of the inherent attributes to human beings began to be developed and taught at different levels. Those characteristics thought to be more desirable were encouraged, and those which were harmful were discouraged. It has been predominantly through the family that values have been taught, by children learning and being influenced by their parents. These values determine the extent to which certain attributes will grow. The amount of kindness and courtesy we project is directly influenced by our values. It is the same for the amount of violence and disrespect we demonstrate. What, then, are the values learned by the children of a mother who is abused by her husband? What behavior is learned by a young child who is beaten by her mother? What does a young girl learn when raped and sexually molested by her father, uncle, or brother?

Many theories abound, but very prevalent is the influence of family life. One aspect of those theories is grounded in the truism that "children learn what they live."

… If a child lives with criticism, he learns to condemn. If a child lives with hostility, he learns to fight. If a child lives with ridicule, he learns to be shy. If a child lives with jealousy, he learns to feel guilty. If a child lives with impropriety, he learns to feel shame. If a child lives with tolerance, he learns to be patient. If a child lives with encouragement, he learns confidence If a child lives with praise, he learns to appreciate. If a child lives with fairness, he learns justice. If a child lives with security, he learns to have faith. If a child lives with approval, he learns to like himself. If a child lives with acceptance and friendship, he learns to find love in the world.[3]

Although some also submit that broken homes and single-parent homes are contributing factors in youth violence, it is apparent that what goes on in the home is much more important. A child from a single-parent home in which good values are instilled and responsibility taught may very well grow up without any violence-associated problems at all. A mother and father who fail collectively to instill appropriate values, or who teach violent behavior by example, may end up with a son or daughter inclined to violence. The greatest lessons of life are learned in the home, and regardless of whether parents are making an effort to teach or not, they are.

We adults now name the young criminals super predators. Perhaps we should think of them as super alones. There are children in America who have never been touched or told that they matter. Inner city momma is on crack; suburban momma gives the nanny responsibility for raising the kids. Papa is in a rage this morning. … Where is there a neighbor who cares?[4]

The statement above is, of course, a gross generalization. The inner city mother, more likely than not, is away from home, at work, leaving an 8-year-old in charge of taking care of the baby while the mother is cleaning the house or tending the children of the suburban mother 12 to 18 hours a day. The suburban mother, in turn, is busy with her own schedule of work and social causes.

Contact Comfort: Love

"Contact Comfort experiments by psychologist Harry Harlow (1905–1981) revealed the long-term devastation caused by deprivation of mother's love and contact comfort, leading to profound psychological and emotional distress and even death. … Harlow's work generated a wealth of research on love, affection, and interpersonal relationships. … His enduring legacy reinforced the importance of emotional support, affection, and love in the development of children."[5] Harlow's work explained and accentuated the importance of contact comfort and social interaction to healthy development.

Harlow is known for his experiments on maternal separation and social isolation of rhesus monkeys. His work emphasized the importance of caregiving and companionship as vital to normal social and cognitive development.

In his surrogate mother experiment, Harlow demonstrated the importance of contact comfort. Baby rhesus monkeys were separated from their mothers and given two surrogate mothers: one made out of wire and another made of terry cloth. He found that the baby monkeys preferred to cling to the terry cloth surrogate even when food was provided by the wire surrogate.

In his social isolation experiments, he again separated baby rhesus monkeys from their mothers and subjected them to partial or total isolation of varying duration. He found that those who experienced partial isolation exhibited abnormal behaviors, such as blank staring, going in circles, and self mutilation. Those who experienced total isolation exhibited severe psychological disturbance, and experienced emotional shock upon being released from isolation. He also found that subsequent attempts to socialize monkeys who were isolated were only partially successful.[6]

Does this mean that, if violence among youths and initiation into gangs is on the rise, the responsibility for the rise rests solely on the parents and the lack of family values, contact comfort, and social integration? Of course not; there are many other factors that contribute to the lifestyle that young people choose to live, and it is just that, a choice. What many people fail to understand is that when children are left to make this choice on their own, they choose poorly.

Sociologist Robert K. Merton, following studies of suicide by Emile Durkheim, discussed what came to be known as the *strain theory* or *anomie.* The strain theory "depicts delinquency as a form of adaptive, problem-solving behavior, usually committed in response to problems involving frustrating and undesirable social environments."[7] Durkheim defined *anomie* as "a feeling of not being personally embedded in society. It marked a loss of the sense of belonging." Merton went further with the strain theory: "… crime and deviance tend to rise as alternative means to success when individuals feel the strain of being pressed to succeed in socially approved ways, but find that the tools necessary for success are not available to them."[8] Primary tools of success are marked with education and job success, often unavailable to large segments of the youth cohort.

The choice in lifestyle will be based on what they observe in the environment around them, and quite often that is violence (domestic violence, gang shootings, video games, movies, and social and news media). Without some support, some guidance, and even some protection and contact comfort throughout their younger years, juveniles know nothing more than to imitate the behaviors they see around them. The fights at school, the bloodshed on television, and the shootings they see in their neighborhoods become their teachers.

The Influence of Drugs and Alcohol

The current trends of alcohol and drug abuse are a major part of youth violence. Not only do juveniles who use drugs and abuse alcohol commit more violent crimes, but they are victimized more often. Many violent crimes having to do with drugs do not involve a person under the influence, but do involve possession, sale, or theft of drugs. "Los Angeles police estimate that at least four city gangs earn over $1 million per week through cocaine sales."[9] "The potential for huge drug-based profits appears to have changed the nature of gangs themselves, making them more prone toward violence and cutthroat tactics. Gang killings, including the now famous drive-by shootings, have become commonplace in our nation's cities."[10]

Violence in School

One of the most obvious concerns pertaining to youth violence today is school violence. With the widespread news media attention and coverage of school shootings, nearly every family in every state where children attend public schools has cause for concern. How could such tragedies occur in upper middle class schools in Littleton, Colorado, and Newtown, Connecticut? And, the concern does not end with the parents and children in public schools. In fact, those most concerned seem to be children/students themselves. Many students are feeling their school will be next on the news. Major school shootings involving mass murder, such as Columbine High School in Littleton and the elementary school in Newtown were in no way "gang related," but the efforts of three disassociated individuals.

However, gang-related violence in schools is a leading cause of concern for administrators, parents, teachers, and students. What is it that causes students to bring violence to school? It only may be the fear of being a victim resulting from a gang-related incident outside of school that causes the violence. For example, a student takes a gun to school "only for protection," then finds himself in a confrontation with a rival gang member that triggers anger in him. Although he may not have been physically threatened, he has given himself the opportunity to act violently by having the gun. The decision whether or not to use that gun at that moment would not be a rational one, especially for a young man who is in an unstable, irrational, "gotta look good in front of the 'hommies' to maintain 'respect'" state of mind. Just the fact the boy has given himself the opportunity places him and others in a dangerous situation.

Influence of Television, Movies, and Video Games on Youth Violence

Since there is no way to directly link a television program or what is seen on the nightly news to a violent crime, this topic is full of controversy. One can read page upon page of arguments that either support or deny that the media is a factor in the amount of violent crime in society. One fact is obvious, however, and that is there is more violence, and more graphic portrayals of violence, in the media today than ever before. The question that looms is how much, if at all, does this influence the behavior of today's youth gangs?

Movies and television programs are overflowing with explosions, gun battles, and bloody fight scenes. Every edition of video games is bloodier and more graphic than a previous rendition. Though this is meant to be fantasy and entertaining, some would argue that it instills a level of tolerance and dulls the senses of the viewer. For example, after worldwide news coverage of the school shootings in Littleton, Colorado, and Newtown, Connecticut, among several other high-profile shootings, the number of "copycat" threats and instances rose to unprecedented levels.

After seeing bloody scene after bloody scene, and gunfight after gunfight, it does not seem so horrible. To a teenage gang member, the message is that death is not real and enables him to approach a car stopped at a traffic signal and shoot and kill the driver in front of his family. Or, on a spur of the moment "lark," seek out and randomly kill a victim walking to a bus stop. The finality of death being unreal to a desensitized youngster.

Although adults have the ability to mentally digest these scenes as fictional and unreal, the immature brain of an impressionable young person shows much less ability to distinguish between what is real and what is not. When the good guy wins on television by brutally killing the bad guy, does a child know that is not how problems are solved in real everyday life? Do children understand that, in reality, most of these acts seen on television hold severe consequences and that there are always more victims to a shooting than just the immediate victim, including himself and his family?

Conclusion

The relationship between America's youth and gang violence is of concern to many, and one not easily understood. Some support the idea that today's youths are much more violent and commit more violent crimes than ever before. Others state that there is little, if any, difference in the violence of youths today. They cite the gangs and youths of earlier generations who were as violent and crime prone as latter-day youths. Every decade, every generation has endured youth street gang problems. Many of the gang members outgrew their violent youths and sought "legitimacy" through more subtle types of crime, such as white-collar crime, and others have managed to leave their criminal pasts behind them and gained respectful lives with families and jobs.

The relationship and frequency of violent crime among youths may not be growing at the alarming rate some believe, but it has long been a problem and will continue to be. Like any type of crime, youth gangs cannot be totally eliminated. The hope is that they can be better understood, and that we can influence today's potential gang members to make the right decisions for their sake and the sake of society.

References

1. June, D. L. 2012. *Protection, Security and Safeguards; Practical Approaches and Perspectives.* Boca Raton, FL: CRC Press/Taylor & Francis.
2. June, D. L. 2008. *Introduction to Executive Protection,* 2nd ed. Boca Raton, FL: CRC Press/Taylor & Francis.
3. Neite, D. L. Online at http://www.scrapbook.com/quotes/doc/11809/350.html (retrieved December 21, 2012).
4. Rodriquez, R. 1996. *The Los Angeles Times,* January 21. Rodriquez, Richard; *The Coming Mayhem: Pre-Teens today are more violent than ever before. In their world—nothing matters. Where are all the adults?* January 21, 1996, *Los Angeles Times* Op.Ed.
5. Harlow, H. Online at http://psychology.about.com/od/historyofpsychology/p/harlow_love.htm (retrieved December 22, 2012).
6. Harlow, H. Online at http://www.alleydog.com/glossary/definition.php?term=Harry%20Harlow (retrieved December 22, 2012).
7. Schmallenger, F. 2006. *Criminology Today: An Integrative Introduction,* 4th ed. Upper Saddle River, NJ: Pearson-Prentice Hall.
8. Ibid.
9. Rogers, C. 1993. *Children in Gangs. Criminal Justice, 1993–1994.* Guilford, CT: Dushkin, pp. 197–199. Quoted in Schmallenger, F. 2006. *Criminology Today: An Integrative Introduction,* 4th ed. Upper Saddle River, NJ: Pearson-Prentice Hall, p. 235.
10. Schmallenger, *Criminology Today.*

Effect of Gang Culture on Juveniles

3

MICHAEL TUIMAVAVE

Contents

There are many complex problems with the modern world—the economy, war, poverty, crime, the health care system, and the list goes on. One thing that is mandatory for survival is environmental adaptation, and an adaptation made to these various issues has been the emergence of street gangs. In 1936, Frederic M. Thrasher (sociologist at the University of Chicago) defined street gangs as "an interstitial group originally formed spontaneously, and then integrated through conflict. It is characterized by the following types of behavior: meeting face-to-face, milling, movement through space as a unit, conflict, and planning. The result of this collective behavior is the development of tradition, unreflective awareness, and attachment to a local territory" (Whitehead and Lab, 2009, p. 103). Street gangs have become so prolific in modern society that gangs have their very own culture, including aspects such as music, art, language, and history. The following research will not necessarily focus on the culture of gangs; rather, the focus will be on the appeal that this gang culture has for juveniles of today and what juveniles can be considered "at risk" of gang membership.

The draw of street gangs impact juveniles in three major ways: socially, psychologically, and criminally. It is through a combination of all three of these factors that the street gang problem has worsened, and the only acceptable solution to this problem is to analyze the street gang and develop a collective solution that will truly address the entire spectrum of the problem.

Juveniles can be influenced fairly easily, and it is this exigent circumstance that gangs exploit. It is the search for relativity and belonging that juveniles seek, and, oftentimes, that is exactly what they find in gangs. Furthermore, there are a number of sociological factors that can encourage youths to become gang affiliated, such as socioeconomic status, family history of gang involvement, and neglect in the home.

Poor socioeconomic standing has been proven to escalate the amount of gang activity in certain areas. A study by Alan Seals (2009) of whether or not gangs are a substitute for legitimate employment states: "The effects of economic incentives on gang participation across different age groups because federal minimum working age requirements create natural 'treatment' and 'comparison' groups within my sample. The age profile of gang members in the NLSY97 [National Longitudinal Survey of Youth 1997], which is 'a unique data set for the study of youth gang activity in the United States because it annually collects detailed information on gang participation and is both nationally representative and current'" (p. 408). This suggests that individual gang careers are relatively short-lived, which is important because it also implies that gangs require a steady supply of new recruits to remain extant.

Studies have shown the rate of gang participation rises until age 16, which is also the minimum legal age required to work most jobs, and then participation gradually declines. This demographic remains constant throughout crime indices reflecting that as a person becomes older, the rate of criminal participation gradually drops off for several reasons. Among the reasons are employment and career opportunities, marriage and family, assimilation into the general community, etc. "It is possible that many individuals are unable to find legitimate employment before age 16, perhaps because of age requirements or transportation constraints, and join gangs to generate income (or pass the time). After age 16, the opportunity cost of gang participation may be higher because legitimate economic opportunities are more plentiful" (Seals, p. 408). This study focuses on the economic factors of the societies in which gangs are prevalent, and found that "even though members can reap financial gains from gang crimes, those who are old enough to have more economic opportunity outside the gang may weigh the costs of gang membership differently. The average age of those who admit gang participation in the past 12 months is 17.2; however, 35.8 percent of this subsample is also below the age of 16 at some point during the survey. If gang members respond to economic incentives, the unemployment rate should have a greater effect on the gang participation decision for those who are legally eligible to work most jobs" (Seals, p. 419).

A second social factor that can influence whether or not a juvenile will become gang affiliated is his home life. A juvenile's household is responsible teaching him certain values and responsibilities to the community. Jack ng (Young, 2001) observes that "community" is sometimes thought of as holesome, homogeneous entity waiting to be mobilized, while 'crime' antisocial behavior' are 'readily recognized by any decent citizen.'" Yet, considered to be "antisocial behavior," and how best to respond to it, pend upon one's relationship to the lines of division that prevail in a rhood" (Silver, p. 29). Furthermore "an inappropriate responsibili- parents and families can divert attention from the multi-domain risk and the importance of structural/contextual factors in shaping cesses" (Bronfenbrenner, 1979) (Aldridge et al., 2011, p. 372)." A t does not receive this education at home has a higher chance of gang membership than that of a juvenile who receives support and education of the community responsibility in the home. This lack of education can be a sort of neglect in the home. "The early work of Thrasher (1936) suggests that the gang provides inner-city youths with a sense of belonging and acceptance. ... The importance of a gang to its members can be seen in the level of group cohesion often found among the group" (Whitehead and Lab, pp. 115–116). This sense of belonging and acceptance can be intensified exponentially if the juvenile comes from a home that has prior gang affiliation.

Gangs have a tremendous affect on the societies in which they operate, especially juveniles that are affiliated. A second factor that is impacted by gang activity is the psyche of affiliated juveniles. Some of the major psychological factors that gang-affiliated juveniles encounter include:

1. Low self-esteem which has a significant relationship with delinquency.
2. Antisocial behavior and aggression.
3. The carrying of a mob mentality while participating in gang-related activities, and this can be detailed through the disregard of nonaffiliates.
4. A responsibility to the gang above everything else.

The terms *at-risk* and *troubled* can be synonymous, especially in regard to gang affiliation and juveniles. Troubled youths are those who carry a sense of detachment with them in their everyday lives. This detachment leads to low self-esteem and can be the predecessor to full-on gang membership. "Low self-esteem has a significant relationship with delinquency, antisocial behavior, and aggression; elements characteristic of gang membership (Donnellan et al., 2005). Some research supports the premise that youths with less confidence and self-esteem, and weak bonds with a prosocial environment and network (i.e., schools and family) are more likely to look toward gangs than youth who are more confident" (Dukes et al., 1997) (Alleyne and Wood, 2010, p. 425). Self-esteem as a driving point can be very strong, because the gang is often viewed as a source where the juvenile can become accepted by a group, and gain a sense of confidence through proving that he or she can maintain his or her status as a member.

Along with self-esteem growth, juveniles feel that they can improve their sense of pride; pride in themselves, as well as pride of their gang. At-risk youths believe that the gang gives them ownership over something. In a sense, they are a part of a team, and that team encourages the sense of pride that juveniles have, along with promoting their self-esteem. Although the pride and self-esteem can be found elsewhere, some juveniles believe that the gang is the only place to get those feelings.

Another by-product of gang affiliation is the mob mentality. Mob mentality can lead to detrimental behaviors, but affiliated individuals have no regard for the consequences they face simply because their behaviors are accepted and promoted by the group. "Previous findings have shown how, once a collective identity has been formed, even the mere awareness of an out-group (possibly a rival gang) is sufficient to motivate the group to defend its reputation (Emler and Reicher, 1995; Tajfel and Turner, 1979; Turner, 1982)" (Alleyne and Wood, p. 432). Tying the sociological aspect to the psychological aspect, neglect in the home leads these juveniles to develop a train of thought that promotes self-sufficiency.

An interview conducted with a young man who "talks about being a child in the inner city of Edmonton and how poverty was a precursor to his gang affiliation: '[When I was 10] that was a hard thing to deal with—having Mom taking off and not being there ... you get up in the morning, sometimes she would be there, sometimes she wouldn't. When she was there, she wouldn't be up to get us ready for school, to cook us breakfast. I would slap something together for me and my little brother, get my little brother dressed, and away we went. [That's how I grew up], seeing my mother and stepfather fight a lot—that's how they handled their problems, by yelling, swearing, screaming, and physically assaulting one another. So I thought, OK, that's how I deal with things'" (Grekul and LaBoucane-Benson, 2008, pp. 66–67). This neglect in the home forces juveniles to seek a caring environment, and they have not been taught right from wrong, subsequently seeking guidance from surrounding gangs.

Upon finding the guidance that is lacking in their home lives, juveniles who have become gang-affiliated develop a sense of obligation to the gang. Gang-affiliated juveniles begin to believe that the acceptance and guidance provided by the gang obligates them to place their gang on a pedestal and do anything they are capable of to pay the gang back for the sense of acceptance they feel. This feeling of obligation leads affiliated juveniles to have little or no regard for the well-being of nonmembers or rival members. This mental state often leads to destructive behavior, and affiliated juveniles "are guilt-free of their criminal behavior, also, gang members cope with their behavior by neutralizing the negative consequences of their actions" (Esbensen and Weerman, 2005; Esbensen et al., 2009) (Alleyne and Wood, p. 425).

This neutralization of the negative consequences of their actions leads to more and more destructive behavior, along with an increased quantity of crime; the quality of the crimes committed becomes more heinous. These trains of thought are encouraged from the top of the gang and trickle down to the foot soldiers of these gangs. A responsibility to the gang is bestowed upon these juveniles, and it is through the belief that they are obligated to commit various crimes because a superior member told them to is quite apparent.

With the gullibility of juveniles, it is not a difficult task for gangs to implant a sense of obligation to these juveniles who are either at-risk or full-blown members. It is the sense of obligation that encourages the criminal mentality of these troubled youths. "Hirschi (1969) suggested that gang members lack the ability to form effective, fulfilling relationships with others. Research on the friends of gang members indicates that gangs do not typically encourage active members to have friends, especially close ones outside the gang (Horowitz, 1983; Miller, 1977; Spergel, 1989) (Craig et al, 2002, p. 55). As mentioned earlier, the neutralization of the negative consequences associated with the criminal behaviors carried out by these juveniles is dangerous. More experienced members are pressing the notion that the gang is responsible for protecting the juvenile and that the gang is the juvenile's family. In return, the juvenile is expected to do whatever is asked of him/her, no matter what it may be. The actions that are required of the at-risk youths and gang-affiliated youths include, but are not limited to, vandalism, theft/robbery, drug trafficking, assault, and, most notoriously, murder. Through the mentality instilled within these juveniles, it is common for the individual who committed the crime to have no sign of immediate remorse for his/her action. Not until an undetermined period of time has passed, and the juvenile has time to reflect on and understand the entire severity of his/her actions, does he/she show some signs of remorse for what he/she has done.

"Gangs are expanding, evolving, and posing an increasing threat to U.S. communities nationwide. Many gangs are sophisticated criminal networks with members who are violent, distribute wholesale quantities of drugs, and are responsible for an average of 48 percent of violent crime in most jurisdictions and up to 90 percent in several others, according to the National Gang Threat Assessment (NGTA) analysis" (NGTA, 2012, p. 9).

Although the threat of gang-affiliated juveniles is very real, accurate measurement of the extent of the gang problem continues to be a problem for the justice system. "A number of problems arise when attempting to assess the extent of gang membership. First, there is no single, accepted definition of what constitutes a gang. Second, many agencies classify individuals as gang members only if the individual self-identifies as such (Egley et al., 2004). Third, many jurisdictions may actively deny the existence of gangs and not collect any data on gangs, thus any count would be an undercount" (Whitehead and Lab, p. 107). Gang members and at-risk juveniles are taught early on that admission of gang affiliation is a sort of certain death if he or she is convicted of a crime.

Documented affiliates of gangs, in a number of states, are held to a different standard in the justice system. "Current law generally defines gangs as any ongoing organization, association, or group of three or more persons, whether formal or informal, having as one of its primary activities the commission of certain enumerated crimes. This measure provides new prison sentence enhancements (including the death penalty) for crimes committed by gang members, changes the standards for prosecuting crimes related to gang recruitment, expands conspiracy statutes to include gang-related activities, allows widened use of 'wiretaps' against gang members, and requires that gang members register with local law enforcement agencies" (Lockyer, 1998, p. 1).

Gangs are held to a different standard in the justice system, and the way gangs choose to combat this is through secrecy. A variation on the "don't ask don't tell" policy of the US military is very much in play for gangs. Denial will be the first reaction of gang-affiliated juveniles, and any hang-around juveniles who seek affiliation will eventually be able to understand the underlying key factors to determine affiliated individuals.

Summary

The draw of street gangs impact juveniles in three major ways: socially, psychologically, and criminally. It is through a combination of all three of these factors that the street gang problem has worsened, and the only acceptable solution to this problem is to analyze the street gang and develop a collective solution that will truly address the entire spectrum of the problem. In the analysis of the different disciplinary data, the solution that has been developed is of collective nature. Responsibility is the most important tool in the solution to the juvenile gang problem of today's society: economic responsibility, parental responsibility, and governmental responsibility to hold harsher punishment for the commission of gang-related crimes will lead to the demise of the juvenile gang problem.

Economically, the local and national governments must pump financial support into programs, such as Gang Resistance Education and Training (G.R.E.A.T) (Ebensen et al., 2011, p. 53), to improve the relationships that juveniles have with authority figures. This relationship is not limited to police or teachers; a responsibility of parents must be set into place. Should parents have responsibility to an extent over the actions of their children, a greater emphasis will be in the home life of these at-risk juveniles to follow the honest lifestyle desired by society. This responsibility acquired by the parents will result in a more caring environment in the home and the at-risk juveniles will no longer encounter the sense of neglect that has forced their psyche to be that of eat or be eaten; an honoring of the family through an honest lifestyle will be felt by the juvenile. This honest lifestyle, in turn, will result in a lower crime rate, and a decline of gang-affiliated crime will be apparent due to the fact that there are fewer juveniles joining these gangs. Although the number of crimes may decline, the intensity of punishment on those crimes committed must be escalated. This escalation will serve as a deterrent for future commission of crimes. Responsibility will create a better social environment for these juveniles to live in, ultimately altering the psychological process of troubled youths, and finally leading to fewer gang-related crimes being committed. Even those crimes committed will carry a punishment so formidable that the affiliated individual will have no choice but to learn responsibility.

References

Aldridge, J., J. Shute, R. Ralphs, and J. Medina. 2011. Blame the parents? Challenges for parent-focused programmes for families of gang-involved young people. *Children & Society* 25 (5): 371–381.

Alleyne, E., and J. L. Wood. 2010. Gang involvement: Psychological and behavioral characteristics of gang members, peripheral youth, and nongang youth. *Aggressive Behavior* 36 (6): 423–436.

Bronfenbrenner–Bronfenbrenner U. 1979. *The Ecology of Human Development*. Harvard University Press: Cambridge, Massachusetts.

Brownfield, D., A. Sorenson, and K. M. Thompson. 2001. Gang membership, race, and social class: A test of the group hazard and master status hypotheses. *Deviant Behavior* 22 (1): 73–89.

Bureau of Justice. 2012. *The mix of circumstances surrounding homicides has changed over the last two decades*. Washington, D.C.: Bureau of Justice Statistics Homicide Trends in the U.S.: Homicide Circumstances. Online at http://bjs.ojp.usdoj.gov/content/homicide/circumst.cfm.

Craig, W. M., F. Vitaro, C. Gagnon, and R. E. Tremblay. 2002. The road to gang membership: Characteristics of male gang and nongang members from ages 10 to 14. *Social Development* 11 (1): 53–68.

Esbensen, F., D. Peterson, T. J. Taylor, A. Freng, D. Osgood, D. C. Carson, and K. N. Matsuda. 2011. Evaluation and evolution of the gang resistance education and training (G.R.E.A.T.) program. *Journal of School Violence* 10 (1): 53–70.

FBI. 2012. National gang threat assessment. Washington, D.C.: Federal Bureau of Investigation. Online at http://www.fbi.gov/stats-services/publications/2011-national-gang-threat-assessment/2011-national-gang-threat-assessment-emerging-trends.

Grekul, J., and P. LaBoucane-Benson. 2008. Aboriginal gangs and their (dis)placement: Contextualizing recruitment, membership, and status. *Canadian Journal of Criminology & Criminal Justice* 50 (1): 59–82.

Howell, J. C. 1998. Youth gangs: An overview. *Juvenile Justice Bulletin*. Office of Juvenile Justice and Delinquency Prevention, August. Online at http://www.ncjrs.gov/pdffiles/167249.pdf.

Lockyer, B. 1998. Gang violence and juvenile crime prevention act of 1998. Sacramento, CA: Legislative Analyst's Office, January 22. Online at http://www.lao.ca.gov/ballot/1997/970898_int.html.

Seals, A. 2009. Are gangs a substitute for legitimate employment? Investigating the impact of labor market effects on gang affiliation. *Kyklos* 62 (3): 407–425.

Whitehead, J. T., and S. P. Lab. 2009. *Juvenile Justice: An Introduction,* 6th ed. Newark, NJ: Lexis Nexis Matthew Bender.

Gang History

4

ROBERT TAYLOR

Contents

Introduction

The influences of gangs, inside and outside of prison, cannot be ignored.

Indeed, while the history of street gangs in the United States can be traced to their emergence on the East Coast around 1783, as the American Revolution ended,[1] today's problem is different. There is also some justification for questioning the classification of these early gangs within the context of what we commonly view as gangs today. The best available evidence suggests that the more serious street gangs likely did not emerge until the early part of the nineteenth century.[2] Some experts suggest street gangs on the East Coast developed in three phases.

The first gang-like groups began to emerge immediately after the American Revolution ended in 1783, but they were not seasoned criminals, only youths fighting over local turf. The beginning of serious ganging in New York City would commence a few years later, around 1820, in the wake of far more large-scale immigration. With large migrations of Latinos and black populations from Latin America and the American South in the 1950's and 1960's, a third wave of gang activity developed in inner cities.[3]

According to a report published in 2009 by the United States Department of Justice,[4] gangs pose a serious threat to public safety in many communities throughout the United States. During the past two decades, gang members have increasingly migrated from large urban centers to suburban areas and other countries. Perhaps one of the most notorious gangs that is now international is the Mara Salvatrucha gang, which originated in Los Angeles and was set up in the 1980s by Salvadoran immigrants in the city's Pico-Union neighborhood. Members immigrated to the United States after the Central American civil wars of the 1980s. This gang has now become problematic in Central America.

Some African-American gangs developed during the 1960s. The Crips, originated in Los Angeles in the mid to late 1960s, and the Bloods street gangs were formed in reaction to the Crips.[5] In the early 1980s, members of both gangs surfaced outside Los Angeles and the rest of California, primarily to sell cocaine. Investigative reports in 1991 placed Crips or Bloods in 32 States and 113 cities.

Gang members are responsible for a growing percentage of crime and violence in many communities. According to the 2009 National Gang Assessment Center, gangs in the United States have swelled to an estimated 1 million members responsible for up to 80 percent of crimes in communities across the nation, according to federal officials.[6]

The National Gang Information Center[7] data also suggests that, while much gang-related criminal activity involves drug trafficking, gang members are increasingly engaging in alien and weapons trafficking. Additionally, a rising number of US-based gangs are seemingly intent on developing working relationships with US- and foreign-based drug trafficking organizations (DTOs) and other criminal organizations to gain direct access to foreign sources of illicit drugs. The US Justice Department's National Gang Intelligence Center study, which has not been publicly released, concluded gangs are the "primary retail-level distributors of most illicit drugs" and several are "capable" of competing with major US-based Mexican drug-trafficking organizations.

The funneling of major drug-trafficking routes from air transport and sea crossing to the overland route via Central America and Mexico has opened more lucrative drug-trafficking opportunities to US gangs along the border and within the southwestern and western regions. These expanded and intensified interactions with Mexico and Central American countries over the past 20 years or so have contributed to the growth of the several street gangs. Concern has been expressed about these gangs expanding into other criminal or terrorist enterprises. Indeed, some of these street gangs are influenced by prison gangs, such as the Mexican Mafia or other criminal enterprises. The Mexican Mafia is not the only prison gang to influence criminal enterprises in the community. Other prison gangs include the Black Guerrilla Family, Nuestra Familia, and the Aryan Brotherhood.

While some might argue that gangs have been around forever and that history, American history in particular, is replete with stories of gangs, gangsters, outlaws, and lawmen, today's gang problem is much different than it was a generation or more ago. Some also might argue that gangs are comparable to nomadic tribes in the Middle East to the extent that they exert their influence on others, either locally or regionally. However, within the context of this work, we will focus on the evolution of gangs in the United States, with the exception of an early reference to gangs in England, or Great Britain, for some historic perspective on the problem.

In understanding this evolution, it is important to focus on the social context of their development. Clearly, there is a similar evolution to gang development in the nineteenth and early twentieth centuries. In many instances, gangs developed around ethnic or cultural lines and often within neighborhoods or communities. Some gangs then evolved from neighborhood groups to economic enterprises, often criminal in nature. Understanding the historic context and development of these gangs is important in understanding how they may evolve in the future.

A Historical Look

Henry Fielding, an English playwright, novelist, and justice of the peace, was an early expert on gangs. He was an appointed magistrate for the city of Westminster and County of Middlesex in 1749. He also founded a detective force known as the Bow Street Runners, which was a forerunner of Scotland Yard. He published a pamphlet in which he wrote about the gangs of thieves and beggars that plagued London in 1751. He wrote, "The Innocent are put in Terror, affronted and alarmed with Threads and Execrations, endangered with loaded Pistols, beat with Bludgeons and hacked with Cutlasses, of which the Loss of Health, of Limbs, and often of Life, is the Consequence; and all without any Respect of Age, Dignity, or Sex. ..."[8]

While the prominence of street gangs in the United States cannot be traced to England, it is interesting to note that the emergence of gangs or violent street thugs is not uniquely an American experience. It also is interesting to note that more than 250 years later, gangs still plague the innocent.

According to some, the history of street gangs in the United States can be traced to their emergence on the East Coast around 1783, as the American Revolution ended.[9] One of the first notorious gangs in recorded American history was the Doan gang. According to an act passed by the Pennsylvania General Assembly in 1783, the Doans were "robbers, felons, burglars, and traitors" to the American cause whose reign of terror throughout Bucks County had to cease.[10] Moses Doan and his followers derived their principal source of income for several years by stealing horses in Bucks County, driving them into Philadelphia, and selling them to the British. They also committed periodic robbery of Whig tax collectors and wealthy Whigs. The Doan gang worked regularly for the British Army as spies and supplied horses to the British Army. In the winter of 1781, Col. William Hart and a group of seven men tracked down Moses Doan at Halsey house and, after a fight, Doan was killed by Capt. Robert Gibson of Fisherville, Pennsylvania.

On May 15, 1787, Abraham and Levi Doan were arrested in Chester County, and after trial in Philadelphia were convicted and taken to Smith's Island and hung on September 24. Thus ended the career of this early gang.

Understanding the historic significance of gangs is important, but acknowledging today's gang problem as much different is an important distinction. There is also some justification for questioning the classification of these early gangs within the context of what we commonly view as gangs today. The best available evidence suggests that the more serious street gangs likely did not emerge until the early part of the nineteenth century.[11]

Criminal gangs, as we know them today, began to form in the nineteenth century. Historians and researchers say this was a result of a growing population, bad economy, a breakdown of the family, massive immigration, and an increase in job competition. It is likely that there were many social and political factors that influenced gang development. This early period of American history was a harsh and difficult time for many, especially new immigrants who were frequently housed together within their own microcommunities estranged from the general population. Life for many was more difficult than they imagined, and death due to poverty and disease was common. For example, a cholera pandemic in New York City began in June 1832, peaked at 100 deaths *per day* during July of that year, and finally abated in December. More than 3,500 people died in the city, many in less affluent neighborhoods, particularly the area known as Five Points.[12]

There was another cholera outbreak in December 1848, whose spread was initially limited by winter weather. But by June 1849, the epidemic killed 5,071 city residents. There were many early Americans who died from various other causes as well, orphaning their children.

With no money to send the children back to their homeland or to other relatives, and with no relatives to care for them in America, children living on the street was a common problem in many cities. Juvenile delinquency became a major concern as scores of homeless children wandered the streets in nearly every large city.[13] Children and teenagers stealing food and clothing was a common problem. Although the youths were banded together, they were more of a nuisance for the communities rather than feared violent groups.

Gangs started to specialize in crime in America's larger cities. These gangs were generally comprised of members of the same race and ethnic background, who banded together for protection, recreation, and financial gain.

They were known to dress in a specific way and used *monikers* or nicknames. Edward Coleman was the first recognized gang leader for a gang called the Forty Thieves. He formed the gang in 1826. He became the first man to be hanged at the newly constructed Tombs Prison in New York City for murdering his wife, a "Hot Corn Girl," in 1838.[14] As the name would imply, girls were hired to sell hot corn on street corners. There were several groups of gangsters in and around the New York Bowery.[15]

Two sets, the Dead Rabbits and the Bowery Boys, became involved in a citywide gang war that lasted for two days in July (4–5) 1857. Taking advantage of the disorganized state of the city's police force, brought about by the conflict between the municipal and metropolitan police, the fighting spiraled into widespread looting and property damage by gangsters and other criminals from all parts of the city. It is estimated that between 800 and 1,000 gang members took part in the riots, along with several hundred others who used the disturbance to loot the Bowery area.

Prior to the Civil War, New York City's government was so corrupt that gangs plundered stores and businesses as well as private homes without fear of the police. Some experts suggest street gangs on the East Coast developed in three phases.[16] The first gang-like groups began to emerge immediately after the American Revolution, but they were not seasoned criminals, merely youths fighting over local turf. The beginning of serious ganging in New York City would commence a few years later, around 1820, in the wake of far more large-scale immigration. The gangs that emerged from this melting pot were far more structured and dangerous. In 1850, New York City recorded more than 200 gang wars fought largely by youth gangs. As early as 1839, Mayor Philip Hone declared: "This city is infested by gangs of hardened wretches"[17] who "patrol the streets making night hideous and insulting all who are not strong enough to defend themselves."[18]

In Herbert Asbury's book, *Gangs of New York*,[19] which was later made into a movie by Martin Scorsese, described the Bowery Boys, Plug Uglies, True Blue Americans, Shirt Tails, and Dead Rabbits (named after their battle standard, a dead rabbit on a pike). The book also described William Poole, the inspiration for William "Bill the Butcher" Cutting, a member of the True Blue Americans, a bare-knuckle boxer, and a leader of the Know Nothing Party, which was fueled by popular fears that the country was being overwhelmed by German and Irish Catholic immigrants, who were often regarded as hostile to Anglo-Saxon Protestant values and controlled by the pope in Rome. Both the fictional Poole and the real one had butcher shops, but Poole is not known to have killed anyone.[20] The book also described other famous gangsters from the era, such as Red Rocks Farrell, Slobbery Jim, and Hell-Cat Maggie, who filed her front teeth to points and wore artificial brass fingernails.[21] As is the case with most new immigrant groups, there was persecution and discrimination in New York in the mid-1800s, particularly toward the Irish. By 1860, New York City had 200,000 Irish, out of a total population of 800,000.[22]

Chinese American immigrants were common enough in New York to have their own community and public venues, but significant Chinese immigration to the city didn't begin until 1869 (the Chinese immigrated to America as early as the 1840s, but in smaller numbers to work on the transcontinental railroad and to chase the dream of riches in the gold fields of California). Discrimination against the Chinese rivaled that of the Irish, but was more hostile because of their ethnicity, culture, and appearance.

After the Civil War, in 1865, New York records indicated a presence of Jewish, Italian, African, and Irish gangs. As the population of immigrants grew, so grew gang membership. Almost every criminal gang of historic note made New York its headquarters. Chinese gangs appeared in California in the mid-1800s. Philadelphia reported gangs as early as 1840. Between then and 1870, Philadelphia became home to more than 100 street gangs. During this time, murder became a test of toughness. Drugs became a part of the scene. By the end of the nineteenth century, gangs started using clothing to distinguish themselves from others.

While these historical references to gangs are interesting, there was no real working definition of gangs at the time. In fact, Mark Twain's fictional character, Huckleberry Finn, discussed the nature of a pre-Civil War gang agreement in Chapter Two:

> Everybody was willing. So Tom got out a sheet of paper that he had wrote the oath on, and read it. It swore every boy to stick to the band, and never tell any of the secrets; and if anybody done anything to any boy in the band, which-ever boy was ordered to kill that person and his family must do it, and he mustn't eat and he mustn't sleep till he had killed them and hacked a cross in their breasts, which was the sign of the band. And nobody that didn't belong to the band could use that mark, and if he did he must be sued; and if he done it again he must be killed. And if anybody that belonged to the band told the secrets, he must have his throat cut, and then have his carcass burnt up and the ashes scattered all around, and his name blotted off of the list with blood and never mentioned again by the gang, but have a curse put on it and be forgot forever.
>
> Everybody said it was a real beautiful oath, and asked Tom if he got it out of his own head. He said, some of it, but the rest was out of pirate-books and robber-books, and every gang that was high-toned had it.[23]

Just as the 1860s ushered in a period of massive immigration, it also is noted as one of the most divisive periods in American history because of the Civil War. The Civil War remains the deadliest war in American history, resulting in the deaths of 620,000 soldiers and an undetermined number of civilian casualties between 1861 and 1865. The Civil War also generated some outlaws who formed gangs.

When the war began in 1861, William Quantrill, who claimed he was a native of Maryland, allegedly became a member of the Missouri State Guard. However, his dislike of army discipline led him to form an independent guer-rilla band by the end of that year. The band was known as Quantrill's Raiders. In the spring of 1865, now leading only a few dozen men, Quantrill staged a series of raids in western Kentucky. He and his group, terrorizing communi-ties, were more like outlaws than confederate rebels. His band of marauders quickly grew to more than 100 in 1862, with both regular proslavery citizens and Confederate soldiers, until he became the most powerful leader of the many bands of border ruffians that pillaged the area.

Several famous would-be outlaws joined his ruffian group, including Frank and Jesse James and the Younger Brothers. Justifying his actions for perceived wrongs done to them by Kansas jayhawkers and the federal authorities, the band robbed Union mail, ambushed federal patrols, and attacked boats on the Missouri River throughout the year. Quantrill rode into a Union ambush on May 10, 1865, near Taylorsville, Kentucky, and received a gunshot wound to the chest. He died from his wound on June 6, 1865, at the age of 27.[24]

Quantrill's actions remain controversial to this day. Some historians view him as an opportunistic, bloodthirsty outlaw. James M. McPherson, one of America's most prominent experts on the Civil War today, calls him and Lt. William "Bloody Bill" Anderson "pathological killers" who "murdered and burned out Missouri Unionists."[25]

The James–Younger gang was another notable nineteenth-century gang of American outlaws that included Jesse James, his brother, Frank, and Cole Younger.[26] The gang had its roots in the Confederate Army, but this group's postwar crimes began in 1866, though it did not truly become the James–Younger Gang until 1868, when the authorities first named Cole Younger and both the James brothers as suspects in the robbery of the Nimrod Long bank in Russellville, Kentucky. The gang dissolved in 1876, after the capture of the Younger brothers in Minnesota after the ill-fated attempt to rob the Northfield First National Bank.[27]

While folklore romanticizes these outlaw groups, adding to the tapestry of American history, these bands were criminals involved in robbery and murder. Their criminality did not make a favorable contribution to our culture or history. Much the same can be said of today's brand of gangs. This post-Civil War period was a difficult time for America.

During the Civil War, 10 percent of all Northern males 20 to 45 years of age died, as did 30 percent of all Southern white males aged 18 to 40.[28] Victory for the North meant the end of the Confederacy and of slavery in the United States, and it strengthened the role of the federal government. Certainly, the social, political, economic, and racial issues of the Civil War decisively shaped the 1870s reconstruction period of America and future cultural issues.

Unfortunately, the war did not resolve all of those social, political, economic, and racial issues. For example, it is believed that the first Ku Klux Klan was founded in 1865 in Pulaski, Tennessee, by veterans of the Confederate Army. Although it never had an organizational structure above the local level, similar groups across the South adopted the name and methods.[29] These various factions formed in different towns, which led to a meeting in April 1867 to codify rules and organizational structure. At this meeting, former

Confederate Gen. Nathan Bedford Forrest was elected Grand Wizard, or supreme leader, of all the Klan. In 1870 and 1871, the federal government passed the Force Acts,[30] which were used to prosecute Klan crimes.

In 1915, William J. Simmons, a lifelong joiner of clubs, was inspired to reorganize the Ku Klux Klan after seeing the movie *Birth of a Nation*, D. W. Griffith's spectacular account of Reconstruction, told from the perspective of the South and adopting the group's mythic vision of a noble and pristine antebellum South.[31] The timing was perfect. The United States was struggling to meet the challenges imposed by a massive influx of immigrants, many of whom were Catholic or Jewish and few of whom spoke English. Appealing to the middle class and claiming to be a "purely benevolent" club, the Klan drew members immediately.

In the late 1800s and early twentieth century, many large urban areas in the United States were the birthplace to new, violent gangs, comprised of criminals willing to do whatever was necessary to make money. Many of these gangs fell upon or developed around ethnic or cultural roots. New York City was an example of one of these urban areas, and the Whyos were one of the city's most powerful gangs.[32] The members were predominantly Irish, but would victimize anyone, regardless of ethnicity. Edward "Monk" Eastman (1875–1920) was another New York brawler who founded and led one of the most powerful street gangs in New York City at the turn of the twentieth century—the Eastman Gang.

Herbert Asbury reports that Eastman distinguished himself as a colorful character in these early days by keeping a messy head of wild hair, wearing a derby two sizes too small for his head, sporting numerous gold-capped teeth, and often parading around shirtless or in tatters, always accompanied by his cherished pigeons.[33] He was a prototype for what would emerge as a major crime figure. He was involved in a variety of criminal enterprises, such as larceny, physical assaults, robbery, and murder. He was one of the first gang leaders to become politically connected and was involved with Tammany Hall. Perhaps this was one of the first major transitions from street thugs to what would later be termed *organized crime*. Along with the organized criminal influence came political influence.

Tammany Hall was a political organization founded in 1786, but its power surged with the influx of millions of Irish immigrants to New York. From 1872, Tammany had an Irish "boss"; however, Tammany Hall also served as an engine for graft and political corruption. Perhaps the most infamous leader of that engine was William M. "Boss" Tweed in the mid- to late nineteenth century.[34] In 1928, a Tammany hero, New York Governor Al Smith, won the Democratic presidential nomination.

While the nineteenth century witnessed the emergence of organized crime, it also witnessed an increase in drug usage, particularly opium and cocaine. An increase in opiate consumption during the nineteenth century was caused by the prescribing and dispensing of legal opiates by physicians and pharmacist to women with "female problems" (mostly to relieve painful menstruation). Between 150,000 and 200,000 opiate addicts lived in the United States in the late nineteenth century, and between two-thirds and three-quarters of these addicts were women.[35]

The first law outright prohibiting the use of a specific drug in the United States was a San Francisco ordinance that banned the smoking of opium in opium dens in 1875. The reason cited was "many women and young girls, as well as young men of respectable family, were being induced to visit the Chinese opium-smoking dens, where they were ruined morally and otherwise."

In the 1890s, the Sears & Roebuck catalog, which was distributed to millions of Americans' homes, offered a syringe and a small amount of cocaine for $1.50.[36] As a result of this domestic problem, the Harrison Narcotics Act (Ch. 1, 38 Stat. 785) became a US federal law that regulated and taxed the production, importation, and distribution of all opiates. The use of the term *narcotics* in the title of the act describes not just opiates, but also cocaine. Some, of course, saw this as an opportunity to create an underground market in prohibited drugs.

After many decades of agitation by temperance societies and the Anti-Saloon League, Congress passed a joint resolution to forbid the use of liquor in the United States. The national law, proposed by Congress during World War I, would become the Eighteenth Amendment to the US Constitution. People like Frances Willard[37] (one of the most famous women of the nineteenth century) dedicated their careers to the "temperance" cause. Since the Eighteenth Amendment itself included neither enforcement provisions nor violation penalties, Congress passed a national prohibition law called the Volstead Act. The act was named for a Minnesota lawyer and congressman who facilitated it. The law gave federal authorities broad enforcement powers. The Volstead Act, passed in 1919, over the veto of President Woodrow Wilson, was a noble attempt to prohibit the sale of alcohol, but the federal government did little to enforce the law. By 1925, in New York City alone, there were anywhere from 30,000 to 100,000 speakeasy[38] clubs dispensing alcohol.[39]

While Prohibition may have been successful in reducing the amount of liquor consumed, it stimulated the proliferation of rampant underground, organized, and widespread criminal activity.[40] As the nation moved into the Great Depression, prohibition became increasingly unpopular, especially in large cities. The bulk of America became disenchanted after the St. Valentine's Day massacre in 1929 in Chicago[41] as part of widespread violence of gang warfare, including bombings and "drive-by shootings."

On March 22, 1933, President Franklin Roosevelt signed into law an amendment to the Volstead Act known as the Cullen–Harrison Act, allowing the manufacture and sale of certain kinds of alcoholic beverages. On

December 5, 1933, the ratification of the Twenty-First Amendment repealed the Eighteenth Amendment, but federal law still prohibits the manufacture of distilled spirits without meeting numerous licensing requirements.[42]

The turn of the twentieth century was a time of change across America, and entrepreneurs in the Detroit area—notably Henry Ford—forged into production of the automobile, capitalizing on the already-existing machine tool and coach-building industries in the city. Early automotive production is recognizable by structures, such as Ford's Piquette Plant (1904) and multiple structures in the surrounding Piquette Avenue Industrial Historic District (including the now-destroyed E-M-F/Studebaker Plant, 1906) and the New Amsterdam Historic District (including the original Cadillac factory, 1905), and small factories, such as the Crescent Brass and Pin Company Building (1905). Along with this industrialization came opportunity for organized criminals.

In Detroit, four Bernstein brothers (Abe, Joe, Raymond, and Isadore (Izzy)), entrepreneurs in their own right and young delinquents, quickly graduated from nuisance types of street crime to armed robbery, hijacking, extortion, and other strong arm work as a part of the Purple Gang.[43] They became notorious for their high-profile manner of operation and their savagery in dealing with enemies.

The Purple Gang was never a tightly organized criminal syndicate, but a loose confederation of predominantly Jewish gangsters. By the early 1920s, the Purples had developed an unsavory reputation as hijackers, stealing liquor loads from older and more established gangs of rumrunners. The Purple Gang always preferred hijacking to rum running, and their methods were brutal. Anyone landing liquor along the Detroit waterfront had to be armed and prepared to fight to the death, because it was common practice for the Purples to take a load of liquor and shoot whoever was with it. In the early years, the Purple Gang preyed exclusively on other underworld operators, thereby insulating themselves from the police.

During the late 1920s, the Purple Gang reigned supreme over the Detroit underworld, controlling the city's vice, gambling, liquor, and drug trade. They also controlled the local wire service that provided horse racing information to all of the Detroit horse betting parlors and handbooks. The gang even became the suppliers of Canadian whiskey to the Capone organization in Chicago. This arrangement was made after Capone was told by the Detroit underworld to keep his operation out of the city. Capone thought it more prudent to make the Purples his liquor agents rather than go to war with the gang. The Purple Gang was active until about 1935.

The Detroit Partnership, also known as the Detroit Combination or the Tocco–Licavoli–Zerilli crime family, is another organized crime group of the American Mafia or Cosa Nostra, or "Our Thing" to its members. Based in Detroit, the group's illicit activities include labor racketeering, gambling, loan sharking, extortion, hijacking, fencing, narcotics, and a number of legitimate businesses that included a race track, trucking and garbage hauling firms, construction companies, restaurants, food supply, and laundry services.

Even though the American Mafia and its remaining crime families have been hit hard by law enforcement over roughly the past 25 years, La Cosa Nostra is still considered by federal law enforcement agencies to be the most powerful and influential organized crime group in America. Large prosecutions and the lack of a decent recruitment pool has left the organization weakened, but not destroyed. In fact, most within law enforcement and Mafia historians know that the American Mafia, with its more than 100 years of organized crime experience and established criminal connections, has bounced back a number of times and should never be counted out. The Detroit Partnership remains one of the original 24 crime families.[44]

Chicago, like Detroit, Philadelphia, and New York, has its early history of gangs. By the early twentieth century, Polish and Italian gangs were the most numerous in Chicago. Polish gangs located in the "Pojay" colony on the Northwest Side battled rival Polish groups across the river in the Bucktown area and southward, where a different Polish gang occupied every block of Milwaukee Avenue down to the industrial area along the Chicago River. These gangs also engaged in territorial skirmishes with Italian gangs of the "Little Sicily" neighborhood to their south. Usually identifying themselves by streets that served as hangouts, several of these Italian gangs reportedly had connections with "Black Hand" syndicates.[45]

The involvement of the Ragen's Colts gang in the race riot of 1919 established a pattern of white ethnic gang behavior that would affect the course of race relations in Chicago through the 1950s. Named after Democratic alderman Frank Ragen of Canaryville, this gang attacked African-Americans residing in a nearby Black Belt neighborhood after African-American votes had helped lift Republican "Big Bill" Thompson to victory in the municipal elections.[46]

However, Chicago is more renowned for its organized crime roots. Big Jim Colosimo[47] was the first man to make organized crime a major Chicago "business." His initial focus was the brothel industry that he built with his first wife, a former madam. Netting around $50,000 a.m.nth, success from his 200-house business led to competition for his cash.

When the Black Hand[48,49] targeted Colosimo with extortion threats, he initially paid. After all, he knew how the game was played because he had been involved with that criminal element at the beginning of his career. However, when threats continued, and worsened, Colosimo called for help. He summoned his nephew, Johnny Torrio, from New York City.

Torrio had a "business" of his own working in New York. After he came to the frontier town of Chicago, Torrio needed trusted people around him. At the top of his list was "Al Brown," better known as Alphonse Capone, also known as "Scarface" because his face had been sliced in a New York saloon fight. Capone joined Torrio in 1920. With the help of Torrio and his crew, Colosimo built a growing business of saloons, brothels, and gambling dens. Of course, it wasn't enough for Torrio to merely share his uncle's spoils.

On May 11, 1920, Colosimo, the man who made Chicago crime big business, was gunned down at his saloon, Colosimo's Restaurant. (The cafe was a popular place, frequented by the likes of trial lawyer Clarence Darrow and opera singer Enrico Caruso.) Prohibition had been in effect just under four months. Colosimo's killer was never arrested, but it was speculated that Frankie Yale made the hit, although he was never charged with the shooting. Most people believed Torrio ordered his uncle's death. Torrio's rein on the gang was short. After returning from a shopping trip with his wife, on January 24, 1925, Torrio was shot in front of his home. Although he didn't die from his wounds, the near-death experience convinced him to step down from his organization. With the words, "It's all yours, Al," he gave control to Capone. It was speculated that Capone was behind the shooting of Torrio.

In another version of the hit on Torrio, Hymie Weiss is credited with shooting him plus coining the phrase, "one-way ride:"[50]

Hymie Weiss was born Earl Wajciechowski in his homeland of Poland in 1898. He emigrated to the United States with his family and the name was changed soon after their arrival. Weiss became buddies with Dion O'Bannion in his teens and the two of them performed numerous burglaries, car thefts, and jewel robberies. The years went by and Weiss became O'Bannion's right-hand man in the ruthless North Side Gang. The gang became involved in bootlegging and had frequent run-ins with Al Capone and John Torrio.

Some crime experts have credited Weiss with building up O'Bannion's booze empire. He also coined the phrase "a one-way trip." In 1921, a fellow gangster named Stephen Wisniewski, hijacked some of O'Bannion's booze and Weiss was tasked with the job of teaching Wisniewski a lesson. Wisniewski was invited to go for a ride with Weiss along Lake Michigan and, somewhere along that ride, he was whacked. Weiss is said to have stated, "We took Stevie for a one-way ride."

After the murder of Dion O'Bannion in November of 1924, Weiss became the boss of the North Side Gang and began plotting the demise of those responsible for the death of his good friend, namely Capone and Torrio. Weiss kept a low profile for two months after O'Bannion's funeral and then on January 12, 1925, made an attempt on Capone's life. Weiss, Schemer Drucci, and "Bugs" Moran tailed Capone's limousine to a restaurant at 55th Street and State where they opened up with their guns and managed to get 26 hits on the limo. The chauffer was hit, but Capone and his two bodyguards were unscathed by the tirade of bullets. Weiss then tried a hit on Torrio in a similar manner and bungled that, too. Torrio's dog was killed, along with his chauffer, but Johnny escaped with just two holes in his fedora.

Weiss made a second attempt on Torrio and was a little more successful this time. On January 24 of the same year, Torrio was ambushed outside his apartment block and was gravely wounded by shotgun blasts and .45 caliber slugs from Weiss and his accomplice, "Bugs" Moran. The two hit men were about to apply "la coup de grace," a shot to the head, when they heard an approaching vehicle. Thinking the oncoming vehicle to be police, or worse, other members of Torrio's gang, they fled. The vehicle was actually a laundry truck. Torrio survived and after two weeks in the hospital, retired.

Weiss continued to try to get Capone. Probably his most famous attempt took place outside Capone's headquarters, The Hawthorne Inn in Cicero. Weiss had a whole cavalcade of cars drive past the Inn and fire over 1,000 rounds into the building on September 20, 1926. One of Capone's bodyguards and an innocent woman bystander were hit but, once again, Capone was unhurt.

Three weeks after the Hawthorne Inn hit, Weiss was killed by Capone hit men. An unknown gunman was lying in wait in the second floor window across the street from Weiss' headquarters—Dion O'Bannion's old flower shop. The gun man opened up on Weiss and three of his men with a machine gun. Weiss arrived dead at the hospital and the coroner counted 10 bullets in his body. He was 28 years old when he died.

A story in *The Los Angeles Times* by journalist Steve Harvey reported that Al Capone, then the "28-year-old kingpin of bootlegging, decided to take a vacation in a balmy burg he had never visited: Los Angeles." His welcoming to Los Angeles was not what he expected. "He was recognized and his visit blazoned in the newspapers, rousing a storm of public protest," biographer John Kobler wrote. "Barely 24 hours after the Capone entourage arrived, the Biltmore manager ordered them to leave."[51*] Los Angeles Police Chief James Davis went the manager one better, giving Capone 12 hours to get out of town. "You're not wanted here," the chief explained.

Just to make sure Capone got the message, Davis dispatched several officers, including E. D. "Roughhouse" Brown, to help Capone pack up. Roughhouse was especially handy with his fists and, "Brown," *The Times* wrote, "was accustomed to act as an unwelcoming delegate to visiting luminaries of the underworld." The police escorted Capone and the out-of-towners to the old Santa Fe train station to ensure their return to Chicago.

Chicago and Detroit were not the only cities with organized crime problems. One of Philadelphia's leading gangsters was Waxey Gordon, born Irving Wexler (1886–1952), who specialized in bootlegging and illegal gambling.[52]

Gordon started his career as a pickpocket and sneak thief as a child, becoming so successful he earned the nickname Waxey for supposedly being so skilled in picking pockets it was as if his victims' wallets were waxed.

---

[*] Kobler, John. *Capone: The Life and World of Al Capone.* Da Capo Press, 1992.

Joining "Dopey" Benny Fein's labor sluggers in the early 1910s, Gordon helped organize Fein's operations before being noticed by Arnold Rothstein, who hired him away from Fein and put him to work as a rumrunner during the first years of Prohibition.

Gordon's success later led him to run all of Rothstein's bootlegging on most of the East Coast, specifically New York and New Jersey, and importing large amounts of Canadian whiskey over the US–Canadian border. Gordon, earning an estimated $2 million a year, began buying numerous breweries and distilleries as well as owning several speakeasies.

After Rothstein's death in 1928, Gordon's position began to decline. He made an alliance with Mafia founders Charles "Lucky" Luciano, Louis Buchalter, and Meyer Lansky. He constantly fought with Lansky over bootlegging and gambling interests, and soon a gang war began between the two; several associates on each side were killed. Lansky, with Luciano, supplied New York District Attorney Thomas E. Dewey with information leading to Gordon's conviction on charges of tax evasion in 1933. Gordon had a large million-dollar operation, which included many trucks, buildings, processing plants, and associated employees, and his business front could not account for this ownership and cash flow and he paid no taxes on it. Gordon was sentenced to 10 years of imprisonment. When he was released, he started a narcotic enterprise in California that led to his arrest and conviction on drug charges. He died in Alcatraz Prison in 1952.

While some of these stories of gangsters are colorful and entertaining, it is important to note that much of what we learn about gangsters is that many had their start as street hoodlums. Just to underscore that point, Frederic Milton Thrasher (1892–1962) was a sociologist at the University of Chicago. He was a colleague of Robert E. Park and was one of the most prominent members of the Chicago School of Sociology in the 1920s. Thrasher's epic work, *The Gang: A Study of 1313 Gangs in Chicago,* was published in 1927.[53] Thrasher observed that "neighborhoods in transition are breeding grounds for gangs." Thrasher's work is recognized as the first sociological and criminological study of gangs. Based on Thrasher's PhD dissertation, the book is a study of gangs in the United States, specifically examining early gang life in Chicago. Thrasher's study discusses what a gang actually is, what life in a gang is like, organization and control in a gang, and the social problems associated with gang behavior.

The second phase[54] of gang growth in Chicago commenced in the 1930s as the result of a steady migration of Mexicans and blacks to northern cities.[55] Black immigrants arrived first, following the U.S. Civil War, to escape Jim Crow laws and the sharecropper's life in the southern states. Between 1910 and 1930, during the "Great Migration" of more than a million blacks from the rural South to the urban North for jobs, Chicago gained almost 200,000 black residents,[56] giving the city an enormous urban black population—along with New York City, Cleveland, Detroit, Philadelphia, and other Northeast and Midwest cities. From 1940 to 1950, the Chicago black population nearly doubled, from 278,000 to nearly 500,000. A majority of the immigrant blacks in Chicago settled in the area known as the Black Belt, a geographic area along State Street on the South Side, where abject poverty was concentrated.

The 1940s were largely defined by World War II. United States isolationism was shattered by the bombing of Pearl Harbor. As President Franklin Roosevelt guided the country on the home front, General Dwight Eisenhower commanded the troops in Europe. General Douglas McArthur and Admiral Chester Nimitz led them in the Pacific. Aside from the war itself, the successful use of penicillin by 1941 revolutionized medicine. Developed first to help military personnel survive war wounds, it also helped increase survival rates for surgery. The Great Depression concluded with the war. Unemployment almost disappeared, as most men were drafted and sent off to war. The government reclassified 55 percent of their jobs, allowing women and blacks to fill them. First, single women were actively recruited to the workforce. By 1943, with virtually all the single women employed, married women were allowed to work. Japanese immigrants and their descendants, suspected of loyalty to their homelands, were sent to internment camps.

Large numbers of black workers were inspired "to leave family and friends and seek their fortunes by working in factories in the North."[57] However, they faced unanticipated and very formidable challenges. Many observers viewed the black migrants as unqualified for the upward mobility paths because of poorer educational and social background than white immigrants before them had used in Northeast cities. However, "the reason for nonassimilation of black migrants into American society was not because blacks were nonurban or unskilled. It was substantially related to racial segmentation of the labor force structured to keep them at what they had been recruited for—entry-level, cheap labor."[58]

Three major street gang organizations were formed in Chicago from the 1940s through the early 1960s (i.e., Devil's Disciples, P-Stones, and Vice Lords). Two of these gangs, the Vice Lords (1958) and the Black P-Stone Nation/Black Stone Rangers (1959), were created in the Illinois State Reformatory School at Saint Charles.[59] The Latin Kings also was formed in this era. Established in 1960, the Devil's Disciples gang splintered into three warring factions between 1960 and 1973: the Black Disciples, the Black Gangster Disciples, and the Gangster Disciples.[60]

Gang wars erupted and, what Chicago viewed as largely a black gang problem, "exploded" in the 1960s, a period of increased gang "expansion and turbulence" in the city with the formation of so-called "super gangs" with 1,000 members or more.[61] Several already sizeable gangs "were joining forces and becoming larger, structured organizations," and each of them controlled large sectors of the city.[62] At this time in the city's history, the major black street gangs were the Black Gangster Disciple Nation, Black P. Stones, Cobra Stones, and El Rukins.

"The Civil Rights Movement was advocating nonviolence, racial pride, and unity. But, in Chicago, black students who were having nonviolent demonstrations in the South had little influence on black street gang members who were having their own distinctly more violent demonstrations."[63] The black gangs that were prevalent in Chicago in the 1960s "lived and acted in a world that overlapped with that of other youths (and the gang members), who were surely participants in a street culture" that promoted racial empowerment and racial unity.[64] This same evolutionary process during this period can be attributed to other urban areas in America as well.

> In New York, some of the same pattern of gang expansion developed, "mass migration of Southern blacks (seeking better employment opportunities and social conditions) landed many of them in urban locales near all white neighborhoods, which sparked interracial conflict. White male youth groups formed and violently resisted racial integration of neighborhoods, which led to black brotherhoods evolving into social protection groups."[65] Under these conditions, "street gangs became entrenched in the social fabric of the underclass."

New York City's gangs also were strengthened during this period by Latino immigrant groups (from Latin America, the Caribbean, Puerto Rico) that moved into areas of the city populated by European Americans—particularly in the South Bronx and Brooklyn.[66]

The Los Angeles experience was a little different. The city became heavily populated with an unusual mixture of native-born urban Americans, Mexican Americans from other parts of the Southwest, new immigrants from Mexico, and third-generation Latinos who had long lived in the intermixed barrios of the city. Indeed, "Los Angeles has long been the Latino 'capital' of the United States, housing more people of Mexican descent than most cities in Mexico."[67]

The influx of black immigrants to Los Angeles came in two waves, between 1915 and 1929 and from 1940 to 1950, with most newcomers coming from the Deep South.[68] "Southern blacks were simply looking for a better life, and the West was considered the land of prosperity because of employment opportunities in factories," according to Cureton.[69] Instead, institutional inequality (in housing, education, and employment) rendered some of Los Angeles off-limits to some minorities.

The first black gangs formed in Los Angeles in the late 1940s were a defensive response to white youth violence in the schools from which they spread south and westward.[70] However, the gangs that subsequently grew in the 1950s and 1960s were far more serious gangs than the earlier ones.

After the Watts Riot of 1965, many of these early gang or club members turned their efforts in other directions. Many political organization and radical movements developed during the years from 1965 to 1969. Bunchy Carter, once a Renegade Slauson (gang from the late 1950s to 1965), became the leader of the Los Angeles chapter of the Black Panther Party. Other key figures that were influential into the black consciousness of the 1960s, were Ron Wilkins, William Sampson, Gerald Aubry, Robaire Nyjuky, and Hakim Jamal. They were all former club members before 1965.

In January 1969, Bunchy Carter and John Huggins were murdered at Campbell Hall on the campus of the University of California at Los Angeles (UCLA) in a dispute with US Organization members. The US Organization, or Organization US, was a black nationalist group in the United States founded by Ron Karenga in 1965. It was a rival of the Black Panther Party in California. The Panthers referred to the organization as the United Slaves, a name never actually used by members of US, but which is often mistaken for the group's official name.[71] George and Ali Stiner of the US Organization were arrested, convicted, and sent to San Quentin prison for their involvement in the murder of Carter and Huggins. In 1971, Karenga, Louis Smith, and Luz Maria Tamayo were convicted of felony assault and imprisoned for assaulting and torturing two women members of US: Deborah Jones and Gail Davis. A May 14, 1971, article in *The Los Angeles Times* described the testimony of one of the women: "Deborah Jones, who once was given the Swahili title of an African queen, said she and Gail Davis were whipped with an electrical cord and beaten with a karate baton after being ordered to remove their clothes. She testified that a hot soldering iron was placed in Miss Davis' mouth and placed against Miss Davis' face and that one of her own big toes was tightened in a vise. Karenga, head of US, also put detergent and running hoses in their mouths, she said. They also were hit on the heads with toasters."[72]

It has been observed that "the end of the 1960s was the last chapter of the political, social, and civil rights movement by black groups in LA, and a turning point away from the development of positive black identity in the city" (p. 668).[70] However, the "deeply radicalized context coincided with the resurgence of new emerging street groups" between 1970 and 1972 (p. 668). Black Los Angeles youths searching for new identities began to mobilize as street groups. This process also widened the base of black gangs into two camps: Crips and Bloods.

The Bloods became particularly strong in the black communities in Southcentral Los Angeles (especially in places on its periphery, such as Compton) and in outlying communities, such as Pacoima, Pasadena, and Pomona.[68,70] By 1972, there were 18 Crips and Bloods gangs in Los Angeles, and these were the largest of the more than 500 active gangs in the city in the

1970s (p. 76).[68] In the 1980s, the most prominent of the Los Angeles gangs were the Crips and Bloods.

There are other competing accounts of how Bloods and Crips gangs formed. Prominent among these is Cureton's (pp. 356–357).[65] Based on his research, former Black Panther president Bunchy Carter and Raymond Washington formed the Crips in 1969 out of disappointment with the failure of the Black Panther Party to achieve its goals. As previously mentioned, this was the same time that Carter was the head of the Black Panther Party, and it is the same year he was murdered. The Crips were originally organized as an association designed to help the community; however, following Carter's death, the Crips' leadership shifted its focus "to drug and gun sales that involved much violence."

While this might be the story told by members of the gang, this was not necessarily the experience of members of the community who saw these groups as low-level criminals engaged in drugs and violence. Street gang feuds soon erupted.

Neighborhood groups who opposed the Crips formed an umbrella organization to unify these groups (Steven R. Cureton 2008). "Hence, the Bloods were born (1973 to 1975), and their philosophy was that a far more ruthless approach was needed to compensate for being outnumbered by the Crips. The Bloods viewed themselves as Crips killers. The Crips and Blood feuds were historic, featuring the rise and fall of peace treaties, community stress, shock, and sorrow over the unforgiving nature of fatal violence." For yet another competing account of Bloods and Crips origins, see Valdez (pp. 186–87).[73] There were many factions of these gangs, including the Hoover Crips, East Side 40th Street Gangster Crips, Hacienda Village Bloods, and 42nd Street Piru Bloods.

Many of the Bloods and Crips gangs regarded one another as mortal enemies and engaged in continuing and often fatal feuds. In succeeding years, hundreds of gangs in the Southwest—and also in other parts of the United States—adopted the Bloods and Crips names. "Today, all West Coast black street gang members affiliate themselves as being either with the Bloods or Crips" (p. 189).[73] While historically the gang influence might be viewed as starting in the east and spreading to the west, influence of the Bloods and the Crips and later some of the prison gangs would mark a shift of influence from west to east. However, there are other gang groups worthy of note.

In recent years, the issue of Asian-American youth gangs has gotten a lot of attention from the media and law enforcement. Interest in this group shares many similarities with other "gang problems" in the black and Latino communities. However, certain ethnic and cultural differences are worth noting. Chinatown gangs around the country (most famously in New York City) have been the subject of much attention and academic research, starting from their initial appearance in the late 1800s and continuing through modern times. Like their Italian, Irish, and Jewish counterparts who came to the United States back in the 1800s and early 1900s, many Asians struggle to adapt to a new country and social environment and challenges of making a living, whether they are immigrants themselves, American-born children of immigrants, or whose families have been in the United States for several generations.

Many Asian immigrants feel overwhelmed, frustrated, depressed, and even angry as they try to adjust to living in the United States. While some Asian youth gangs may start out as just social groups of friends and acquaintances, more commonly, larger and more established gangs actively recruit new members into the gang. Once the new member finds a sense of belonging and acceptance, including the perks to the gang life, such as sex and drugs, it's often very hard for him or her to give it up. Some (although not all) Asian youth gangs also may have connections to, or even be controlled by, larger and more formal Asian organized crime groups who themselves manage elaborate prostitution, gambling, smuggling (including illegal aliens), extortion, and other gang activities around the world (Chinese "triads" or "tongs" or *Wah Ching*).

In the Los Angeles area, the Wah Ching gang has a reputation for ruthlessness among the local Asian gangs. This has put it at odds with another rival Asian gang in Los Angeles, the Asian Boyz (ABZ) that also aligned themselves with the Vietnamese Boyz (VBZ) in opposition to Wah Ching. Wah Ching's move from its original home in the San Francisco Bay area to the southern California region is probably one of the sources of the disputes over gang turf.

Currently, the gang has shown signs of mixed ideology. Despite the fact that *Wah Ching* in Chinese literally means Chinese youth, there are still some individuals of non-Chinese descent who claim Wah Ching. The gang now consists of a great number of Vietnamese members, and the gang's rival, the Vietnamese Boyz, holds a great number of Chinese members. It is rumored that their reasoning for this is that it is the Chinese youth gang, and that the members working or fighting for the gang do not have to be of Chinese ethnicity. Members of the gang have been involved with arms trafficking, burglary, drug trafficking, extortion, illegal gambling, loan sharking, murder, prostitution, and software piracy. The gang has alliances with black street gangs and black prison gangs (Black Guerrilla Family).

Street gang activity grew significantly across the South from the 1970s through the 1990s, but remained dispersed across the region (p. 26).[74] According to The National Gang Intelligence Center's assessment, several Southern states saw sharp increases in the number of new gang counties by 1995: Florida (23 percent), South Carolina (15 percent), Alabama (12 percent), and Texas (8 percent). In addition, gang activity emerged in multiple cities in a number of southern counties by 1995, including Dallas County, Texas (18 cities); Broward County, Florida (15 cities); Palm Beach County, Florida

(11 cities); Dade County, Florida (8 cities); and St. Louis County, Missouri (6 cities). From the 1970s through 1995, the Southern region led the nation in the number of new gang cities, a 32 percent increase, versus increases of 26 percent in the Midwest, 6 percent in the Northeast, and 3 percent in the West (p. 32).

By 1998, the states with the largest number of gang-problem cities were California (363), Illinois (261), Texas (156), and Florida (125) (p. 60).[74] Of these, only two, California and Illinois, reported large numbers of cities with gang problems in the 1970s. The states with the largest number of gang counties in 1998 were Texas (82), Georgia (61), California (50), Illinois (42), and Florida (40), with the South replacing the Northeast as the region with the most top-ranking states (p. 63). Hence, the Southern region appeared to catch up with other regions in the prevalence of gang activity just before the turn of the twenty-first century.

Not all gang activity is limited to the streets, and in some instances it crosses over between the street and the walls of our jails and prisons. Prison gangs are criminal organizations that form inside the penal system and still function within correctional facilities inside the United States today. The original five groups of gangs began forming in the 1960s and 1970s. One main reason for the creation of many, if not all, of these prison gangs was to come up with a way in which inmates could protect themselves from other possible threats. Most prison gangs do more than offer simple protection for their members. Most often, prison gangs are responsible for any drug, tobacco, or alcohol handling inside correctional facilities. Furthermore, many prison gangs involve themselves in prostitution, assaults, kidnappings, and murders. Prison gangs often seek to intimidate the other inmates, pressuring them to relinquish their food and other resources.

In addition, prison gangs often exercise a large degree of influence over organized crime in the outside or, as they refer to it, the "free world," larger than their isolation in prison might lead one to expect. Since the 1980s, larger prison gangs have consciously worked to leverage their influence inside prison systems to control and profit from drug trafficking on the street. This is made possible based on the logic that individuals involved in selling illegal drugs face a high likelihood of serving prison terms at some point or in having friends or family members in prison. The cooperation of drug dealers and other criminals can be secured due to the credible threat of violence upon incarceration if it is not provided. Prison gang members and associates who are released are usually expected to further the gang's activities after their release and may face danger if they refuse and are returned to prison, such as on a parole violation.

The War on Drugs also led to large numbers of drug addicts serving prison terms, providing gangs with a significant method of asserting control within prisons, by controlling the drug trade.[75]

There are five major prison gangs in local and federal prisons. They are, in alphabetical order, the Aryan Brotherhood, Black Guerrilla Family, the Mexican Mafia, Nuestra Familia, and the Texas Syndicate. Before the 1960s, most prisons in the United States were racially segregated. As prisons began to desegregate, many inmates organized along racial lines.[76]

The Aryan Brotherhood is believed to have been formed by a group of Irish bikers in 1964 at San Quentin State Prison. They decided to strike against the blacks who were forming their own militant group called the Black Guerrilla Family. By the 1990s, the Aryan Brotherhood had shifted its focus away from killing for strictly racial reasons and focused on organized crime, such as drug trafficking, prostitution, and sanctioned murders. They took on organized crime-like powers, and may be more powerful than the Italian crime families within the prison system.[77]

For example, while incarcerated in Marion Federal Penitentiary in 1996, after being assaulted, former Mafia Gambino crime family boss John Gotti allegedly asked the Aryan Brotherhood to murder his attacker. Gotti's attacker was immediately transferred to protective custody and the planned retaliation was abandoned.[78]

In 2002, more than 40 leaders of the Aryan Brotherhood gang were simultaneously rounded up from prisons all over the country and brought to trial under the federal Racketeer Influenced and Corrupt Organizations Act (RICO). Among them was Dustin (Mickey Mouse) D. a fearsome member known to often visit Disneyland.[79] The intention of the roundup was to bring death sentences for at least 21 of these gang members, to cut off the leadership of the gang, in a manner similar to tactics used against organized crime. However, none of the members received death sentences.

The Black Guerrilla Family (BGF) was founded in 1966 by George Lester Jackson (1941–1971), a convict who became a left-wing activist, Marxist, author, and a member of the Black Panther Party. Jackson achieved fame as one of the Soledad Brothers, who were three African-American inmates charged with the murder of white prison guard John V. Mills at California's Soledad Prison on January 16, 1970.[80] Jackson, Fleeta Drumgo, and John Clutchette were alleged to have murdered Mills in retaliation for the shooting deaths of three black prisoners by another guard, Opie G. Miller, during a prison fight in the exercise yard three days prior.

One of the inmates killed by Miller was W. L. Nolen. Jackson and Nolen were the original founders of the BGF while they were incarcerated at San Quentin State Prison in California. Activist, UCLA university professor, and author Angela Davis took up the cause of the Soledad Brothers after reading about the case in February 1970, and became the chair of their defense committee.[81] Davis said, "The situation in Soledad is part of a continuous pattern against blacks in the black community."

On August 7, 1970, George Jackson's 17-year-old brother Jonathan Jackson and others burst into a Marin County courtroom with an automatic weapon. He successfully freed prisoners James McClain, William A. Christmas, and Ruchell Magee, and took Judge Harold Haley, Deputy District Attorney Gary Thomas, and three jurors hostage as a part of a demand for the release of the Soledad Brothers. Haley, Jackson, Christmas, and McClain were killed as they attempted to drive away from the courthouse. Eyewitness testimony suggests Haley was killed by the discharge from a sawed-off shotgun that had been fastened to his neck with adhesive tape by the abductors. Thomas, Magee, and one of the jurors were wounded.[82] The case made national headlines.

Angela Davis, accused of buying the weapons, was later acquitted of conspiracy, kidnapping, and murder. Magee, the sole survivor among the attackers, eventually pleaded guilty to aggravated kidnapping and was sentenced to life imprisonment in 1975.[83]

On August 21, 1971, Jackson met with attorney Stephen Bingham on a civil lawsuit Jackson had filed against the California Department of Corrections. After the meeting, Jackson was escorted by Officer Urbano Rubico back to his cell when Rubico noticed a metallic object in Jackson's hair, later revealed to be a wig, and ordered him to remove it. Jackson then pulled a Spanish Astra 9 mm pistol from beneath the wig and said, "Gentlemen, the dragon has come." This was a reference to one of Ho Chi Minh's quotes.[84] Jackson then ordered Rubico to open all the cells and, along with several other inmates, they overpowered the remaining guards and took them hostage, along with two inmates. Six of the hostages were later found in Jackson's cell murdered, including guards Jere Graham, Frank DeLeon, and Paul Krasnes, and two white prisoners. Guards Kenneth McCray, Charles Breckenridge, and Urbano Rubico had been shot and stabbed as well, but survived.[85] After finding the keys for the Adjustment Center's exit, Jackson, along with fellow inmate and close friend, Johnny Spain, escaped to the yard where Jackson was shot dead and Spann surrendered. Jackson was killed just three days prior to the start of his murder trial for the 1970 slaying of guard John Mills. While Jackson has long been dead, the violent prison gang he helped found lives on.

The Mexican Mafia (*La Eme*) originated in the mid-1950s at the Duel Vocational Institute in Tracy, California. The prison, originally built to house young male offenders, soon became the home of many Mexican-American street gang members mostly from barrios, or neighborhoods, in East Los Angeles. Approximately 13 Mexican-Americans from East Los Angeles, including gang members from the Maravilla street gang, formed the original core of the gang called *Mexikanemi*, Aztec for "he who walks with God in his heart." Luis "Huero Buff" Flores is credited with being the initial leader of the gang.[86] As the organization grew, it rapidly evolved into a criminal organization involved in extortion, narcotics trafficking, and murder, both inside and outside the prison system walls. Before 1960, white inmates enjoyed control over most of the trustee positions that offered them many prison luxuries. But, more importantly, the whites controlled the prison underworld. The Mexican-American inmates wanted more freedom and, more importantly, to control the prison drug trade.[87]

Today, the Mexican Mafia has spread from California to at least seven other states, including Texas, Arizona, and New Mexico. Since its founding, the group has grown to include between 200 and 400 "made" members in California and is considered the most powerful prison-based gang in the state. It controls narcotics distribution inside and outside prison walls and enforces its edicts on the streets through murders and mayhem carried out by members of affiliated street gangs, which number in the tens of thousands.

The Texas chapter of the Mexican Mafia was founded in a Huntsville prison in 1984 by Heriberto "Herbie" Huerta. Huerta was serving three life terms for murder conspiracy and racketeering when he was given permission by the California chapter to establish his own branch in Texas. Huerta also wrote the constitution that is followed by members to this day, and continues to collect and manage revenue generated by criminal activities.[88]

Within about 10 years of its founding, the Mexican Mafia faced the first real challenge to its authority in the California prison system. Northern California Latinos felt abused by the largely Southern California gang. During September 14–16, 1968, there were a series of incidents at San Quentin Prison that started over a pair of dress shoes that led to what is referred today as "The Shoe War."

"Pie Face" Ortega told the following story on videotape after he was debriefed by the Gang Task Force in the mid-1970s. An inmate named Hector "Mad Dog" Padilla, from San Jose, California, fought with Robert "Robot" Salas from Hazard in Southern California. Salas was Ortega's crime partner. While the fight was serious and quickly involved others, neither one was killed. From that point forward, a new prison gang known as Nuestra Familia Mexicana came about, consisting of former Mexican Mafia and many Northern California inmates who fought with La Eme. Major rioting followed, with several inmates killed and wounded. In fact, the first public record of the Mexican Mafia was by San Quentin Warden Louis "Red" Nelson in an article in 1968. Nelson said, "We have put an end to this group, that they call themselves, the Mexican Mafia."

According to Chris Blatchford, "By 1961, administrators at Duval Vocational Institute (DVI), alarmed by the escalating violence, had transferred a number of the charter Eme members to San Quentin, hoping to discourage their violent behavior by intermingling them with hardened adult convicts."[89] It didn't work. For example, the story goes that "Cheyenne Cadena arrived on the lower yard and was met by a 6'5", 300-pound black inmate who planted a kiss on his face and announced this scrawny teenager would now be his 'bitch.' Chy returned a short time later, walked up to the unsuspecting predator, and stabbed him to death with a jailhouse knife (shank). There were more than a thousand inmates in the yard. No witnesses stepped forward, and only one dead man entertained the idea that Cadena was anyone's bitch."[90]

Cadena and Joe "Pegleg" Morgan, who became his best friend and mentor, led the gang to prominence in the California correctional system by terrorizing other unorganized ethnic inmate groups, gaining a monopoly over the sale of drugs, pornography, prostitution, extortion, and murder for hire.

Cadena continued to run the Mafia's activities and began to look beyond the walls of prison, envisioning a statewide monopoly of crime. He struck an uneasy alliance with George Jackson and the Black Guerilla Family and became active in Latino political organizations like the Brown Berets. Cadena made overtures to unite La Eme with the rival Nuestra Familia, but his peace talks with *the farmeros* were frowned upon by Joe Morgan and other senior Eme leaders. In response, they ordered the murder of two Familia leaders just prior to an important peace conference between Cadena and Death Row Joe Gonzalez, a leader of Nuestra Familia, at the Chino Reception center. As an aftermath of this, on December 17, 1972, Cadena was set up by Familia assassins as he left his cell in Palm Hall at the Chino Reception center. He was stabbed an estimated 50 times on the tier and thrown off a third story tier onto the concrete floor below and stabbed another 20 times.

The Mexican Mafia collaborated with others in skimming money from the *Get Going Project,* a taxpayer-funded drug treatment program. This Get Going, along with another taxpayer funded program in the Lincoln Heights area of Los Angeles called Community Concern, were involved in extortion, narcotics, and murder. These programs had one thing in common. They were all being run by "reformed" criminals. The most notorious of these was Get Going located on 127 South Utah Street in Boyle Heights, just a few blocks from the Hollenbeck police station. Get Going was founded by Michael Delia, a convicted bank robber and associate of Jimmy "The Weasel" Fratianno and Jimmy Coppola, both Cosa Nostra operators. Ellen Levitt eventually married Michael Delia and changed her name. Ellen Delia was a brilliant writer of grant proposals. One person who hired her said that when "she walked in the door, and the money would follow."

By 1977, Get Going founder Ellen Delia, who was a naïve community activist, was determined to expose the infiltration of her beloved program. Shortly before an appointment with the California State Secretary of Health and Welfare Services, Delia was murdered. Her husband conspired to have Alfie Sosa kill her. Ironically, the car that drove her to that drainage ditch on Elkhorn Boulevard in Sacramento was bought and paid for by a government grant. In essence, she helped finance her own killing. Her collection of evidence on Italian and Mexican Mafia infiltration of the Get Going program was never recovered. Michael Delia and other members of the Mexican Mafia prison gang were implicated in the killing of Ellen Delia.

Monterey Park, California, police began surveillance of the Delia residence. When Armando Varela and defendant Alfred Sosa drove to that residence, the officers detained them, discovered a gun in the car, and arrested Varela and Sosa. Sosa, the triggerman on the Ellen Delia execution, got a life sentence in March 1982. Sosa, according to testimony given by informants, was also Delia's boyfriend. That was probably the reason she got into the car with him. She trusted the guy.

While the Mexican Mafia was created to protect Mexicans in prison, there was a perceived level of abuse by members of La Eme toward the imprisoned Latinos from rural farming areas of Northern California.[91] The gang is believed to have been founded in Soledad prison in 1965. Founders of the group were Haero Morgan, Robert Joseph Gonzales, Bobby Joe Barkley, and Freddy Gonzales. The gang's initial guidelines were designed to protect members and create a brotherhood. The spark that led to the ongoing war between Nuestra Familia and members of the Mexican Mafia, as was mentioned previously, involved a member of La Eme allegedly stealing a pair of shoes from a Northerner. This event put into motion the longest-running gang war in the state of California.[92]

Nuestra Familia (Spanish for our family) is a criminal organization of Mexican American prison gangs with origins in Northern California.[93] Nuestra Familia (NF) and La Eme continued to fight one another; inmates belonging to Hispanic street gangs were strongly encouraged to choose sides upon entering the California prison system. Those from Central and Northern California tended to side with NF, and those from Southern California with La Eme. By the late 1970s, Hispanic street gang members entering the prison system became known either as Nortefios (Northerners) or Surefios (Southerners), depending upon where they lived when they were arrested. Nortefios were generally from north of Bakersfield, California, and Surefios were from Bakersfield and points south.

Nuestra Familia has some influence over much of the criminal activity of thousands of Norteño gang members in California.[94] The gang's main sources of income are distributing cocaine, heroin, marijuana, and methamphetamine within prison systems as well as in the community, and extorting drug distributors on the streets.[95]

The Texas Syndicate (or Syndicato Tejano) is a mostly Texas-based prison gang that is generally Hispanic in origin. The Texas Syndicate, unlike La Eme or Nuestra Familia, has been more associated or allied with Mexican immigrant prisoners, known as "border brothers," while La Eme and the NF are comprised mostly of US-born/raised Latinos. The Mexican cartel gang, Los Zetas, has been known to hire US gangs, such as the Texas Syndicate, to carry out contract killings.[96]

Development of the Texas Syndicate[97] was initially motivated by self-protection against the historical "building tenders" in prison. After building tenders disappeared, the Syndicate's activities turned to drug trafficking, extortion, prostitution, protection, gambling, and contract murder. Released or paroled members who generate money for the Texas Syndicate must surrender a 10 percent tax of all proceeds toward the gang in prison.

Texas Syndicate has a paramilitary structure, headed by a president and vice president elected by the general member population. There are about 8,126 Hispanic members who operate across Texas, including specific reports of members in the Coffield Prison Unit, about 60 miles southwest of Tyler, and at the Allred prison unit outside of Wichita Falls. Each prison unit is controlled by a chairman, who oversees a vice chairman, captain, lieutenant, sergeant of arms, and numerous soldiers. Ranking members in prison are automatically demoted to the level of soldier upon institutional reclassification.

Texas Syndicate members are required to follow a constitution, stipulating that members:

1. Be Texan
2. Always remain members
3. Place the Texas Syndicate before anything else
4. Understand that the Texas Syndicate is always in the right
5. Wear the Texas Syndicate tattoo
6. Never let a member down
7. Respect other members
8. Keep all gang information within the group [98]

Leadership is determined by democratic vote, requiring unanimity. Recruitment is achieved by demonstrating a "homeboy connection," passing a background check to make sure the prospect is not an informer, and receiving a unanimous vote.

We have briefly touched upon early gang development from the beginnings of this country's founding through the 1920s and 1930s. A third wave of gang activity developed in the 1950s and 1960s when Latino and black populations arrived en masse.[99]

Before concluding this chapter, it is important to mention an emerging threat from gangs. So-called transnational gangs are a concern throughout the Western Hemisphere. Criminal street gangs have evolved to pose significant security and public safety threats in individual neighborhoods, metropolitan areas, nations, and across borders. Such gangs—widely known as *maras*—are no longer just street gangs. They have morphed across three generations through interactions with other gangs and transnational organized crime organizations (e.g., narcotics cartels) into complex, networked threats.[100]

While street gangs are generally viewed as local criminal nuisances with varying degrees of sophistication and reach, some gangs have evolved or morphed into potentially more dangerous entities with a reach well beyond the local community. In many of the world's cities, especially in the "lawless zones" of cities where civil governance is weak, and insecurity and instability dominate, organized armed groups such as gangs, maras, or pandillas reign supreme.

These so-called transnational gangs reside at an intersection between criminal activity and war. They are a by-product of the significant changes in societal organization that result from the confluence of globalization and technological advances that alter the nature of conflict and crime; favor small, agile groups; and fuel the privatization of violence.[101] The evolution of transnational gangs in Central America and Mexico are significant. Among these transnational gangs is Mara Salvatrucha (MS-13), originally from the MacArthur Park neighborhood in Los Angeles and which now operates throughout North and Central America.

Eighteenth Street (Calle 18, Mara 18, or M-18) is another export from Los Angeles spreading across North and Central America with elaborate, flexible, and redundant organization and leadership, functioning as networks with extensive transnational linkages.[102] These gangs have their own internal culture (symbols, tattoos, graffiti), recruit, perform internal logistics functions, conduct attacks, collect intelligence, perform information operations (websites), and arm their members with heavier small arms (AK-47s, M-16s, and grenades).[103]

They benefit from networked dynamics and city-to-city interconnectedness, exploiting new spatial and geographic relationships afforded by globalization. Once the province of inner-city ghettos, some gangs have evolved from a sole interest in turf or localized crime to gain in sophistication, political interest, and international reach. They thrive by exploiting seams in law enforcement and judicial structures, immigration (often by forced deportation), and technologies that foster communication, and have become global criminals, threatening local stability and potentially fueling broader networked conflict.

Gangs have been found to be generationally linked, and recent research by Sullivan and Bunker[104] is essentially a situation report on third-generation gangs in Central America. It also includes background on the Los Angeles (LA) nexus, and transnational gang migration, in the context of third-generation gang studies. Gangs, of one sort or another, are a part of the fabric of historical and contemporary society. It is just a simple conclusion to believe gangs and their brand of lawlessness and violence will continue to have future threat potentials.

References

1. Sante, L. 1991. *Low Life: Lures and Snares of Old New York*. New York: Vintage Books.
2. Ibid.
3. Adamson, C. 2000. Defensive localism in white and black: A comparative history of European-American and African-American youth gangs. *Ethnic and Racial Studies* 23: 272–298.
4. US Department of Justice. 2009. National Gang Threat Assessment. Washington, DC, Document ID: 2009-M0335-001.
5. Ibid.
6. Williams, S. T., and T. Smiley. 2007. *Blue Rage, Black Redemption*. New York: Simon & Schuster, pp. xvii–xix, 91–92, 136.
7. Bureau of Justice Statistics. 2010. *National Gang Information Center Bulletin*, May.
8. Fielding, H. 2009. *An Enquiry into the Causes of the Late Increase of Robbers, etc.: With Some Proposals for Remedying This Growing Evil (1751)*. Whitefish, MT: Kessinger Publishing.
9. Sante, *Low life*.
10. McNeally, T. A. Forthcoming. *The Doan Gang: The Remarkable History of America's Most Notorious Loyalist Outlaws*. Yardley, PA: Westholme Publishing.
11. Ibid.
12. Duffy, J. 1968. *A History of Public Health in New York City: 1625–1866*. New York: Russel Sage Foundation, p. 440.
13. New York City Rescue Mission.
14. Sifakis, C. 2005. *The Encyclopedia of American Crime*. New York: Facts on File Inc.
15. Worth, R. 2002. *Gangs and Crime*. Philadelphia, PA: Chelsea House Publishers.
16. Sante, *Low life*; Adamson, C. 1998. Tribute, turf, honor and the American street gang: Patterns of continuity and change since 1820. *Theoretical Criminology*.
17. Teeter, R. 1995. 19th century AD. *Adolescence*, summer.
18. "Gangs, crime, smut, violence." 1990. *The New York Times,* September 20.
19. Asbury, H. 1928. *The Gangs of New York: An Informal History of the Underworld* 1928. (Reprinted by Dorset Press in original format, 1989.)
20. Herbert Asbury website The Gangs of New York.
21. Gangs of New York at the Internet Movie Database. Online at http://en.wikipedia.org/wiki/Internet_Movie_Database.
22. Bayor, R. H., and T. Meagher, eds. 1996. *The New York Irish*. Baltimore, MD: Johns Hopkins University Press.
23. Twain, M. 1885. *Adventures of Huckleberry Finn*. New York: Charles L. Webster and Company.
24. Mills, C. 2001. *Treasure Legends of the Civil War*. Apple Cheeks Press.
25. McPherson, J. M. 2008. Was it more restrained than you think? The New York Review of Books, February 14.
26. Stiles, T. J. 2002. *Jesse James: Last Rebel of the Civil War*. New York: Knopf Publishing, pp. 249–258.
27. Dyer, R. 1994. *Jesse James and the Civil War in Missouri*. Columbia, MO: University of Missouri Press.

28. Huddleston, J. 2002. *Killing Ground: Photographs of the Civil War and the Changing American Landscape.* Baltimore, MD: Johns Hopkins University Press.

29. Horn. 1939, p. 9. The founders were John C. Lester, John B. Kennedy, James R. Crowe, Frank O. McCord, Richard R. Reed, and J. Calvin Jones.

30. Library of Congress. *A century of lawmaking for a few nations: U.S. Congressional documents and debates, 1774–1875.* Statutes at Large, 22nd Congress, 2nd Session, p. 632. No. 1833-03-02.

31. Lang, R., ed. 1994. D.W. Griffith's The Birth of a Nation. In *The Birth of a Nation* (pp. 250–293). Piscataway Township, NJ: Rutgers University Press.

32. Sifakis, *The Encyclopedia of American Crime.*

33. Ashbury, The Gangs of New York.

34. Riordin, W. L. 1963. *Plunkitt of Tammany Hall: A Series of Plain Talks on Very Practical Politics.* New York: E. P. Dutton, pp. 91–93.

35. Kandall, S. R., MD. *Women and Addiction in the United States—1850 to 1920.* New York: Albert Einstein College of Medicine. Online at http://archives. drugabuse.gov/pdf/DARHW/033-052_Kandall.pdf.

36. Cockburn, A., and J. St. Clair. 1998. *Whiteout: The CIA, Drugs and the Press.* Brooklyn: Verso Books.

37. Bordin, R., and B. Anderson. 1986. *Frances Willard: A Biography.* Chapel Hill, NC: University of North Carolina Press.

38. A "speakeasy" was a club that to gain entrance, a person would whisper, "Joe sent me," or some other code word, and one would be admitted to drink illegal alcohol.

39. United States National Archives. 2008-02-14. Online at http://www.archives. gov/education/lessons/volstead-act/.

40. Von Drehle, D. 2010. The demon drink. *Time Magazine*, May 24, p. 56. Online at http://www.time.com/time/magazine/article/0,9171,1989146,00.html.

41. Four of Al Capone's men, some wearing police uniforms, entered a garage at 2122 N. Clark Street owned by gangster George "Bugs" Moran and killed seven men, Chicago February 14, 1929. It became known as the St. Valentine's Day Massacre. Online at http://history1900s.about.com/od/1920s/p/valentines.htm (retrieved December 12, 2012).

42. Aaron, P., and D. Musto. 1981. Temperance and prohibition in America: An historical overview. In *Alcohol and Public Policy: Beyond the Shadow of Prohibition,* eds. M. H. Moore and D. R. Gerstein (pp. 127–181). Washington, DC: National Academy Press.

43. Kavieff, P. R. 2005. *The Purple Gang: Organized Crime in Detroit 1910–1945.* Fort Lee, NJ: Barricade Books.

44. Kelly, R. J. 2000. *Encyclopedia of Organized Crime in the United States.* Westport, CT: Greenwood Press.

45. Thrasher, F. 1927. *The Gang: A Study of 1,313 Gangs in Chicago.* Chicago: University of Chicago Press.

46. *Chicago Daily Tribune* (1872–1963); March 3, 1954; ProQuest Historical Newspapers.

47. *Encyclopedia Britannica.* 2011. James Colosimo. Online at http://www.britannica.com/EBchecked/topic/126602/James-Colosimo.

48. Lombardo, R. M., assistant professor of criminal justice at Loyola University.

49. Several extortion rackets run by immigrant Sicilian and Italian gangsters in the Italian communities of New York City, Chicago, New Orleans, Kansas City, and other US cities from about 1890 to 1920. It consisted of sending threatening notes to local merchants and other well-to-do people—notes printed with black hands, daggers, or other menacing symbols and extorting money on pain of death or destruction of property. *Encyclopedia Britannica, Inc.* For more information, visit Britannica.com.

50. Weiss, H. One-way ride. Online at http://www.gangland.net/weiss.htm (retrieved December 23, 2012).

51. Kobler, J. 1992. *Capone: The Life and World of Al Capone.* Cambridge, MA: Da Capo Press.

52. Fried, A. 1980. *The Rise and Fall of the Jewish Gangster in America.* New York: Holt, Rinehart and Winston.

53. Thrasher, *The Gang.*

54. Adamson, C. 1998. Tribute, turf, honor and the American street gang: Patterns of continuity and change since 1820. *Theoretical Criminology* 2 (1): 57–84.

55. Howell, J. C., and J. P. Moore. 2010. History of street gangs in the United States. *National Gang Center Bulletin,* Office of Juvenile Justice Planning.

56. Miller, B. J. 2008. The struggle over redevelopment at Cabrini-Green, 1989–2004. *Journal of Urban History* 34: 944–960.

57. Marks, C. 1985. Black labor migration: 1910–1920. *Critical Sociology* 12: 5–24.

58. Ibid, p. 22.

59. Dawley, D. 1992. *A Nation of Lords: The Autobiography of the Vice Lords,* 2nd ed. Prospect Heights, IL: Waveland.

60. Block, C. R., R. and Block. 1993. *Street Gang Crime in Chicago. Research in Brief.* Washington, DC: US Department of Justice, National Institute of Justice.

61. Chicago Crime Commission. 1995. *Gangs: Public Enemy Number One, 75 Years of Fighting Crime in Chicagoland.* Chicago: Chicago Crime Commission.

62. Chicago Crime Commission. 2009. *The Chicago Crime Commission Gang Book.* Chicago: Chicago Crime Commission.

63. Perkins, U. E. 1987. *Explosion of Chicago's Black Street Gangs: 1900 to the Present.* Chicago: Third World Press.

64. Diamond, A. J. 2001. Rethinking culture on the streets: Agency, masculinity, and style in the American city. *Journal of Urban History* 27: 669–685.

65. Cureton, S. R. 2009. Something wicked this way comes: A historical account of black gangsterism offers wisdom and warning for African American leadership. *Journal of Black Studies* 40: 347–361.

66. Sullivan, M. L. 1993. Puerto Ricans in Sunset Park, Brooklyn: Poverty amidst ethnic and economic diversity. In *In the Barrios: Latinos and the Underclass Debate,* eds. J. W. Moore and R. Pinderhughes (pp. 1–25). New York: Russell Sage Foundation.

67. Moore, J. W., and Vigil, D. 1993. Barrios in transition. In *In the Barrios: Latinos and the Underclass Debate,* eds. J. W. Moore and R. Pinderhughes (pp. 27–49). New York: Russell Sage Foundation.

68. Vigil, J. D. 2002. *A rainbow of Gangs: Street Cultures in the Mega-City.* Austin, TX: University of Texas Press.

69. Ibid.

70. Alonso, A. A. 2004. Racialized identities and the formation of black gangs in Los Angeles. *Urban Geography* 25: 658–674.
71. Hayes, F. W., III, and J. L. Jeffries. 2006. US does not stand for United Slaves! In *Black Power in the Belly of the Beast*, ed. J. L. Jeffries (pp. 74–75). Chicago: University of Illinois Press.
72. Scholer, J. L. 2001. The story of Kwanzaa. The Dartmouth Review, January 15. Archived from the original on December 30, 2007. Online at http://web.archive. org/web/20071230053918/http://dartreview.com/archives/2001/01/15/the_ story_of_kwaanza.php.
73. Valdez, A. 2007. *Gangs: A Guide to Understanding Street Gangs,* 5th ed. San Clemente, CA: LawTech Publishing Co.
74. Miller, B. J. (2008). The struggle over redevelopment at Cabrini-Green, 1989– 2004. *Journal of Urban History*, 34, 944–960.
75. Hagedorn, J. M. 2008. *A World of Gangs: Armed Young Men and Gangsta Culture.* Minneapolis, MN: University of Minnesota Press.
76. Holthouse, D. 2005. Smashing the shamrock. *SPLC Intelligence Report,* fall.
77. Grann, D. 2004. The brand. *The New Yorker*, February 16. Collected in *The Devil and Sherlock Holmes.* 2011. New York: Vintage Books.
78. Hughes, J. 2002. Aryan Brotherhood makes home in state. *Denver Post,* November 24.
79. Grann, D. 2004. The brand. *The New Yorker*, February 16.
80. Various authors. 1970. Prison guard is beaten to death. *Beaver County Times,* January 17.
81. Biography. 1995. *Angela Davis Legal Defense Collection 1970–1972.* New York Public Library. Online at http://archives.nypl.org/scm/20821
82. Time Magazine. 1970. Justice: A bad week for the good guys. *TIME,* August 17.
83. Associated Press. 1975. Magee gets life term. *The Milwaukee Journal,* January 23.
84. Andrews, L. 1999. *Black Power, White Blood: The Life and Times of Johnny Spain.* Philadelphia: Temple University Press, p. 158.
85. Cummins, E. 1994. *The Rise and Fall of California Radical Prison Movement.* Stanford, CA: Stanford University Press, p. 155.
86. Valdemar, R. 2010. History of the Mexican mafia prison gang. *Police Magazine.*
87. Rafael, T. 2007. *The Mexican Mafia.* New York: Encounter Books.
88. Online at tomdiaz.wordpress.com.
89. Blatchford, C. 2008. *The Black Hand: The Bloody Rise and Redemption of "Boxer" Enriquez, a Mexican Mob Killer.* New York: HarperCollins.
90. Ibid, p. 6.
91. An end to the cycle. *Monterey County Herald.*
92. Modern prison gangs. Online at http://publicsafety.wikia.com/wiki/ NorteñosHistory.com.
93. Federal indictments crack vast prison crime ring. *The Press Democrat.* http:// publicsafety.wikia.com/wiki/Norteños.
94. Reynolds, J. 2010. Operation knockout: Gang raid targets Nuestra Familia in Salinas. *Monterey Herald* Salinas Bureau, April 23. Online at http://www.mon-tereyherald.com/ci_14943640.
95. Gangs in the United States. 2005. *Narcotics Digest Weekly,* October 4, 1–12.

96. Mosso, R. 2008. "El MIlenio" "FBI: *Los Zetas: Problema de seguridad nacional para EU,* January 9.
97. Gangs in the United States.
98. Adamson, C. 2000. Defensive localism in white and black: A comparative history of European-American and African-American youth gangs. *Ethnic and Racial Studies* 23: 272–298.
99. Blatchford, C. 2008. *The Black Hand: The Bloody Rise and Redemption of "Boxer" Enriquez, A Mexican Mob Killer.* HarperCollins.
100. Sullivan, J. P. 2006. Maras morphing: Revisiting third generation gangs. *Global Crime* 7 (3–4): 487–504.
101. Sullivan, J. P. 2001. Gangs, hooligans, and anarchists: The vanguard of netwar in the streets. In *The Future of Terror, Crime, and Militancy,* eds. J. Arquilla and D. Ronfeldt (pp. 99–126). Santa Monica, CA: RAND.
102. Sullivan, J. P. 2000. Urban gangs evolving as criminal netwar actors. *Small Wars and Insurgencies* 11 (1), spring.
103. Manwaring, M. G. 2007. *A Contemporary Challenge to State Sovereignty: Gangs and Other Illicit Transnational Criminal Organizations in Central America, El Salvador, Mexico, Jamaica, and Brazil.* Carlise, PA: Strategic Studies Institute, US Army War College, December.
104. Sullivan, J. P., and R. J. Bunker. 2007. Third generation gang studies: An introduction. *Journal of Gang Research* 14 (4): 1–10; Bunker, R. J., and J. P. Sullivan. 2007. *Subject Bibliography: Third Generation Gangs and Child Soldiers.* Quantico, VA: FBI Library.

Religion and Criminal Gangs
A Perspective

5

GREGORIO ESTEVANE

Contents

Religion has always been a part of criminal organizations, criminal street gangs, organized crime, unorganized crime groups, or individuals involved in criminal gang-like behaviors; historically, presently, and most likely for the foreseeable future.

Historically, we can reference far back in ancient recorded history to find examples of a blending, like poison and ceremonial wine, of religion and criminal activities.

According to the stories of the 20th dynasty (BCE) criminals, as translated from *La Vie Quotidienne en Egypte* (Hachette, 1946) by Pierre Montet (French Egyptologist):

> … Not just common people committed tomb robberies. Times were difficult during the late Ramesside period. The administration was in disarray and salaries rarely paid on time, if at all. Social upheaval and civil war brought with them sharp price rises so it is no wonder that scribes and priests involved themselves also in this "redistribution of wealth."
>
> One such gang included a priest named Pen-un-heb, and four Holy Fathers of the God, Meri, and his son[s] Peisem, Semdi, and Pehru. They began by stealing the golden necklace of a statue of Osiremire Sotepenre, which after melting, left them with four *deben* and six *kit* of gold, which the old Meri divided between them. Another gang of priests, scribes and herdsmen robbed the *House of Gold* of Osiremire Sotepenre. The priest Kaw-karui and four of his colleagues occasionally removed some gold with which they bought grain in town. A herdsman after threatening the priests, received a bull they had

bought for five *kit* (about 45 grammes) of gold. A scribe, Seti-mose, who over-heard their quarrel, blackmailed them and extorted four and a half *kit* of gold.[1]*

In times of Roman and Jewish antiquity, the relationship of religion and crime was no less malignant, as stated by Martin Goodman (p. 407)[2] as he talks of *sicarii* practicing "terrorism within Jewish society." A Latin plural of *Sicarius* "dagger-men" or later "contract killer," *Sicarii* is a term applied, in the decades immediately preceding the destruction of Jerusalem in 70 CE, (probably) to an extremist splinter group of the Jewish zealots, who attempted to expel the Romans and their partisans from Judea using concealed daggers.

The Sicarii used stealth tactics to obtain their objective, concealing under their cloaks a *sicae*, or small dagger, from which they received their name. At popular assemblies, particularly during the pilgrimage to the Temple Mount, they stabbed their enemies (Romans or Roman sympathizers, Herodians, and wealthy Jews comfortable with Roman rule), lamenting ostentatiously after the deed to blend into the crowd in order to escape detection.

The Crusaders of the middle ages were not all zealots to the higher cause of forgiveness of mass murder and plunder in the name of a Christian God, a cause that would forgive all atrocities under some manmade interpreta-tion of a divine pardon and guarantee of one's soul going to heaven. Many Crusaders, though religious, were criminals induced by personal greed and blood lust under the guise of religion.

Many hardened criminals became crusaders to escape punishment at home or scheming debtors joining the Crusades to escape their creditors or the criminal justice system.

According to Uri Dowbenko's critique of *The Templars and the Assassins: The Militia of Heaven* by James Wasserman:[3]

> The Crusades were simply a power grab by the Roman Church under the guise of a contrived "religious" war. As a political tool of the Roman Church (the aptly named "Church Militant"), the Templars revealed their pretensions of piety and religiosity to be completely void, when they murdered the Cathars in southern France in 1244. Their true nature as mercenaries in the service of the Illuminati (the grossly iniquitous Roman Catholic Popes) became perfectly clear, when they exterminated their fellow Christians. Finally, double-crossed by the wily Philip the Fair, the ill-fated Templars and their leader Jacques de Molay, the 23rd and last Grand Master, have forever branded the Templars as a gang of dead losers. ... The Templars were thoroughly identified with the Crusades, Wasserman writes. ... This degenerate and murderous behavior, then, is the legacy of the Templars and the Assassins, who killed in the name of their Gods of Death.

---

* *La Vie Quotidienne en Egypte* by Pierre Montet.

Thus, it would not be surprising to see how modern Mexican drug cartels would borrow on the original Knights Templar, branding the fusion of piety and crime into a toxic modern mixture of religion and crime, as outlined in the 2012 investigative report by InSight Crime, *Organized Crime in the America's Knights Templar:*[4]

The Knights Templar (modern Mexican drug cartel) announced their arrival to Mexico's criminal underworld in March 2011, three months after the Familia's leader, Nazario Moreno Gonzalez, was killed, when they hung banners throughout Michoacán, saying that they would now be carrying out the altruistic activities that were previously performed by the Familia Michoacána. ... The group takes its name (Knights Templar) from a medieval military religious order that was charged with defending pilgrims journeying to the Holy Land, whose members were known both for their piety and for their fearlessness on the battlefield.

The choice of name is part of the Knights Templar's bid to be seen as more than just a drug gang. Members use Roman warrior-type helmets during induction ceremonies, and distribute propaganda promoting themselves as champions of the fight against materialism, injustice, and tyranny. The group even announced a temporary ceasefire ahead of Pope Benedict XVI's trip to Mexico in March 2012. ... Despite their claims, the Knights Templar are heavily involved in drug trafficking, extortion, and kidnapping, having taken over many of the operations once run by the Familia.

In addition to drug trafficking, the Knights receive a large amount of income from extorting businesses in their areas of influence. The Knights' extortion activities are aided by its influence over local government officials, achieved through intimidation, and handing over kickbacks from drug profits. Some of the group's influence also may be based in local loyalties.

While the Knights Templar have not developed the brand recognition of the Familia, which was fueled by contributions to social projects like building schools and roads, the group appears to be dedicated to changing this. In April 2012, the Knights hung up banners claiming that they were responsible for negotiating a drop in the price of basic foods, a clear attempt at gaining the favor of locals.[4]

Religiosity and criminality have long merged seamlessly to unfurl the banner of crime as a cause to rally a fractured populous, in the hopes of legitimizing crime as a duty of God's law.

Pirates of the seven seas and beyond have often mixed that potent cocktail (like a Molotov cocktail) of religion and criminal activities, as seafaring gangsters from ancient times to modern buccaneers.

In medieval times, religion was infused with criminality, pitting European Christians against Muslims of the Ottoman Empire. Naval medieval warfare, on both sides, deployed corsairs (fast and deadly military and pirate ocean-sailing vessels) to attack enemy shipping lanes, and these former naval men saw the vast booty (gold and treasure) that could be their very own; evolving from holy emissaries into criminals clothed in religious vestments solely for the capture of piracy's glimmering ornamentation.

According to Cindy Vallar,[5] "The Barbary corsairs came from Algiers, Tunis, Tripoli, and Salé along the northern coast of Africa. Whenever Janissaries, the warriors on Barbary ships, boarded an enemy vessel, the *khodja* (purser) 'read out verses from the Koran in a loud voice.'"

The corsairs' Christian counterparts came from religious orders, most notably the Knights of St. John of Jerusalem (eventually known as the Knights of Malta) and the Knights of St. Stephen. Livorno (also known as Leghorn) was a haven for Christian corsairs who sailed under the Duke of Tuscany's flag. Sometimes their raids crossed that gray line between privateering and piracy, and both sides sometimes attacked friendly ships rather than just those of their enemies:

> According to documents dated 6 June and 11 June 1607, in the *Venetian Calendar of State Papers,* the duke "receives, shelters and caresses the worst of the English men who are proclaimed pirates by the King. ... Priests, themselves, were more often than not the victims of piracy, rather than pirates. One exception was Eustace the Monk (also known as The Black Monk). As a Benedictine, he became Count Renault of Boulogne's administrator. The count accused Eustace of a crime; he fled to Jersey, one of the Channel Islands, and was declared an outlaw. He became a privateer in the employ of King John of England in 1205 and sailed the English Channel, demanding protection money from ships and attacking those who opted not to pay.
>
> In 1212, when his men attacked English towns, he fell out of favor with the English king and changed sides, becoming a privateer for Philip II of France. Five years later, English forces captured Eustace off the coast of Sandwich and executed him.[5]

The pirates of China were well-versed in weaving the silks of religion and gang crime together as one, as outlined in the 1858 Fanny Loviot book of her capture by Chinese pirates (*A Lady's Captivity among Chinese Pirates,* National Maritime Museum, 2008):

> Every junk ... is furnished with an altar. On this altar, they (Chinese Pirates) burn small wax-lights, and offer up oblations of meat and drink. They pray every night at the same hour, and begin with a hideous overture played upon gongs, cymbals, and drums covered with serpent skins. First of all, I saw a young Chinese come forward with two swords, which he stuck upright in the very centre of the deck. Beside these he then placed some saucers, a vase filled with liquid, and a bundle of spills, made of yellow paper, and intended for burning. A lighted lantern was next suspended to one of the masts, and the chief fell upon his knees before the shrine.

After chanting for some time, he took up the vase and drank; and next proceeded, with many gesticulations, to clink a lot of coins and medals together in his hands. The paper spills were then lighted and carried round and round the swords, as if to consecrate them. These ceremonies completed, the captain rose from his knees, came down to the after-part of the junk, waved the burning papers to and fro, and threw them solemnly into the sea. The gongs and drums were now played more loudly, and the chief seemed to pray more earnestly than ever; but as soon as the last paper was dropped, and the last spark extinguished, the music ceased, the prayer came to an end, and the service was over. Altogether it had taken quite twenty minutes (pp. 110-111).

This reevolution of religious and criminal gang behaviors, so colorfully illustrative in the golden age of piracy from the 1500s to the 1700s, closely resembles the subcultures of modern cartels' penchant for religiosity with a lust for the finer things in life, pious prayers, harmonized into screeching, malodorous murder in the blink of an eye.

As illustrated in Emily Collins thesis of 2004:[6]

… Pere Labat, a Dominican priest from France, traveled to the West Indies as a missionary. … While traveling to various islands to preach, he was captured by buccaneers and ended up sailing with them. Although he stayed with the pirates, he continued his practice as a priest and preached from pirate ships and gave communion. … Labat's records are particularly important to understanding the role of religion in Caribbean piracy. Labat's memoirs describe an instance when Captain Daniels and his crew kidnapped and ransomed a group of settlers, including Pere Lucien, a cure of Saints (i.e., a person of spiritual faith).

Daniels did not wish harm to his captives. He only ransomed them in order to obtain food for him and his men. Once he obtained food and drink for his vessel, Daniels requested the cure to say Mass for them. The request of Mass alone illustrates Daniels' religious nature, yet what happened after Mass continues to confirm the importance of Christ to the captain. When one of his men became offensive during the Elevation and swore, Daniels shot this crew member through the head and made an oath that to any other "who showed disrespect to the 'Sainte Sacrifice,' he would do the same too."

Daniels and his men showed their gratitude for the service by rewarding the cure with presents and a slave for his willingness to set up an altar on the ship to say Mass for these buccaneers. Another account of religious observance on Captain Daniels' ship was when he shot a crew member dead for using the Lord's name in vain during a Mass service given by Labat.

Although Labat was shaken by this violence during a service, this drastic response by Daniels illustrates how serious he felt matters of religion should be taken. Through Labat's memoirs and the books written about pirates, the respect and importance of Christianity during the Golden Age of Piracy among Caribbean buccaneers becomes apparent. Despite the common misperception of pirates as immoral, irreligious seafarers based on the stories of a few infamous individuals, many pirates were, in fact, religiously motivated individuals.

… Many Caribbean freebooters exhibited many Christian ideas and practices throughout their raiding, pillaging, and plundering. Overall, many buccaneers viewed religion as an important part of their lives and held great respect for their respective religious figures.

Modern piracy, as a continuation from the Golden Age of piracy has all the hallmarks of criminal gang activities bootstrapped to ideas of godly entitled divination. In looking at Somali piracy off the Horn of Africa and the pirates' professed religiosity melded into the hardness of steeled bullets and Bibles, little has changed over time, and there has been little if any ability to effectively fight these modern-day pirates.

Somalia has been a lawless state since the early 1990s, with an all too convenient finger pointing to the intelligence establishment's inability to point to clear, unambiguous, and unimpeachable links or alliances among the pirates, tribal warlords, village chieftains, and known terror networks. As long as the pirates are officially perceived as nothing more than organized criminal entrepreneurs making the most of Somalia's lack of security and police infrastructure, Somali piracy will continue.

Somali pirates have extorted billions of dollars in an incensed mixture of al-Shabaab religious extremism and criminal piracy. From the perspective of Joshua E. London:[7]

In a 1786 meeting in London (future presidents) Thomas Jefferson and John Adams, met with Sidi Haji Abdul Rahman Adja, the Tripolitan ambassador to Britain. They met to negotiate a peace treaty and protect the United States from the threat of piracy from the Barbary States, modern-day Morocco, Algeria, Tunisia, and Libya.

Ambassador Adja answered them in unmistakable terms "… that it was founded on the Laws of their Prophet, that it was written in their Koran, that all nations who should not have acknowledged their authority were sinners, that it was their right and duty to make war upon them wherever they could be found, and to make slaves of all they could take as prisoners, and that every Musselman [Muslim] who should be slain in battle was sure to go to Paradise."

… The Islamic basis for piracy in the Mediterranean arises from an old doctrine relating to the physical or armed Jihad, or struggle. Although the piratical activities of Barbary degenerated over the centuries from pure considerations of the glory of Jihad to less grandiose visions of booty and state revenues, it is important to remember that the underlying religious foundations of the institution of piracy remained central. Even after it became commonplace for the pirate captains or their crew to include renegade Europeans, it was essential that these former Christians "turn Turk" and convert to Islam before they could be accorded the honor of engagement in "*al-Jihad fil-bahr*," the holy war at sea.

The peoples of Barbary continued to consider the pirates as holy warriors even after the rulers began to allow nonreligious commitments to command their strategic use of piracy. The changes that the religious institution of piracy underwent were natural, if pathological. Just as the concept of Jihad is invoked by Muslim terrorists today to legitimize suicide bombings of noncombatants for political gain, so too *al-Jihad fil-bahr* served as the cornerstone of the Barbary states' interaction with Christendom.

Centuries of failure and military disadvantage have shifted the institution of Muslim piracy from being primarily *al-jihad fil-bahr*, or the holy war at sea, to the more rewarding notion of *al-jihad bi-al-mal*, or the financial holy war (raising money for Muslims and jihad warriors). Fundamentally, however, little has changed about their motives or their strategy.[7]

Beyond early American policing and political problems of international buccaneering religious gangs, America had an ever-increasing domestic gang problem with religious dissonant undertones threatening the harmonic democratic foundations of the time.

The early American experience of religious and criminal gangs was artfully captured in the American movie *Gangs of New York*. Based on Herbert Asbury's 1928 nonfiction book, *The Gangs of New York* (Vintage Books) dramatically paints in hues of bloody red, Protestant gangs versus Catholic gangs' urban warfare in disturbing lightless penumbras of early American gang culture. In 1846, in Lower Manhattan's Five Points, a territorial war between the "natives" (those born in the United States) and recently arrived Irish Catholic immigrants came to a head in Paradise Square. The natives were led by Bill (the Butcher) Cutting, a Protestant nativist. The leader of the Irish gang, the Dead Rabbits, was known as "Priest" Vallon.

These two American criminal street gangs had strong religious hatred between their Protestant and Catholic belief systems as well as being street crime competitors over criminal proceeds in a very close-quartered environ. American natives were historically linked to English Anglican and Protestant rivalries with the Catholic Church dating back to Henry VIII, the English Tudor king who broke away from the Catholic Church, spurning long and blood-drenched religious wars.

This Catholic versus Protestant rivalry became even more compounding and complex as the arriving Irish Catholic immigrants to a new America brought with them a historical hatred of the native American Anglican Protestants in nightmarish memories of the infamous Oliver Cromwell who waged a savage religious/military genocidal war on behalf of England's Protestant majority onto its Irish Catholic territorial peoples.

According to author and journalist Pete Hamill:[8]

... The Irish hoodlums established the nexus between New York crime and New York politics that would last more than a century. A path was established among the Dead Rabbits, the Plug Uglies, the Bowery Boys that continues all the way to today's Latin Kings, Crips, and Bloods.

According to Paul S. Boyer, a US cultural and intellectual historian:[9]

The period from the 1830s to the 1850s was a time of almost continuous disorder and turbulence among the urban poor. The 1834–1844 decade saw more than 200 major gang wars in New York City alone, and in other cities the pattern was similar.

As early as 1839, Mayor Philip Hone said:[10]

This city is infested by gangs of hardened wretches ... [who] patrol the streets making night hideous and insulting all who are not strong enough to defend themselves.

These mid-nineteenth century, American-born gangs, scarred with religious rivalries, would soon see a new gang competitor arrive in America in the form of Italian immigrants.

The first published account of what would evolve into the Italian Mafia in the United States came in the spring of 1869 from *New Orleans Times*, which reported, "... that the city's Second District had become overrun by well-known and notorious Sicilian murderers, counterfeiters, and burglars, who, in the last month, have formed a sort of general co-partnership or stock company for the plunder and disturbance of the city."[11]

Mafia groups in the United States first became influential in the New York City area, gradually progressing from small neighborhood operations in poor Italian ghettos to citywide and eventually international organizations. The Black Hand was a name given to an extortion method used in Italian neighborhoods at the turn of the nineteenth to twentieth centuries. It has been sometimes mistaken for the Mafia itself, which it is not.

Giuseppe Esposito was the first known Sicilian Mafia member to immigrate to the United States. He and six other Sicilians fled to New York after murdering 11 wealthy landowners, and the chancellor and vice chancellor of a Sicilian province. He was arrested in New Orleans in 1881 and extradited to Italy.

New Orleans was also the site of the first Mafia incident in the United States that received both national and international attention. On October 15, 1890, New Orleans Police Superintendent David Hennessy was murdered execution-style. It is still unclear whether Italian immigrants actually killed him or whether it was a frame-up by nativists against the reviled underclass immigrants. Hundreds of Sicilians were arrested on mostly baseless charges, and 19 were eventually indicted for the murder. An acquittal followed, with rumors of bribed and intimidated witnesses.

The outraged citizens of New Orleans organized a lynch mob after the acquittal, and proceeded to kill 11 of the 19 defendants. Two were hanged, nine were shot, and the remaining eight escaped. The lynching was the largest mass lynching in American history. From 1890 to 1900 in New York City, the Sicilian Mafia developed into the Five Points Gang and were very powerful in the Little Italy region of the Lower East Side. They were often in conflict with the Jewish Eastmans of the same area. There was also an influential Mafia family in East Harlem. The Neapolitan Camorra was very active in Brooklyn, also. In Chicago, the 19th Ward, which was an Italian neighborhood, became known as the "Bloody Nineteenth" due to the frequent violence in the ward, mostly as a result of Mafia activity, feuds, and vendettas.

Although the Black Hand was not a secret society, there were many small Black Hand gangs. Black Hand extortion was often (wrongly) viewed as the activity of a single organization, because Black Hand criminals in Italian communities throughout the United States used the same methods of extortion.[12-17]

The relationship between the Mafia inside the country of Italy, and the Mafia's strong Catholic practice (though without direct Church consent) has a long-standing history.

In July 2010, in Rome, Monsignor Giuseppe Fiorini Morosini, bishop of Locri Gerace in Calabria, spoke out after more than 300 alleged mobsters, including the 80-year-old Godfather Domenico Oppedisano, were arrested in a police blitz earlier that month. Surveillance footage released by police showed the graying boss being "sworn in" under a statue of the Virgin Mary at Polsi near Reggio Calabria. In his letter to bosses of southern Italy's 'Ndrangheta crime group, Monsignor Morosini demanded that they stop gathering at the shrine. "We have seen images of your illegal gatherings and divisions of power," he wrote.

"We had always thought that these meetings at holy shrines were folklore, but now we have had to rethink. What sense is there in having meetings and ceremonies at a shrine to the Madonna where, while the faithful pray and reflect in God, you plan your activities which God and the Virgin Mary cannot bless?" he asked.

He ended his letter by reminding the mobsters that the Church was "always willing to welcome you with open arms because it is the only institution that believes in the possibility of your conversion." Religion and the Mafia have a long-shared history. Mobsters follow rituals, including burning prayer cards of saints while promising: "As this card burns, so will I if I betray secrets." Members of the mafia are known to carry prayer cards in the belief they will offer divine protection from police or enemies.[18]

Other interesting examples of Italian-based Mafia and Vatican financial scandals have surfaced in recent years:

> In the scandals two decades ago, Sicilian financier Michele Sindona was appointed by the Pope to manage the Vatican's foreign investments. He also brought in Roberto Calvi, a Catholic banker in northern Italy. Sindona's banking empire collapsed in the mid-1970s and his links to the mob were exposed, sending him to prison and his eventual death from poisoned coffee. Calvi then inherited his [Sindona's] role. Calvi headed the Banco Ambrosiano, which collapsed in 1982 after the disappearance of $1.3 billion in loans made to dummy companies in Latin America. The Vatican had provided letters of credit for the loans. Calvi was found a short time later hanging from scaffolding on Blackfriars Bridge, his pockets loaded with 11 pounds of bricks and $11,700 in various currencies. After an initial ruling of suicide, murder charges were filed against five people, including a major Mafia figure, but all were acquitted after trial. While denying wrongdoing, the Vatican Bank paid $250 million to Ambrosiano's creditors. Both the Calvi and Sindona cases remain unsolved.[19]

One of America's infamous Catholic ordained priests and alleged Mafia member illustrates the pairing of crime and Catholicism in the life of Antonio D'Andrea:

> Born Antonio D'Andrea in Valledolmo, Sicily, in 1872, to a large family; he studied law at the University of Palermo in Palermo, Sicily. In 1897, D'Andrea immigrated to the United States, briefly settling in Buffalo, New York. He later attended seminary at St. Mary's Academy in Baltimore and St. Bonaventura's Academy in Allegheny, New York. In June 1899, D'Andrea moved to Chicago, where he was ordained a priest and appointed pastor of St. Anthony's Italian (Independent) Catholic Church under Bishop Anton Kozlowski.
>
> His brother Orazio (Horace) also became a priest. In Chicago, D'Andrea met a young German woman, Lena Wagner. D'Andrea fell in love with Lena, left the priesthood, and married her in Milwaukee. However, after their marriage, Lena suddenly disappeared. D'Andrea suspected that the people who sheltered Lena after her parents' deaths were holding her. With help from the police, D'Andrea and Lena were reunited. Now that he was no longer a priest, D'Andrea decided to become a teacher of modern languages. Interestingly, his brother Louis also left the priesthood and married.
>
> In 1919, D'Andrea became president of the Chicago chapter of the Unione Siciliana, a charitable organization dedicated to helping poor Sicilian immigrants. However, D'Andrea used the Union as another means to increase his political base. He also ran for ward committeeman in the 19th. After he was elected, the Illinois Supreme Court negated the election, and D'Andrea lost the

support of John Powers, one of the ward's aldermen. D'Andrea then decided to run again for alderman against Powers.

Powers was an Irish saloon-keeper who had been alderman since 1888. He was popular with the Italian community, and this led to the so-called Aldermen's Wars. Murders and bombings became political weapons. The violence reached such a point that D'Andrea condemned it and dropped out of the race. On May 11, 1921, D'Andrea was shot and killed while entering his apartment. Mike Merlo, who was vacationing in Italy when he heard the news, immediately ordered the assassin's murder. After his return to Chicago, Merlo became the Mafia boss and Unione Siciliana president. D'Andrea's nephew, Philip D'Andrea, later became a member of (the Chicago Outfit) under boss Al Capone.[20]

Of course, this does not mean to infer that the Catholic Church is tied to the Italian Mafia; rather, it shows that religion and criminal gangs, including individual gangsters, have a rather unholy union of crime wedded to religion.

Modern media and Hollywood stretches this inference in movies, such as the *Godfather* series, as in scenes of Michael (the Godfather) in a baptism ceremony with a priest blessing, while the mob kills its adversaries in bloody scene after scene.

Latino Gangs

Catholicism unfortunately has been co-opted by US-based Latino-American criminal street gangs in the ornate Virgin of Guadalupe and other Catholic tattoos framed side-by-side with crazed and carnal criminal street gang tattoos.

With Mexican and other Latin nationals becoming Americans after the Mexican–American War of the mid-nineteenth century, in areas like Los Angeles, it would be almost a century later (1920s to World War II) that these same marginalized, languishing Latinos, stranded behind the "railroad tracks of the bad side of town," would emulate those same Italian-American mobsters made so popular in graphic, bullet-ridden gangster movies.

Two other historic events in Los Angeles of the 1940s would prove pivotal in the development of Mexican American gangs in the Southwest: the Sleepy Lagoon murder and the Zoot Suit Riots.

With the Zoot Suit Wars of Los Angeles and corrupt criminal justice in the Sleepy Lagoon case (1940–1942), some Latino's would soon find themselves in hostile urban and prison environments that were venom-laced with racism and poverty with few resources, if any, for these LA Latinos to obtain the American Dream. Many of these languid Latinos would soon turn toward organizing groups and clubs for protection and would soon graduate into criminal-bent gangs, all the while incorporating their long-held and confused adoration of the Church and its teachings.

Sleepy Lagoon was a popular swimming hole in what is now East Los Angeles. A Mexican youngster was killed there in 1942, and members of the 38th Street Mexican gang were arrested and charged with murder by the Los Angeles Police Department.[21]

Unfortunately, the criminal trial resembled a "kangaroo court," in which five of the gang members were convicted and sentenced to prison. "Mexican street gangs changed forever because of these convictions. The jail sentences also acted as a glue to unite the Mexican community in a common cause, a fight against class distinction based on prejudice and racism, a fight against the establishment."[22] The 38th Street gang members' cause continued in prison. They maintained their dignity and "demonstrated a type of gang pride and resolve never seen before. These behaviors also elevated the incarcerated 38th Street gang members to folk hero status in the Mexican community. The street gang members especially held them (the convicted) in high esteem."[23]

The Zoot Suit Riots had a similar unifying effect for Mexican-Americans. Zoot suits were a fashionable clothing trend in the late 1920s and popularized in the nightclubs of Harlem (p. 96).[24]

The exaggerated zoot suit included an oversized jacket, with wide lapels and shoulders, and baggy pants that narrowed at the ankles, typically accompanied by a wide-brimmed hat. The style traveled west and south into Mexico and, most likely, was introduced into California via the El Paso Mexican street gang population. By 1943, the Anglo community, the police, and the media began to view the zoot suiters as a savage group that presumably had attacked vulnerable white women and also was said to be responsible for several local homicides (Katz and Webb, 2006, p. 44). Military personnel and citizen mobs chased and beat anyone wearing a zoot suit—Latino and black youths alike—during a five-day riotous period (p. 68).[25]

To further understand how this evolution of Latino gangsters merged Catholicism and crime, it is helpful to understand that criminals always seek a power edge, and what stronger ally of ultimate power can there be than God and his church as your gang ally?

From the gold crucifixes worn with cool zoot suits in the 1940s, to the intricate tattoos of the Virgin of Guadalupe on some gang members today, religious icons have long formed an integral part of Latino youth culture. Holy images can be found throughout Southern California, especially where the Latino population is concentrated. Rosaries dangle around a teenage girl's neck. The face of Christ ringed with a crown of thorns is etched on a young man's arm.

Mesmerizing murals of the Virgin of Guadalupe blaze throughout the housing projects of East Los Angeles, offering spiritual comfort to those within her gaze. What can those images tell about a gang member's religious upbringing and beliefs? Are religious symbols being distorted to serve as accessories to a life of crime? Or are the images of Jesus and Mary on tattoos and in graffiti being redefined in a contemporary spiritual light? Father Gregory Boyle of Dolores Mission Catholic Church in Boyle Heights, Los Angeles, who runs a neighborhood business (Homeboy Industries) employing former gang members, says that he does not believe a lot of thought goes into the religious icons that gang members sport. He senses that youths simply seek a spiritual comfort not being provided by people around them. "They have a more complex take on religion that doesn't translate into church attendance," he said. "There's a deep, dark hole inside them. It's not difficult to see that they hope protection will come from those images. They are asking, 'Please God, protect me. Somebody, protect me.'"

But Jose M. Lopez, professor of Chicano and Latino studies at Cal State Long Beach, believes the tattoos and religious rituals of gang members have a more complex level of meaning. At a recent academic conference on religion and politics, Lopez connected gang members' religious images with the history of religious development in Latin America. Young people reinterpret the icons to suit their time and space, he said. "The manifestations of religious icons and artifacts found in gang life tell more about youth culture than almost any other single factor," Lopez said. "These kids are defining their religious inheritance with these images. … We're missing the whole picture if we think gang life is just about drugs and violence. Religion is an important aspect of it."

Lopez traces the roots of religious conquest in Latin America back to the indigenous gods of the Aztec and Olmec civilizations.

The establishment of Catholicism by Spanish colonialists created a clash of religious beliefs that native people attempted to resolve by incorporating Catholicism and their own beliefs into a single religion. Although the indigenous gods were multiple deities, powerful and vindictive, the European God was gentle and forgiving, conceptualized as either a baby in the arms of the Madonna or a man nailed to a cross. Lopez believes the contradiction between those two images of Gods caused confusion that runs through Latino culture and still influences the minds of young Latinos today. "It's our religious heritage, and we are trying to make sense out of it," said Lopez, who has served as an expert witness in several trials because of his knowledge of gangs. "That's how it gets distorted and reinterpreted."

Former gang member Robert Martinez sports a tattoo of Christ on his left arm, a symbol that he says many teenagers use as a form of protection. Most gang members are religious, but have only a limited understanding of Catholicism, says Martinez, who is now a member of the Boyle Heights Christian Center. Basic elements, indeed, are embedded in their heritage, but rarely nurtured.

"It's a form of respect. If somebody has Jesus Christ on his arm, nobody is going to mess with him," Martinez said. "We all believe in God, but we never talk about it. Everybody's afraid they're going to die and want to be ready."

Javier Stauring, the Catholic chaplain at Central Juvenile Hall, sees the conflict in the minds of many of the younger Latinos convicted of crimes. "They do not have a complete picture of who God is," he said. "Most of these kids don't have parents. Their image of God is a punishing God. He's a God who is keeping tabs on them for what they have done. My feeling is that they need to be angry with him before they form a complete picture of him as loving and forgiving."

Tattoos are seen by some gang members as gestures of faith for which they expect something in return, says Lopez. "It's an offering. They are telling God, 'Look, I did this for you. Now, you owe me one.'" Lopez also believes religious rituals are redefined by gang members who might, for example, light a candle so a drive-by shooting will be successful. Some religious leaders may denounce such practices as sacrilegious, but Lopez urges a closer look. "Is it really distorted?" he asked. "How different is that from a businessman lighting a candle for a successful deal? Or from a soldier saying a prayer before going to war?" Lopez said he believes churches and religious leaders are missing a great opportunity to use these icons as a vehicle to talk to youths about faith.

Stauring, of Juvenile Hall, has similar concerns. He said young people are caught between a mother who orders them to go to church on Sunday and an institution to which they often can't relate. "Something has to change. The Catholic Church needs to start opening their doors and designing new activities for these kids," Stauring said. "They need to realize that these are our sons and daughters. They are the church."[26]

A diametrically oppositional counterclockwise movement can be seen in the daylight-to-darkness temporal change of gangs from a Christian God to gangs and satanic worship.

One such Los Angeles gang, MS13, originated out of war-torn refugees from Central America in the 1970s and 1980s right into the barrios of Los Angeles. Many of the first generation teens, living in the Rampart area of Los Angeles, benignly started to emulate American rock culture by growing their hair out, listening to Black Sabbath-style music, and throwing up the devil's horns sign with their index and pinky fingers; not as devil worshippers (which they were not), but as rowdy and rebellious LA teen rockers!

These young Central American LA mischievous teens soon violently collided with the deadly reality of violent Latino American criminal street gangs (18th St.), in frightened realizations that in order to survive they would have to band together. Soon that band of teen rockers was transformed into the internationally infamous gang MS13—the ultimate violent criminal gang with their tattoos of devil and satanic imagery.

However, unlike other Mexican-American gangs that utilized Catholic imagery in the literal and figurative branding of their bodies, with mixed gang and religious tattoos of the church, these newer Central American gang members adorned their tattooed bodies with imagery of the devil, devil horns, and other satanic emblems of evil.

Black Gangs

An interesting example of African-American gangsterism and religion can be seen in the Black P Stones (BPS). Originally a Chicago-based gang, they used a Presbyterian church as headquarters, meeting place, and arsenal, using religion as a front for criminal activities.

While in prison, the gang leader of the BPS, Jeff Fort, converted to Islam and renamed the gang in parallel as the El Rukns. Reinterpreting the original word *Stone* in the gang name, as a stone from the ancient and holy Kabala, Prince Malik (Fort had changed his name as well) would provide historical and religious power to his international criminal gang.

In later years, as the El Rukns, this organization ran a hybrid mosque/ disco, which, likewise, contained an arsenal and functioned as the fortified base for the gang's various criminal enterprises. The Black P Stone Nation has always recognized a use for religion. Whether this use ever went beyond mere camouflage, like a clerical collar worn for the purposes of a scam, remains an open question, and it's not a question that gets answered. A chronicle of the shifting organization that, helmed by Jeff Fort (later Prince Malik), cornered a sizeable chunk of the Chicago heroin market, provided protection for Martin Luther King and Jesse Jackson, defrauded the government on funding for Great Society social programs, was identified with praise by Louis Farrakhan as the Nation of Islam's "Angels of Death," and eventually plotted to bomb select Chicago buildings and shoot down airplanes over the Chicago skies—though no resume should neglect the routine work of murder, extortion, and theft.

This makes the religion, with its embrace of Orientalist imagery and esoteric texts, sound more like the African-centered outreach program for school children that author Lance Williams founded, and is, at the very least, an idealized simplification of a complex religious movement. While the Blackstone creed borrowed directly from the writings of Ali*, insisting "all members must obey the laws of the government," when the El Rukns recited this creed, they either had some elaborate exegesis in mind or were plain dissembling. "Whether the tenets of Islam were practiced by the El Rukhns at

* Ali ibn Abi Talib: '13th Rajab, 22 or 16 BH – 21st Ramadan, 40 AH; September 20, 601 or July 17, 607 or 600 – January 27, 661) was the cousin and son-in-law of the Islamic prophet, Muhammad, ruling over the Islamic Caliphate from 656 to 661. A son of Abu Talib, Ali was also the first male who accepted Islam. Sunnis consider Ali the fourth and final of the *Rashidun* (rightly guided Caliphs), while Shias regard Ali as the first Imam after Muhammad, and consider him and his descendants the rightful successors to Muhammad, all of whom are members of the *Ahl al-Bayt*, the household of Muhammad. This disagreement split the *Ummah* (Muslim community) into the Sunni and Shi`i branches. *The History of al-Tabari Biographies of the Prophet's Companions and their Successors*, Tabarī, translated by Ella Landau-Tasseron, pp.37-40, Vol:XXXIX *Encyclopædia Britannica Online*. Encyclopædia Britannica, Inc. ArchiBiogrved State University of New York Press, 1998.

the individual level can be argued; nevertheless, Islam was, without a doubt, fundamental to the spirit of the organization." Perhaps, depending on what "fundamental to the spirit" means. Central to the imagery and rhetoric? Sure. Defining of the practice and worldview? Not so much.

The contradictions of righteousness and impiety became the foundation of the El Rukns. They prayed in their mosque. They sold drugs. They practiced entrepreneurship. They kept a stockpile of weapons. They celebrated their women at an annual feast with cake and adulation. They got arrested for murder. They started a security firm. They held community meetings. Chief Malik ran the organization as if he were the head of a monarchy. He actually sat on a throne at the El Rukns' headquarters.[27]

Are Tattoos Haram in Islam?

A question often asked is: Are tattoos *haram* (forbidden) in Islam?" The answer is that permanent tattoos are haram in Islam and the Prophet of Allah has cursed the person who has tattoos done on them and the one on whom tattoos are done.

So, having tattoos done and tattooing is a major sin. The reason for it being haram has not been given, but some scholars believe that it may be because it is changing the creation of Allah. The curse is not permanent, but it is lifted when a person sincerely repents to Allah for this mistake. So, one should not feel doomed because they committed this mistake when they were in days of Jahilia (ignorance).

Although the reasons for the prohibition are not mentioned, scholars have outlined various possibilities and arguments:

- Tattooing is considered "mutilating" the body, changing Allah's creation.
- It inflicts unnecessary pain, and introduces the possibility of infection.
- It covers the natural body, and is, therefore, a form of "deception."
- Nonbelievers often adorn themselves this way, so it is "imitating the *kuffar*."

As for things which are not permanent, such as henna painting on women's hands, feet, and so on, they are not regarded as tattoos and are allowed in Islam.

Persons can become Muslim even if they have had tattoos done to them or if they were involved in tattooing. You do not have to remove them in order to become a Muslim. You can pray, do *wudhu,* and do all your Islamic duties even if you have tattoos. This is because Islam erases all sins that a non-Muslim committed before he or she became a Muslim.[28]

Even as BPS migrated to Los Angeles in the 1970s, led and founded in its West Coast chapter by T. Rodgers, a blend of Islam, Black Panther ideology, and gansterism amalgamated itself. "We will always have a sense of respect of women, the dignity of all our African Black Princes, and a sense of struggle, mixed with street justice."[29]

Hate Groups/Gangs

White gangs in America have a long hooded history of hijacking religion (at gunpoint, if needed) and using the two to create power and fear in some of the most appalling ways. According to Wyn Craid Wade:[30]

> The number one source of knowledge for the Ku Klux Klan (KKK) is the Holy Bible. Members of the Klan believe in the literal truth of the Bible. One KKK member once wrote, "The Klansman pins his faith to the Bible as the revealed will of GOD." Many active Klansmen were ordained ministers. In the early 1980s, new religious fundamentalists used very similar rhetoric about Christian supremacy.
>
> Ordained ministers in the Klan preach the Christian aspect of the Ku Klux Klan to members. These clergymen have been trained in the church and added their own views to their religion to create an interpretation of the Bible that fits the creed of the Ku Klux Klan. Reverend Bailey Smith, the president of the Southern Baptist Convention, announced in 1980, "God Almighty does not hear the prayer of a Jew." He continued, "God can't possibly hear the prayer of someone who does not believe Jesus Christ is the true Messiah." The Klan takes direct action against those who do not share its beliefs or those who it simply views as inferior based on its readings of the Bible.
>
> Rituals and ceremonies are very important and commonly used by the Klan. For example, an elaborate initiation ritual is carried out for new members, and the custom of wearing white robes and hoods sets the members apart from other citizens and provides for them a special identity. Cross burning is a very common practice of the Klan. This ritual is used mainly as a form of fear and intimidation. This ritual has also been called "cross lighting," a term used by David Duke and other Klansmen in the 1970s to illustrate that "Christ is the light of the world."
>
> Most members already have a strong sense of white supremacist thought in their heads before they join the Klan.[30]

Skinheads, or Neo Nazis, Take the KKK to a New Level of Religious and Gang Madness

Vacillating between pre-Christian Odinism and white Christian historical explanations of the lost tribe (Aryans) of Abraham, Skins and Neo Nazis are finding new uses for religion in their gang culture.

Religion is a factor that prevents the skinheads from becoming a unified movement. Racist skinheads tend not to be particularly religious, yet the growth of racist religions has allowed them to justify their hate. After the 9/11 attacks, many Americans learned firsthand how a perversion of Islam could be used as a rationale for massive violence. Domestic racists also have twisted other religions to justify their beliefs. For example, Christian Identity (CI) belief rewrites the Christian Bible as a racist manifesto ending in a prophesized race war. CI skinheads cast themselves as religious warriors in a racial war they believe will end with the defeat of their enemies.

Racial war and related themes are commonly celebrated by tattoos worn by skinheads; Hammerskins are often found with Biblical passages tattooed on their bodies. Still, the irony that the pacifist religion of Christ, a Jew, was being perverted into a racist creed was not lost on some white supremacists. Many of them actively despised Christianity in any form, seeing it as a theology of weaklings seeking to turn the other cheek. Looking for a pre-Christian European faith to claim, some skinheads began moving toward Viking paganism in the 1990s. As in radical Islam, the way to heaven (Valhalla) was to die in combat. What these religions have in common is a fanatical belief in anti-Semitic conspiracy theories. Everything from national elections and affirmative action to rap music and Mexican restaurants are seen as part of an evil plot. Young skinheads, religious or not, are easily pulled into this simplistic worldview and given a justification for hate.[31]

One of several elements that distinguish white supremacy mixed with religion from other types of criminal gangs is the use of religion as an overt political objective. Political motivation, mixed with a potent use of crime, fear, and religion, will undoubtedly continue to exhibit itself in more horrific criminal acts than that of the Oklahoma City Bombing—a criminal expression mixed with white religious fanaticism.

> The mixture of criminality and magico-religious practices has become a growing phenomenon among street gangs and drug cartels. It is understandable that members of organizations like MS-13 would gravitate toward using "anti-Christian" symbolism in their graffiti and tattoos. "Demonized" symbols help promote fear and communicate an air of "power" toward those outside of these subcultures.
>
> Are members of the cartels discovering that magico-religious practices can be incorporated into their deadly narco-culture or are these spiritual traditions that they grew up around and now simply bringing them into gang life? Allegations that Mexican authorities may be involved in some of these magico-religious practices comes as no surprise.
>
> Police in the city of Tijuana, across the border from San Diego, tattoo their bodies with Voodoo symbols, believing they can repel bullets. … Army raids on homes of police working for cartels have found ornately adorned Santeria-type altars covered with statues and skulls stuffed with money paying homage to gods and spirits. … Many police see a need to shield themselves from witchcraft used by drug gangs who mix Caribbean black magic and occultism from southern Mexico using things like human bones, dead bats and snake fangs to curse enemies and unleash evil spirits. …[32]

The origins of the Santa Muerte are a mystery and that may be linked to centuries old customs. Journalist José Gil Olmos in his book, *La Santa Muerte. La Virgen de los Olvidados* (virgin of the forgotten), writes of a Catholic Church document reporting indigenous people having rituals with a skeleton in 1797 as presatanic.

Some say the skeletal saint's origin may be the legacy of Mictlantecuhtli and Mictecacihuatl, the Aztec god and goddess of the dead and rulers of the underworld realm of Mictlán. There are cases in which murders of rivals have been offered to the Santa Muerte. Olmos writes that most believers condemn violence and view the death saint as a protector. But there have been deaths linked to the Santa Muerte followers.

Malverde is a saint worshiped by drug traffickers, criminals, prisoners and others that are noncriminals usually associated with the poor in need of extra spiritual leverage. The accounts of the true life of Malverde differ, with him being portrayed as a railway worker or a construction worker who became a bandit before being hanged in Culiacan in 1909.

Many drug traffickers carry symbols of Malverde and Mexican prison cells are often decorated with his image. Where Jesus Malverde's legend began is also where drug smuggling began in earnest in Mexico. It is only logical that the region's bandit saint would sooner or later become associated with drugs, drug smugglers, and drug dealers. Today he is revered by almost all Mexican-born drug smugglers. Jesus Malverde's legacy is definitely a mixed one. On the one hand, he is the patron saint of drug smugglers, the "Narco Saint." To law enforcement, particularly in the United States, he is seen as an emblem of crime and drugs, a tipoff to assist them in finding drug traffickers. But to thousands upon thousands of Mexicans and Mexican nationals, he is not known as "Narco Saint," but as "the Generous One" and "the Angel of the Poor." These people look to Malverde's miraculous intervention in their lives to help them live on day-by-day and perhaps to one day find a better life. Jesus Malverde protects them from the many dangers with which they are in constant struggle.[33]

Mexico's epidemic of violence first erupted in 2006, according to most accounts. But an ex-Muslim from India, who serves as a Christian pastor along the Texas-Mexican border, believes the problem began much earlier, with human sacrifice, witches, and the adoration of death in ancient Aztec days. "A large majority of the Valley's population is Catholic, but the Catholicism here is mixed up with ancient pagan rites, witchcraft, false religions like Santeria, Voodoo, Palo Mayombe, and other demonic cults, and the worship of false saints like 'Saint' Death and Jesus Malverde," Elijah said. "Basically, it all adds up to Satan worship, which feeds the violence and every other problem, like poverty, drought, hunger, chronic ill health, lack of jobs, and hopelessness," ... there's so much demonic activity, it has to be dealt with in order to reach the lost, according to Elijah.[34]

Muslim street gangs can and are utilized by political extremists seeking to gain power in North Africa and other Islam religious majority-based countries. Make no mistake about it, whether you are talking about Iran, Pakistan, Algeria, or other similarly situated Muslim majority countries, these street gangs are no different than the street gangs of Los Angeles. These Muslim gangsters have strong or confused religious convictions, but their main purpose remains true to most criminal street gang's goals: fear, violence, drug sales, extortion, illegal activities for profit, murder, and many more crimes as the main criminal activities of these Muslim gangsters.

As outlined by John Hagedorn:[35]

> … a political example of gangs is the Muhajir Quami Movement (MQM), a party representing Pakistani migrants from India after the 1948 partition. By the 1980s, Karachi had become a major port for the shipment of heroin from Afghanistan to the West and guns from the West to Afghanistan. The fall of the military regime led to democracy in 1988, and the MQM grew as the voice of what is called a new ethnic group. Its success, in no small part, Oskar Verkaaik argues, was due to small groups of friends who partook in the violence and "fun" and recruited other youth to the MQM banner. The MQM won the local elections [in] Hyderabad, but the military takeover of Pakistan's government led [to] the party's fracturing. Accused of abusing power during its heyday, in the aftermath of General Muhammad Zia-ul-Haq's police state, "the MQM fell apart into locally organized groups resorting to antistate militancy and crime.

These undulating movements, from using street Muslim gangsters to twisting voter's arms during elections (reminiscent of the Gangs of New York in the nineteenth century), by power-seeking parties, and then turning those street gangsters into secret police thugs now in positions of real political power, indicate how those once out of power the same Muslim street gangsters return to the streets as criminals again. This is profoundly illustrates that religion is merely an anecdotal back story to the real main plot—murderous criminal street gangs that happen to have some religious beliefs.

This comparative look at religion and the criminology of gangs is but a small sampling of common factors that many cultures and criminal subcultures share in the unholy union between religion and dangerous criminal gangs. Many more theories need to be explored and added into the mix in the study of these unique neo-religious gangster behaviors. Many different theories to explain criminal behavior have been around as long as recorded history, such as:

- Aristotle (BCE): "Poverty is the parent of revolution and crime (an environmental view of the antecedents of crime)."
- Sir Francis Bacon (1600s): "Opportunity makes a thief," pointing out the power of the situation to affect behavior.
- Voltaire and Jean-Jacques Rousseau (1700s): "Free will, hedonistic decision making, and the failure of the social contract produces criminal behavior."

And many more explanations need to be added to the core of the classical theory of criminology and criminal gangs.

However, before leaving this very brief introduction of religion and criminal gangs, it must be pointed out that many religious leaders from the beginnings of time to the present have known of the misuse and misunderstood use of criminal-based religion by gangs and criminally minded gang members. These "good seeking" religious leaders of all faiths have long combated this fire and brimstone with a more potent form of religion—that of religion for goodness regained as one of the ultimate powers.

A heralding angelic example of this is Father Greg Boyle, a Jesuit priest and the founder and executive director of Homeboy Industries, a nonprofit organization in Los Angeles that works with former gang members to help transform their lives, create positive communities, and "find the person they are really meant to be."

Father Boyle quotes Mother Theresa saying, "The problem in the world is we have just forgotten that we belong to each another." He also loves to say, "Nothing stops a bullet like a job." For the past 20 years, Father Boyle has mentored and counseled more than 12,000 gang members who pass through Homeboy each year to learn job skills, get their gang tattoos removed, and attend therapy sessions on everything from alcohol abuse to anger management.[36]

Another divine example is Victory Outreach Ministries International, founded by Sonny Arguinzoni in 1967, in Los Angeles. He is an ordained minister of the Assemblies of God. Victory Outreach is a ministry that exclusively reaches out to drug addicts and gang members.

God's Anointed Now Generation (G.A.N.G.) is a revolutionary, faith-based approach by Victory Outreach in getting kids away from the mindless destruction of street gangs. More than a simple youth club, G.A.N.G. energizes kids to want to do good.[37]

To add to the choir of change from gangs to good deeds is Ansar El Muhammad (aka Brother Stan) who spent most of this childhood in Compton and Venice, California. He got involved in gang activity at a very young age, which led to 15 years of a nonproductive lifestyle. His influence came from family members who were entrenched in negative activities for two generations. This type of behavior ultimately led to violence, drug use, and incarceration.

After serving time in a federal penitentiary, Brother Stan recommitted himself to the life-giving teachings of the Most Honorable Elijah Muhammad and the Nation of Islam through Louis Farrakhan's study course: Self-Improvement: the Basis for Community Development.

In 1999, Brother Stan was one of the key organizers in developing a community-based organization to serve gang members and their families and addressing the issues that were affecting the Los Angeles community.

The Help Establish Learning, Peace, Economics, and Righteousness Foundation (V2K H.E.L.P.E.R. Foundation) offers a range of programs:

- Targeting 14-to 25-year-olds, this gang intervention effort was created in 1997 to provide counseling, mentoring, parenting classes, anger management, and life skills training, and after-school activities, such as sports, art programs, and field trips.
- Trained gang intervention workers connect directly with gang members to provide crisis intervention to defuse potentially violent situations, develop peace treaties between rival gangs, and provide alternative, positive opportunities, including occupational training, employment, and drug and alcohol abuse treatment referral services.
- Safe Passage Staff is on-site at Venice High School (Venice–Los Angeles) to ensure "safe passage" between home and school in neighborhoods where intimidation, drug dealing, and shootings occur far too often. Staff members engage surrounding businesses and organizations to build a "safety net" with them.

Though controversial to some, the Safe Passage program is life-saving to LA's kids that are in gangs or are marginally associating (criminally, not socially) with the gang lifestyle.[38]

An exemplary example of Kung Fu, Buddhism, Taoism, and other harmoniously aligned areas of oneness and good is the dedication to antigang intervention through Sifu (Master Instructor) Sharif Bey. Sifu Bey at age 5 began his martial arts training in Tae Kwon Do and Wing Chun Kung Fu. He was introduced to Hung Ga Kung Fu in 1984. He absorbed the Kuntao teachings of GGM Reeders, as taught by Ed "Tiny" Sealy, through his representative, Randy Elliot. In 1989, Sifu Bey began following Grandmaster Yee Chee Wai. After years of dedicated study, practice, and participation, Sifu Bey was invited to participate in the Bai See (BaiShi) ceremony and, in 2000, became a disciple of Grandmaster Yee. In 2008, in recognition of years of dedication, Sifu Bey was inducted into the Governing Board of Yee's Hung Ga International Kung Fu Association.

In 2000, he began to teach publicly and, in 2004, founded Syracuse Kung Fu. As an avid supporter of the community's youths, Sifu Bey designed and implemented a number of programs, including a gang intervention program that not only provides mediation, court advocacy, and conflict resolution services to youths, but also gang intelligence training for youth professionals.[39]

Rev. Heng Sure was ordained as a Buddhist monk in 1976. For the sake of world peace, he undertook a "three steps, one bow" pilgrimage from South Pasadena to Ukiah, California, traveling more than 800 miles while observing a practice of total silence. Rev. Sure obtained an MA in oriental languages from UC Berkeley and a PhD at the Graduate Theological Union in Berkeley.

He serves as the director of the Berkeley Buddhist Monastery and teaches on the staff at the Institute for World Religions.

Rev. Sure is actively involved in interfaith dialogue and in the ongoing conversation between spirituality and technology.

So, that's what this black belt Rev. Sure and his companion walked forth with. "If you use these, you will find them inexhaustible," their teacher said. And, they were sorely tested on this. Again and again and again, people threw stones, punches, insults, and threats.

Walking through some of the toughest parts of town, they encountered dope pushers, alcoholics, hardened street gangs—troublemakers at large— aching for an excuse, any excuse to fight. Looking down the barrel of a gun and meeting it with the Four Hearts, that takes a certain sort of strength, integrity of spirit, and unwavering conviction. That is what Rev. Sure and Heng Ch'au took with them. They say that is what kept them alive.[40]

Native American's have one of the fastest growing criminal gang problems in all parts of the United States. As a means to turn away the bad spirits of gangsterism, the Native American Youth and Family Center has specialized, intensive, and ongoing outreach to those troubled and involved with gangs, such as Gang Prevention and Outreach:

> The Gang Prevention and Outreach program serves youth ages 11 to 19 who want to keep their feet on a good, healthy, and safe path. Youth receive support to increase school attendance and enjoy healthy peer and family relationships. This fosters strength in youth and helps them to avoid possible gang affiliations and police or juvenile crime involvement. Case management services and outreach to children, their families, and other important individuals in their lives are provided.[41]

Countless other religious and nonreligious groups, of all forms and persuasions, know of the gang members' plight, which seems hopeless, yet these groups provide help and understanding as a way out of the self-destructive gangster life.

References

1. Montet, P. 1946. *La Vie Quotidienne en Egypte.* Paris: Hachette.
2. Goodman, M. 2008. *Rome and Jerusalem: The Clash of Ancient Civilizations.* New York: Alfred A. Knopf, p. 407.
3. Wasserman, J. 2001. *The Templars and the Assassins: The Militia of Heaven.* Rochester, VT: Destiny Books. Critiqued by Uri Dowbenko, 2002.
4. Online at http://www.insightcrime.org/groups-mexico/knights-templar# modusop (retrieved December 30, 2012).
5. Vallar, C. 2005. *Pirates and Privateers: Exploring the History of Maritime Piracy.* Self-published.

6. Collins, E. 2004. Eyes on God and gold: The importance of religion during the golden age of Caribbean piracy. Master's thesis, University of North Carolina, Department of History.
7. London, J. E. 2009. Somali pirates and the Islamist Jihad. *The Cutting Edge*, April 20. Online at www.the cuttingedgenews.com/index.php?article=11267
8. Hamill, P. 2002. Trampling *City's History,* December 15.
9. Boyer, P. S. 1992. *Urban Masses and Moral Order in America, 1820–1920.* Cambridge, MA: First Harvard University Press.
10. Lockwood, C. Gangs, crime, smut, violence. 1990. *The New York Times,* September 20.
11. 1869 from *New Orleans Times.*
12. FBI. *Organized Crime.* Washington, D.C.: Federal Bureau of Investigation. Archived from the original on October 10, 2010.
13. Barret, D., and S. Gardiner. 2011. Structure keeps Mafia atop crime heap. *The Wall Street Journal,* January 22.
14. Pontchartrain, B. <year> *New Orleans Know-It-All.* Online at www. Bestofneworleans.com.
15. Under Attack. *American Memory.* Washington, D.C.: Library of Congress.
16. *Milestones of the Italian American Experience.* Washington, D.C.: National Italian American Foundation.
17. Sagepub.com.
18. Pisa, N. 2010. Italian bishop asks Mafia to stop using holy shrines for initiation ceremonies. *The Telegraph,* July 26. Online at http://www.telegraph.co.uk/news/worldnews/europe/italy/7909315/Italian-bishop-asks-Mafia-to-stop-using-holy-shrines-for-initiation-ceremonies.html (retrieved December 30, 2012).
19. Public Intelligence. 2010. Vatican bank may have used clergy as fronts for mafia, corrupt businessmen. December 13. Online at http://publicintelligence.net/vatican-bank-may-have-used-clergy-as-fronts-for-mafia-corrupt-businessmen/(retrieved December 30, 2012).
20. Warner, R. N. 2009. The dreaded D'Andrea: The former priest who became the windy city's most feared mafia boss. *Informer: The Journal of American Mafia History,* 2 (2), April.
21. Op Cit; Valdez, 2007, pp. 98–99.
22. Ibid.
23. Ibid.
24. Op Cit; Valdez; Page 96.
25. Howell, J. C., and J. P. Moore. 2010. History of street gangs in the United States. *National Gang Center Bulletin,* Bureau of Justice Assistance, May (4): 1–24.
26. Ramirez, M. 1999. The gangs and their God. *The Los Angeles Times,* May 8. Online at http://articles.latimes.com/1999/may/08/local/me-35168.
27. Moore, N. Y., and L. Williams. 2011. *The Almighty Black P Stone Nation: The Rise, Fall, and Resurgence of an American Gang.* Brooklyn, NY: Lawrence Hill Books.
28. Online at http://www.muslimconverts.com/cosmetics/tattoos.htm (retrieved January 2, 2012).
29. Personal interview with T. Rodgers (2004 to present).
30. Wade, W. C. 1987. *The Fiery Cross.* New York: Simon and Schuster.
31. Blazak, R. 2007. *Essay: The Racist Skinhead Movement.* Montgomery, AL: Southern Poverty Law Center.

32. Emmott, R. 2010. *Mexican police ask spirits to guard them in drug war.* May 24. Online at Reuters.com/article/2010/03/19/us-mexico-drugs-idUSTRE6213Z2201.
33. Butler, A. 2006. "Jesus Malverde: The Narco Saint." *Yahoo Voices.* Accessed from http://voices.yahoo.com/jesus-malverte-narco-saint-42822.html.
34. Cook, E. 2012 Free Republic.
35. Hagedorn, J. 2009. *A World of Gangs, Armed Young Men and Gansta Culture.* Minneapolis: University of Minnesota Press.
36. Boyle, Fr. G. 2011. *Tattoos on the Heart: The Power of Boundless Compassion.* New York: Free Press.
37. Online at http://www.sonnyarguinzoni.org.
38. Online at http://helperfoundation.org/gangintervention.html.
39. Online at http://www.taichifest.com/zhangsanfengfestival/index.php?option=com_content&view=article&id=87&Itemid=132.
40. Online at http://www.urbandharma.org/sitemap.html.
41. Online at http://www.nayapdx.org/.

Seven Pathways Into and Out of Gangs

AARON KIPNIS

Contents

Editor's Note: According to myth and legend, "Blood in, Blood out" has been the philosophy of many gangs. This saying simply means the way into a gang is by killing and leaving by way of being killed. Some gangs initiate new members via a violent process called "jumping in," during which the initiate is forced to fight two or more members in a brutal and often near fatal attack. This is a means of proving "worthiness" or, in the vernacular of some gangs, "earning your bones."

Introduction

Why would anyone join a gang? This is a reasonable question for reasonable people. Gang membership exposes its members to dramatically higher rates of violence, addiction, injury, disability, police surveillance, arrest, incarceration, and sudden death. Gang membership is not reasonable. It is, however, understandable from a psychological point of view. To make any substantive change in gang culture, we must understand the deep psychology of gang membership and the pathways that lead into and out of gang culture.

Gangs, of a sort, have existed throughout history. Consider a Neolithic band of young men who left the comfort and relative safety of their cave dwelling to track down and kill an Aurochs bull, which stood six feet high at the shoulder. The hunters averaged five feet tall and took on these huge beasts with spears and clubs. In the fury of the hunt, they could be trampled, gored, kicked, accidentally stabbed by another hunter, or driven off a cliff. Skeletal remains show injury was frequent. Some hunters did not return. Those who did brought a large quantity of protein needed for the tribe to survive. Additionally, they procured rawhide for clothing and shelter, bone for tools, fat for lamps, and other needed supplies. Only a skilled, very committed crew of courageous young men could pull off such largess for their community. They were heroes. In part, because of this deeply entrenched tendency toward male toughness, daring, cooperation, and courage, humanity has survived over the ages.

Hunting groups naturally evolved into bands of warriors over time. Once agriculture took hold in human development so did the invention of wealth. As grain could be stored in large silos, a tribe, which formerly relied on only what they could hunt and gather, could now store a year or more of a food supply in one site. This surplus created leisure and the capacity for many members of society to do something else other than produce food, and this creation of wealth created something worth stealing. Small bands of hunters became raiders of stored goods. Military units formed in response to protect the wealth of the larger community.

Street gangs today evoke police units in response. Street gangs selfishly serve their own needs at the expense of the larger community; police "gangs" (like the hunters of old) generously serve the needs of the whole community. While one group exploits the innocent and the other protects them, the need to belong, to have membership in a "tribe," is a universal longing. If youths cannot find membership in a prosocial group, many feel it better to belong to an antisocial group than to operate alone. Historically, being solo often resulted in failure to thrive. Today, when families fall apart and social institutions fail to meet the needs of youth at risk, many gravitate to gangs rather than risk the pain of isolation that comes from lack of affiliation with any meaningful group.

Author's Story

My own family fell apart when I was 3, and society offered me very little assistance or protection. I spent years in various foster homes. During my adolescence, when not residing in juvenile institutions, I spent most of my time living on the streets of Hollywood or San Francisco. The outcast and the outlaws were my friends and family. I lived in tenements with Hell's Angels and other gang members, drug dealers, runaways, prostitutes, and thieves.

I stole from shops. I slept in abandoned buildings and cars. I ate out of Dumpsters, "dined and dashed" at restaurants, burgled homes and cars, sold drugs, and did whatever else I could to survive as a teenager alone on the unforgiving city streets. Understandably, the police repeatedly arrested me.

During my detentions, I witnessed numerous beatings, sexual assaults, bloody suicides, stabbings, desperate escape attempts, and young men driven insane from solitary confinements. In these institutions, I quickly learned that gang affiliation could afford some protection from predation and that it was hard to survive on your own. Even though I was white and Jewish, I successfully pretended to be Mexican and, through gang affiliations in jails, suffered less than other white boys.

The horrors I witnessed in my youth propelled me into adulthood with a drive to find alternatives to the juvenile justice system. Most conditions that I encountered as an "at-risk" young man have steadily worsened, as our society has largely pursued ineffective intervention strategies for gang-prone youths.

Today, American boys suffer higher rates of homicide, suicide, incarceration, functional illiteracy, school failure, child poverty, gang involvement, gun carrying, drug abuse, violent victimization, sexual assault, and homelessness than the youths of any other Western industrialized nation. The only other nation with similar incarceration rates is Russia. However, Russia never has been known as the "land of the free."

After my first arrest, a judge made me a ward of the state of California. I remained on probation or parole from ages 11 to 23. Most friends from this period died long ago from the perils of street life. But I survived. I even thrived. And so can most boys at risk. They do need, however, some specific help, offered at the right time in the right way. It is my personal and professional belief that the majority of difficult, troubled, angry, criminal, and even violent young men in gangs can lead whole and productive lives when given the right opportunities and leadership.

Unlike most gang-prone youths, I received a college education. A compassionate parole officer found a grant to cover minimal educational expenses. Los Angeles City College admitted me—a 19-year-old with only a ninth grade education. From there, with other grants, loans, and jobs, I worked my way through the California State University system and private institutes, culminating my studies with a PhD in clinical psychology.

Over the years, I have worked with many gang-affiliated boys. Most share a common past—they were neglected as children. Many were emotionally, sexually, or physically abused. This does not excuse their violence. However, the more insight we gain into issues that generate anger and violence, the better we are able to prevent or treat it. My focus here is primarily on young male psychology and gangs, though much also is applicable to girls who are a minority of gang members, often as affiliates to male gangs.

Just as Dante explored seven levels of Hell, this chapter investigates seven paths that can lead into or out of gangs: (1) home, (2) school, (3) the street,

(4) juvenile institutions, (5) drugs, (6) the prison system, and (7) leadership (on the pathways out). Crossing each of these paths are critical junctions where gang-prone boys can either be diverted toward community and life or, tragically, be pushed closer to gangs, alienation, isolation, incarceration, and death. For most, the first pathway begins at home.

First Pathway to Gangs: Child Abuse and Neglect

Abused children, or those who merely witness domestic abuse, are highly overrepresented among youths suffering academic, emotional, and economic failure. They have higher rates of alcohol and drug abuse, juvenile arrests, and gang involvement than similar nonabused children. Abused boys are three times as likely to become violent. They grow up to become the majority of incarcerated felons and men on death row.

Girls represent the majority of sexually abused children. The majority of children who are medically neglected, seriously injured, or murdered are boys. Protection of boys from domestic violence should be a priority of our social programs. However, boys are far less likely than girls to tell anyone about abuse. It is egodystonic—not in accord with their traditional gender identity—for boys to complain about pain. Nationally, annual reports of child abuse and neglect now exceed a record 3 million. As a precursor to future incarceration, neglect is as damaging to boys as physical abuse.

Children who live with both biological parents have the lowest reported rates of maltreatment. Children living with single mothers, particularly those with a nonbiological male in their home, suffer the highest abuse rates. Child poverty dramatically exacerbates these rates, as do alcoholism and drug addiction. My own teenaged parents met all these criteria, as do the parents of most gang members. The connection between distressed parents with insufficient social support and increased incidences of future gang involvement for their children is blatant.

Coming mostly from young family systems that fail to thrive, more than 350,000 American boys are in government-run foster care. For many children, this intervention fails to stop their downward spiral. Most of them experience multiple placements and go through a bewildering process of disorientation from which, in my personal and professional experience, it is hard to recover. This background, too, is a virulent medium for the incubation of antisocial behavior that can lead to gang involvement. I was in more than a dozen such homes. Eighteen months after discharge, one in four former foster kids reports having been beaten, seriously hurt, or incarcerated; a third have not completed high school; and half are unemployed. The need most abandoned children have to belong to a family of some sort is profound. Gangs are, albeit dysfunctional, families. Gang leaders appear, at first, to offer some protection to youths who feel they have no adult advocates or protectors.

Contrary to popular opinion, hate is not the organizing principle of most gangs. Though elaborately disguised, it is more often fear. In his study of white, racist youth gangs, sociologist Rafael Ezekiel noted that almost every one of the boys he interviewed was fatherless, poor, and undereducated. Most lived in decaying neighborhoods where they were an ethnic minority and had little hope for the future. Abuse and neglect by parents was rampant in their histories.

Boys who present a hard-edged, violent posture to the world around them are not necessarily "looking for trouble." Many gang members develop a menacing demeanor as an unconscious defense designed to keep the violence in their world at bay. Often, it is merely a sociopathic façade covering an inner experience of profound anxiety. Males tend to enforce their physical boundaries through looks, gestures, and postures. The more threatening the environment, the more stereotypical these nonverbal signals tend to be. Urban gang graffiti, gang "colors," and hand gestures signaling gang affiliation are modern extensions of this "marking" behavior by males who feel threatened by the potential intrusion of other males into their territory. It is primate behavior.

Boys have good reason to be afraid. Our adolescent male death by homicide rate averages 50 times that of Japan's and 12 times that of most other industrialized societies. Some costs are involved in better protecting child welfare. However, the investment is considerably less than the resources needed to contain the criminal behavior of gang members. Broken homes, fatherlessness, poverty, neglect, abuse, parental substance abuse, and criminality all funnel boys toward the wastelands of gang culture.

Second Pathway to Gangs: School Failure

The ecology of neglect toward boys in public school today is evident in many arenas. As compared with girls, boys have lower grade averages and significantly lower reading and writing scores. Boys are suspended, expelled, referred to special education, and drop out of school at rates about four-to-one over girls. Because challenging boys are referred to programs in which the staff usually has the lowest level of training, the poorest tools, and most dilapidated facilities, our highest-risk students tend to become the least well cared for. Economically disadvantaged schools have the highest male dropout rates and lowest male reading scores, as much as four grade levels below affluent schools. Gangs often proliferate in these districts, where boys are also the majority of school violence victims. I dropped out in the ninth grade because my living situation made me too distressed to focus. Throughout college, however, I got straight As. Clearly, my problem was not academic. Nevertheless, I spent countless days in detention receiving welt-raising swats and writing "I will not (name of infraction)" sentences 500 times. All the rest of those classmates in detention with me were boys.

Zero-tolerance regulations are having a severe negative impact on boys today. Parents find few educational alternatives after a student is expelled because of truancy, drugs, tobacco, alcohol, weapons, bad language, fighting, acting out, or sexual harassment. Because adults, not kids, commit the vast majority of drug abuse, sex crimes, weapons carrying, and violence, we are now holding school boys to higher standards of behavior, greater scrutiny, and punishment, and lower standards of legal protection than adults.

More than 15 percent of eighth-grade boys are suspended or expelled from school each year. In many urban schools, more than one-third of the black male students are annually suspended or expelled. Latino boys have the lowest high school graduation rates. These young men of color also disproportionately populate most gangs.

Of course, teachers must remove disruptive boys from classrooms at times. They distract other students. If suspended from campus, however, they are free to roam the streets. With in-school suspension, boys get up, go to school, and get their classwork. There, they could receive tutoring and counseling, something many failing, gang-prone boys need to succeed, instead of being dumped on the streets or shipped to other districts.

American boys now score in lower ranks of literacy than boys in any other industrialized nation. Nationally, two out of five children cannot read well enough to keep up in school. Low literacy is closely tied to failure in all academic, economic, and social arenas, and boys' involvement in the disruptive activities that channel them out of educational institutions and into gangs. About 70 percent of boys in juvenile institutions suffer from unremediated learning disabilities, while roughly 80 percent of convicted felons and gang members are high school dropouts.

As former Education Secretary Richard Riley once said, "Prisons are full of high school dropouts who cannot read," yet Congress "continues to dilly-dally and dawdle rather than enact a bill to build a corps of reading tutors." Many boys need a strong classroom presence that can contain and direct their aggression with caring firmness. Highly spirited, gang-prone boys need one-on-one periods or small-group instruction, realistic expectations, clear behavioral limits, frequent changes in activity, and opportunities to burn off excess energy. In many schools today, physical recreation is merely 15 minutes a day. Many schools have no functioning outdoor equipment. Some host no physical activity at all. Gangs offer adventure for bored and restless boys.

We could recruit literate young men, from groups overrepresented by school failure and underrepresented by educators, for teacher training programs. We should stop kicking salvageable boys out of school and onto the streets. We could provide in-school suspension programs with tailored curricula and teachers/counselors well trained to work with noncompliant boys.

Given the right opportunity, most gang-prone boys are fully capable of learning and changing their lives in a positive direction. They need the dedication, direction, and support of caring adults who can point them toward a better life. Education, even a highly resourced one, is always far cheaper than the tolls gangs take on society.

Third Pathway to Gangs: Homelessness and Poverty

For many boys, the streets become their next arena of education. Most low-level drug dealing and minor property crime—the cause of the majority of young male incarcerations—take place on the street. Crimes against people also propagate in unsupervised arenas. Most initial police contacts happen on the street, as does gang induction.

Though America is affluent, more than 20 percent of our children live in poverty, a prime cause of their homelessness. One in four urban homeless are children. Many were discharged from foster care or youth corrections without any housing or employment waiting. Many emergency shelters are reluctant to house young men. Gangs are waiting.

Educational outreach, job training and living wage employment, transitional living programs, counseling, affordable housing, and health care for homeless boys are all sorely needed. Without safe and simple access to these services, children needlessly suffer and become increasingly vulnerable to gang induction. The documented costs of increased hospitalizations, mental health services, substance abuse, violence, crime, gang membership, and incarceration for this population far exceed the investment needed to create zero tolerance toward child homelessness. If we are going to promote intolerance of any kind, this would be a good arena to practice.

Today, guns are increasingly the great pacifiers for boys who legitimately feel threatened by street violence. Many boys who tote weapons have a profound feeling of isolation, alienation, and a perceived lack of protection from others who attack their safety. According to the Centers for Disease Control and Prevention (CDC), nearly 20 percent of all ninth- to twelfth-grade US students periodically carry weapons to school.

I worked with a local, 15-year-old gang member, Ramón, who says, "You need to be 'strapped' [carry a gun]. If someone 'draws down' [pulls a gun] on me, I've gotta pull my 'gat' [gun], too. Otherwise, wind up in the wrong place, you wind up dead, too." Paradoxically, in any community, schools are still the safest places for boys to be. A great deal of weapons carrying at school is an attempt to assure street safety on the way to and from school. When we kick increasing numbers of boys out of schools, where they are suddenly transported from safety and hope to the danger and despair of the streets, we practically ensure an increase in the level of youth victimization, violence, and gang participation.

Homicide is now the second leading cause of death for all 15- to 24-year-olds and the leading cause of death for African-American and Hispanic youths. One out of four homicide victims is younger than 24. Our youth homicide rates are 10 times Canada's, 15 times Australia's, and 28 times that of France or Germany. Handguns kill 13 children a day in the United States and 13 people a year in Sweden. In a nation where there are now more guns than people, gun control could be a good idea. It won't eliminate gangs, but it would certainly reduce their lethality.

Many gang-prone boys need a regular opportunity to talk openly about the serious issues that trouble them and distract them from education. After several months in one of our after-school youth councils, Ramón, said, "I'm talking now to homies from the other side. I'm not packing [carrying a gun] anymore. We are just trying to be cool with each other." That underfunded school, however, has had to move three times in four years and still has no permanent home. These kids don't miss the message that they are of the lowest priority. Whatever the approach, schools and after-school community-based programs remain the last lines of defense for boys at risk for initiation into street life and gangs.

More than 10 million children of working parents are home alone after school. More than half of all juvenile crime occurs between 2 and 8 p.m. Many gang-affiliated boys live in homes that are essentially crash pads with family members only marginally involved in their lives. Unsupervised boys on the street are more likely to be recruited into gangs and generate more police contacts for noncriminal activity than more socially integrated boys. They are much more likely to be incarcerated for the same crimes that divert more affluent youths into mental health treatment.

Often, a negative encounter is a street youth's first experience with police. This can make them cynical about justice. Inequity, in any arena, tends to breed contempt for the law. When I lived on the street, police harassed me continually. Admittedly, I looked like trouble. When we create opportunities for alienated young men to come into positive contact with public safety officials, however, it can go a long way to bridge the divide between gang members and the law. Police officers who demonstrate that they regard young men as a part of the community they "protect and serve" can win their respect. After all, boys on the street have the highest victimization rates of all citizens.

In community law enforcement, cops walk the street and live in the same neighborhoods they patrol. They know the boys by name and where they live. Positive community policing can forge human relationships with gang members while better ensuring public safety at the same time. Midnight basketball games, often sponsored by police organizations, create a context where gang members and police officers can forge positive relationships with one another. When a pilot program in Arizona kept basketball courts open until 2 a.m., juvenile crime dropped about 50 percent. The cost of the program was 60 cents per boy. One of my graduate students created a program for gang members and police officers to act together in Shakespeare plays. It levels their playing field and creates community.

That poverty breeds crime is a truism so blatant as to appear trite. Even so, we have done little to deal effectively with this precursor to crime, focusing instead more on its effects. We will spend four times as much to incarcerate a boy as to educate him. As blue-collar jobs evaporate and entry-level jobs require greater technical skills and education, these fading bastions of work for young men make them the fastest growing segment of the economically disenfranchised. More than 12 million American males are currently impoverished. Most property crime—the highest arrest category for juvenile males—is fueled by poverty.

Publicly funded work programs that once restored unemployed men to dignity are meager today. "Jobs not jails" would be a good slogan for a political candidate who really cared about reducing violence and gang involvement. Gangs offer disenfranchised young men economic opportunity through criminal enterprise. An increase in entry-level employment opportunities for young men, in jobs with upward mobility and a living wage, would be sure to undercut gang induction. The costs would be considerably less than that of criminalization of boys who fall through the safety nets of home, school, and community, and onto the streets.

Fourth Pathway to Gangs: Juvenile Justice

Many people believe that the need to keep expanding juvenile institutions is inevitable. However, prisons, juvenile or otherwise, are not an indelible fact of life. The time is overdue for the leaders of a new era to revise our juvenile justice system. The crumbling, dark and dank basement cell I first occupied in the Los Angeles Juvenile Hall was built in 1903.

The bulk of public money, however, continues to go toward punitive restraint, a practice that has little or no efficacy in reducing violence. Many fear that humanistic treatment of young offenders reads as "soft on crime." Politicians pander to voters' fears, urging more police and prisons, as though this will magically solve the deep-rooted economic and social problems that cause most violent crime and gang involvement.

A year of youth imprisonment costs roughly the same as a year at a university. I've done both. The latter is better. Recovering gang members need opportunities to give back to their communities instead of returning from abusive lockups with a desire for revenge against a culture that subjected them to neglect or even torture. Numerous learning and behavioral studies demonstrate that punishment is the least effective means for creating lasting change in people. Positive reinforcement for new behaviors has the greatest efficiency. Incarceration frequently severs boys' few threads of continuity with jobs, housing, social support systems, and family. Rehabilitation programs could move youthful offenders out of remote, isolated institutions into secured environments near populations that can provide educational and social services, community volunteer programs, and regular interactions with family members. There is much we can do.

Some years ago, I hosted a series of public dialogues with social workers, teachers, police, probation, government, clergy, and the gang members of our region in Southern California. We named these gatherings "Boys to Men: It Takes the Whole Village." We invited local gang members and the boys in probation camps and juvenile hall, who came under guard. Adult mentors also brought one boy each whom they felt had successfully made the transition from juvenile justice to our community in their programs. With more eloquence than I could have ever imagined, these boys informed the professional community about what had changed their lives and what they thought other boys like them needed from the community.

One former gang leader, Arturo, now the director of a gang diversion program, said, "I had no heart. Anyone [who] tried to show me love, I put my walls up. Babatunde [my mentor] is a strong man. He gave me a chance, guidance, love, a job. He gives me focus, showing me how to be a man, walk the walk, and be a father to my son. If I didn't have my son, I'd be in the joint. All I knew was drugs. I'm trying to break the cycle. Everything I do in my life now I do for that little man [my son]."

When I offer fatherhood trainings at juvenile detention centers, I always note both high rates of premature fatherhood among the boys as well as histories of fatherlessness or victimization by abusive or neglectful fathers. Once we make that connection clear, I often ask, "Do you want your own son to be here in 15 years?"

To a man, they say, "No way!"

"So," I reply, "What are you going to do to change your behavior so you can protect your own children from this place?"

That always gives them pause. This encounter produces more buy-in to significant behavioral change than any other approach I've tried. When young men are treated with respect and given the educational and economic opportunities that can enable them to help their children, a surprising number rise to meet the challenge. They often do so with pride and commitment once given clear opportunities and support to fully participate in family life. Leaving the gang to become a better father is also one of the only universally acceptable excuses to exit gang life.

Another boy told one of our assemblies, "I grew up in the 'life.' My dad was a gang member. I'm only 17, but I feel 30 or 40. My fear is getting out of the gang. I want to make something out of my life, get a good job. I'm afraid I'll end up six feet deep. I want to be able to just walk down the street without looking behind my back."

Almost every boy who spoke at our events later said it was the first time that people in authority had ever listened to him or indicated that he had anything of value to offer. Did these conferences help lower gang membership and violence in our community? The rates, in fact, did significantly drop, but we can't prove it was due to our efforts. We did, however, clearly open up lines of communication between groups that seldom respectfully talk to one another. The incarcerated young men saw their former cohorts being honored and valued for trying to get their lives together, and several said that the stories they heard gave them hope.

We are social animals. It is dehumanizing to deny an individual all human contact and subject them to abuse. Some men meet injustice and violence against themselves or those they love with violence of their own, just as some nations go to war when attacked. This, of course, doesn't justify violence, but it helps us to know better how to treat it. Intensive supervision in the community is a proven, viable alternative for the majority of boys sent to juvenile jails.

Many evolutionary psychologists theorize that boys are naturally aggressive—biologically programmed as hunters. However, it is a dangerous theoretical leap to conclude that boys also are innately violent. Theories vary, but in my experience, young male violence generally happens when parents, educators, and other concerned adults fail to direct young male aggression into positive channels and protect boys from abuse. The California Wellness Foundation notes that the state spends $2 billion a year on police, courts, and jails, just responding to juvenile crime. However, funds allocated for the prevention of youth violence are merely $116 million. We can do better.

Youth correctional institutions, by any name, are still prisons. Youth prisons occupy a narrow penal territory between lower-level offenders in juvenile facilities and men in adult prisons. Historically, the philosophy in youth prisons leaned more toward rehabilitation than adult prisons. In most states, however, juvenile penal laws become more stringent each election year. As one astute criminologist puts it, "What began as an attempt to eliminate delinquency ended up as a practical method for getting rid of delinquents."

Once a boy makes the leap from juvenile institutions and probation to youth corrections and parole, chances are high he will remain on the prison road for life. Over half the "wards" of the California Youth Authority (CYA) are back in custody within 24 months of release. Most of the rest return in time or matriculate to adult prisons. I was first committed to CYA when I was 15 for "status" offenses, such as runaway, curfew violations, living without adult supervision, and probation violation. It remains one of the most utterly terrifying experiences of my life. I keep my honorable parole certificate framed right next to my PhD.

The climate toward young male offenders and gang members, in particular, has steadily become more punitive over the past few decades. Recent state and federal bills aim to significantly expand the processes by which boys can be tried and convicted as adults and to abolish federally funded juvenile rehabilitation while increasing juvenile prison construction.

There is no clinical or forensic evidence that adult-level prosecution or incarceration reduces juvenile violence in any way. Young men tangled up in youth corrections enter lockup like uranium. They have a potential for destructiveness, but most have not fully realized it. Young men leave prison like plutonium: The constant bombardment by concentrated streams of violence in prison dangerously enriches a boy's latent potential for harm, breeding ever-increasing levels of societal violence in an endless feedback loop.

If we want to break the cycle of violence, however, we could provide protection from subjugation to assault, torture, and rape in locked facilities. We could implement programs designed to heal young lawbreakers' lives, rather than merely punish them or break their spirits. Youth prison, as it stands today, only prepares young men for admission to adult prison, and they are prime recruitment facilities for gangs. Ultimately, as police states of other cultures have demonstrated, no amount of law enforcement can permanently contain the social upheavals that occur in reaction to injustice.

For the tens of millions of us with arrest sheets, the slope toward reincarceration is slippery and steep. The system is sticky. It's hard to jump out. A great deal of new violence happens in response to the posttraumatic stress disorder (PTSD) men suffer from incarceration. Though gang members rarely admit it outside our councils, some would rather get shot or shoot someone else than risk rearrest. As a boy in Youth Authority for car theft once told me, "My father is in prison, my mom works all day. You want me to give up my gang when I get released? Whose gonna be my family then? You?"

If we do not help marginalized boys to change course, as I was helped, the majority will careen along this path until they slam against the gates of the adult prison system. Since the early 1970s, when I began to turn my life around, California's prison population has increased sevenfold. One could infer that the chances I had for diversion away from prison have become increasingly rare.

In order to help boys at risk for incarceration and gangs, we could build secure, small-scale, community-based juvenile facilities instead of expanding state institutions far from family and local resources. We could make free job training, like high school, available to all young men who seek it and open more doors to education for dropouts, because viable education and employment are the best defenses against crime. We could provide substance abuse treatment, therapy, education, parenting education, and literacy and vocational training in all locked juvenile facilities to help break generational cycles of poverty and violence. We could reduce caseloads of probation officers so they can provide intensive supervision and integrated support services for young men returning to the community. We should assure zero tolerance toward the abuse of boys behind bars so they do not leave with a heart of vengeance against society.

Fifth Pathway to Gangs: Drugs

Most gang members have substance abuse problems; many are addicts. The psychology of substance abuse, however, is complex. As such, it eschews simplistic solutions. Illegal drugs are dangerous and can destroy lives, as can alcohol, tobacco, prescription drugs, and motorcycles. Today, however, the widespread criminalization of young addicts appears abundantly more harmful, costly, and generative of violence than drug use itself. Drug offenders now represent the majority of federal prisoners and more than one-third of state and county prisoners, more than those incarcerated for all violent crime categories combined. In California, more "three strikes" prisoners are doing 25 years to life for marijuana than murder.

Despite massive campaigns and countless ruined lives, teen substance abuse remains prevalent, though consistently less than adult abuse. Adolescent substance abuse rates rise and fall over the years, with no sustained, long-term trend toward reduction. Citizens who do not use antidepressants, tranquilizers, and other psychiatric medications; pain medications; diet pills; caffeine; tobacco; alcohol; or some illegal substance are likely a minority. The type of drug, level of use, population who uses it, method of distribution, manufacture, regulations, laws, and other features of substance use keep shifting. "Just say no or go to jail" for certain substances, however, does not rise to a stellar psychosocial treatment methodology. Most young, male drug users are nonviolent, at least before incarceration. Zero tolerance equals zero success. We can do better.

Drug-savvy kids dismiss most antidrug programs as a joke, an insult to critical thinking. These programs could be extremely valuable to those same youths, however, if designed for harm reduction instead of law enforcement's goals. Numerous program reviews demonstrate that zero tolerance is a total failure, recapitulating our protracted, failed "war on drugs." The growing intolerance toward addicts appears more to reflect blind ideology than enlightened leadership offering thoughtful and workable solutions to difficult social problems. Almost half of recently surveyed 17-year-olds report having used marijuana, and three-quarters of high school seniors reported using alcohol during the previous year.

Without intensive treatment, total lifetime abstinence is unrealistic for many addicts. Inexpensive and quick drug testing is sending record numbers of young parolees to prison instead of treatment. In many states, as many are returned to prisons from parole as for new felony convictions—most for failed drug tests.

The billion dollars or so spent annually for youth-oriented, antidrug media campaigns could send 80,000 to 150,000 gang-prone youths to college or trade school, provide a year of quality outpatient drug treatment for 350,000 young addicts, or provide wages for one million mentors or reading tutors to spend a few hours with a gang member or "wannabe" each week. Although there is no positive correlation between incarceration and reduced drug involvement, there is a clear, direct relationship between level of education and drug abuse. The less of the former, the more of the latter.

Treating the underlying social and psychological conditions that provoke youths to seek the temporary pain relief of drugs could be more effective than forcing hundreds of thousands into the criminal justice system. The problem isn't that law enforcement has failed to make addicts and gang members afraid enough, the real problem is that these young people are not hopeful enough. A campaign for hope calls for different tactics than a war.

Today, many boys feel caught in dichotomies between gangsters' allure and mainstream invitations. Particularly in our inner cities, young men often feel they must choose between outlaws, who provide acceptance, community, and economic opportunity, and a mainstream culture that often rejects or condemns them. The glamour of rap music artists, with their excess of drugs, sex, and money, attracts countless young men. Many hang their identities on the profiles of gang members who seem to have escaped our decaying inner cities. These boys need jobs, education, spiritual guidance, and a clear road to a bountiful world before seeds of doubt will be cast on drug culture affiliations that, albeit falsely, promise a better life.

"Gangsta" ethos obscures the Cimmerian sinkholes swallowing gang members today. Crack, coke, smack, or speed—it doesn't matter. If not medically supervised, all of these lead to oblivion. The protracted use of street drugs, with their wide variance of purity, is suicide on the installment plan. Many marginalized youths feel little reason for living. That gaping void in the soul is the biggest drug lure of all. For a few moments, drugs obscure the demoralizing lacuna in a bad boy's psyche. However, like subterranean termites, drugs eat farther into psychological foundations already weakened by adverse social circumstances.

Every time we disenfranchise a boy from the mainstream, for whatever reason, we create a potential new drug user or gang member. Social exclusion is a more powerful generator of drug abuse than any street corner recruitment. Many young men crave risk as an opportunity to display their courage, a traditional means of inclusion in male culture throughout the world.

Drug dealing is very social, intense, engaging, vivid, and dramatic. Dealing and drug use are very seductive to young men who lack strong hopes or ties to other sources of social inclusion. Economic opportunity and the attention of older males seduce many lost boys into this dangerous trade.

My father inducted me into drug dealing, and I was happy and proud to do it then, because it won his respect. Then he went to federal prison and I went to college. There I found new respect from other older men and women for engaging in prosocial activities.

Drug abuse is widely distributed among most economic, racial, and cultural groups. Boys from racial minorities, however, suffer the most severe consequences for drug use, particularly if they are gang-affiliated. Affluent addicts avoid drug sweeps and other street hazards. They more easily raid parent's medicine cabinets, obtain legal prescriptions, and use drugs in more secure environments. Socially advantaged addicts receive better legal representation and health care. Judges often view enfranchised whites as better candidates for diversion to treatment than low-income or minority addicts. African-Americans are 13 percent of the US population, yet 40 percent of drug arrests. They serve longer prison terms for the same crimes as whites. Gang affiliation often lengthens sentences. Black teenagers are surveilled, stopped, searched by police in greater numbers, and, once arrested, are seven times more likely to be charged with a felony than white teens who commit the same crime.

The billions spent on drug wars have not diminished supply or increased prices. Drug prohibition generates billions for drug lords. It is young men in the lower ranks of gangs, however, dealing small quantities on the streets, who constitute the easiest police targets and the majority of arrests. Many gangs are little more than drug-dealing enterprises. Minority boys in inner-city neighborhoods are the primary casualties of both the drug war and gang recruitment. They are flooding our prisons.

When meaning is absent, insanity, violence, and criminality rush into the vacuum like thunder chasing lightning. When we avail boys with no other creative opportunity for self-definition, a bad-boy identity can provide a powerful sense of meaning. The graffiti wallpapering of our cities is, in part, an outpouring of that quest for expression and recognition. For many, it feels better to be part of a gang, even a violent one that puts them at risk, than to suffer the existential anxiety of having no strong definition at all.

When there is more to lose, some people become more motivated to protect their lives. For example, many Vietnam veterans came home with narcotics addictions. Those young men who came home to intact families and communities, with good access to economic and educational opportunity, were significantly less likely to remain addicted than those who returned to less hopeful circumstances. Drug addiction is not simply physiological dependence; it is deeply tied to social, emotional, familial, economic, physical, mental, and spiritual health. Opportunities for personal growth can undercut the psychological conditions that lead to substance abuse. A great deal of harm can be simply reduced by policy changes.

Germany, Ireland, the United Kingdom, Australia, Switzerland, New Zealand, and other nations are exploring varying degrees of decriminalization. The Frankfurt Resolution, drawn by international policy experts, states: "A drug policy which treats addiction exclusively as a law enforcement problem, and makes abstinence a precondition for the granting of assistance, is doomed to failure."

Most well-informed health experts today agree that the collateral trauma, injury, disruption of families and communities, fiscal drain, infliction of mental illness, disease, and death that occurs from drug criminalization far exceeds the harm caused by drugs themselves. Decriminalization would cause prices to plummet. Many experts believe it could halve our prison population and free law enforcement to focus on more serious crime. If profits were eliminated, gang-turf violence would decrease, making neighborhoods safer. That proved true in Holland when they legalized soft drugs and decriminalized hard drugs. On average, each nonaffluent, hard-drug addict commits 50 robberies and 85 burglaries each year.

Beyond organized crime, the only other groups who directly benefit from criminalization of drugs are prison workers unions. The RAND Corp. calculates that $34 million invested in treatment could reduce cocaine use as much as $380 million spent on interdiction or $250 million on enforcement. When drug offenders also receive job training, recidivism further falls 25 percent, even for those with long criminal records. Of all resources available, criminalization appears to be most costly and least productive as a method to reduce drug use.

Drug courts represent a bridge between the disparate philosophies of "treatable patient" versus "dangerous criminal." As distinct from criminal courts, drug courts attempt to draw youths away from drugs through treatment, education, community involvement, close supervision, and various sanctions. Drug courts lean toward real justice, utilizing a policy of "harm reduction" over the deterrence through fear that dominates our national drug enforcement policy. At one-tenth the cost of imprisonment, taxpayers save $7 to $11 for every dollar spent on treatment.

The best way to fund gangs and encourage poor and minority youths to join them is to keep drugs illegal. Harm reduction, education, treatment, and decriminalization are merely first steps toward reducing boys' use of pain-relieving drugs. Until our society addresses the social issues and environmental contexts that drive so many young men into despair and self-medication of their pain, I doubt anything will have much significant effect.

Sixth Pathway to Gangs: Adult Prisons

When I got here, a guard told me, "Boy, if you want to survive here you better get your self a big, tough boyfriend right away." (Malcolm, 17, starting 15 years in adult prison for small quantity drug sales.)

Once a gang member arrives at adult prison, hope for his future dims. Imprisonment signals that we failed to forge crossroads along the prison highway that could have turned him toward community. For some, there was little any of us could have done to divert their destinies toward prison. However, most who pass those gates embody our collective failures in parenting, education, counseling, community support, legislation, economic policy, and juvenile justice. Today, more than 2.3 million Americans are behind bars, and more than 4 million are on probation or parole, one violation away from reincarceration.

In a nation that prizes openness, prisons remain a largely obscured world with closed borders. If we care at all about gang-prone youths, however, it is important to know what awaits them, particularly in light of a widespread push to sentence more gang-affiliated youths to adult prisons. Many state prisons are filled to 150 percent of capacity. Criminologist Elliot Currie, professor at the University of California, Irvine, notes that the severity of Texas's "punitive scale" ranks it between United Arab Emirates and Nigeria. Not surprisingly, tensions are mounting in many prisons. They are unsafe for guards and inmates, both of whom suffer high assault rates. In response, new, ultrasecure, "super maximum" prisons, set far from human habitations, have been created for "problem" prisoners—often gang leaders or affiliates. Similar to practices used to extract information from terrorists confined in Abu Grab and Guantanamo Bay, some prisons use protracted solitary confinement to coerce gang members to inform on others.

A US federal court found "a pattern of needless and officially sanctioned brutality" at Pelican Bay, and a United Nations' torture expert has reported "cruel, inhuman, and degrading treatment" there and at other US supermax sites. As this goes to press, thousands of inmates are on a protracted hunger strike in an attempt to draw attention to supermax conditions, which Federal Judge Thelton E. Henderson says "may well hover on the edge of what is humanly tolerable." I worked on the death penalty case of one young man driven violently psychotic by nine months of solitary confinement. He entered prison as a nonviolent, teenaged burglar who 10 days after discharge participated in a horrific murder.

One reason America imprisons more of its citizens than any other nation is that we can afford to, spending more than $60 billion a year managing current prisoners. We pour billions more into prison construction, county jail administration, judicial systems, law enforcement, and the probation, parole, and social service agencies needed to deal with released prisoners. In recent decades, California has built 23 prisons and one university. In 1984, the higher education budget was two-and-one-half times that of corrections; now they are equal. This budgetary transfer from classrooms to cells is increasingly true in other states, as well, for the first time in US history. Five times as many African-American males are now in California prisons as are in public higher education.

Contrary to conventional wisdom, the US Department of Justice indicates that there is no definitive relationship between crime and incarceration rates. Incarceration rates, however, are linked to total numbers of young men and their employment rates. As spending on prisons steadily rose over recent decades, job-training funds plummeted. Moreover, rehabilitation incentives, such as sentence reductions for good behavior, education, and drug and alcohol recovery programs have declined dramatically. Higher education programs for prisoners fell from 350 nationwide in 1990 to only a few today. On the average, however, most prison wardens agree with me and want to see the development of more prevention programs, the repeal of mandatory minimum sentences, judges granted greater discretion, and an expansion of alternatives to incarceration.

Of all the indignities I encountered in the criminal justice system, none was greater than the constant threat of rape. Rape in prison is the most psychologically damaging experience most young men ever endure. Even though the majority of prisoners are there for nonviolent crimes, incarcerated young men are often repeatedly raped, by multiple perpetrators, over a period of years with no hope of escape or justice. Just like battle-shocked war veterans, we turn these traumatized young men onto the streets with no opportunity to heal the after-effects of protracted sexual torture.

Research estimates that roughly one in five male prisoners is sexually assaulted during his incarceration; a number at least matching the numbers of sexual assaults against free women. One of the only ways to avoid such a fate is to join a gang in prison and doing whatever they want you to do to secure their protection.

Torture, rape, degradation, unjustified shootings, sensory deprivation, electric shock, chemical sprays, injurious physical restraints, beatings, medical neglect, forced prostitution, slave labor, and the abuse of psychiatric medications do nothing to rehabilitate prisoners or ensure public safety. Even men who have perpetrated horrible crimes should have the opportunity to make productive use of their time, at least to make whatever restitution they can to their victims and their families. If not for humanity's sake, we should change the system simply to protect the rest of us from released prisoners, because most of them are someday.

Besides ruling the day-to-day lives of most prisoners, prison gangs have enormous influence on street gang activity. Most gang members cycle in and out of prison. They must serve the dictates of prison gang "shot callers" while on the street to assure protection once incarcerated themselves. In many cases, they serve to protect family members already in prison. Prison gangs perpetuate cycles of violence for generations. Many incarcerated boys tell me that they are the sons, nephews, and even grandsons of OGs (original gangsters, the charter members of gang culture). The fact that many of their relatives are dead, disabled, or imprisoned does little to dissuade their gang involvement. In many ways, gangs are extended families, a kinship system in which members regard one another as siblings, the only family tradition they know.

When gang members refer to someone as a "Homeboy," or simply "Homes," it basically means, "This boy is from my home territory; he understands my cultural context. He is my brother. With him, I stand united against all enemies." These sentiments are not unlike the feelings of men in police or military corps, for whom the city or nation is the "hood." As in prison, many young men in the community feel they must curry the protection of a neighborhood gang. For those living in gang territories, there is often little choice. Just as governments draft young men to fight in national conflicts, gang membership looms as forced conscription in an urban war.

Just as my willingness to fight in CYA demonstrated my worth, new members of gangs must demonstrate their courage. Gang initiation ("jumping in") frequently involves stoically taking a fierce beating by the gang's members. Often it also means committing a daring crime, even a murder. In a similar, but more socially integrated way, soldiers must often prove their fearlessness in training, hazing, and combat to be included in elite units or to gain rank.

Most adolescent boys search for some form of masculine identity and male community wherever they can find it. They crave affiliation with a group of same-aged boys and a few older males. Most young men still seek opportunities to prove their courage, strength, and other "traditional" attributes of masculinity. If the community does not provide them membership in a productive group of men, many will join a gang rather than risk the psychological and physical dangers of remaining unaffiliated.

About 80 percent of gang members lack a father present in their lives, as is true for the majority of all boys arrested for violent crimes. In fact, one of the chief predictors of youth crime in a community today is the percentage of father-absent households. Social scientists also correlate fatherlessness with higher rates of youth suicide, teen pregnancy, mental illness, substance abuse, poverty, and school failure, dropout, suspension, and expulsion. The United States leads the world in both fatherlessness and incarceration of young men.

In our economically challenged communities, fathers are often discouraged from family involvement by social welfare laws that reduce aid if fathers are at home, bias against fathers in custody and visitation rulings, family agencies that virtually ignore them, and incarcerations that devastate family relations for men in custody. Children living in single-parent homes have increased from 5 million to more than 17 million in the past three decades. Coincidentally, the quadrupling of our prison populations and proliferation of gangs rode tandem with this trend. Nevertheless, the bulk of crime prevention and gang eradication funds continue to pour into law enforcement, tracking, punishment, and prisons.

When drug use is the primary reason for reincarceration of a parolee, we could offer treatment as an alternative. We also could build smaller, secure, community-based prisons where inmates can get rehabilitative support from family, local volunteers, educational institutions, and community agencies instead of isolating them far from the cities. We should not allow adolescents to be imprisoned with adults, and should separate predatory prisoners from those more vulnerable to predation.

The costs for the above are secondary to the human and fiscal cost of recidivism. Most prisoners were already marginalized prior to incarceration. Upon release, few are better equipped to succeed; most are worse off. Freedom can be startling, disorienting, and overwhelming. Ex-prisoners need supports to make the transition to productive citizenry.

Because most prisoners reoffend and return, prison and parole themselves create a self-propagating pathway to gangs, more of a circular driveway, actually, than a path. In prison, low-level gang members grow up to become gang leaders and serious criminals. There are limits to what the average reader can do to help those behind bars. However, there is a great deal that any one of us can do to help gang members become good men once they are released or before they go away.

Seventh Pathway is a Road Out of Gangs: Mentoring

Many "male mentoring" programs across the nation are working to change the social conditions driving so many young men into gangs and violence. "Retired" gang members also have formed numerous local and national grassroots groups. They help negotiate gang truces and divert current gang members and young "wannabes" into productive paths. These grassroots programs, usually operating with shoestring budgets, have been seriously overlooked by social statisticians for their contributions to reducing violent crime in recent years. Government tends to falsely attribute crime reduction solely to increased policing and incarceration.

Mentors in these groups report that socially nurturing behavior emerges from troubled boys when they can connect with a sense of "male honor." Through respectfully appealing to a boy's manhood, by modeling a responsible model of masculinity, older men can reach the unreachable. This is in contradistinction to the justice system, which often modifies behavior by instilling fear and shame through increasing levels of constraint and degradation and attacks on young offenders' sense of masculinity.

Successful mentors, however, learn to channel and redirect young male pride and toughness. They create meaningful community and relationships that young men thereby naturally want to preserve and protect.

National gang authority Steve Nawojczyk (program administrator in the Community Services Section of the Arkansas State Division of Youth Services) calls gangs "the 5-H Club. They are homeless, helpless, hungry, hugless, and hopeless. They create their own subsociety because they don't fit into ours. Many youth join gangs because they don't have anything else to do. Gangs are the strongest where communities are the weakest."

To facilitate positive change, we could offer gang members good education, job skills training, parenting and relationship skills training, employment opportunities, drug recovery, and other interventions that restore hope. When we create opportunities for self-determination instead of merely condemning gang members, things change.

Jeff Prieto was "jumped into" a local gang, the Barrio Hoods, when he was a teenager. Drugs, violence, pervasive feelings of anger, and alienation from Anglo culture filled his life. One day, a "special education" teacher in his school said to him, "If you're going to just sit there, read something." He loved to read, but reading was not "cool." So, he read in secret, in the library, and learned a great deal on his own.

When he was a high school senior, not one school counselor ever talked to him about the possibility of college. He never even imagined it himself. But, one day a visiting Chicano rights activist saw that Jeff had potential and practically forced him to fill out a college application. He was accepted to UCSB (University of California, Santa Barbara), graduated in law from UCLA, and received an additional graduate degree from Princeton.

He says, "I was in the gang for social and economic reasons. But the strongest draw was an overwhelming feeling of power. We used to say, "*Somos chicos pero locos*" [we are small, but we are crazy]. Our wildness made us feel strong.

"Even in college the pull back to the street was powerful. I didn't fit in at school. Many middle-class people acted like I did not belong there. I thought that maybe I was not intelligent. I felt divided and I dropped out. I threw away the opportunities people fought hard to give me.

"How did I finally get out of the gang? Familia [family], amigos [friends], and carnales [brothers] helped me take heart. True friends don't grab you as they are going down so they won't be lonely. True friends lift you up, they help you find your dreams. So, I went back to school. It was hard. I stayed up late every night and studied. My sons grew up in married student housing.

"*Cholos* [Chicano gang members] have heart. But they are fighting for something they do not own. The city owns the streets, not the gangs. There is something, however, that does belong to them and is worth fighting for: their future. It takes a real man to stand up for the [neighbor] hood, but it takes more to stand up in school. Education is the key. There is power there, like what I felt in the gang. How we educate our children today will determine how our community is in the future. The real battle in our culture today is not between gangs, it is for the hearts, minds, and souls of the children in our community."

Many gang members without good education and job skills feel that being an outlaw is their only recourse. That is why Father Gregory Boyle started Homeboy Bakery in Los Angeles. He invited gang members, some from rival gangs, to work there and learn a trade. It had a profound effect in weaning a number of them away from crime and violence.

The film industry, in which I worked for several years, has a program called City Lights that reaches out to gang-prone young men. Candidates first go through rites of passage designed to evoke responsible "manhood." They also learn about anger management, communication, grooming, and other basic workplace survival skills. Then they learn a good trade. Former O.G. "Crazy Ace" was a young felon with two strikes on his record. On leaving prison, he wanted out of gang life and to dedicate himself to caring for his daughter. After City Lights mentors got ahold of him, he said, "I used to dream about a good future. But I couldn't see it. Now I can."

In the outcry against gangs, it is seldom noted that there are varying levels of involvement: (1) prison leaders, (2) prison members, (3) street leaders, (4) hard-core members, (5) affiliates and spouses, (6) wannabes, (7) young boys at risk, and (8) children of members. Most at-risk boys, 14 years old and younger, are between levels 5 and 8. This is the time we should be pouring resources into their lives to offer them clearly viable and stable alternatives to gang initiation.

One-shot programs don't work. Just saying "no" doesn't work. Criminalization and incarceration won't turn the tide. Gangs offer cultural pride and self-rule. They challenge a dominant culture, often perceived by disenfranchised youths more as an oppressor than a source of opportunity. Gangs are attractive because they fill an essential need in adolescent male psychology for membership, acceptance, display, recognition, pride, a sense of mission, and a feeling of power.

Gangs provide community for lonely boys, economic opportunity for poor boys, adventure for bored boys, action for restless boys, protection from violent males outside the gang, and connection with powerful (in their social context) older men. So, for all the despair they can bring, gangs are attractive to disenfranchised boys.

Just one trustworthy, committed, honest, caring, and capable adult who will hang in with gang members through all their ups and downs can make the critical difference between a boy positively moving toward community or trying to destroy it. In my case, a parole officer named Vincent Price liberated me from my despair in the CYA. He was the only professional to come along, in my two years of incarceration, who genuinely cared and was willing to help. He lobbied to get me released to a new program—the first CYA halfway house.

I was 16 and wanted to attend college. However, I had only a ninth-grade education. Even though I was motivated and capable, school officials said I lacked sufficient credits for admission. Many boys gravitate to crime as their options for a good future narrow. With Mr. Price's help, I instead secured a full-time job working as a clerk for the same school system that would not accept me as a student. I later successfully petitioned the court to designate me as an emancipated minor. That meant I could leave the home, get my own apartment and no longer be subject to arrest for living on my own or being out after curfew. I worked hard until I was 18 and could attend L.A. Community College, which did not require a high school diploma. I completed my associate of arts degree, transferred to state college, and spent the next 20 years working my way through higher education until I earned my PhD.

For many former felons or gang members who are good men today, some sort of spiritual experience turned the direction of their lives. So, in paying full homage to the power of good parenting, education, counseling, real justice, community support, and economic opportunity, it would be remiss not to acknowledge the power of a spiritual community or teacher to restore a boy's moral compass to working order.

Intrinsic to bad-boy psychology is a deep emotional constraint. Sociopathy is the extreme of this complex, in which a boy's "emotional body" has been buried alive, extinguishing whatever spark of moral conscience he may have once had. Most gang members find themselves in hostile territory. Broken homes, mean streets, pathologizing schools, undertrained counselors, indifferent communities, police scrutiny, gang violence, punitive institutions, jails, and prisons are all bars of their emotional prisons. Their thirst for freedom, release, and transcendence is deep.

One way the hunger for relief can actualize itself is through an unconscious but profound longing for death. Not unlike a powerful sex drive, there also exists a death drive that can take over someone's life. Hard drugs, shootouts, suicide attempts, criminal activity, poverty, poor medical care, selfabuse, and incarceration all contribute to giving gang members early death rates comparable to soldiers in combat.

There are many routes out of the ghettos that leak into our hearts and take residence in our souls. An impoverished interior life recapitulates the landscape of a bankrupt environment inside a bad boy's heart and mind. When our inner life is deadened, we project deadness into the world. Coming alive in our emotional and spiritual life, however, is one antidote to despair.

For many young men, a felony conviction is tantamount to a lifetime sentence to poverty. In this computer age, it stays on record forever. Every time police officers run a record check for a traffic stop, they learn they have a felon. Thus, they are more likely to extensively investigate. Felons are subject to more scrutiny than the average citizen who also may be in violation of some law. Our legal system does not display a strong belief that people can redeem lives once in error.

I am disturbed by the current move to deny loans to students with drug convictions. Had that been true in my era, I'd probably be dead. Without education, there is little hope for those of us who have gotten off to rough starts. During my university years, through social osmosis, I gradually acquired a new identity. Though some make miraculous turns on a dime, most personal growth happens incrementally. An acorn becomes a sapling. It adds annual rings of growth. Then, bang, there's an oak with acorns of its own to give back to the earth. Thanks, in part, to a string of student loans and the lower fees of the California university system in my era, I acquired a good education. Ultimately, I earned enough through honest work to finance doctoral studies and to repay all student loans. I now pay taxes instead of consuming them.

Integrated after-care, with a spectrum of services, is essential to break the chain of criminality and despair in the previously incarcerated. Confinement in our penal institutions is so traumatic that, without help, few of us stay harm-free or secure productive independence from the system. Integrated precare for those at risk for incarceration is equally imperative to divert young men from the prison road.

In our culture today, various events mark adolescent boys' passages into adulthood. For some, it is high school graduation. For others, it's the independence and responsibility that comes with a car. Some feel that their first sexual experience or parenthood marks that transition. Joining the army, going off to college, getting a job, leaving home, all, for some, make them feel they have crossed over into an adult world. Among gang members it is often "making their bones"; committing their first crime on behalf of the gang, but none of these events properly conveys a transition from boyhood into a mature and responsible adult role.

The boy-to-man transition isn't clearly marked in our culture. An approximation is the image of a Boy Scout collecting enough merit badges to become an Eagle Scout. It is something hard won and highly admired by the adults of that community. It gives boys an opportunity to demonstrate their talent, courage, strength, discipline, integrity, and usefulness.

In a Jewish boy's bar mitzvah, his rite of passage is witnessed by his family and community. The rabbi declares, "Today you are a man." Thousands of years ago, that was probably true for a 13-year-old boy. Confirmation for Christian boys has a similar function. Today, however, the day after a boy's bar mitzvah, his mother still tells him to take out the trash. The confirmed boy still has to go to school in the morning. The Scout is only admired at jamborees. In any case, few gang members experience any of the above. I was behind bars on bar mitzvah day.

If a boy cannot win the respect of his elders, he will turn toward other means to command the attention he craves. Gang initiation has more in common with the traditional rites of passage than most institutional approaches today. When a boy is initiated into a gang, he gets a new family. He becomes part of a powerful tribe. His "jumping in" ceremony confirms his courage. Therefore, he is regarded as a man by the other homies. The fact that gangs expose him to danger feels inconsequential compared to the emotional power membership conveys.

For thousands of boys today, incarceration marks their transition to adulthood. Prison tattoos mark, to all "initiates" who can read them, their induction into the gang fraternity. So, we are left with a challenge. On one hand, most contemporary attempts to draw gang members across the bridge to responsible manhood are too irrelevant to our time and their culture to be effective. The powerful initiation approaches of gangs, on the other hand, suck boys into a vortex of belonging. Whether in South Chicago or Littleton, Colorado, they create affiliation inside the group by setting boys against the world.

According to anthropologists, such as David Gilmore, most young males do not experience manhood as an intrinsic birthright. It must be won. Most importantly, young men need to know they are seen, valued, needed, and that they have an important role to play that is essential to society. Boys to Men programs try to develop ways to create meaningful male-affiliation groups, with mature male leadership, dedicated to the common good of the community.

If powerful and successful men steadily admire, support, and praise them as they try to become better men, many claim that role instead of looting their environment for survival or simply as the outward expression of anger, frustration, and despair. Successful leaders of Boys to Men programs have learned a few things from their experiences. To be effective with gang members, we could do the following:

- Meet them as they are instead of how we think they should be.
- Accentuate the positive in anything they do while speaking with them directly, simply, openly, and honestly.
- Treat them with respect, knowing the sum of a young man's worth is greater than his worst act.
- Create diverse collaboratives to provide integrated services, which weave a strong net of support for boys at risk.
- Use recovered gang members in leadership positions and incorporate their input into program design and implementation.
- Provide real, sustainable opportunities for economic advancement and social inclusion.

Many young men who lose their way need sustained services from multiple arenas before they can get on the good-man track. They also need room to fail without the specter of unredeemability looming as a consequence. One-shot programs rarely work. Brash get-tough laws with sound-bite slogans do not breed justice. Halfhearted interventions foster more disappointment and cynicism than they cure. Every time a mentor, teacher, parent, or social servant walks away from a young man in trouble, for whatever reason, they drive another nail in his coffin. Real change usually takes time.

Gang members are elements of a system. The majority of their behavior is linked to preventable economic, social, familial, educational, institutional, medical, and legal issues. Pathologizing, criminalizing, dehumanizing, demonizing, and disenfranchising gang members has proved ineffective as a strategy for provoking lasting positive change.

One need not have a PhD in psychology to help many of these boys. A compassionate heart and courage to risk a little goes a long way. I hope this chapter will encourage us all to try, in whatever way we can, to at least look out for the life of one young man in our community, beyond our commitments to our own children.

Editor's Note: Portions of this chapter were excerpted from the author's book, *Angry Young Men: How Parents, Teachers and Counselors Can Help Bad Boys Become Good Men* (Jossey-Bass, 2002).

Gang Culture in the United States

7

MOHAMAD A. KHATIBLOO

Contents

Introduction

In recent years, gangs have become increasingly real in many regions of the world as a major problem contributing to crime and violence. The perceived relationship between gangs and violence has led major international organizations like the World Health Organization, the Pan-American Health Organization, the Organization of American States (OAS), the Canadian International Development Agency (CIDA), and the United States Agency for International Development (USAID) to explore potential solutions to the problem. While gang research has a long and rich history in the United States and has recently begun to flourish in Europe, gangs have not been the focus of sustained empirical research elsewhere, including parts of Central and South America. Scholars have lamented the paucity of research on the contributions of gangs to violence in both North and South America.

Much of what is known about gangs has come from research in developed nations, particularly the United States. Researchers have invested considerable energy studying how factors, such as communities, peers, drugs, families, subculture, and the organizational structure of gangs, influence gangs and gang-related outcomes. Over the past decade, researchers have begun to examine the extent of the gang problem in Europe and characterize how it compares with other nations. Much of this work has been conducted by the

Euro Gang Working Group, which has developed common instruments and methodologies to examine the scope and nature of the gang problem in different nations. The group's work has resulted in several volumes of research. They have made substantial progress in understanding the issue of definition, gang structure and organization, individual gang member characteristics and risk factors, neighborhoods, immigration and ethnicity, and the impact of groups and gangs on individual delinquent behavior, primarily at the national level (Allan, 2004).

It was not until fairly recently that researchers began to collaborate on cross-national gang research. To the researcher's knowledge, there have been only four cross-national quantitative studies examining gangs, all of which were conducted in developed countries and relied on samples of juvenile gang members. Various researchers examined the scope and nature of gang problems among high-risk youths from Denver, Colorado, and Berman, Germany, and school samples participating in the US-based Gang Resistance Education and Training (GREAT) and the Netherlands Institute for the Study of Crime and Law Enforcement (NSCR) School Project.

Both reported similar rates of gang joining across countries, and both found that gang members were significantly more likely to be involved in delinquency than nongang members. However, some of the authors reported that German gang members reported fewer drug sales than American gang members. They indicated that Dutch gang members belonged to gangs that were less organized than American gangs. Most recently, Uberto Gatti and his associates compared the prevalence and characteristics of deviant youth groups in Italy to those in France and Switzerland (Gatti, U., Tremblay, R. E., Vitaro, F., and McDuff, P.). Both studies were coordinated efforts and used the International Self-Report Delinquency Study (ISRD-2) instrument to collect data from students. These studies found that participation in deviant youth groups varied by nation, with France reporting the highest levels of gang membership, followed by Italy, then Switzerland. In all three countries, respondents involved with an uncommon youth group were significantly more likely to be involved in delinquency and to have been a victim of a crime than those not involved in an uncommon youth group (Bell, 1985). Issues related to gang culture in the United States and the revolution of these gangs will be discussed in detail.

The History of Gang Culture in the United States

Over the past three decades, public policy on gang membership and gang crime overwhelmingly has emphasized suppression and deterrence over prevention and intervention. Typical law enforcement antigang strategies meant to increase apprehension and prosecution include enhanced or saturation patrols in gang neighborhoods, specialized intelligence and operations units, multiagency collaborations and task forces, vertical prosecution, and increased use of civil abatement strategies like gang injunctions. California led the nation in implementing gang-specific legislation that increased sentences for crimes committed by gang members, established new penalties for gang recruitment, and witness intimidation in concert with moves toward more punitive sanctions for youthful offending more people.

In 1989, the California legislature passed the Street Terrorism Enforcement and Prevention Act. This bill defined a "criminal street gang" in California law and provided sentencing enhancements for "gang" crimes stipulated in the statute. In 2000, 62 percent of California voters supported the passage of ballot measure Proposition 21, which further increased gang crime penalties, required convicted gang member registration, and increased penalties for certain violent offenses, while also reducing the age at which juveniles could be tried in adult court, changing the types of probation available for juvenile felons, and reducing juvenile confidentiality protections (Gavazzi, 2006).

On the national level, 50 percent of states have laws that provide for enhanced penalties for gang-related crime. The US Senate passed S. 456, the Gang Abatement and Prevention Act of 2007. The House referred the bill that same year to the Subcommittee on Crime, Terrorism, Homeland Security, and Investigations. Its stated purpose is to increase and enhance law enforcement resources committed to investigation and prosecution of violent gangs, to deter and punish violent gang crime, to protect law-abiding citizens and communities from violent criminals, to revise and enhance unpardonable penalties for violent crimes, and to expand and improve gang prevention programs.

This bill that was introduced and eventually died, was to enact a national definition of criminal street gang and gang crime and establish federal penalties of imprisonment for gang crimes for life (murder, kidnapping), 30 years (any other serious violent felony), 20 years (other violent felony), or 10 years (any other offense). Although increasing prison sentences also may reflect goals of incapacitation or retribution, we assert that the assumption of the effectiveness of deterrence from increased apprehension, prosecution, and punishment are the foundation of popular support for these antigang crime policies. Ultimately, gangs were thought to be a state and local issue, not a federal issue. The common grasp of deterrence principles and their ready application to antigang response was noted by some researchers in 2007 (Dodge, 2006).

The purpose of suppression is to reduce gang-related activity by current gang members, and to reduce the number of people who choose to participate in gangs by providing for swifter, more severe, and more inescapable punishment. The guiding assumption is that, in the words of Malcolm Klein, "the targets of suppression, the gang members and potential gang members, will respond 'rationally' to suppression efforts and will weigh the consequences of gang activity, redress the balance between cost and benefit, and withdraw from gang activity." Klein issues a major challenge to proponents of deterrence-based gang responses. The well-documented, negative influence of delinquent peers on youth behavior is powerful in gangs, and the decision to engage in criminal activity is further affected by status threats and affiliation challenges, group cohesiveness, protection and loyalty norms, and other group processes.

Indeed, the spontaneous and criminal nature of much gang violence contradicts an image of the rational, calculating gang youth, weighing the certainty and severity of potential punishments for gang crime.

Given the pervasive patterns of suppression policies and the considerable body of scholarly work on deterrence, the lack of empirical assessments of deterrence processes among gang members is surprising. The work aims to address this gap between collaborative policy and social research. Specifically, various authors investigate whether there is empirical support for the viability of deterrence among gang members as compared to other youthful offenders. This chapter seeks to examine the common wisdom of policymakers that gang members' and young offenders' perceptions of certainty and severity of punishment for crimes are related to their intentions to commit these crimes in the future (Esbensen, 2000).

Past Deterrence Research

The principles of deterrence (i.e., swiftness, certainty, and severity of punishment, as they relate to criminal offending) have been researched for more than 30 years. A timely review by a few researchers concluded that many cross-sectional studies found support for the certainty component of deterrence, but mostly failed to find a severity effect. However, some of them concluded that support for the deterrent effect of perceived certainty is most likely to be found in those studies that are methodologically weakest. They noted that deterrence effects detected among bivariate correlations are reduced dramatically, or disappear completely, with more sophisticated models and the inclusion of other important predictors of crime. Few authors concurred that panel design studies find that neither perceived certainty nor severity are significant predictors of crime and that extralegal factors, such as informal sanctions, socialization, and moral considerations are the best predictors of crime.

More recently, few authors have reported the results of a meta-analysis of 40 empirical studies on deterrence effects (certainty, severity, a composite of certainty and severity, and nonlawful sanctions). These scholars systematically assessed the conditioning effects for the sample, model specification, and research design characteristics in these 40 studies. Therefore, these potential effects were the subject of extensive debate in the deterrence literature. Their five main conclusions were:

1. The mean effect size between deterrence variables and crime are "modest to negligible" (typically between 0 and −0.20).
2. Deterrence effect sizes are substantially reduced and often eliminated in multivariate models.
3. Deterrence effect sizes fluctuate according to methodological practices across studies, especially sampling of college students versus general samples and controls for competing theories and past criminal offending.
4. Certainty of punishment is the most consistently supported deterrence domain and tends to be most predictive of white-collar offenses.
5. The threat of nonlawful sanctions is a fairly robust predictor, suggesting the promise of combining deterrence theory with other (self- or informal) control theories.

The results of the researchers' analyses provide a tremendous opportunity to take stock of understanding of the conditions under which the threat of acceptable sanctions influences criminal behavior. Their review highlights a major omission in this empirical literature: No assessment of the effects of deterrence domains of certainty, severity, or nonlawful sanctions was possible for juvenile offenders because too few studies were available. Deterrence research has relied heavily on testing exceptional school and undergraduate students. The findings from these samples may not readily generalize to seriously delinquent youths.

Similarly, some of the authors and students argued that the studies, which test the general population, may misinterpret the deterrent effect because they include individuals who were unlikely to engage in criminal behavior. There have been a few studies that utilize seriously delinquent populations. A few of them even used previously incarcerated adults, known drug users, and high school dropouts, and found no effect of the risk of sanctions on behavior for these groups. They concluded from their investigation of juvenile and adult arrestees that adults were more receptive to deterrence messages and that, among juveniles, the deterrent impact of risk of arrest or punishment lessens as youths become more experienced with violent subcultures.

Some of them utilized analyses of the longitudinal Denver Youth Survey (1986–2012) of high-risk youths to identify modest effects of perceived certainty of arrest on offending. Finally, some tested a sample of inner-city high school students and found that peer behavior and severity of parents' punishments were significant predictors of self-reported delinquency, but that perceptions of risk of arrest (certainty) were not. The study's author also found that "internalized norms" (otherwise referred to as morality) mediated the impact of peer behavior and parental sanctions on delinquency. Numerous studies have found measures of morality to be among the strongest predictors of the frequency of offending behavior or perceptions of future offending.

However, none of these studies sampled high-offending or gang-involved youths (Gavazzi, 2006).

Results from studies utilizing an adult-offending population should be generalized to juvenile offenders with caution. Some of these studies test a type of criminal, for example, those who are active burglars, batterers, or property offenders. Youthful offenders are not specialists in their offending and often offend in groups, which may imply a different mechanism of decision-making involved in adolescence. Juveniles are likely influenced by peers, status and identity issues, and other potential situational contexts, such as drug and alcohol use, in ways that are different from adults. These influences may render deterrence processes less effective in adolescents and even less effective for gang members. There has been a serious effort to identify "determinable offenders." Many scholars believe that deterrence will not work on the entire population of people, but there is disagreement as to which individuals are not detectable. Some studies suggest that frequent offenders may be "undeterrable," whereas other research finds that crime-prone individuals (i.e., those with low self-control and high impulsivity) may be more sensitive to the threat of authorized deterrents than are other individuals.

Overall, past research on perceptual deterrence suggests a minor association between the perceived threat of legal sanctions (especially certainty) and levels of offending. The strength of this relationship in a population of juvenile offenders and gang members is not well known. Given the current policy climate of increasing punitive sanctions toward juveniles and gang members, studies that examine the deterrent effect of such sanctions in samples of young offenders are critical and timely. Prior research is unambiguous about the importance of including extralegal factors, such as morality, and nonlegal sanctions, such as the risk of social condemnation, and to consider the role of prior criminal offending in the examination of deterrence effects on future offending. The current study tests these relationships in a delinquent juvenile sample that permits the first systematic investigation of these issues with gang members (Guerra, 1997).

The Influence of Gang Members in the United States

One of the most trustworthy findings in criminological research is that a small subset of offenders is responsible for a large proportion of crime. Gang members, in particular, represent a group of individuals who are routinely involved in a disproportionate amount of crime and offending, and, therefore, have been the target of a great deal of attention from law enforcement and community crime prevention programs. The US Department of Justice has made gang prevention and intervention a primary focus and has endorsed a targeted public health approach to combat gangs under the assumption that "targeting a small, high-risk population can have significant, broader benefits. The logic behind this move toward intervention and prevention services targeted at high-rate offenders, especially youth most at risk of future gang membership, is quite simple. If one can prospectively identify youth most at risk of becoming gang members and successfully direct prevention and intervention services at these individuals before the onset of their gang careers, it can produce a positive impact for both the individual and society.

Potential benefits to such an approach are numerous, including reduced financial costs to both individuals and society through decreased losses associated with victimization, decreased public spending on incarceration and correctional supervision, as well as increased physical and psychological well-being for members of the community (Kennedy, 1997).

This move to a public health model of targeted crime prevention is perhaps best documented in the city of Los Angeles' efforts to use a survey instrument to decipher which youths are most likely to become gang involved. The hope is that through the use of risk assessment instruments, practitioners can more efficiently identify youths likely to become gang involved than can be done through subjective physical assessments. The development of risk instruments has proliferated greatly over the past decades, and evidence suggests that such instruments outperform human judgments concerning the risk for continued disruptive behavior.

Mounting evidence also suggests that there are risk factors for gang membership, which can be identified prospectively, lending credence to a public health approach to gang prevention. Some researchers suggest in their study on the identification of chronic juvenile offenders, to achieve the advantages of the rational decision-making model of risk classification and of prediction, one must ensure that the entire process is valid (Howell, 2005).

While the logic behind targeted interventions directed at gang members appears sound, the most fundamental policy question is whether practitioners have the ability to identify youths most at risk of becoming gang involved, both prospectively and efficiently. While advances in risk assessment devices have been made over the past decades, such that use of these instruments clearly outperforms subjective human risk assessments, the probability for human error has not been eliminated from the process of identifying youths at risk of gang membership. In an ideal world, every youth could be screened for risk factors associated with gang membership and receive intervention and prevention services related to their needs. Such practices, however, are not widespread and do not appear imminent, given both budgetary and staffing limitations across US jurisdictions. As some researchers concluded, specific organizational concerns (e.g., staff expertise, size, coordination, and cooperation) in a given juvenile justice jurisdiction limit how many juveniles can be screened to identify subsets of acute offenders for interventions.

Thus, human error is still a distinct possibility at the front end of the screening process, where practitioners must identify youths they believe could benefit from a formal risk assessment. This requires contact between the youth and agent responsible for making such recommendations, as well as gaining the youths and parents' permission to carry out such a screening. Given these potential hurdles, even in light of significant progress in the development and implementation of risk-screening instruments, youths most at risk for gang membership may be systematically underserved by such programmatic efforts. Unfortunately, this link in the chain of targeted prevention and intervention services, which precedes risk assessment and prevention programming, has not been minutely examined and, thus, could undermine the theoretical advantages of this strategy (Kennedy, 1997).

Risk Factors for Gang Membership

Popular discourse usually associates gangs with their involvement in violence, or the threat thereof. While the media may exaggerate or overemphasize some features of gangs and their related violence, there is little doubt that gangs and their members are associated with a disproportionate amount of violent crime. What is often lost in this discussion of the association between gangs and their responsibility for committing acts of crime and violence is their disproportionate level of violent victimization. Whether it has been measured through self-reports of nonlethal violence or a report on the probability of falling victim to homicide, gang membership is correlated with a disproportionately high level of violent victimization. For instance, various authors in their review of the literature on the association between gangs and violence, report that "... gang homicide rates are estimated at up to 100 times that of the broader population." This reality suggests that effective gang prevention can benefit the community at large, but can be especially advantageous for members of these groups.

There are two distinct issues that complicate the identification of youths most at risk of gang involvement. First is the fact that even in communities plagued by gang activity, only a small proportion of youths will ever become gang members. The determination of what sets these individuals apart from those that resist gang membership, therefore, must be done on an individual basis. After all, youths, in neighborhoods with a documented gang problem, will share many of the same community-level risk factors often associated with increased criminal activity and will most reasonably share a great deal of similarity in external appearance and demeanor. Secondly, very few youths have no risk factors associated with violence and gang membership, especially those that live in chronic gang communities, meaning that the identification of youths with one or two risk factors associated with gang membership provides little discriminate validity for proper risk classification. An identification of the small subset of youths most at risk of becoming active gang members, therefore, can be very difficult. Prospective studies, however, have documented some unique characteristics of gang versus non-gang youths, which can aid in the identification of youths in need of targeted prevention and intervention services, which we describe next (Klein, 2007).

Risk factors for delinquency and gang membership is typically divided into five finest domains: individual, peer, family, school, and community. Factors such as antisocial beliefs (e.g., negative views of police), techniques of neutralization, prior delinquency, and the experience of negative or traumatic life events (e.g., death or loss of a loved one), illness, or suspension or expulsion from school have been found to increase the probability of gang membership in adolescence.

While risk factors associated with the family domain have been inconsistently associated with gang membership in the literature, issues related to poor parental management, such as poor supervision and lax disciplinary practices, have been implicated across studies. The role of peers in the genesis of delinquent and criminal behavior, on the other hand, enjoys consistent support in the literature. Specifically, associating with delinquent peers is one of the strongest correlates of individual involvement in delinquency and violence, while commitment to delinquent peers also has been found to increase the probability of youth violence and gang membership. School risk factors can be further broken down into both individual and environmental domains.

While the influence of school-related risk factors has been inconsistent in the literature, from an individual standpoint, the negative effect of low bonding and attachment to school, little commitment to school activities, and poor academic performance have received some support across data sources. From an environmental standpoint, poor school climate (e.g., inconsistent discipline, inadequate supervisory support, substandard teachers) and perceptions of disorder (e.g., antisocial behavior on school grounds, victimization) at school are associated with increased involvement in delinquency and gang membership. As was discussed earlier, few youths have no risk factors associated with delinquency and gang membership (McCorkle, 1998).

There also appears to be no unique predictors of gang membership that can systematically distinguish risk of gang membership from risk of involvement in delinquency and violence. This led researchers to examine the impact of accumulated risk on the probability of gang membership. According to this body of research on the cumulative effect of risk on the likelihood of gang membership, the more risk factors associated with an individual, the greater the probability of gang membership. More specifically, researcher Esbensen and his colleagues found that the risk for gang membership was especially pronounced for this youth with seven or more risk factors, compared with those youths with zero or one risk factor. Further yet, it appears that the accumulation of risk factors across domains is also important, such that the risk of gang membership increases as individuals are exposed to risks in multiple domains.

Overall, for those charged with identifying youths most at risk for gang membership, it appears that the accumulation of individual risk factors, as well as the accumulation of risk factors across domains, is the best predictor of gang membership; no single risk factor can efficiently predict gang membership (Maxson, 1998).

Emerging Issues in Gang Culture in the United States

Gang research suffers from scant attention to data on two critical issues when applied to international comparisons. The first of these understands the role of the highly varied immigration/ethnicity/national origins effects on gang formation and support. The second is the enhancement of theory in explaining street gang issues. Looking at theory first, the progression of efforts in American research has all but stalled since 1965. In the remarkable data collection effort in Chicago, Short and Strodtbeck, in 1965, put to the test the three dominant theories of the time: opportunity structure, strain, and cultural deviance.

Each failed the test of explaining much of the variance in gang variety. Since then, Klein's (1995) minitheory of gang cohesiveness, Sanchez-Jankowski's (1991) defiant individualism concept, application of Wilson's urban underclass theory, and Hagedorn's theory in 2008, has applied more recent emphasis on globalization of gang culture, and each has offered some grist for the mill. Yet, no overarching theoretical structure has emerged. Spergel's (1995, 2007) revitalization of broad social disorganization theory has failed to direct his efforts to convincing empirical evidence for its explanatory value. The interactive, life-course developmental perspective advanced by Thornberry, Krohn, Lizotte, Smith, and Tobin (2003) seems a more promising approach (Smith, 1999).

The far more recent emergence of European street gangs and gang research has not as yet paid much attention to theory. Instead, it has concentrated on such issues as the prevalence of gangs and patterns of gang crime. International Self-Report Delinquency Study (ISRD II) is a tool that is concerned with the collection of data for analyzing the results in order to obtain proper findings for the study. For gang culture in the United States, some of the facts were collected by using ISRD II that was necessary to obtain reasonable findings on this issue. With the inclusion of social control, ordinary activities, and collective efficacy variables in the data collection, people may see some theoretical advance in cross-national gang theory, as these variables are applied to the ISRD II inclusion of the Euro gang definition's operationalization in that massive survey. Still, at this point, there is a great need and an apparent opportunity for theoretical gang work in comparative contexts.

Even more obvious is the opportunity for advances in understanding the role of ethnic and national origins in gang matters. Unlike the United States, where black, Hispanic, and some Asian groups have garnered almost all of our attention, comparative studies, especially in Europe, must account for a wide variety of minority statuses along with a number of instances of indigenous Caucasian groups. With the guest worker influx following World War II, the failure of so many of them to return to their homelands and the gathering of their family members in the different countries, and the liberal refugee policies that brought yet more immigrants, Europe has increasingly found itself less white and more diverse (Esbensen, 2000).

Assimilation problems, ghettoization, and just plain ancient culture clashes created a mass of socially excluded youths ripe for gang formation. Further, as ethnic gangs appeared more common, so did indigenous populations' backlash against the non-European groups. In addition, these minority populations were so diverse in their origins and subcultures that no single policy could be applied to them, other than right-wing-based repression and ethnocentrism.

Just to provide a few examples, European gangs often (separately) derive from Algerians, Turks, Moroccans, Jamaicans (Afro-Caribbean), Chinese, Pakistanis, Ausiedlers (Eastern European of German descent), Southern Italians in northern Italy, Finns in Sweden, Central and South Americans, Surinamese, and Chileans. A science or theory of ethnicity and street gangs must be broad enough to encompass such diversity of origins yet sensitive enough to account for the differences within such diversity. This is a serious challenge, only recently engaged by writers brought together for various purposes (Swanson, 2009).

Politics, Policies, and Practices

There are a number of issues that either reflect or impinge upon the nexus of street gang realities and public policies. One of these is the problem of contrasting street gang patterns with other group patterns of equal or greater visibility to the media and policymakers. In Europe and elsewhere, for example, there is an interest far exceeding that in the United States in football (soccer) hooligans. Similarly, there is a repeated interest among multinational organizations (the United Nations [UN], EU, and Interpol) in adult criminal gangs and conspiracies that threaten international commerce, and at the other end of the spectrum are various youth subcultures with little commitment to criminal or delinquent pursuits. If street gangs are to be studied and understood in their own right, they must be differentiated from these gang-like groups that clearly call for different public policies and practices (Chesney-Lind, 1994).

The European Gang Program was conducted in Europe and in many parts of the United States to obtain relevant data related to criminal activities performed by various gangs in America. The program assisted the researchers and even the authorities in gathering maximum information about the criminal activities that were taking place across the entire country. In the very early stages of the E.G. Program, there was something of a split between two camps as to whether Europe had a street gang problem or not.

While at first the split seemed to be between the American researchers and their European counterparts, it later became apparent that the major distance was between those actually engaged in gang research (most Americans and some Europeans) and those relatively new to gang research. The issue was crystallized by discussions about whether or not the term *gang* should be used at all in the European context. Those opposed to the term and less commonly active in the research were concerned that a "gang" program could help to create a moral panic about street gangs, that there was the danger of a national stigma, and that European delinquent groups were not like the stereotypic image of traditional American street gangs.

Further discussions, numerous empirical descriptions of US and European gangs, and very careful delineation of the E.G. Program's definition of gangs have largely dispelled the original split among the program's participants, but not among many media spokespeople and public officials. The denial of street gangs is still commonplace and likely reduces the perceived need to study and respond to them. Comparative gang researchers are in a position to reduce the gang denial trend by allowing their data to infiltrate public discourse about gang problems. It is a matter of stereotypes versus empirical realities (Thornberry, 2003).

Not surprisingly, this need for clarification also has to do with what is generally accepted as "valid" information. Media reports are made to sound authoritative, but seldom by reference to scientifically drawn data. Police reports are made to sound authoritative on the basis of the street experience of the officers, thought to be the closest window on gang structures and behavior. Yet, seldom do those relying on police reports think to question the representativeness of the police observation of gang members they encounter and as for the politicians. One way or another, those of us in the research field need to consider how to get our data into the hands of these others, as uncomfortable as that process may be.

However, we, ourselves, are not always so pure. For instance, there is among us a tendency to overpattern the conclusions about the nature of gangs. Some offer two examples as dissimilar to each other as is possible. The first is the recent work of Hagedorn in 2007 and 2008, which makes much of the effects of globalization on gangs throughout the world, and takes an ideo-logical stance toward gang definitions that allows cartels and boy soldiers and "our" gangs to be subsumed under the same umbrella. Any "science" of gangs is obliterated in this approach (Freng, 2007).

The contrasting example is provided by Junger-Tas and her colleagues in the ISRD II analysis plans (2010). The main purpose of this ISRD II program was to gather data on criminal gang activities that was not only taking place in the United States, but to also obtain information about the criminal activi-ties performed in other countries. To bring some sort of social order to the delinquency data collected in some 30 countries, the analysts have grouped those countries into societal types or models of society: Scandinavian, Southern European, Anglo-Saxon, and Central European in one instance, and an expanded grouping of six national clusters in another. The purpose is both to ease the analytic burden as well as to refer delinquency patterns to broad social structures.

This overpatterning may, or may not, clarify street gang differences; the jury is out until the data are in. American and some European research sug-gest that the group processes inherent in street gang structures trump differ-ences in ethnicity, national origin, and geography. Thus, different national, political, and social responses to gang problems may be overstating assumed differences in a range of similar phenomena (Dodge, 2006).

A reference should be made toward the gender issues in street gangs. American research is slowly but surely coming to grips with the often over-looked place of girls in the gang world. European research still largely ignores the gender issue. Yet, there may be a unique situation worthy of attention on the Continent due to two factors. The first is the perceived greater interest among European analysts in "masculinities." The second is the presence of many Muslim populations framing the gang prevalence. It is a significant component of Muslim culture both to shelter girls and to forbid their par-ticipation in many public settings, especially in the company of young males.

Researchers' emphasis on both factors and cultural barriers place people in a state of extra ignorance about European female gang participation. The implications for policy and practice escape me. The need for focused research on comparative gender issues does not. The one final problem brings people to a close of this discussion. Whereas US gang writing is replete with descriptions of gang prevention, intervention, and suppression programs, European litera-ture is not. The massive investment in these programs in America has failed to yield much by way of useful guidelines for policy and practice. The paucity of known programs in Europe offers a new opportunity to assess program effec-tiveness. Therefore, it is a challenge for comparative gang researchers who are willing to expand their concerns to include public policy initiatives.

As they collect gang data, accounting in the process for the complexi-ties enumerated in this discourse, they will be in a position, which is poorly advantaged in the United States, to seek implications for both broad policy and local gang control practices. It is a tall order not to every researcher's liking. Still, many researchers noted several years ago that time-extended, cross-disciplinary, and cross-national endeavors can be successful when persistence is coupled with patience, when scientific rigor is handled with goodwill (Vigil, 1998).

The Role of Youths in Gang Culture

Living in these chasms, foreign-born and second-generation youths were the most likely to join gangs. Unlike their parents, these youths came "into contact with a motley collection of diverse customs on the one hand and new situations on the other. Cultural organization, not race or class, was the key. It is not because the boys of the white middle and wealthier classes do not form gangs, but because their lives are organized and stabilized for them by American traditions, customs, and institutions to which the children of the immigrants do not have adequate access. Then the assimilation factor was part of the city's metabolic processes. To Chicago school pioneer Ernest W. Burgess, it entailed "disorganization and organization that may be thought of as in reciprocal relationship to each other, and as co-operating in a moving equilibrium of social order toward an end vaguely or definitely regarded as progressive. Gangs were way stations on the path to cultural integration."

Free markets and the liberal state, as well as a guiding hand from civil society institutions, would transform old-world subjects into equal possessors of rights and freedoms, no matter what their religion, race, language, or culture. The city was a synecdoche for America, and the reorganization of new urban residents into a cohesive society and polity was the essence of Americanization. All could be incorporated, old world superstitions left behind (Warr, 2002).

It was perhaps not all; blacks were nearly absent from Thrasher's Chicago. Furthermore, the model of incorporation failed to capture the generative nature of the encounter between migrants and the industrial city. There the race was to borrow Partha Chaterjee's (Indian scholar/professor) words that had no mere survivor from a premodern past, no product of a lag in cultural reorganization. Even if engagement with urban life transformed migrants into modern citizens as Thrasher hoped, no universal trajectory of assimilation denuded them of other ways of belonging. Instead, migrants' contact with the institutions and peoples of the city resulted in both inclusion and exclusion. Race did not disappear. Rather, in Thomas J. Sugrue's (American historian) formulation, "In the postwar city, blackness and whiteness assumed a spatial definition." The urban encounter made racial difference a defining variable of the twentieth-century metropolis.

Andrew Diamond's *Mean Streets* (2009) argues that explaining gangs requires people to confront race. He examines the "power of culture," working-class youth subcultures, and the street gangs that took root in them in shaping Chicago's social and political geography from the interwar period through the 1960s. In examining the relationship among gangs, race making, and politics, Diamond challenges studies, such as Eric Schneider's *Vampires, Dragons, and Egyptian Kings* (2001), that argues the masculinity was the *sine qua non* of working class youth behavior. Diamond concedes that the "intertwined predicaments of class and masculinity" provided the spark that ignited a culture of street combat during the interwar period, but maintains that the "search for respect" ultimately came to be "perceived or felt in racial rather than class terms."

Gangs formed an "infrastructure within which sensibilities of racial anger formed and circulated." Moreover, they expressed these sensibilities through violent resistance to integration. Racial formation occurred in the changing cityscape, black, white ethnic, and Latino youths defined themselves, each other, and their urban neighborhoods through struggles over space (Zatz, 1987).

Historians and sociologists have examined the relationship between gangs and politics at two key moments. John Hagedorn (2008) argues that interwar ethnic gangs, such as Chicago's Hamburg Athletic Association, whose president from 1924 to 1939 was Richard J. Daley, were integrated components of urban political machines. By contrast, scholars lament the failure of black and Latino gangs to incorporate themselves within the broader political movements in the 1960s and 1970s. For Schneider (2001), individual resistance trumped collective action; movement politics "did not transform gangs from apolitical defenders of turf into a vanguard for community change."

Hagedorn's darker narrative suggests that racism materializing in Mayor Daley's 1969 "war on gangs" was the key to black gangs' failure to similarly assimilate. Daley's war stopped the black Conservative Vice Lords from becoming "legitimate." Instead, in the 1970s and 1980s, it survived by creating an institutional structure to profit from drug sales.

These portraits of the politics of street gangs do not adequately capture the historical experience of Chicago youths, who navigated more variegated terrains. *Mean Streets* explores what Walter Johnson describes as "the way that cultural forms functioned as mechanisms of creating the political solidarity necessary to collective action." Diamond defines gangs loosely as "formal or casual organizations of teenage boys and young men." Formal gangs play a prominent role around the 1919 riot and from the 1950s forward; they disappear during the later interwar period and during World War II. Even where gangs are central to the narrative, Diamond does not always clearly distinguish their impact from working class male youth subculture, more generally. Nonetheless, they convincingly demonstrate the importance of these youth activities to the development of racial consciousness and race-based political mobilizations (Bell, 1985).

Youth subculture existed "somewhere betwixt and between, and *Mean Streets* is a history of the pursuits that flourished in both public (street, parks, beaches) and commercial (movies, dance halls) venues." Diamond tells a ground-level history of whiteness as made and experienced by ethnic youths and the similar process by which black youths developed their own solidarities. The details are thick and the analysis dizzying. The idea that interlaces them pace contemporary theories of multiculturalism is the irony that youths forged racial boundaries through regular interracial contact.

The visits of Irish-American gangs to black and tan cabarets, for example, allowed the transgression of racial boundaries, thereby reifying them. Ethnic youths measured their status as Americans, as men, and perhaps even as whites, exploring and articulating new racial self-understandings that differed from those of their immigrant elders. State institutions shepherded the emergence of generational subcultures. The passage of the Compulsory Education Act of 1897 provided the wedge, and the growing truant police and new juvenile court became the hammer.

Youth culture developed in schools and, in some cases, against them. For many foreign-born parents, compulsory schooling threatened community byways: As the number of 15- to 17-year-olds in school skyrocketed, so did the threat that boys would adopt "American ways." Diamond claims that territorial conflict allowed gangs to define their places within the racial hierarchy. He contests the received wisdom that the 1919 race riot and the post-World War II housing riots (originally described by Arnold Hirsch) were defensive, communal responses to black invasion or "reactionary reflexes of ethnic solidarity." Instead, in "Irish Canaryville, Polish Packingtown and the Bush, Italian Little Sicily and Little Italy," identity-based politics emerged from the struggle to use and define space.

These identities were not simply "black and white," which remained unsettled concepts on the temporarily integrated South and West Sides into the 1950s. What's more, Puerto Rican and Mexican youths demonstrate the multifocal nature of race-making after World War II, as their demands for inclusion often reinforced black exclusion (Allan, 2004).

Gang Violence Battles

Whether gang violence was political is ultimately a relational question, and Diamond (2009) recognizes that many battles had no such meaning. However, when groups of young men chose to "define themselves against one another and engage in rituals of racial hatred and violence," they often acted politically. The nihilistic elements of their violence are inseparable from what Steven Hahn (2007) describes as "collective struggles for socially meaningful power."

In history, debate over what constitutes politics frequently centers on actors, such as slaves, whose behaviors were traditionally recognized as prepolitical. Labeling an act as political valorizes its significance to struggles against tyranny. *Mean Streets* shows how race-making through territorial violence reworked Chicago's political landscape in both oppressive and liberatory ways.

The increasing assertiveness of black youths from the mid-1950s forward was a factor in white collective identity, such that, by the 1957 Calumet Park riots, "whiteness had never before seemed so much like an end in itself, where black students demanded Black Power in their schools, white students immediately responded with calls of their own for White Power, leaving little middle grounds. Youth groups, whether just neighborhood cliques or more tangibly defined gangs or clubs," Diamond says, "were the most vigilant and the most effective entities in consolidating and maintaining struggles for racial separation." They embedded race in the landscape of Chicago; physical acts of exclusion and inclusion constituted a practice of politics.

Gang warfare and political activism among black youths were two sides of the same coin, back payment for years of "grassroots white intimidation and police intransigence." By the mid-1960s, lines of political influence were tangled; gang members, Black Power advocates, and student movement leaders all drew on a protean language of racial identity and community control. Gangs used Black Power rhetoric to attract more members, just as Black Power leaders traded on gang imagery to attract followers. This cross-fertilization resonates with Diamond's deeper history of the creation of black youth subculture, explaining why these "Black Power sensibilities" burned so intensely. Black Power "represented the continuation of the same logic of turf control that had organized black street gangs since the 1950s."

These conflicts eventually implicated state behavior. Police and schools were the most visible institutional actors in the youth domain. Mainstream civil rights leaders recruited gang members as potential allies, but struggled to contain the youths' energies. The actions of young black men remained by turns destructive (the civil violence of antipolice riots) and productive (the schools movement). When city forces began to use violence themselves, the involvement of street gangs in illicit activities made gang youths vulnerable. However, state repression did not alone decide the political fate of black gangs. The logic that linked race, space, and power also shaped the contradictions that emerged from this turn toward the state. Within the liberal political arena, the effectiveness of the logic of racial solidarity for black mobilization did not translate into similar efficacy in "developing alliances across racial and ethnic lines."

Diamond (unlike Thrasher) emphasizes the inescapable role of politics in shaping the integration of urban migrants, but his account ends with the 1960s. New books by João Costa Vargas (2006), John Hagedorn, and Karen Umemoto (2006) describe a different era, beginning in the 1970s, in which a new metropolitan order emerged. Understanding the relationships among gangs, race, politics, and the contemporary city requires making "sense of the patterns of inequality that grew out of the economic, demographic, and spatial transformation of American cities in the second half of the twentieth century."

If Chicago was the paradigmatic outdoor laboratory of industrial America, Los Angeles, the setting for Costa Vargas's *Catching Hell in the City of Angels* and Umemoto's *The Truce,* is in the vanguard of contemporary cities. Los Angeles is physically sprawling and culturally heterogeneous, characterized by the development of high- and low-technology industries, thriving financial and business services, and burgeoning low-cost personal services. The city remains deeply divided along lines of class, race, and gender. These variables exist elsewhere, but no city (to borrow the city's official slogan) brings it all together like Los Angeles (Bellair, 2005).

Despite the disintegration of the old urban process, today's urbanizing world is producing gangs faster and in myriad forms and shapes, according to Hagedorn (p. xxiii). These gangs are successors to Thrasher's, but, beginning in the late 1950s, scholars and public-policy makers narrowed their object of study. They replaced the race-neutral (though often white, ethnic) face of the gang with a black or Latino one, and they made delinquency part of the definition of the gang. Despite the fact that self-reports identify "relatively equal distributions of white and black gangs in urban areas," gangs are understood today to be primarily as a criminological problem pertinent to "disenfranchised inner-city minorities."

Delinquent black and Latino gangs in poor neighborhoods are the sole object of concern here, and, in part, these authors replicate the problematic framework that dominates gang studies. They also challenge it by implicating incarceration and intensive policing in the creation and management of economically and socially precarious urban populations. Such strategies described variously as the "culture of control," governing through crime and the rise of the carceral state have honed the edges of inequalities already extant by the 1970s.

American welfare provision, racial politics, and penal policy combined to explosively increase the number of people under state supervision. These changes in state policy are "at bottom a political project," as Loïc Wacquant (2009) contends. They have produced a new governing structure, which couples aggressive penal policy to the withdrawal of the welfare provision for the poor in favor of "the 'free market' and the celebration of 'individual responsibility'."

Gang-Related Complexities

For those undertaking comparative or cross-national studies that are specifically of street gangs, the complexities, noted above in general comparative studies, are likely joined by a series of other issues. First and foremost is the requirement to use a common definition of street gangs. For instance, the definitions used in prominent studies in Montreal, and the American national sample used by the National Youth Gang Center, reveal two problems. One is cross-national diversity and creativity in gang definitions. The other is the noncomparability of such definitions at the cost of scientific knowledge-building about gangs.

An alternative approach has been designed by a working group in the E.G. Program yielding a common street gang definition now in use in many studies in numerous countries, e.g., the United States, England, Holland, Germany, France, Italy, Russia, Switzerland, and Norway. The E.G. Program street gang definition, after seeing the Introduction in Klein and Maxson (2006) and the Euro gang website, specifies a minimal number of defining variables as opposed to descriptor variables, and separates street gangs from other youth groups as well as from other "gangs," such as terrorist groups, prison gangs, motorcycle gangs, and adult organized crime groups and cartels. A common definition yields comparable data from which a science of street gangs can emerge (Howell, 2005).

To date, the comparative Euro gang studies have been retrospective. They have used already collected data from already similar, but not identical, instruments and gang definitions in locations selected by convenience rather than by joint design. Conclusions have been illuminating but hardly definitive. It is past time to see prospective study designs in which commonalities (in definition, instrumentation, and sampling) are deliberately implemented.

Cross-national gang studies also could benefit from planning for longitudinal designs, such that patterns of gang joining, membership fluidity, gang structures, gang member behavior, gang transformation, and gang desistance can be measured. Within such designs, repeated measurements over time on the same individuals and groups other differential problems of interest may emerge, such as differences in gender patterns, differences in ethnicity and national origin, and age-related changes. The ultimate design aim might be the launching of prospective, longitudinal, and comparative research. This would require a team of planful, dedicated scholars willing to devote some years to the enterprise (Curry, 2000).

At the group level, a number of the common descriptors of street gangs and gang members lend themselves readily to data collection. One of these, related to the youth group definition of these groups, is a set of age factors. Among these are ages of joining gangs, peak or median ages, and ages of desistance from gang activity. Other demographic variables would include the gender mix and ethnicities and national origins. Common group characteristics include rivalries and territoriality, longevity of gang existence, and crime levels and patterns versatility, frequency, drug involvement, and violence levels.

Officials often rely on such indicia (indications) as hand signs, colors, clothing, tattoos, gang names, individual monikers, special argot, and similar peripheral descriptors that people find of lesser value. Much of the above relates directly to the use of the gang typology, whose derivation and validation has been described in detail in Klein and Maxson (2006). The five street gang types (traditional, neotraditional, compressed, collective, and specialty) have been described in both the United States and a number of European countries.

In consort with the European gang definition of street gangs, the typology handily facilitates the cross-gang and cross-site descriptive characteristics needed in comparative work. Finally, since illegal activities constitute one of the definers of street gangs, collection of delinquency and crime data is a required expectation for comparative studies. Cross-site examples can be found in Weerman and Esbensen (2005), Huizinga and Schumann (2001), Klein, Weerman, and Thornberry (2006), and Blaya and Gatti (2010). While the Euro gang youth survey and others contain very adequate measures of criminal involvement, the carefully constructed and validated ISRD II survey, to my mind, offers the best measure yet devised and tested across 30 countries (Dodge, 2006).

References

Allan, E. 2004. *Civil Gang Abatement: The Effectiveness and Implications of Policing by Injunction*. New York: LFB Scholarly.

Bell, D. 1985. The intake dispositions of juvenile offenders. *Journal of Research in Crime and Delinquency*.

Bellair, P. 2005. Beyond the bell curve: Community disadvantage and the explanation of black-white differences in adolescent violence. *Journal of Criminology*.

Blaya, C., Gotti, U. (2010). "Deviant Youth Groups in Italy and France: Prevalence and Characteristics." *Eur J. Criml Policy Res*. 16:127–144.

Chesney-Lind, A. 1994. Gangs and delinquency. *Crime, Law, and Social Change*.

Costa Vargas, J. 2006. *Catching Hell in the City of Angels: Like and Meanings of Blackness in South Central Los Angeles*. Minneapolis: University of Minnesota Press.

Curry, G. 2000. Self-reported gang involvement and officially recorded delinquency. *Journal of Criminology*.

Diamond, A. J. 2009. *Mean Streets: Chicago Youths and the Everyday Struggle for Empowerment in the Multiracial City, 1908–1969*. Oakland: University of California Press.

Dodge, K. 2006. *Deviant Peer Influences in Programs for Youth: Problems and Solutions.* New York: Guilford Press.

Esbensen, F. 2000. *Preventing Adolescent Gang Involvement.* Washington, D.C.: Office of Juvenile Justice and Delinquency Prevention.

Freng, A. 2007. Race and gang affiliation: An examination of multiple marginality. *Justice Quarterly.*

Gavazzi, S. 2006. Gender, ethnicity and the family environment: Contributions to assessment efforts within the realm of juvenile justice. *Journal of Family Relations.*

Guerra, N. 1997. *Intervening to Prevent Childhood Aggression in the Inner City.* New York: Cambridge University Press.

Hagedorn. 2007. *Gangs in the Global City.* University of Illinois Press. Champaign, Illinois.

Hagedorn. 2008. *A World of Gangs: Armed Young Men and Gangsta Culture.* University of Minnesota Press.

Hahn, S. 2007. *A Nation Under Our Feet: Black Political Struggles in the Rural South from Slavery to the Great Migration.* Harvard University Press, Cambridge, MA and London, UK.

Howell, J. 2005. Moving risk factors into developmental theories of gang membership. *Youth Violence and Juvenile Justice.*

Huizinga, D. and Schumann, K.F. 2001. "Gang membership and Bremen and Denver: Comparative Longitudinal data." In *The Eurogang Paradox Street Gangs and Youth Groups in the U.S. and Europe.* Ed. M.W. Klein, H.-J. Kerner, C. L. Maxon, and E.G.M. Weitekamp. Kluwer, Dordrecht, Netherlands.

Junger-Tas, J. Marshall, Enzmann, I. H., Killias, D., SSteketee, M., and Gruszczynska, B. (eds.). (21010). *Juvenile Delinquency in Europe and Beyond: Results of the International Self-Report Delinquency Study.* Springer. New York.

Kennedy, D. 1997. Pulling levers: Chronic offenders, high-crime settings, and a theory of prevention. *Valparaiso University Law Review.*

Klein, M.W. (1995). The American Steet Gang. Its Nature, Prevalence, and Control. Oxford University Press. New York.

Klein, M. 2007. *Variations on a Theme of Gang Control.* Bologna, Italy: European Society of Criminology.

Klein, M.W, and Maxson, C.L. (2006). *Street Gang Patterns and Policies.* Oxford University Press. New York.

Maxson, C. 1998. Vulnerability to street gang membership: Implications for practice. *Social Service Review.*

McCorkle, R. 1998. The political and organizational response to gangs: An examination of a 'moral panic' in Nevada. *Justice Quarterly.*

Sanchez-Jankowski, M. 1991. *Islands in the Street: Gangs and American Urban Society.* Berkeley, CA: University of California Press.

Schneider, E. C. 2001. *Vampires, Dragons, and Egyptian Kings: Youth Gangs in Postwar New York.* Princeton, NJ: Princeton University Press.

Short, J. F. and Strodtbeck, F. L. (1965). *Group Process and Gang Delinquency.* University of Chicago Press. Chicago, Illinois.

Smith, W. 1999. Prediction of recidivism among 'second timers' in the juvenile justice system: Efficiency in screening chronic offenders. *American Journal of Criminal Justice.*

Spergel. 1995. The Youth Gang Problem: A Community Approach. Oxford, UK: Oxford University Press.

Spergel. 2007. *Reducing Youth Gang Violence: The Little Village Gang Violence Reduction Project*. Lanham, MD: Rouman Altamira Press.

Swanson, C. 2009. *Cities in Crisis 2009: Closing the Graduation Gap*. Bethesda, MD: EPE Research Center.

Thornberry, T., Krohn, Lizotte, Smith, and Tobin. 2003. *Gangs and Delinquency in Developmental Perspective*. New York: Cambridge University Press.

Umemoto, K. 2006. *The Truce: Lessons from an L.A. Gang War*. Ithaca, NY: Cornell University Press.

Vigil, J. 1998. *Barrio Gangs: Street Life and Identity in Southern California*. Austin, TX: University of Texas Press.

Wacquant, L. 2009. *Punishing the Poor: The Neoliberal Government of Social Insecurity*. Durham, NC: Duke University Press.

Warr, M. 2002. *Companions in Crime: The Social Aspects of Criminal Conduct*. New York: Cambridge University Press.

Esbensen, F.-A. Weerman, F. M. 2005. *Europen Street Gangs and Troublesome Youth Groups*. Lanham, MD: Alta Mira.

Zatz, M. 1987. Chicano youth gangs and crime, creation of a moral panic. *Contemporary Crises*.

If Drug Abuse Is the Answer, Then What Is the Question?

8

MICHAEL S. ODEN

Contents

Human social behavior and several life changing events can contribute how drug abuse can become an important component of an individual's life. There also will be discussions about why one would consider using illicit drugs, when their drug use originally began, the length of time an individual consumed illicit drugs, and the social/emotional needs that were met by using drugs.

Introduction

Illicit drug use is considered an epidemic in America. Those who continue to have or had the unfortunate opportunity to become seduced by drugs over an extended period of time understand the devastation this behavior can cause an individual and his/her family. The reasons for extended drugs use may vary. Therefore, the focus will be on what has been discovered throughout my investigation as a supervision probation officer for drug and alcohol offenders. Since drug abuse can be attributed to many areas, a segment of this discussion will be those events where drug use impacted the lives of these individuals. The objective is to disclose several truths about drug use and its origin.

Introduction to Behavior

Definition of behavior:

> The manner of acting or controlling yourself.
> The action or reaction of something under specific circumstances.
> The behavior of small particles can be studied in experiments.
> The aggregate responses or reactions or movements made by an organism in any situation.[1]

"The first few years of life are critical for building social and emotional responses to life. If a child fails to get warm responsive contact with another person during those years, the disadvantages may never be fully overcome."[2]

In other areas regarding behavior, what tends to set a precedent is imprinting over logic and rational thinking. In other words, our thoughts lead to words, our words lead to actions.

Throughout history, many people have written about behavior. That being said, here are my experiences as a probation officer who has interviewed more than 6,500 drug and alcohol offenders. When the California Proposition 36 (Drug Treatment as an Alternate to Criminal Prosecution) caseload of drug and alcohol offenders was introduced to me, I had the belief that there had to be a reason why certain individuals consumed illicit drugs for extended periods of time. One had to wonder why someone would choose to go down that road where the end result was usually a painful, mind-numbing, and life-diminishing experience where the consequences were high. It was at this juncture of their drug use where an individual would inevitably lose his family, job, relationship with children, self-respect, etc. Certain questions regarding their behavior would need to come to the forefront, such as: "Don't they see what they are doing to themselves?" "Why don't they just stop?" "What are you gaining by participating in this behavior?" These are just a few of the questions that would continually surface as the clients would relate to their drug abuse experiences. This is where the process of understanding the "whys" of their behavior began for me.

Our experiences when we are growing up provide us with imprinting moments that affect us in a variety of ways. After many interviews with the clients, there appeared to be an underlying pattern as to how their behavior was affected by what they experienced from their caretakers during their formative years. This discovery made it clear that there was a direct correlation regarding the client's current behavior, which was usually life-diminishing, and how their behavior was directly related to what social/emotional needs were met or not met from the caretaker.

It is important to understand that how we navigate in the world is directly related to how the world is presented to us, which, in the majority of cases, begins in the home. With these clients, the common denominator that continued to reveal itself was the lack of a caretaker, usually the paternal figure, and, at times, the maternal figure. It was this emotional upheaval and uncertainty of the family structure that oftentimes propelled the individual to behave in a manner that was more about survival then about connecting with family members or the outside world. It was during this time in childhood where most of the imprinting and mirroring would have the most impact on the client/child. Since our parents are our initial teachers, they are the individuals who have the greatest impact on how a child views the world. Now, in most instances, as indicated by the clients, the majority of men were not available to have an impact on the client's childhood development. Most of the fathers of my clients were either in state prison, county jail, distant while in the home, disappeared in the streets, or dead. The male impact, or lack thereof, from this experience as a probation officer, has caused the client to interpret his world as the "no father syndrome." My clients would create a belief about themselves that "he doesn't love me," "he doesn't care about me," or that "I am worthless." These are only a few images the clients would carry in their minds, throughout their lives, which would directly impact how they interacted in their world. It was apparent through the interviewing procedure that the majority of the disruptive behavior by the client is caused by what the parent says or does not say to the child. It also was evident in how the child held on to and interpreted that information in regard to how he/she believed himself/herself to be valued beings.

Language is one of the most powerful forms of communication we use as humans to interact with one another. Parents are one of the few individuals whose words can impact the way children will view themselves and how they will relate to the world around them. It appears the "behavioral pathology" or, to put it in laymen's terms, "life-diminishing behavior" that clients exhibited in the past or since childhood is directly related to how caretakers connected, related, or validated the clients during their formative years.

In regard to the clients, the destructive behavior comes from years of numerous social/emotional needs not being met by the caretaker. The client has, for many years, believed that he/she is not validated, given self-worth, or has a sense of belonging from his/her caretaker. Because of this belief, the client is unable to make decisions that would benefit his/her life and is usually "stuck" emotionally and, therefore, is unable to make the necessary changes to transform his/her circumstances. When a client has experienced many years of dysfunction (not getting social/emotional needs met by the caretaker), the client has few options to deal with the situation that only he/she can understand and, yet, not really understand "why" he/she has participated in this life-diminishing behavior. One of the ways clients manage their unmet needs from the caretaker is by consuming illicit drugs to numb the negative emotions that arise out the experience. In other words, the client does not want to continue his/her confrontation with the reality as to where the emotional pain originates. Other ways clients mirror these experiences, besides abusing drugs, is by exhibiting violent behavior, sabotaging their own success, or having many short-term relationships where they are unable to become vulnerable or intimate with their partner or their own children. This behavior is directly related to how the client views himself/herself.

The phrases: "Why can't they just get over it?" or "They are adults, they should be able to move on" are just a few of the common statements people repeat when they see a person behave in a destructive manner for a long period of time when abusing drugs. They do not understand that people behave in a certain manner, albeit life-diminishing, because they actually believe they are getting certain needs met by participating in that behavior. These are commonly known as "nice dead people." These people do not know where this behavior originated so they can change it. This behavior can only be altered if the individual is made aware it and is given understanding of the behavior. It is at this juncture that the majority of the clients will actually change their behavior, in this case drug/alcohol abuse, which they have been repeating for many years out of pure habit and familiarity.

Divorce and the Child

Children who are well-tended in early childhood grow up with better social and emotional ways of meeting the world. Even in adult relationships, we tend to each other's needs in ways that sustain long and healthy lives, according to Taylor (2002).[2]

Is there a direct correlation between the fractured family nucleus and extensive drug abuse? The impact of divorce on children and how they would eventually surrender to excessive drug use in their future is one of several subdivisions that will be discussed.

The clients who experienced divorce stated that they saw the world as an unpredictable, dangerous place to live when they were trying to make sense of their new circumstances that stemmed from the divorce. The most popular view the clients had of themselves is that they were the cause of the divorce. For multiple reasons, children appear to blame themselves for the breakup of the mother and father. The upheaval and breakup of the family has to be one of the most devastating events a child can ever experience. How a child reacts to this traumatic event usually surfaces later on in life or in the adult world. The majority of the clients stated they never really got over the divorce of their parents as they were growing up. Several factors that caused their anxiety was how the parent responded to the divorce, how the parent related the separation to the child, and if the parent made the child feel safe, just to name a few. When asked about their drug use, the clients rarely thought to look into an earlier period of their lives to get an understanding of the origin of the problem. The clients usually had the tendency to believe their drug use began because they wanted to experiment, gain acceptance from their peers, escape their current reality, or their drug use was more of a social matter. These may be valid responses; however, the genesis of the drug use, in this case, would usually begin when a life-changing event occurred.

When discussing their behavior during adolescence or preteens, after a divorce, the clients usually divulged that they had a lot of freedom and individuality as children/teenagers due to having one parent and that parent was usually working. The social/emotional needs were unable to be met by the caretaker(s) and, therefore, they looked for other ways to gain acceptance, or even find emotional safety. It was at this preadolescent or adolescent stage where the child would begin his journey in long-term drug use with others to fit in or to numb the emotional pain he/she experienced from the shattered family.

It was interesting that during these interviews the client would always make the ever-popular statement that he/she hung out with the "wrong" group. The clients would be informed that they were the "right" group, otherwise you would not have associated with them in the first place. It was mentioned to them that they were getting something out of the "deal" by associating with certain peers. They were meeting a particular social/emotional "need" at that time.

The Fatherless Child

In the quest to discover another reason why the clients began their drug use and the emotion that was attached to their excessive drug use, there appeared to be the pattern of the "absent father" in more than 90 percent of the cases. The impact a father has on a child, especially a boy, did not fully resonate until the stories of these individuals were brought to the forefront and how each client longed for the attention and influence of his/her male role model. It can be understood that 85 percent to 95 percent of these individuals did not know their father, never connected with their father, or were somehow abused by their father in a verbal or sometimes physical manner. Comments such as, "You will always be a fuck up," "You will never amount to anything," or "You are as stupid as the rest of them," were consistent reminders of their self-worth. When asked the question, "What kind of relationship did the clients have with their father as a child or during adolescence," the typical response was that they "had a great relationship with their father" or that "he provided for me." In order to get the clients to reveal more of their past, another question that was asked was, "How did you relate to your father or how did he relate to you when you were living with him at that time?" Instinctively, the clients would respond by saying, "He was a great dad and I loved him." This is the part of the conversation where the discussion of what needs the father was unable to meet, at that time, were explained and exposed to the clients. It was at this time that the clients would become emotionally uncomfortable due to realizing the truth, for the first time, about their relationship with their fathers and how certain social/emotional needs were actually never met. The majority of the clients had a difficult time, initially, coming to terms with the truth that their relationship with their fathers was not as they had envisioned. It was at this point the clients began to purge all the emotions that they had been harboring inside over the years and, for the first time in their lives, they realized that they never had the emotional connection with the fathers. It is at this point in the discussion where the clients would begin to "shift" in a manner that they would begin the healing process. The clients now begin to understand how not having fathers impacted their lives at a young age. The clients also can now pinpoint when their drug abuse began and, most importantly, "why" they have abused drugs for an extended period of time. The truth is that drugs masked, covered up, or numbed the emotional pain attributed by the lack of the male caretaker and the needs that were unable to be met at that time.

It was important for the clients to have an understanding and awareness of how not having their fathers in their lives was the direct cause for them to behave in the manner that was life-diminishing. They needed to see the truth about how they envisioned their lives and what the actual truth was. This process usually took a few tissues to wipe away the tears, but once they got past this section, the remaining interview would be about healing their emotional wounds of the past, and the absent father syndrome would no longer impact their present-day lives. Will they have the scars from what their fathers did or did not give them? Absolutely. However, once they have been given empathy and understanding about their fathers' failure to meet their social/emotional needs, they can now, for the first time in their lives, take the blame and shame of themselves.

"My Mother Worked Two Jobs!"

If there was an equation that was the underlying theme that exemplifies the clients and how this equation was relative to their life-diminishing behavior (i.e., drug use, high school dropout, abusive relationships, abandoning their children, etc.), it would look like this: Absent father (death, state prison, working long hours, running the streets) plus overworked/stressed mother (make ends meet by working two jobs, caring for multiple siblings, receiving welfare, emotionally overwhelmed, not receiving any type of support) equals no caretaker at home. A child with no caretaker to create boundaries or to meet the social/emotional needs of the child creates a situation where freedom and choice are abundant in their reality. This lack of influence by the caretaker creates an atmosphere of limitless freedom, which, in turn, leads to antisocial behavior of the individual. This is the last segment of the formula: life-diminishing behavior (bullying, gang activity, early pregnancy, criminal activity, hostile/violent relationships, and **drug use**), which leads to state prison, county jail, or death.

Absent father + Overworked/stressed mother = *Nobody home* + *Life-diminishing behavior* = state prison, drug abuse, gangs, criminal behavior

There were many clients who could relate to having one caretaker in the home. Many clients stated that because there was no supervision in the home, they tended to push the boundaries in regard to staying out late, using drugs, committing crimes, and even joining gangs, because at last they could connect with someone. It was apparent that too much autonomy, independence, and choice is a disaster waiting to happen when given to an adolescent who was not taught the importance of boundaries.

In addition to the father being absent, the single mother was usually too drained to connect with the child in any way due to the demands of her job. With that reality, the child was usually left to fend for himself/herself, which usually meant finding connection elsewhere (neighborhood gangs) because he/she couldn't get the interpersonal needs met by the immediate caretaker.

Physical Abuse and Sexual Abuse

There were clients who decided to tell their story/the truth about the emotional devastation they have endured at the hands of a sexual predator. When asked when their drug use began and why, it was at this juncture that the information received was not quite what was expected from the clients. For those clients who had this experience, the initial response would vary between a loud, gut-wrenching roar, to a fetal cry, to tears streaming down their faces. For the majority of the clients, it was the first time they had ever told someone about their sexual abuse. This was the initial point during the interview when the healing process would begin.

By using excessive amounts of alcohol, methamphetamine, heroin, cocaine, etc., was all that was needed to numb the fear, emotional pain, and memory of a sexual predator as a child. It was at that time in their lives, children of 6 to 9 years of age, where they were vulnerable to the size, and trust of the individual who defied their trust. The majority of these clients were sexually violated by babysitters, their mothers' boyfriends, uncles, fathers, and mothers; usually someone they knew personally. Each client held on to that image for many years, never confiding in anyone as to what was truly happening, emotionally, inside him/her. The reaction of each client was that of survival. Most the clients mentioned they never trusted anyone after the incident. These clients would be afraid to get close to anyone for fear of being abused again; trust was their most feared need. They couldn't manage a regular relationship due to trust issues, which affected past and present relationships.

Once it was established that this is where the great emotional pain began we could now attribute these traumatic events to their drug use. When the clients disclosed their traumatic events, the response to the client was: "That event was the beginning of your drug problem." Initially, the client would give a puzzled look as if there were something strange in what was said. They would ask, "What do you mean, my drug problem?" So, the next queries would be:

"Notice when the drug use began."
"Understand what feelings surfaced when you remembered the event
    and what you needed to do to make that feeling or memory go away."
"When you began to consume drugs, where did the experience take you?"
"What did you get out of using drugs excessively?"

The usual response was: "It got me put in jail," "It messed up my life." It appeared there needed to be a clearer manner in which to ask the question. So, the question was asked from another perspective. "Why did you need to use chemicals to alter your state of mind and body?" A stricter question that was asked was: "Why did you need to continuously escape?" After some thought, they began to get a better understanding of where this question-and-answer session was headed. Other questions that were asked were:

"What about your real-world experiences you didn't want to face?"
"Think about a time in your life when the drug use began."
"Understand what feelings surfaced when you remembered the event
    and what you needed to do to make that feeling or memory subside."

After some thought, they began to see the unpleasant journey that was necessary to make in order to make sense of their drug use. This is where they began to name the unfortunate events of the past that they did not want to confront. It was at this point these clients began to realize that it was not the consumption of drugs that was going to be discussed, but the tragic event(s) that caused the drug use.

Conclusion

Drug use in America is considered an epidemic. About three-fourths of drug users have employment, and almost half of the American population knows someone who has a drug problem. No matter where you look, people from all walks of life are involved in illicit drug abuse. There have been clients who were college graduates, executives, attorneys, and daughters and sons of millionaires. Then there are those clients who grew up in and around an environment of poverty and gang relationships and know only about struggle and survival. These known facts tell the story that no one is immune to drug abuse; it is everyone's concern.

The subsequent investigation has uncovered several factors why individuals have chosen to use drugs. These aspects can range from a divorce in early childhood, parents abandoning the home, sexual abuse/exploitation, neglect, death of a family member, and physical and emotional abuse, etc. It is apparent that these events have a direct correlation to the initial cause of excessive drug use and the emotional and psychological toll these experiences can have on an individual. These events are considered the catalyst to cover up, hide, and mask the emotional pain these clients experienced from past tragic episodes. Therefore, it is highly likely that drug abuse is a symptom that stems from a tragic event or experience as opposed to believing the individual is an addict, has a disease, or may never recover. Drug abuse comes from somewhere. If one were to look at the cause instead of the effect, one would find the truth behind excessive drug use.

References

1. Online at http://www.wordnetbwe.princeton.edu/perlwwebwn.
2. Taylor, S. 2002. *The Tending Instinct: How Nurturing is Essential to Who We Are and How We Live.* Henry Holt, NY.
3. Online at www.eurekalert.org/pub_release/2002-07/.

Use of Technology by US Gangs

9

MOHAMAD KHATIBLOO

Contents

It is a reality that US-based gangs are continuing to use technology to advance their operations. They are using social media to recruit, intimidate, and communicate with the people whom they want to join their group. The US gangs have even realized the importance of technology that can turn out to be very useful for most of their activities. Though the option of technology is expensive, its benefits are quite high for these elements. However, there are various principles that indicate the use of technology has increased considerably by most of the criminal gangs in the United States. The investigation carried out by the FBI has acknowledged the fact that the role of technology has proved to be quite effective for many gangs operating in America. The social media tools, such as Facebook, Twitter, and other mediums, have been utilized as well as by the criminal gangs for carrying out their illegal operations (Kennedy, 1997).

Furthermore, U.S. gangs are moving into new crimes based on technology, such as credit card fraud, identity theft, computer crime, etc. These gangs have identified these areas as one of their best targets. The major reason is the benefits they receive in the form of large amounts of money obtained by these criminals. This is not only the case in the United States, but in Europe as well. The use of technology has increased dramatically by most of the gangs in the

United States. The criminal activities in Europe have even experienced an upward trend in the past few years, and the law enforcement agencies must try hard to take action against these criminal elements. It has been identified that the role of technology is quite high in most of the criminal activities that have taken place on a large scale. This is the world of global technology, and it is providing lots of benefits, but some negative elements in the society are even misusing it. Law enforcement agencies need to play a strong role in this regard (Zatz, 1987).

Impact of Criminal Activities in Entire American Region

At the root of Central America's problem is the geographic reality that, like Mexico, it exists between the world's largest consumer of illegal drugs the United States, and the world's largest producer, South America. Under normal circumstances, that would be bad enough. Unfortunately, after the civil wars, insufficient attention was paid to building professional, apolitical police forces, reforming judiciaries, rooting out corruption, building ministries that work effectively, and creating economic opportunity fueled by the accumulation of human capital through an intensive focus on broad-based education and training. The local private sector remained self-interested, doing little to lend its voice or resources for fundamental reform. The region also failed to take full advantage of the promise of its free-trade agreement with the United States, Central America Free Trade Agreement–Dominion Republic (CAFTA-DR), by slow-walking for political reasons the steps it needed to take toward true regional economic integration and a focus on competitiveness (Maxson, 1998).

At the same time, the United States contributed to the problem by deporting hardened criminals back to the region who had been thoroughly indoctrinated into gang culture in the United States and its prisons. This is a potent mix, and governments have largely proved incapable of responding effectively. Without realistic prospects for economic gain, the young and unemployed either attempt the dangerous, illegal journey to the United States or throw in with the drug gangs that have proliferated and transformed the region into one of the most dangerous worldwide. Astoundingly, Central America's homicide rate is more than four times the global average. Corruption and impunity are rampant.

The press is self-censoring for its own physical safety in the face of intimidation and gruesome killings of journalists by drug traffickers. Police and security forces are thoroughly penetrated by the gangs, and entire zones, such as Guatemala's huge northern Peten region, have little or no government presence As the institutions of democracy strain, the specter arises that at some point, perhaps sooner than later, the citizens of the region will seek leaders who promise improved physical security and job creation without the niceties of democracy or a strict adherence to human rights. Given the significant bipartisan effort to midwife democracy in Central America, this would be a major setback for US policy. Timely, then, that regional leaders, including Secretary of State Hillary Clinton, met in Guatemala in 2010 to discuss the crisis. As part of an overall effort that approaches $2 billion in pledges, the United States offered some $300 million both in reprogrammed and new money for citizen security initiatives. That is a promising start, an acknowledgement of the seriousness of the issues (Gavazzi, 2006).

Various Operations Carried Out by the US Gangs

The possible scenarios in which the US-based gangs will eventually be approached by international terrorists to gain access to the United States and targets are one of the most serious operational issues in the countries. The US gangs might fail for the sake of the promise and realization of large cash payments. However, they would assist other groups to help and aid these operatives in the following manner.

The biggest assistance given is the secure transportation provided to these criminal elements in the country. This is a huge concern for law enforcement agencies, as these criminal gangs use this option as their first step for carrying out various criminal operations in the country. The setup also is launched by keeping the operatives in safe houses and providing support to the people who are living in the safe shelters in these mysterious places. There are even some groups that provide aid to these criminal elements for keeping their weapons safe and secure along with the proper placement of some dangerous explosive materials. The key issue in this aspect is the logistics that serve as a basic platform for these criminal elements. The ideal setup provided by some of the criminal elements to other criminal gangs based in other countries turns out to be the biggest concern for police and other investigating departments.

The strategy developed by these groups is done with a proper plan by making it easier for these criminal gangs to perform their negative activities without any problem. They also take steps to forward the operatives to carry out their missions of target destruction in the United States. However, in the realization of the fact, that by aiding such terrorists, the gang hierarchy will appreciate the full strength and might even make it quite difficult for law enforcement agencies to take proper action against these elements.

Law enforcement agencies find it hard to take effective action against criminal gangs that facilitate further ideal situations for them. However, the US federal government must take this issue seriously and must try its best in handling this issue in the best possible manner. Even though it is not possible for the US authorities to completely finish the activities of these criminal elements, they must try their best to take action against these people (Klein, 2007).

The issue of US gang culture is gaining a lot of value in the last few years and the latest technology is making the work of these terrorists quite easy, which is a huge concern for law enforcement agencies. Even though police have all the sources to take action against these criminal gangs comprised of different groups, the gangs have prepared their logistical operation quite well. These gangs are investing further money to improve their operations and are even expanding beyond the borders. Some of the countries who are having terrible criminal activities histories are even providing support to various criminal elements in the United States.

Federal authorities also are aware of this fact, but they are still struggling to take action against these criminal elements. In the end, it can be said that the US government can report much vital information to some of the important authorities. However, the gangs know that they can be rounded up and even thrown in prison (in large numbers), and the money-making operations (drugs, taxing enforcement, prostitution, money crimes, murder for hire, etc.) will all cease when all members are locked in federal prison. The US government now labels US gangs as terrorists and cuts off all operations, resulting in significant downsizing and possible elimination of their operations. It is quite clear that a lot depends on the US government in cracking down on all of these criminal activities taking place in the country.

The above paragraphs would be based on the arrests that have taken place in the last several years. It would show the extent of actions taken by the US government and will also give an idea about the future operations that the government will need to take to curb these criminal acts. Therefore, it is quite clear that the US government must take concrete action against the criminal gangs operating in the country (McCorkle, 1998).

Gangs and Arrest

Few social statuses are expected to increase the risk of arrest as much as gang membership. Street gangs in America represent a public enemy of sorts, depicted as nearly synonymous with a delinquent lifestyle in the literature. These views are no doubt shared by police agencies, whose agents receive training and directives to deal with gangs. For example, a current trend in police suppression of gangs is to "arrest on sight" where civil gang injunctions are imposed, making mere membership an arrest risk. The distinct physical appearance cues of most gang youths and their group-oriented nature help to facilitate their targeting by police. Recognition of street gang subculture has become standard in police work, perpetuating the long-held rivalry between the police and gangs. Yet, despite being the epitome of delinquent youth sub-culture, the effect of gang membership on arrest frequency is not well demonstrated in the delinquency literature (Bellair, 2005).

Volatile Gang Effect

While gang youths would seem to invoke greater police scrutiny than non-gang youths, evidence on membership as a risk factor for arrest is quite limited. One group of studies evaluated arrest data for cities and found little to no difference in the number and types of charges filed against gang and nongang youths. Other recent studies purported a link between gang membership and arrest, which fail to execute a rigorous test by not controlling for delinquency. Therefore, the increased delinquency levels of gang youths are not truly accounted for, and whether or not they deserve to be arrested is not assessed.

Studies have provided a crucial test and have obtained conflicting results. Two published articles using data from the Seattle Youth Study found that gang membership is not a significant risk factor for juvenile arrest. The predominant explanation offered for this counterintuitive finding was the low priority given to youth gangs by Seattle police at the time of data collection—1978 to 1979. Using Chicago data from 1987 to 1988, police officers reported that self-admitted gang involvement did increase the odds of arrest. With conflicting results reported for different periods in Seattle and Chicago, whether gang membership significantly increases arrest risk controlling for delinquency is yet to be determined. These few studies inform the current approach, the first to provide a critical test with national-level data (Chesney-Lind, 1994).

Racial Minorities and Arrest

Of the various treatments of race in the crime literature, the microperspective provides the best framework for the current study. Racial profiling and ecological contamination are useful paradigms for thinking about police minority group relations. Research shows that police cognitively organize their patrol areas by race and class, and many share the belief that minority neighborhoods are more crime-prone. To the extent minority youths are targeted by police while on routine patrol, this perspective is useful. However, since most delinquency cases with police contact are citizen-initiated and not police-initiated, this research is perhaps better served by conceptualizing less intensive forms of bias, such as differential treatment of minority subjects. Patrol officers have greater discretion over legal action on less serious crimes, for example, which may provide room for harsher treatment of racial minorities (Cicourel, 1976).

Black Youths and Arrest

Historically, the black youth arrest rate is consistently much higher than that of white youths. However, the black youth arrest rate appears to be too high for their self-reported delinquency level. Their self-reported, serious offense rate is typically double that of whites, yet black youths are arrested for index offenses four times as often, down from six times the rate through the 1990s. Moreover, the racial difference in self-reported offending is not always significant. Researchers have offered various hypotheses over the years to explain the discrepancy between self-reported offending rates and arrest rates of black youths. For some, it reflects differences in patrol of black and white communities. Others have considered possible differences in demeanor toward police by race. Some field studies suggest that it reflects the bias of citizens who make stronger demands for arrests of black youths than for white youths. Still, others have suggested that black youths underreport their delinquency in survey data, though conflicting evidence has since been offered.

Like many early studies on racial differences in youth offending, modern efforts of considerable sophistication also fail to tease out race effects in delinquency. For example, a handful of multilevel studies show that an individual's race loses its statistically significant relationship with violence and other serious forms of delinquency once contextual items, such as neighborhood disadvantage, are accounted for. Nonetheless, race is a serious predictor of individual-level juvenile arrest in virtually every published study in the contemporary delinquency literature that examines this issue (Curry, 2000).

Hispanic Youths and Arrest

The historical limitations of official and survey data have stunted arrest research on Hispanics. National-level arrest data are not available for this group. In many prominent surveys, Hispanic youths were not adequately sampled to generalize to the population and, therefore, were dropped from the study. Recent developments in survey data have helped to remedy the latter situation. The data used here over samples of Hispanics, making possible one of the first national-level studies on the arrest risk posed by the juvenile's Hispanic ethnicity status. There is a small body of research on Hispanics in the early stages of juvenile processing, most on cities. Findings from recent studies deviate from earlier ones in that they do find arrest penalties for Latinos. Early on, some researchers found that Mexican-Americans were no more likely to be arrested than whites in one medium-sized Midwestern city in the 1950s. They also failed to observe a pattern in decisions to file petitions for Mexican, black, and white youths in various Southern California cities. They, however, found that Hispanic youths in two New Jersey counties experienced a higher risk of arrest than white youths, but a lower risk than black youths. This midrange arrest penalty was recently observed by researchers (Huizinga, 2007) for Hispanic youths in Rochester and Tapia, California, using data for the nation. They also showed that blacks and Latinos were targeted for curfew arrests at a grossly disproportionate rate compared to white and Asian youths in Ventura, Fresno, and Santa Clara counties in California. Finally, in their examination of postarrest intake decisions for youths in Los Angeles, they found that intake officers filed petitions for blacks and Mexican-Americans more often than for white youths (Decker, 2010).

Street Gangs in Deterrence

Few studies have directly assessed deterrence processes among gang members. Some of the researchers considered demographic and perceptual correlates that might affect gun behaviors, such as possession, carrying, and use among juvenile and adult arrestees. They found that gang membership was particularly influential among juveniles and appeared to overwhelm any impact of perceptual deterrence. Past gang research suggests that social processes within gangs might subvert deterrence efforts or, in fact, backfire. Gangs have oppositional cultures, representing "an institutionalized rejection of the values of adult authority." Moreover, by focusing attention on gangs, crime policies may inadvertently increase the status associated with gang membership and solidify youth identification with the group that elicits such attention by authorities.

Gang researchers have observed that the norms of street gangs are explicitly antisocial. The researchers and their colleagues determined that gang members expressed less guilt and mobilized more techniques of neutralization for committing deviant behaviors than did other youths. Further, gang dynamics and norms actively encourage members to participate in violence and crime. Some of the authors interviewed 99 busy street gang members in St. Louis, Missouri, that illustrates how deeply the norms of violence rest in the consciousness of these youths. When asked to offer recommendations for the most effective ways of responding to gangs, the modal response included some form of violence, several on the order of "kill us all." Street gang members' motivation to commit crimes is rooted in group norms and supported by their social identities apart from the individuals' own perceptions or inclinations. From the point of view of group dynamics, regardless of the deterrent influence of legal sanction threats on juvenile offending in general, among gang members, the threat of legal sanctions or even social sanctions is likely to be discounted. Strong collective social identities, such as gang membership, have a powerful and pervasive influence on individuals' perceptions and behaviors and, for gangs, the collective norms motivate members to challenge rather than be determined by threats of legal sanctions (Howell, 2005).

The predictive power of perceptual deterrence on intentions to offend in the near future among gang members is contrasted here with other youthful offenders' intentions. People expect that gang members are more likely to report the intention to offend in the future, an expectation borne from a long line of research indicating higher involvement in criminal activity. The discussion of this finding holds for different samples, geographic locations, gang definitions, and offending indicator. The issue that engages readers here is whether these intentions are influenced by deterrence processes differently for gang offenders than for nongang offenders. In light of the research depictions of oppositional culture and group process within gangs, it is predicted that deterrence, including certainty and severity of punishment, will be less predictive of future offending among gang youths than among nongang youths (Freng, 2007).

Strategy for Handling Gang Membership

A prominent strategy for the prevention of criminal and delinquent behavior is to target youths most at risk for future involvement in serious acts of crime, violence, and gang membership. To this end, criminal justice organizations have initiated interagency collaborations that make use of the various resources and powers available across local service providers. An assumption of this strategy is that agencies involved in these projects have the ability to identify youths in this select group of would-be serious, violent, and chronic offenders and provide them with appropriate services. In other words, the existence of organizational rationality is fundamental to the success of comprehensive programs that would attempt to effect system change.

Results from the current study suggest that the ability of local agencies to identify youths most at risk for delinquency and gang membership should not be taken for granted. Officials in Cuyahoga County, Ohio, contracted with numerous social service providers in their local jurisdiction to provide services to youths most at risk for gang membership, yet such a population proved difficult to locate and include in their initiative. Indeed, a comparison group of African-American males in the general school-based population were more at risk than the targeted group of adolescents on three of the four risk factor domains, 7 of the 12 corresponding subdomains, and accumulated more risk across domains, as measured by the GrADS software, ver. 1.0.

Thus, it is clear that those served by the initiative were not reflective of the intended target population. Although the reasons for this failure to involve the most at-risk youths in the community are difficult to pinpoint in the current study, interviews with Cleveland officials highlighted some of the challenges. The original plan was to administer the GrADS risk assessment tool with all ninth graders in the Cleveland Metropolitan School District (CMSD) and, particularly, in the high school serving the neighborhood targeted in the antigang initiative. However, this proved difficult, given privacy issues and questions about sharing of information that would be collected in schools with the justice system and social service agencies.

It also was difficult to systematically administer the risk assessment tool in schools, which were described as stressed with the numerous demands facing urban school systems. As one respondent stated, the school in the target area was stressed out. Principals and staff felt overwhelmed already, making it difficult at times to ask for more. They were unable to rely on a basic screening process like the schools for conducting the assessment, but wanting to serve youths in need in a high-crime neighborhood, the program tended to rely on referrals from a variety of sources. The end result may indeed have been programs comprised of youths in need who may have benefitted through participation, but it does not appear that the youths most at risk for gang involvement were included (McCorkle, 1998).

The failure to target youths most at risk for delinquency and gang membership is likely to lead to little to no programmatic effect. A recent meta-analysis by Lipsey (<year>) found three substantive factors that are associated with positive program effects, and they include the treatment provided, the quantity and quality of the services, and the risk level of the youths targeted for service.

In fact, Lipsey's review and analysis of the literature suggests that delinquency risk is one of the few individual characteristics associated with programmatic effects, in that programs that target higher risk youths produce larger effects than those that target relatively low-risk individuals. Beyond the risk of reduced programmatic effects associated with targeting low-risk youths, such practices also have been found to have harmful, iatrogenic effects.

For instance, few researchers found that low-risk youths who provided services through the youth/family accountability model reported higher levels of delinquency than the control sample, whereas the program associated with a 16 percent reduction in recidivism among comparable high-risk youths. Evidence presented in Dodge et al. (2006) suggests that such unintended negative programmatic effects may be due to mixing low- and high-risk youths together, and thus providing youths, who might otherwise not be exposed to more seriously delinquent peers, an opportunity to develop such friendship networks, resulting in increased delinquency consistent with a delinquency balance perspective.

In the end, the failure to identify and include youths most at risk, for future delinquency and gang activity is likely to lead to little overall impact, and has the potential to backfire in press, making things worse for youths included in the intervention (Esbensen, 2000).

An evaluation of other targeted gang interventions and delinquency prevention programs has suggested that youths targeted for service were likely not those who posed the greatest risk for future gang involvement or offending. A recent evaluation of Pittsburgh, Pennsylvania's, One Vision One Life Program found that targeting practices were anything but strategic, in that the most frequent mechanisms through which clients became involved in the program were through self-selection (33 percent) and referrals by family members (24 percent). As might be expected, self-selection or referral of individuals by family members is not an adequate strategy for interventions targeted at the highest risk youths.

A review of selection bias in intervention research by Larzelere et al. in 2004 noted that programs that instituted random assignment practices for target selection produced significantly lower overall effect sizes on the likelihood of future arrest than nonrandomized quasi experiments when controls for pretreatment differences were not included. Such evidence suggests that problems associated with sample selection, such as targeting success-prone clients, while excluding those individuals who may be more difficult to change, a practice commonly referred to as *creaming*, are widespread in crime and delinquency interventions (Paternoster, 1986).

Impact of the Strategies on Youths

In moving forward, the development of strategies, or best practices, for identifying youths most in need of preventative services is of utmost importance if people are to realize the potential gains associated with targeted prevention and intervention initiatives. Given the comments of US Attorney General Eric Holder in 2009 and the recent history of federal efforts in this regard, the philosophy of targeting those most at risk for continued or future offending appears to be the reigning paradigm, and, thus, efforts to improve practitioners' abilities to implement such strategies with fidelity must address the issue of identification. Without systematic and, perhaps most importantly, practical solutions for identifying at-risk youths in a population where few youths have no risk factors for delinquency and gang membership, people are destined to repeat the same mistakes that have been documented in the current study and elsewhere. The efficiency promised through targeted prevention and intervention initiatives, after all, hinges on the ability to identify youths most at risk for serious, chronic, and violent offending.

An area of difficulty for those personnel and agencies charged with identifying the appropriate population for targeted criminal justice interventions is the confluence of risk and need in communities chosen for interventions, such as the Comprehensive Anti-Gang Initiative. Given the focus on disadvantaged, high-crime neighborhoods, the need for social services, including job training and placement, after-school activities, and counseling, are nearly ubiquitous.

In other words, many youths in these areas are in need of services, but only privileged youths are at risk for serious, chronic, and violent offending. Maynard-Moody and Musheno's (2003) research on the selection of clients into social services highlights how those in need, but not necessarily at risk, might come to receive a greater degree of services. As Maynard-Moody and Musheno described it: "Motivation clearly makes a client, ex-offender, or kid much easier to handle, because street-level workers typically define motivation in terms of cooperation. The motivated citizen-client is nonetheless deemed morally superior to the unmotivated. Conversely, the unmotivated, regardless of their need or circumstance, are deemed unworthy" (Piliavin, 1986).

Decker and Curry in 2002 highlighted this dilemma faced by social service agents in their evaluation of a targeted intervention in St. Louis, Missouri, when they described how many of the youths failed to show up for their placements, were often late for appointments, and when they arrived were disruptive. In all, while targeted interventions can be successful when implemented correctly, full implementation of programs with high-risk youths can be very difficult. When contracting with local social service providers, whose mission often extends beyond that of crime prevention, it is important to articulate a clear plan for target selection.

Research has highlighted the potential limitations associated with multiple stakeholders collaborating on such endeavors, in those even fundamental processes predetermined to execute targeted initiatives, such as defining common goals and techniques by which these objectives should be achieved can present significant roadblocks for successful implementation. For instance, the social service providers included in the current study did not always specialize in serving clients particularly at risk for crime and delinquency, but instead provided generalized services that focused on the needs of those in the local population. Consequently, standard operating procedures in these organizations were not to exclude clients with documented needs, and thus reliance on routine screening practices would cast a wider net than required under the Comprehensive Anti-Gang Initiative. It clearly articulated that practical methods for selecting cases must be part of future targeted intervention strategies.

As suggested by Le Blanc in 1998, given the low-base rate of youths at risk for involvement in serious, chronic, and violent offending, and by extension gang membership, multiple gating is likely necessary to identify the youths best served by targeted interventions. Multiple informants and multiple-variable domains seem preferable because of the complexity of the influences at work in leading youths down the path of gang membership.

Given the noted influence of accumulated risk across domains (e.g., family, school, and neighborhood), informants from as many of these domains as possible should be included to intervene in the lives of youths. The confluence of opinions from numerous stakeholders should increase the predictive accuracy of the decision to include and exclude youths from interventions. To be sure, there is also a place for standardized risk assessment using instruments such as the one used in the current study (Rosenthal, 2000).

While the current study highlights a potential problem in the notorious implementation of targeted gang interventions, it is not without limitations. First and foremost, while all of the respondents in the two samples used in the current analyses are from the same metropolitan area, the data do not allow for a direct comparison of the neighborhoods or schools in which the respondents lived. Due to issues of confidentiality, all identifying neighborhood and school information was cleaned from the comparison data before analyses could be conducted.

The lack of neighborhood or school identifiers introduces the possibility that sample selection procedures are responsible for our unexpected results. While this remains a slight possibility, the selection procedures purported to be used for the targeted and nontargeted samples should alleviate such concerns. That is, the gang intervention under study targeted what deemed the most at-risk neighborhood in the Cleveland metropolitan area in a number of domains, including violence, gang presence, school failure, and a lack of adequate social services. From there, those chosen to participate in the initiative were supposed to be the most at-risk youths from this particularly distressed community. On the other hand, the nontargeted, school-based sample was derived from available subjects from across the Cleveland Metropolitan School District (CMSD).

Such a sampling technique is notoriously biased, but in a way that should underestimate the level of risk of the general school-based population in the CMSD. Reliance on available subjects (also referred to as convenience sampling) has been found to exclude high-risk individuals, as these youths are least likely to be available or volunteer to, participate in school-based surveys. In the end, while a direct comparison of the neighborhoods and schools from which the two samples were collected is impossible given data restrictions, the observed sample similarities and differences across risk domains remain substantive. The current study highlights the need for more research on the best practices for implementing targeted interventions. Implementation of multiple gating strategies and systematic processes for assessing risk, including the use of actuarial risk assessment devices, such as those used in the current study, are imperative if the benefits associated with targeted interventions are to be realized (Sanchez-Jankowski, 1991).

Future Implications for the Current Topic

Whether gang members experience arrest risks beyond what is warranted by their delinquency level remained in dispute after conflicting findings across two study sites. The current study finds support for undue arrest risk experienced by gang members and racial minorities using survey data for the nation. Given that street gangs predominate in minority communities, the absence of any studies to date that examine the interaction of gang membership and race on juvenile arrests is surprising. Researchers have examined this interaction to help fill that gap, and new insights to the effort to discover sources of DMC with the justice system.

At first glance, it is not entirely clear whether the main effect of gang membership is evidence of undue targeting or the expected effect, given its vilified status in society. That is, it is not clear whether gang membership constitutes a legal variable or a social variable. Based on the recent trend toward criminalization of active gang member status, with many places in the United States enacting civil gang injunctions as a suppression tactic, this might be the expected effect. In this sense, the targeting of gang youths for arrest might be more defensible than the targeting of minority youths, but the great overlap in these populations complicates the matter substantially.

While they are often the signifiers of gang membership, it is not the subcultural elements, such as race, group cohesiveness, gang apparel, and so on, that are criminalized, per se, but elevated criminal behavior that makes these youths the target of suppression. With delinquency and criminal history controlled in these models, however, the most distinguishing characteristic of gang membership is removed (theoretically, at least), arguably leaving only the social components of membership. Thus, it is specified as an extralegal variable here, informed by various plausible lessons from the gang literature.

Summary

All of these factors contribute toward the concept of reevolution of gangs that will need further studies in comprehending the best result for the literature. There is a need to constantly monitor the activities of the gangs in an effective way in order to take timely action. This is the reason why it can be said that gang culture in the United States has its own importance and there is a need for proper strategies by the government to tackle this issue in the best possible way in the future. Therefore, all the issues and aspects related to gang culture in the United States have been discussed in detail.

References

Allan, E. 2004. *Civil Gang Abatement: The Effectiveness and Implications of Policing by Injunction*. New York: LFB Scholarly.

Bell, D. 1985. The intake dispositions of juvenile offenders. *Journal of Research in Crime and Delinquency*.

Bellair, P. 2005. Beyond the bell curve: Community disadvantage and the explanation of black-white differences in adolescent violence. *Journal of Criminology*.

Chesney-Lind, A. 1994. Gangs and delinquency. *Crime, Law, and Social Change*.

Cicourel, A. 1976. *The Social Organization of Juvenile Justice*. New York: John Wiley & Sons.

Curry, G. 2000. Self-reported gang involvement and officially recorded delinquency. *Journal of Criminology*.

Decker, S. 2010. *Gangs, Groups, and Guns: Small Arms Survey 2010*. Cambridge, MA: Cambridge University Press.

Decker, and Curry. 2002.

Dodge, K. 2006. *Deviant Peer Influences in Programs for Youth: Problems and Solutions*. New York: Guilford Press.

Esbensen, F. 2000. *Preventing Adolescent Gang Involvement*. Washington, D.C.: Office of Juvenile Justice and Delinquency Prevention.

Freng, A. 2007. Race and gang affiliation: An examination of multiple marginality. *Justice Quarterly*.

Gavazzi, S. 2006. Gender, ethnicity and the family environment: Contributions to assessment efforts within the realm of juvenile justice. *Journal of Family Relations*.

Guerra, N. 1997. *Intervening to Prevent Childhood Aggression in the Inner City*. New York: Cambridge University Press.

Howell, J. 2005. Moving risk factors into developmental theories of gang membership. *Youth Violence and Juvenile Justice*.

Henry, K.L. and Huizinga, D.H. (2007) "School-related risk and protective factors associated with truancy among urban youth placed at risk." *The Journal of Primary Prevention* 28 (6), 505–519.

Kennedy, D. 1997. Pulling levers: Chronic offenders, high-crime settings, and a theory of prevention. *Valparaiso University Law Review*.

Klein, M. 2007. *Variations on a Theme of Gang Control*. Bologna, Italy: European Society of Criminology.

Larzelere, R., Cox, R., Ketevan, D., and Mandara, J. 2004. "Do Childhood Outcomes of All Disciplinary Enforcements Vary by Ethnicity." Paper presented at the Annual Conference of the National Council on Family Relations, Nov. 5, 2008.

Le Blanc. 1998. Social and psychological characteristics of gang members. *Journal of Gang Research*, 5(3), 15–28.

Lipsey, M.W. 2009. The primary factors that characterize effective interventions with juvenile offenders: A meta-analytic overview. *Victims and Offenders*, 4, 124–147.

Maynard-Moody and Musheno. 2003.

Maxson, C. 1998. Vulnerability to street gang membership: Implications for practice. *Social Service Review*.

McCorkle, R. 1998. The political and organizational response to gangs: An examination of a 'moral panic' in Nevada. *Justice Quarterly*.

Paternoster, R. 1986. The use of composite scales in perceptual deterrence research: A cautionary note. *Journal of Research in Crime and Delinquency.*

Piliavin, I. 1986. Crime, deterrence, and rational choice. *American Sociological Review.*

Rosenthal, L. 2000. Gang loitering and race. *Journal of Criminal Law and Criminology.*

Sanchez-Jankowski, M. 1991. *Islands in the Street: Gangs and American Urban Society.* Berkeley, CA: University of California Press.

Smith, W. 1999. Prediction of recidivism among 'second timers' in the juvenile justice system: Efficiency in screening chronic offenders. *American Journal of Criminal Justice.*

Swanson, C. 2009. *Cities in Crisis 2009: Closing the Graduation Gap.* Bethesda, MD: EPE Research Center.

Thornberry, T. 2003. *Gangs and Delinquency in Developmental Perspective.* New York: Cambridge University Press.

Vigil, J. 1998. *Barrio Gangs: Street Life and Identity in Southern California.* Austin, TX: University of Texas Press.

Warr, M. 2002. *Companions in Crime: The Social Aspects of Criminal Conduct.* New York: Cambridge University Press.

Zatz, M. 1987. Chicano youth gangs and crime, creation of a moral panic. *Contemporary Crises.*

Street Gang Graffiti 101

10

KEN DAVIS

Contents

Introduction

Noah Webster, the father of American scholarship and education, defines graffiti as "the unauthorized writing or drawing on a public surface." However, this definition takes on a different meaning when the writer is not your average person. What if this person is a prolific graffiti vandal, a prolific graffiti vandal belonging to a graffiti crew, or a member of a notorious gang?

I designed this chapter to assist those that are suddenly thrust into the world of street gang graffiti. Most people find this task difficult because the subject is complex. My education about graffiti began in the early 1990s. During this decade, I was introduced to graffiti from two viewpoints: graffiti as an art form and graffiti vandalism as a public nuisance. From the vantage point of graffiti as art, I was a proud cofounder and field coordinator for Off the Wall, a community-based graffiti art program sponsored by the Yonkers Community Action Program and Youth Service Bureau (Fitz-Gibbon, 1992).

This graffiti art program lasted for approximately 10 to 12 years, giving a "canvas" to various graffiti artists and writers, as well as a few gang members (Ferris, 2002). From the perspective of vandalism as a sign of community blight, I was one of the graffiti/gang officers working within the Yonkers Police Department's Community Affairs Division (Allen, 1993). From 1996 to 2000, we apprehended approximately 250 prolific graffiti vandals and identified several street gangs, along with their members. During that time, this unit was deemed the city's first line of defense against street gangs (O'Connor, 2000).

As I look back now, I realize that both unexpected introductions were "divine interventions." In my next career shift, I couldn't wait for another divine intervention. Similar to web groups on the Internet, I had to immerse myself into three focal groups. I will refer to these groups as "circles of enthusiasts." So, what is a circle of enthusiasts? It's a group that consists of anyone or anybody, known or unknown, possessing exceptional knowledge of a specific field. Thanks to the Internet, and one of its popular search engines, I was able to find them.

In the category of graffiti-related issues, my circle of enthusiasts included the No Graf Network, T.A.G.S. (The Anti-Graffiti Symposium–Canada), Metro-Area Graffiti Task Force (Denver, Colorado), the California Graffiti Task Force, one outstanding graffiti coordinator working with Metro North Railroad, and two outstanding graffiti investigators working within the New York Police Department's Special Investigation Unit (Brooklyn, New York).

In the category of gang-related matters, my circle of enthusiasts consisted of the California Gang Investigators Association, Connecticut Gang Investigators Association, East Coast Gang Investigators Association, GANGINFO Network, Gang Prosecution Symposium (Redondo Beach, California), Middle Atlantic/Great Lakes Organized Crime Law Enforcement Network (MAGLOCLEN), Midwest Counterdrug Training Center (Johnston, Iowa), Midwest Gang Investigators Association, National Association of School Resource Officers, National Gang Crime Research Center (Chicago, Illinois), New Jersey Gang Investigators Association, New York Gang Investigators Association, Northeast Counterdrug Training Center (Fort Indiantown Gap, Pennsylvania), State of New York Division of Criminal Justice Services, Texas Gang Investigators Association, and the Police Discussion List.

Finally, in the category of gang graffiti, my circle of enthusiasts consisted of an online database of personnel derived from an online search engine. In other words, I would insert the key phrase *gang graffiti* into the Google Alert's search box. As the online article appeared in my inbox, I selected the information pertaining to my desired topic (gang graffiti). I read the article, daily, extracting names of people who seemed to possess an exceptional knowledge of the specifics of gang graffiti. As of now, it stands that some law enforcement agencies know the difference between gang graffiti and tagging graffiti. In knowing so, a percentage of prosecutors are beginning to apply gang injunctions and enhancements on those generating gang graffiti. In some incidents, gang injunctions and enhancements are being applied to prolific graffiti crews.

The quest for various circles of enthusiasts has defined my agenda and eventually my curriculum vita in becoming a graffiti/gang specialist. Still, to this very day, I attend and present at graffiti- and gang-related conferences with the same intensity as a prolific graffiti vandal eyeing a clean, high-visibility surface.

In order to ease you into your introduction into the world of gang graffiti, I will begin with several subtopics: the truth about graffiti art and graffiti vandalism, subcultures and their subcultural principles, the graffiti identity and the gang identity, street gang graffiti gallery, glossary 1 (graffiti formats), glossary 2 (the culture), and online/offline resources.

The Truth about Graffiti Art and Graffiti Vandalism

Before you begin identifying and analyzing gang graffiti, you need to understand the several principles centered on graffiti and its vandalism characteristics. The first principle is simple. Graffiti is illegal. In New York state, writing, painting, scribbling, or defacing anyone's property without the owner or caretaker's permission is classified as Making Graffiti (NYSPL. 145.60.02) or Criminal Mischief (NYSPL 145.00). Graffiti done with permission can be interpreted as "graffiti art." Graffiti done without permission is considered "graffiti vandalism."

However, within the subcultur, graffiti art and graffiti vandalism is decided by the format of the graffiti being generated. For example, graffiti formats like complex throw-ups, pieces, or productions are deemed as graffiti art. Even if the author generated one of these graffiti formats without the property owner's permission, the perception is that these graffiti formats represent graffiti art. Graffiti formats like tags, territorial acronyms, tag name/attached to an acronym, moniker/attached to an acronym, simple throw-ups, or common throw-ups are normally used for graffiti vandalism. With or without the property owner's permission, the perception is that these graffiti formats represent graffiti vandalism.

Inside any subculture, there are subcultural principles; they govern the way in which things operate within a specific graffiti culture. Graffiti, in its simplest form, conveys self or collective worth. Even in its simplest form, graffiti is governed by subcultural principles.

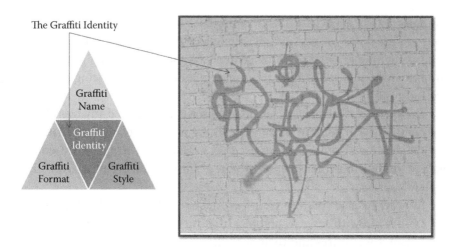

Figure 10.1 The chosen graffiti name (Slick), selected usage of a graffiti format (tag) and preferred usage of a graffiti style (wild-style).

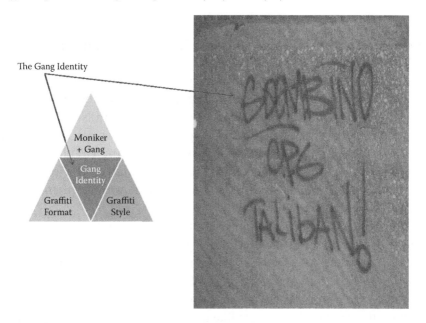

Figure 10.2 Gang member, GOOMBINO, conveying his membership in two groups—Cottage Place Gardens (CPG) and Taliban.

Various Subcultures and Their Subcultural Principles

Since my introduction into the world of graffiti and its vandalism characteristics, I have identified three types of graffiti cultures (extreme, common, and hip-hop) inside my jurisdiction. In brief, the extreme graffiti expresses cultural or racial biases; the common graffiti communicate heterosexual,

Figure 10.3 Writer-based graffiti crew. Hiper, Comp, Slogan and Stomp show that they are members of TBC (To Be Creative).

Figure 10.4 Artist-based graffiti crew. Fame City (FC) is pictured here. This is a complex throw-up.

homosexual, and nonsexual comments; and the hip-hop cultures convey graffiti generated by taggers, graffiti crews, street gangs, street teams, and graffiti artists. One prominent graffiti investigator, Sgt. Dwight Waldo of the San Bernardino Police Department, identified five graffiti cultures (communicative, hate, gang graffiti, tagging, and art) within his jurisdiction. Another popular graffiti investigator, Lee Barnard of Southern California, has came across various graffiti cultures (hate and occult groups, gangs, taggers, tag bangers, and party crews) during his investigations.

Figure 10.5 Territorial acronym for Black Villain Assassins.

Figure 10.6 SORE belonging to OFB/Out For Blood.

Figure 10.7 Simple message.

Figure 10.8 Roll call. In some instances gang members will omit their moniker to conceal their identity while promoting the group's existence.

Figure 10.9 Upper left photo demonstrates Moniker Gang graffiti showing membership in Get Money Gangsters (GMG) and Cottage Place Gardens (CPG).

Figure 10.10 Young Gunz graffiti.

As you continue to explore graffiti and its vandalism characteristics, you will begin to see other graffiti-related cultures. Other examples of graffiti cultures will include ad-busting, guerrilla, cultural jamming, go-go graffiti, grafedia, psy-geo-conflux, reverse graffiti, bathroom, stencil-like, etc. In addition to your ongoing exploration, you will realize that specific graffiti cultures are attached to certain geographic locations (urban, suburban, and rural). Eventually, you will begin to realize the differences between tagging and street gang graffiti.

Whether historical or contemporary, each type of graffiti culture maintains its own set of subcultural principles that can be classified into three categories: creation, construction, and circulation. Inside the tagging graffiti culture, these same subcultural principles direct the graffiti participant toward individualism, and eventually "fame." While attempting to gain notoriety, the graffiti participant develops the graffiti identity. His/her graffiti identity is comprised of their chosen graffiti name (Slick), selected usage of a graffiti format (Tag), and preferred usage of a graffiti style (Wild-Style) (Figure 10.11). Just like in the tagging graffiti culture, there are subcultural principles that govern how to create, construct, and circulate street gang graffiti to promote fear and cohesiveness, aka the family-like atmosphere (Figure 10.12). Whenever the gang member decides to partake in generating graffiti, his or her gang identity will be comprised of their chosen moniker, for instance, Goombino, selected usage of a graffiti format (moniker/acronyms), and preferred usage of a graffiti style (public).

Somewhere between the graffiti identity and the gang identity is a place for the graffiti crew. Most publications will identify the basic graffiti crew as

Figure 10.11 Arabian Knights Posse (AKP) + Vatos Locos (VL) + Puro Vatos Locos (PVL) gang graffiti.

Figure 10.12 Territorial acronyms.

a loosely knit group with the desire to cause large volume of graffiti vandalism damages.

I have noticed two profound differences between street gangs and graffiti crews. First, as compared to graffiti crews, street gangs possess a higher value on establishing leadership, management, and criminality protocols. Graffiti making to them is a secondary protocol. The only similarity between the average street gang and average graffiti crew is that several of their graffiti formats promote and advertise group cohesiveness.

As for graffiti crews, I have identified two types of graffiti crews: writer-based and artist- based. Writer-based graffiti crews tend to generate graffiti associated with graffiti vandalism; whereas artist-based graffiti crews will generate graffiti associated with graffiti art. Some graffiti enthusiasts will stress that "back in the day" graffiti gangs possessed both artistic skills and fighting skills. Other graffiti and gang enthusiasts will offer theories pertaining to their existence. The majority of these theories are centered on the street gang and graffiti crew's evolution, coexistence with other groups, violence, criminal opportunities, and membership size. As of now, you should know that certain graffiti formats and graffiti styles are designed to promote and advertise art, vandalism, individualism, and group cohesiveness. In other words, specific graffiti formats and specific graffiti styles are attached to prolific graffiti vandals, prolific graffiti crews, and street gangs. Those specific graffiti formats and specific graffiti styles affixed to street gangs are categorized as territorial acronyms, moniker attached to territorial acronyms, simple messages, and roll calls.

We will now learn about the four categories of graffiti formats generated by street gangs throughout Westchester County (New York). It is not the various graffiti formats that distinguish the group's racial or cultural background, it is the specific symbols and totems inserted and specific graffiti styles embedded within these graffiti formats.

The Gang Name (aka Moniker)

The gang identity is similar to the graffiti identity comprising the name, format, and style. For clarity purposes, I will refer to the gang name as the "moniker." I am only doing this because most gang-related conferences refer to the gang member's subcultural name as the "moniker." The majority of graffiti-related conferences utilize the term "tag name" to represent the graffiti participant.

Gang members are not obsessed with their monikers as graffiti participants are preoccupied with their tag names. In the gang culture, gang members adhere to subcultural principles that reinforce the 3 Rs (respect, reputation, and retaliation). In the graffiti culture, graffiti participants adhere to subcultural principles reinforcing the 3 Cs (creation, construction, and circulation).

As opposed to the graffiti identity, the gang identity is formed differently. Personalities are recognized by the [monikers] applied to the members of the gang. Individual peculiarities, which have an important effect in determining the status, are likely to give color to the boy's whole personality. He is named accordingly, and his [moniker] often indicates the esteem in which he is held by the group (Thrasher, 1927). Some examples of this gang-related concept will include:

- Porky (a fat boy)
- Slim (a slender boy)
- Shorty (a small boy)
- Sheik (a handsome boy)
- Goofy (a peculiar, unmanly boy)
- Rocky (a hard boy)
- Wop (ethnic background)
- Blackie (complexion)
- Whitey (complexion)
- Red (complexion)
- Dopey (drug addict)

At times, some monikers will have an oxymoronic appearance, such as:

- Tiny (a huge male)
- Mr. Big (a small male)
- Peace (a real fighter)

Very rarely is the graffiti identity obtained in the above manner. It's like an abstract. The graffiti participant's tag name can emerge from various sources, such as the word's phonic sound, structural appearance, meaning, etc.

Gang Graffiti Format

The gang member, as opposed to the graffiti writer, will utilize several fixed graffiti formats. Regardless of the geographic locations, these graffiti formats will be similar in all gang graffiti. The street gang graffiti format can be categorized into four categories:

1. Territorial acronym
2. Moniker
3. Moniker/territorial acronym
4. Simple messages

The gang member's moniker is related to its group, for example, as a puzzle piece in its entire puzzle. Thus, the gang moniker is rarely viewed alone on a surface. His or her moniker is constantly integrated within other graffiti formats to show group participation. In some instances, gang members will omit their moniker to conceal their identity while promoting the group's existence.

Whenever the gang moniker is viewed in public, it generally takes the form of a signature: simple throw-up or common throw-up along with the group's acronym, symbol, or totem.

The Gang Graffiti Style

In the tagger's graffiti culture, there are numerous types of graffiti styles. Within my experience, I have documented approximately 116 various types. The most common mistake is that the graffiti format is mistaken for the graffiti style or visa-versa. The most repeated graffiti styles used on surfaces today are public, semiwild, and wild styles.

Public style means that the general public could easily read it. *Semiwild* style means that intermediate and beginner writers can read it, while, at the same time, it's teasing or daring the general public to understand it. *Wild style* means membership only. Only die-hard graffiti writers or artists can decipher it. In the gang culture, the majority of graffiti will be done in public or semiwild style because gang members want you to understand their graffiti; knowing that they exist, their message, and how strong they are. If the gang graffiti appears to be semiwild, it can be for several reasons, some of which are centered on cultural influences or the gang member's state of mind at the time.

The most misunderstood perception about gangs lies within the notion of cultural influences. Let me state that every culture on this planet retains a percentage of gangs. Some street gangs will maintain a monocultural or racial background, while other street gangs will maintain an integrated status.

Gang Graffiti Style: Additional Elements

Gang participants will insert specific symbols, totems, numbers, colors, and quotes into their graffiti. These items will be arranged in a certain way to reflect their opinion. Items displayed in a regular fashion means respect or support; items expressed in an irregular manner means disrespect or adversary. These same items can be categorized as mainstream, hip-hop/tagging/gang culture, and graffiti instrument elements. For example, the numbers 5, 6, 13, and 14 are known in mainstream society as quantity indicators. However, in the gang culture, the number 5 represents "people," the number 6 represents "folk," the number 13 represents southern (*sureño*), and the number 14 represents northern (*norteño*). All are indictors of specific gang associations. In the world of white supremacy, gangs will utilize the number 14, in which the term "14 words" stands for *"we must secure the existence of our people and future for white children."* A three-point crown in the tagging world will mean he/she is king of a specific geographic location, spot, or line. In the gang world, the crown can mean a status within a particular gang or the particular gang itself. Even the presence of a three-point, five-point, or six-point crown bears significance. Three-point crowns are associated with Dominican or Mexican gangs; five-point crowns are connected with gangs under the People Nation, especially Latin Kings; six-point crowns are associated gangs under the Folk Nations.

At times, the graffiti instrument used to display gang graffiti can enhance the level of the gang's destructiveness. For example, the level of damage intensity can be perceived in this order: pen, marker, spray paint, acid paste, or carving tool. Some tend to believe that gang graffiti inscribed on paper with a pen is less threatening than gang graffiti inscribed on a surface with spray paint. Don't be fooled. All gang graffiti should be treated the same. It behooves you to know what symbols, totems, numbers, colors, and quotes are associated with graffiti vandals, graffiti crews, and street gangs in your community.

Gang Graffiti Gallery (1990–Present)

The photographs in this photo gallery are divided into four categories: territorial acronyms (ta), moniker/territorial acronym (mta), simple messages (sm), and roll calls (rc). Once you have examined and analyzed these images, you will be able to identify and analyze gang graffiti within your community.

Territorial Acronyms (TA)

Territorial acronyms (TA) generally take the form of bold/simple letters, numbers, letters/numbers, or the actual group's name. Territorial acronyms will define the specific group's claimed area, alliances/adversaries, and other graffiti formats (Figure 10.11 to Figure 10.29).

Moniker/Territorial Acronyms (MTA)

This type of graffiti format connects the gang member(s) to their specific group. They act as mini or partial roll calls. Moniker/territorial acronym and tag name/territorial acronym are very similar. However, gang members will generally display one or two acronyms, whereas graffiti participants can exhibit two or more acronyms. It pays to known what groups, graffiti crews, and street gangs inhabit your community (Figure 10.30 to Figure 10.47).

Simple Messages (sm)

Simple messages provide several functions for the gang, such as displaying their allies or enemies, criminal intentions, deaths (RIPs), or other timely events. Most of the time, their graffiti messages consist of brief sentences, omitted letters, upside down or right-side up symbols, or crossing out symbols or totems (Figure 10.48 to Figure 10.64).

Figure 10.13 Tag of Nine-Trey Gangsters (NTG) + Gangster Killer Bloods (GKB).

Figure 10.14 Strip Boys graffiti.

FIGURE 10.15 East Side Crips.

Figure 10.16 Amor de Rey (King Love) a slogan of the Latin Kings.

Figure 10.17 Gray Place Gangsters (GPG) mark a garage.

Figure 10.18 Cholos-18th Street crossing out SUR13/Sureno-13.

Figure 10.19 Chicano Nation (CN) crossing out Aztec Pride.

Figure 10.20 The Lawrence Posse (TLP).

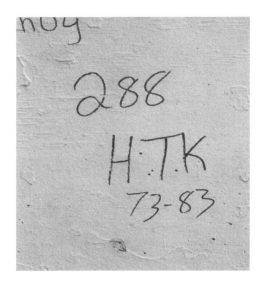

Figure 10.21 Riverdale Ave + HTK/Hard To Kill (73-83 Highland Ave).

Figure 10.22 KDL/King Demons and Lords—Four-Sided Triangle.

Figure 10.23 ABI/Albanian Boys Incorporated.

Figure 10.24 RP/Ravine Posse + BS/Buddha Squad + BHW/Body Hurting Warburton; ta 16–LHP/Locust Hill Posse.

Figure 10.25 NSA/Nino Sin Amor.

Figure 10.26 DST/Downing Street + Raza Loca + 203.

Figure 10.27 HB/Hoover Boys crossing out LOA/Leaders Of All.

Figure 10.28 GMF/Grimy Mother F**kers + F**K + CSG/Cliff Street Gangsters.

Figure 10.29 SKEEFLOW belonging to YB/Young Bloods.

Figure 10.30 NUSE belonging to AKP/Arabian Knights Posse.

Figure 10.31 Deng Dog belonging to Hash Kings (H/K).

Figure 10.32 SHAME belonging to Back Breaking Squad (BBS).

Figure 10.33 MATE belonging to Back Breaking Squad (BBS).

Figure 10.34 NEZ and SEES belonging to The Lord's Table (TLT).

Figure 10.35 SENE belonging to LB/Lake Avenue Boys.

Figure 10.36 P-DOUBLE belonging to CPG/Cottage Place Gardens.

Figure 10.37 PUPPET belonging to TVS/Traviesios.

Figure 10.38 JUEZ and GOOFY belonging to VL/Vatos Locos.

Figure 10.39 AVIN and KR belonging to DIK/Da Ill Kids.

Figure 10.40 ESKO belonging to LP/Lawrence Street Posse.

Figure 10.41 FOXX belonging to CPG/Cottage Place Gardens.

Figure 10.42 PHENO belonging to 527/Emit Burke Gardens.

Figure 10.43 JROD belonging to LHP/Locust Hill Posse.

Figure 10.44 ROACH belonging to VL/Vatos Locos.

Figure 10.45 BILLY belonging to Nine Tray Gangsters (Gangstas).

Figure 10.46 A depiction of two homicides. The message is to keep silent, not to snitch to law envorcement.

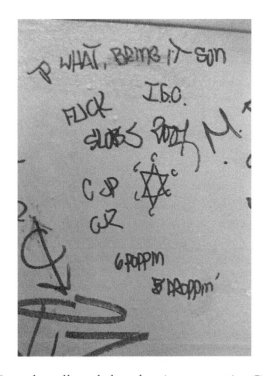

Figure 10.47 Several small symbols and sayings supporting CRIPs.

Figure 10.48 A memorial for a fallen comrade.

Figure 10.49 Small throw-up.

Figure 10.50 RIP for Tookie Williams, a CRIP who was executed in 2005.

Figure 10.51 A foul message to THO/The Hot Ones from TLP/The Lawrence Street Posse.

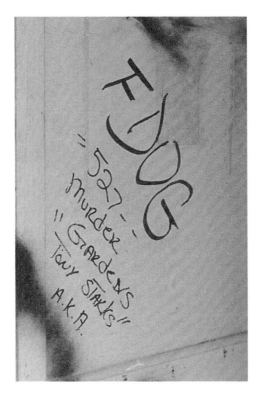

Figure 10.52 A message that reveals a gang member's identity as FDOG.

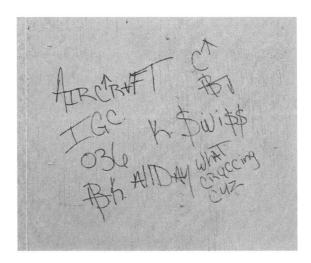

Figure 10.53 Several symbols and totems supporting the CRIPS. K-SWISS = Kill Slobs When I See Slobs.

Figure 10.54 A foul message to SG/Strip Girlsz, auxiliary group to the Strip Boyz gang.

Figure 10.55 A support for the Bloods Street Gang; Bloods up, redrum is murder spelled backwards.

Figure 10.56 RIP for fallen gang member K-Boogie of Saratoga Avenue.

Figure 10.57 Cluster tags representing the Latin Kings; TT/Taino Tribe, ALQN/ Almighty Latin King and Queen Nation, upside-down pitchfork, '05 = 2005, and five-point-crown.

Figure 10.58 RIP for E-Money Wallace of the street gang RZL/La Raza.

Figure 10.59 A memorial for an Arabic friend (Basam, AKA SLIM) who worked in a store within the territory of the TLP/The Lawrence Street Posse.

Figure 10.60 A three-leaf clover representing P&S/Puff and Spliff.

Figure 10.61 A roll call representing HB/Hoover Boy.

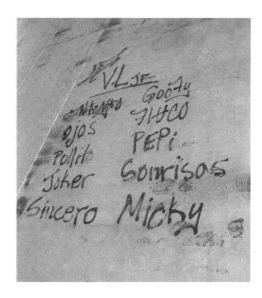

Figure 10.62 A roll call representing VL/Vatos Locos.

Figure 10.63 A roll call representing BHW/Body Hurting Warburton's membership (Kev Joints, Monk, Water, Tore, etc.).

Figure 10.64 A roll call on behalf of CC/Chestnut Crew's roster (Big-LOS, Hot-Rod, Lopez, and P-Rock).

Roll Calls (rc)

These specific graffiti formats convey the group's core membership. The basic roll call will consist of a territory acronym or symbols representing the group. Any graffiti format listing three or more gang members should be considered a roll call; any graffiti format listing one individual should be considered a moniker/territorial acronym, aka placa. Sometimes, gang members will insert their allies rather than other gang members into their roll call.

Figure 10.65 A roll call representing CN/Chicano Nation's membership (Lobo, Bebe, Ozo, Dado, etc.).

Figure 10.66 A roll call on behalf of TL/Tulco's membership (Junior, Grenas, Baby, Gallo, Pachuco, Nino, etc.).

Figure 10.67 A roll call.

Figure 10.68 A roll call representing 28/A peer group (Lil-nom, Lil-C, JAZZO, Mickey, and Q.T.).

Figure 10.69 Roll call for AP/Aztec Pride's membership (Chuco, Trivis, etc.).

Figure 10.70 A roll call on behalf of LC/Los Cholos and GFM/Grand Familia's membership (Kasper, Osito, and Oso).

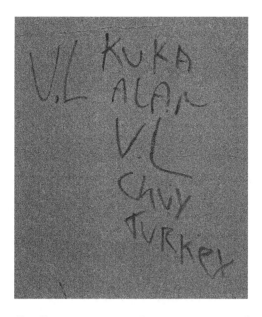

Figure 10.71 A roll call representing VL/Vatos Locos roster (Kuka, Alan, Chuy, and Turkey).

Figure 10.72 A roll call representing TRB/True Ruthless Bitches' membership (Thelmita, Casper, Baby, Cupcake, Nina, and Mama).

Glossary 1: Graffiti Formats

For the purpose of this publication, I use the term *graffiti format* instead of the term *graffiti symbols*. Why? During my experiences, I discovered that the term *graffiti format* offers a stronger clarification of "multiinterpretation," more so than the term symbol. The latter term offers the viewpoint of "a single interpretation." For example, a symbol or totem can be inserted within a format; however, a format cannot be inserted in a symbol or totem.

Cluster of tags: Any graffiti format that appears to contain numerous tags. A close up investigation can reveal this format to be a huge roll call, bunch of simple messages, or placas.

Common throw-up: A variation of the throw-up, graffiti format, consisting of one outline color and one fill-in color. This type of graffiti format can be constructed by a graffiti or gang participant.

Complex throw-up: A variation of the throw-up, graffiti format, consisting of multioutline colors and multifill-in colors. This type of graffiti format is normally constructed by a graffiti participant.

Gang cultural elements: Any distinct design, symbol, or totem linked to a specific group within the gang culture. They are inserted into any one of the four gang graffiti formats. Some examples include the 3-, 5-, or 6-point crown, numbers 13 or 14, 5 or 6, 14 words, laugh now and cry later clowns, pitchforks, heart with wings, 6- or 5-point stars, etc.

Figure 10.73 Common tag.

Figure 10.74 Simple throw-up.

Graffiti formats: Is one-third part of the graffiti identity or gang identity. The basic graffiti format should be viewed as a "generic form" in which the individual inscribes his or her subcultural name (tag name or gang name) and graffiti style upon it. In the tagger's world, the four most common graffiti formats is the tag, throw-up, piece, and production. In the gang's world, the four most common gang graffiti formats are the territorial acronym, moniker attached to an acronym, simple message, and roll call.

Graffiti instrument elements: Any distinct mark or trace, intentionally or unintentionally, associated with a specific graffiti instrument; used to enrich the graffiti format or graffiti style portion of the individual's identity. Some specific elements will include the width of the spray line, drippings, or etching marks, etc.

Figure 10.75 Simple throw-up.

Figure 10.76 Complex throw-up.

Mainstream elements: Any distinct pattern, design, or totem commonly recognized by the general public; used to enrich the graffiti format or graffiti-style portion of the individual's identity. Some examples may include alphabet lettering, cartoon characters, basic designs, and objects.

Moniker/acronym: A graffiti format that depicts the gang member's name and their specific group. At times, this type of graffiti format is referred to as a "placa."

Piece: A huge graffiti format consisting of multioutline and fill-in colors; they can take the form of a pictorial or abstract format. This type of graffiti format is normally constructed by a graffiti participant.

Production: A bigger variation of the piece. The production, like the piece, can take on a pictorial or abstract look. Generally, the production

Figure 10.77 A complex throw-up, pieces.

Figure 10.78 Graffiti as art.

maintains one solid background color. This type of graffiti format is normally constructed by a graffiti participant.

Roll call: A graffiti format that conveys the group's partial or complete roster. At times, gang members will insert other gangs (allies) into their roll call. This type of graffiti format is normally constructed by a gang participant. However, the graffiti participants also will utilize this graffiti under certain conditions.

Signature: The most basic graffiti format (tag) conveying the graffiti or gang identity. This type of graffiti format can be constructed by a gang or graffiti participant. However, a gang participant will usually insert their signature with other gang formats. The gang identity is rarely viewed alone on a surface.

Simple message: A graffiti format that conveys the group's criminal intentions, allies and enemies, or fallen members. This type of graffiti format can be constructed by a gang or graffiti participant. A street gang's simple messages can also signify their past, present, or future dealings.

Figure 10.79 Tag name plus acronyms.

Figure 10.80 Common throw-up.

Simple throw-up: A graffiti format that consist of one outline color, and the color surface acts as the fill-in color. This type of graffiti format can be constructed by a gang or graffiti participant.

Slap-tag: A graffiti identity inscribed on a self-adhesive label or sticker. This type of graffiti format is normally done by a graffiti participant. Slap-tags are usually purchased at office supply stores or taken from postal facilities.

Stencil: A graffiti format produced by a cardboard stencil and single color spray paint. This type of graffiti format is normally done by a graffiti participant.

Tag name/acronym(s): A graffiti format that depicts the graffiti participant's tag name and his or her specific graffiti crew, or graffiti crews. Just like the moniker/acronym, this, too, is sometimes referred to as a "placa."

Figure 10.81 Stencil graffiti format.

Tagger graffiti: Graffiti formats normally generated by graffiti participants. Their graffiti formats will consist of the tag, throw-up, stencil, slap-tag, piece, and productions. Graffiti participants can include the graffiti writer, graffiti artist, graffiti writer/artist, writer-based graffiti crew, or artist-based graffiti crew. For the purpose of this manual, hip-hop graffiti and tagger graffiti will be considered the same.

Glossary 2: The Culture

Gang graffiti: Graffiti formats are normally generated by street gangs. The four most common gang graffiti formats are territorial acronyms, moniker/acronyms, simple messages, and roll calls. At times, gangs will combine them, such as a territorial acronym attached to a simple message, a territorial acronym attached to a roll calls, etc.

Gang identity: Is comprised of three parts: gang moniker, graffiti format, and graffiti style. Note that not all gang members participate in the graffiti making process.

Graffiti art: Any graffiti format displayed on a surface with the owner or caretaker permission, or any graffiti format produced on a canvas. This graffiti-making process is referred to as *piecing*.

Graffiti artist: Any graffiti participant that generates graffiti formats for the purpose of graffiti art. See terms: complex throw-up, piece, and productions.

Graffiti crime: The illegal act of displaying graffiti formats on a surface without the owner or caretaker's permission. In New York state, graffiti crimes will be listed as Making Graffiti (NYS Penal Law 145.60), Criminal Mischief (NYS Penal Law 145.00–145.15), or Unlawful

Posting Advertisements (NYS Penal Law 145.30). Check the criminal legislation in your state.

Graffiti enthusiast: Any person with exceptional knowledge or desire pertaining to all or a specific graffiti culture. Graffiti enthusiasts may include graffiti participants, investigators, researchers, critics, groupies, and sworn or nonsworn personnel.

Graffiti identity: Is comprised of three parts: tag name, graffiti format, and graffiti style.

Graffiti name: One-third part of the graffiti identity; it's the graffiti participant's chosen subcultural name, aka tag name.

Graffiti participant: Any person who participates in the legal or illegal activities of generating graffiti. The three basic categories are graffiti writers, graffiti artists, graffiti writer/artists. Sometimes the graffiti participant is referred to as a tag-banger.

Graffiti specialist: An expert, or sworn or nonsworn personnel, within the fields of graffiti apprehension, prosecution, prevention, intervention, restoration, restorative justice, or information management.

Graffiti style: One-third part of the graffiti identity or gang identity; it's the stylish manner in which the individual inscribes his or her chosen subcultural name and preferred graffiti format during the graffiti-making process. The three most common graffiti styles are public, semiwild, and wild styles. In the tagger's world, there are approximately 116 documented graffiti styles. Graffiti styles associated with gang graffiti is limited.

Graffiti vandalism: Any graffiti format displayed on a surface without the property owner's permission. The graffiti-making process for graffiti vandalism is referred to as tagging, bombing, or getting-up. Graffiti vandalism is a crime.

Graffiti writer: Any graffiti participant who generates graffiti formats for the purpose of graffiti vandalism. At times, he or she is referred to as the prolific graffiti vandal.

Hip-hop culture: An era that began sometime in the 1970s. It consists of four activities: graffiti making, djaying, master of ceremonies (McEing), and break dancing. They are referred to as the "four elements of hip-hop." Other elements associated with the hip-hop culture may include beat boxing, clothing fashion, language, knowledge, or entrepreneurialism (getting paid by any means necessary).

Hip-hop elements: See tagging culture elements.

Hip-hop graffiti: See hip-hop culture or tagging culture.

Old school graffiti: Graffiti formats and graffiti styles associated with a certain era.

Street gang: Three or more individuals that are constantly engaged in criminal activities; they are generally united under one name, color, or totem. For the purpose of this publication, the four basic gang graffiti formats also are generated by the following groups: delinquent gangs, hybrid gangs, modern groups, and locality-based groups.

Subcultural principles: Any written or unwritten laws that graffiti or gang participants adhere to to gain individual or collective notoriety. As for graffiti participants, subcultural principles will govern the creation, construction, and circulation of the graffiti identity. As for gang participants, subcultural principles can be viewed as the 3 Rs (reputation, respect, or retaliation).

Tagger graffiti: Graffiti formats normally generated by graffiti writers and writer-based graffiti crews, or graffiti artist and artist-based graffiti crews, without being gang-related. At times, the media may express the process of tagger's graffiti as extensive graffiti tagging, graffiti spree, tagging war, series of graffiti writing, multiple graffiti incident, graffiti strike, rash of graffiti vandalism, series of graffiti bombing, widespread graffiti vandalism, making graffiti marking, eyesore of signature, string of graffiti vandalism incident, gang-style tagging, graffiti wave, or numerous counts of graffiti.

Tagging cultural elements: Any distinct pattern, design, or totem linked to the hip-hop graffiti culture or the tagger's culture. Some examples include shines, 3-point crown, halo, clouds, bits, breaking points, extensions, chips, arrows, b-boy or b-girl cartoons, hearts, etc.

Territorial acronym(s): A graffiti format that conveys the group's name or claimed region within a jurisdiction (see ta [territorial acronyms] series).

Offline Resources

Christensen, L. 1999. *Gangbangers: Understanding the Deadly Minds of America's Street Gangs.* Boulder, CO: Paladin Press.

Davis, K. 2011. *TAG 18.3: Graffiti and Its Vandalism Characteristics Within the City of Yonkers, NY, 1990–2000.* Graffiti & Gang Specialist.

Grody, S. 2007. *Graffiti LA Street Styles and Art.* New York: Harry N. Abrams.

Phillips, S. 1999. *Wallbangin: Graffiti and Gangs in LA.* Chicago: University of Chicago Press.

Savelli, L., R. Cekada, and A. Mottola. 2007. *Graffiti Pocket Guide.* Flushing, NY: Looseleaf Law Publications.e

Valentine, B., and R. Schober. 2000. *Gangs and Their Tattoos: Identifying Gangbangers on the Street and in Prison.* Boulder, CO: Paladin Press.

Online Resources

Alsonso, A. *Gang graffiti*. Online at Alex, http://www.streetgangs.com/graffiti/.
Nawojczyk, S. *Street gang dynamics*. Online at http://www.gangwar.com/dynamics. htm.
National Gang Crime Research Center. *Gang profiles*. Online at http://www.ngcrc. com/profile/profile.html.
Walker, R. *Gangs or us*. Online at http://www.gangsorus.com/graffiti.html.

References

Allen, M. 1993. Yonkers cop studies the graffiti on the wall. *Gannett Suburban Newspapers*, October 17, p. 3A.
Barnard, . 2007. *Understanding and Investigating Graffiti*. Parker, CO: Outskirts Press.
Ferris, M. 2002. Graffiti as art, as a gang tag, as a mess. *The New York Times–Westchester Weekly*, September 8, section 14.
Fitz-Gibbon, J. 1992. Off the wall idea not so crazy. *Gannett Suburban Newspapers*, August 16.
O'Connor, J. V. 2000. Special unit quells gangs in Yonkers. *The New York Times–Westchester Weekly*, April 30, section 15.
Thrasher, F. M. 1927. *The Gang: A Study of 1,313 Gangs in Chicago*. Chicago: University of Chicago Press.
Waldo, D. (Sgt). 2005. *Taggers & Graffiti Investigations*. San Bernardino Police Department, CA.

11

In Defense of a Gang Member
Sample Gang Expert Witness Report

GREGORIO ESTEVANE

Contents

The following is an example of a report to a defense attorney by a gang expert witness.

In re: *People v. Frank (Last Name)*
Superior Court County of Los Angeles
Case #
Long Beach, Dept E

Purpose

The purpose of this expert evaluation is to show that the gang definitions, gang membership definitions, nongang crimes allegedly committed by gang members and nongang members may or may not reach the requirements of P.C. 186.22.* Gang crime statistics, academic literature, socioinvestigation into client's day-to-day lifestyle, and research on and inside the alleged gang allow separately or collectively to better assess if a client's alleged actions are or are not at the direction of, in association with, or for the benefit of a gang.

In addition, the purpose of this evaluation is to analyze the foundations and basis for the police gang experts' sworn expert witness testimony provided at trial and or at preliminary hearings.

Standard

Legal Standard of Review: Beyond a Reasonable Doubt

There must be some competent evidence to support each and every element of the offense, or the finding must fail. Though circumstantial evidence may be considered in making the determination, all inferences must be reasonable, and any inferences that derive from speculation, conjecture, or guesswork must be discarded.

Police gang expert speculation alone that an alleged criminal event was at the direction of, in association with, or for the benefit of a gang is insufficient to support the enhancements.

California Penal Code section 186.22 (b) applies when a person commits a crime for the benefit of, at the direction of, or in association with a criminal street gang, and that person specifically intends to assist further or promote criminal conduct by gang members.

The prosecution's only evidence on this point may be the opinion testimony of its gang expert officer. The police gang experts will undoubtedly testify that the client allegedly committed the crime for the benefit of, at the direction of, or in association with the gang and that the client had the specific intent to further his or her criminal conduct.

There are no facts, only the opinions of the prosecution police gang expert testimony, or cause to believe that the client had specific intent to commit a crime for the benefit of, at the direction of, or in association with a criminal street gang. The police gang expert is only using the client's past association to create a false nexus to the current allegations.

---

* See Appendix C.

Section 186.22 (b) criminalizes conduct, not mere association. Here, the prosecution is merely bootstrapping prior association, e.g., drinking in a bar where an alleged Mexican Mafia member was also drinking, to the current charges. In essence, " it is dirtying up the defendant with prior conduct" without any other facts that create specific intent (where none exists) for the current gang enhancement.

Even if assuming the client admitted gang membership or criminal association with the Mexican Mafia, which the client vehemently denies, that association only is insufficient. The second element of subdivision (b) of section 186.22 requires that the defendant have "the specific intent to promote, further, or assist in any criminal conduct by gang members" (facts that show there was direction of, association with, or benefit to the gang).

Evidence of Gang Membership Alone Is Insufficient

Gang membership alone does not show that a crime is committed for the benefit of, at the direction of, or in association with a criminal street gang. Gang enhancements require "some evidentiary support," other than merely the defendant's record of prior offenses and past gang activities or personal affiliations, for a finding that a specific crime was committed with specific intent for the benefit of, at the direction of, or in association with a criminal street gang.

Consequently, even if the court assumes that the client is an active or even past gang member, that alone is insufficient to support the gang enhancement.

The only evidence concerning the purpose of the alleged crimes will be the opinion testimony of the police gang expert. The police gang experts will, opine that this was "only" part of gang intimidation; that there could not be any other alternate explanation, such as personal motivated conduct.

However, no evidence was presented to show that any particular gang was involved at the scene of the crime, nor was a particular gang identity mentioned at the scene of the crime, before, during, or after the incident; or that there was any gang bragging, gang graffiti, witness interviews of gang-intimidated public people, or gang acceptance of responsibility after the incident that would benefit the gang's reputation.

To derive specific intent from only the police expert testimony is overreaching. Nowhere is there any indication in the alleged crime that it was directed by any gang, gang leader, or gang member.

Nowhere is there any fact that this alleged crime was done in association with gang members.

Further, the police gang expert will admit at trial that not all crime is gang-related even when committed by gang members. For instance, a Mexican Mafia associate could kill another out of pure personal revenge for insulting his wife, by way of example, and if that victim of the killing was a Mexican Mafia associate as well, this would still not qualify as a P.C. 186 crime.

The Court of Appeal considered a similar question in the 2007 *People v. Albarran* case. In *Albarran*, a known gang member and an accomplice shot at a house during a private party hosted by a man from another gang.

The prosecution relied solely on the expert testimony to prove gang benefit. The expert testified that Albarran was a gang member, had gang tattoos, a gang moniker, and gang graffiti in his home.

Though no gang names or signs were displayed during the incident, the gang expert "insisted that the shooters would gain respect within the gang absent such evidence," and that "by word of mouth, word on the street, it was known the … gang was at the party."

In reversing the gang enhancement conviction, the Court of Appeal held, "[T]here was insufficient evidence to support the contention that this shooting was done with the intent to gain respect. … [T]he motive for the underlying crimes, in particular the shooting … was not apparent from the circumstances of the crime,"

Despite the expert's opinion that the crime was committed to gain respect, the court disagreed, holding:

> "… this shooting presented no signs of gang member's efforts in that regard; there was no evidence that the shooters announced their presence or purpose—before, during or after the shooting." The court also found it significant that "[t]here was no evidence presented that any gang members had 'bragged' about their involvement or created graffiti and took credit for it." In conclusion, the Court ruled "[t]here is nothing inherent in the facts of the shooting to suggest any specific gang motive. In the final analysis, the only evidence to support the "respect" motive is the fact of (defendant's) gang affiliation.

Here, there is no evidence that the client used any gang name term, gang graffiti, gang name, gang bragging, or a gang purpose at any time specifically. There is no suggestion that the gang members bragged to others or sought to take credit for this crime. Like *Albarran*, here there is no evidence to suggest that the client's actions were motivated by any specific gang motive.

Just as the expert's testimony in *Albarran* (**People v. Albarran (2007) 149 Cal.App.4th 214**iled to prove gang's benefit, the expert's conclusory statements that a shooting confers a a gang benefit fails "to suggest a gang motive".

Moreover, *In re: Frank S. (name)* held that expert opinion testimony on the issue of specific intent was improper. While the fact finder may rely on expert testimony about gang culture and habits to determine a gang allegation, the court cannot rely on expert opinion alone to show that "a specific individual possessed a specific intent."

In *Frank S.*, a gang expert testified that Frank, who was charged with illegal weapons possession, was a gang member. Frank had identified himself as a gang member during intake, wore gang clothing, and admitted that he carried the knife to protect himself against other gang members.

The expert testified that the minor possessed the weapon to protect himself against rival gang members and to assault rival gangs, and those weapons help the gang members protect themselves if they should be assaulted.

In reversing the gang allegation, the Court of Appeal found "no substantial evidence supporting the specific intent element."

The court expressly found that "[w]hile the evidence established that the minor has an affiliation with [the gang], membership alone does not prove a specific intent to use the knife to promote, further, or assist in criminal conduct of gang members."

The recent Ramon Vs. People v. Ramon;No. F054603; 175 Cal.App.4th 843 (2009) case also supports an interesting gang enhancement conclusion. There, Ramon and another gang member were driving a stolen car and were in the possession of guns on gang turf when stopped. The Court of Appeal reversed the conviction.

Thus, the police gang expert opinion as to why the client was shooting without some indication that the targets were gang members is improper expert testimony. Indeed, the police gang expert does not even try to suggest these people are likely members. The police gang expert's reliance on the client's alleged gang status is not enough to show gang benefit, as illustrated by *Albarran*, *Frank S.*, and *Ramon*.

The prosecution has the burden of proving beyond a reasonable doubt the elements of California Penal Code section 186.22. Therefore, the prosecution has the burden of proving beyond a reasonable doubt that the client had "specific intent" to commit a felony "for the benefit of, at the direction of, or in association with any criminal street gang, with the specific intent to promote, further, or assist in any criminal conduct by gang members. ..." (Penal Code section 186.22 (b)(1)).

People v. Gardelely, 59 Cal. Rptr. 2d 356, qualifies expert witnesses to testify at criminal street gang trials. Gardeley states the following:

> Under Evid. Code, ß 801, expert opinion testimony is admissible only if the subject matter of the testimony is "sufficiently beyond common experience that the opinion of an expert would assist the trier of fact (Evid. Code, ß 801, subd. (a)).

The subject matter of the culture and habits of criminal street gangs meets this criterion.

An expert generally may render opinion testimony on the basis of facts given in a hypothetical question that asks the expert to assume their truth.

Such a hypothetical question must be rooted in facts shown by the evidence, however.

Expert testimony also may be premised on material that is not admitted into evidence, so long as it is material of a type that is reasonably relied upon by experts in the particular field in forming their opinions (Evid. Code, ß 801, subd. (b)).

Of course, any material that forms the basis of an expert's opinion testimony must be reliable, because an expert's opinion is no better than the facts on which it is based. So long as this threshold requirement of reliability is satisfied, even matter that is ordinarily inadmissible can form the proper basis for an expert's opinion testimony. And, because Evid. Code, ß 802, allows an expert witness to "state on direct examination the reasons for his opinion and the matter ... upon which it is based," an expert witness whose opinion is based on such inadmissible matter can, when testifying, describe the material that forms the basis of the opinion.

Prosecutor and Police Standards of Gang Evidence

A 2009 University of California Hastings College of the Law article in the *Hastings Race and Poverty Law Journal* (7 Hastings Race & Poverty L.J. 111) illustrates the power that prosecutors' gang experts have in gang trials.

> Prosecutors often call gang experts to testify for two purposes: (1) to give testimony involving statutory gang allegations under the STEP Act, and (2) to give testimony involving some other material issue which may be in dispute, such as identity, motive, bias, or knowledge.

The police officer gang expert has considerable evidentiary power. While testifying, the gang expert will often justify his or her opinion by making universalizing assertions about the nature of gang culture that transcend the gang at issue.

While California Penal Code sections 186.22(a), (b), and (d) are not identical, each of the provisions have certain required elements in common. Described most broadly, they each require proof of the existence of a "criminal street gang" and proof that the offense in question was gang-related. The "gang-related" requirement takes two forms, depending on whether the prosecution is attempting to prove the substantive offense (section 186.22(a)) or attempting to prove the sentence enhancement or alternate penalty (sections 186.22(b) & (c)).

For the substantive offense, gang expert testimony is used to prove that there was a pattern of gang activity by the members of the gang; that the defendant had knowledge of that pattern; and that he or she willfully promotes, furthers, or assists in felonious conduct by members of the gang. Further, there must be a showing that the defendant was an active participant.

In order to satisfy the gang-related element for the enhancement and alternate penalty, the prosecution's police gang expert must prove that an offense has been committed for the benefit of, at the direction of, or in association with a criminal street gang.

In sum, police gang experts will often testify to one or more of four elements when testifying in a case where the defendant is charged with an offense under the California Street Terrorism Enforcement and Prevention Act (STEPAct):

1. Existence of a criminal street gang
2. Commission of the crime for the benefit of, at the direction of, or in association with the gang
3. Commission of the crime to promote, further, or assist the gang
4. Active participation of the defendant in the gang

Defense Gang Expert Witness versus Police Gang Expert Witness Are Not the Same

As a fundamental pillar of the adversarial system, a defense attorney has an obligation to make every ethical effort to introduce reasonable doubt.

In the matter at hand, failing to call an expert witness to rebut the testimony of the prosecution's gang expert witness could be a failure to adequately represent his/her client.

Defense gang experts—whether having gained their experience in the streets as investigators, in the halls of academia, in research, as former gang members, as nonprofit gang interventionists, as news reporters specializing in the gang beat, at outreach centers like Father Greg Boyle's Homeboy Industries, as part of religious antigang outreach (churches of all faiths), as social workers, as defense investigators, as the police, or in other ways—do NOT evaluate the alleged gang enhancements charges in the same manner as the police gang expert, and such defense experts should not be held to the lower police gang expert standard either in qualifying as an expert or in their substantive testimony and opinion on the alleged gang enhancement(s).

Rule no. 1 for gangs: *Do not talk or rat to the police.* Violation of this rule can and often has led to a gang-imposed death penalty for cooperating with the police. Therefore, police are more often than not at the bottom of the list of those with gang knowledge. Police testimony that they speak to gang members all of the time, unfortunately, is an attempt to overcome what the police know they can, by force of law, stop alleged gang members or associates speaking with the police; however, the police rarely get inside gang information on or what the gang is doing. "Ratting" or giving the police actionable information is quite different than being forced to talk to the police.

The defense gang expert, by contrast, is literarily invited to the dinner table of the gang members, gang leaders, and gang families at their homes, with the police gang expert rarely, if ever, having access to the inner workings of the gang, gang members, or gang family members.

Defense gang experts are focused on the behavior, background, and lifestyle of the client. With those client behaviors and lifestyles *not* being gang related, they rarely delve into the specifics of a particular gang, i.e., history, boundaries, graffiti, signs, or similar areas.

The defense gang expert assertion is most often twofold: (1) the crime does not fit a gang crime, with the crime more closely resembling crime motivated by personal benefit (not gang benefit); and (2) whether the client's motivation in committing the crime was personal (not in association with, at the direction of, or for the benefit of a gang), regardless if the client is a gang member or not, as gang members commit personal crimes more often than gang crimes.

The defense gang expert defense standard is to prove that the client's lifestyle and behavior is nongang related, not to prove the details or history of the alleged gang.

Therefore, it is unhelpful to the jury, in the legal defense of an accused person, to attempt to render a defense gang expert to the same standards of expertise as that of the police gang expert, as police methodologies and basis of their police expert opinions are diametrically opposed. Additionally, standards and techniques differentiate police gang experts from defense gang experts in determining if the alleged crime could be articulated as personally motivated (not gang motivated, thus not qualifying as directed by, associated with, or benefitting a gang), regardless if the client is an actual gang member or not; this is in stark contrast to cop experts who usually operate with gang member-based theories only.

Gang members more often than not commit crimes that are personally motivated, without regard to direction, association, or benefit to any gang, as illustrated in police department and county sheriff's annual crimes stats that mark gang-motivated crimes as a very small portion of overall crime. Gang stats from 2008 show that only approximately 20 percent of all aggravated shootings were gang related, thus, approximately 80 percent of all shootings [gang member- and nongang member-based] were nongang related. These gang illustrations are similar for most cities in California; gang crime is a very small percentage of overall crime.

Ultimately, if the defense gang expert comes to an expert opinion on the gang allegation for the defense, it is couched in terms of the client's nongang behavior and the facts surrounding how the crime was committed because, most often, the defense gang expert has much more indicia of a personal benefit-oriented crime in contrast to that of a crime that is directed by, associated with, or benefiting a gang. Thus, there is little focus or defense expertise needed on the actual gang, gang history, territory, gang signs, or other gang specific data, because the defense expert focus is on the behaviors of the client and the personal nature of the alleged crime, not the specific gang.

Defense Gang Expert Foundation/Quantitative and Qualitative Methods of Analysis

A defense gang expert opinion may rely on any, or more, of three analytical methods alone or in combination thereof in rendering an expert gang opinion:

1. **Academic** data analysis, research, publications, surveys, review of books, other materials that relate to what may or may not be indicia of gang membership or activities that can be for personal gain and not for the benefit of the gang.
2. **Sociogang evaluation/qualitative investigative field work:** Field interviews of family members, friends, religious leaders, employers, coworkers, or neighbors; and sporting activities, community service activities, educational endeavors, investigation into medical or mental treatments and others.
3. **Contact or research on gang/former members:** Original gangsters (OGs [gang leaders]), gang interventionists, or other aspects having knowledge of the alleged gang and or its members. The information may determine a lack of any direction, association, or benefit relationship with the alleged gang by the client at the time of the alleged offense(s).

Definition of Gang Crime
Classically, there are at least two definitions of gang crime:

Gang-related crime is where all crimes are committed by individuals, who are believed to be members of a criminal street gang, and are treated as gang-related, regardless of the offense or the circumstances surrounding the crime.

Gang-motivated crime includes only crimes that have been committed for the benefit of, direction of, or in association with the gang or as part of a gang function.

Typically, many quasi-modern thinking law enforcement/prosecutorial agencies trend toward gang-related filings with strategic methods at trial that outline a protracted discussion of the terror of the gang, in contrast to whether the crime was truly gang-motivated.

In 2001, criminology experts Cheryl Maxson and Malcolm Klein examined police reports in South Central Los Angeles and found that a motive-based definition reduced by half the amount of gang homicides committed by gang members. Consider the following illustrative examples:

1. A gang member shoots and wounds another gang member for transgressions with his girlfriend (a gang member as well).
2. A gang member (who is angry that day) spontaneously assaults and kills a person for no apparent reason.

Neither of the above two examples would count as gang-motivated crimes under the gang-motive definition. In example 1, the motive had nothing to do with the gang and was rather an event of highly personal jealousy. In example 2, the crime was initiated spontaneously by the angry individual, who happened to be a gang member.

Paradoxically, both of these crimes would unjustly count as gang crimes under the gang-related (member-based) definition of a gang crime.

Therefore, "gang-motivated methodologies can give us a clearer answer as to what is a gang crime or is not. In using hang-motivated methodologies, we also can further extract out gang-directed crimes that are commissioned or orchestrated by gang leaders, or the gang as a whole, that which advances the interests of leaders or the gang as a whole" (Justice Policy Institute, 2007).

Gang and Nongang Violence

A review of the research on gang violence reveals an overall misconception about the rate of gang violence.

According to Miethe and McCorkle (2002), between 1989 and 1995, defendants who are alleged to be gang members accounted for just 6 percent of violent crimes and 5 percent of drug charges in Las Vegas. Fritsch, Caeti, and Taylor (2003) found that Dallas gang-related offenses accounted for less than 10 percent of serious violent crime. And, in California, Kent et al. (2000) came to the same conclusion in studies of a gang task force in Westminster, California, that showed rates of gang violence at 7 percent to 8 percent of all crime.

These data are in stark contrast to the media frenzy that "... those hordes of gangs are enveloping our cities" and is consistent with the National Crime Victimization Survey (Ziedenberg, 2005) that shows that gang members were responsible for only a small share (6 percent) of the violent crime from 1998 to 2003.

The Federal Bureau of Investigation's (FBI) Uniform Crime Reporting (UCR) program recorded more than 14 million serious (Par 1) violent and property crimes in 1993 nationally from cities across the United States. Only

3.1 percent to 4.1 percent (440,000 to 560,000) of these 14 million crimes were attributed to gang members nationally.

Another factor to consider when assessing gang violence is whether the gang violence is actually a benefit for the gang.

In *Youth Gangs in American Society*, Sheldon, Tracy, and Brown (2004) stated that "... acts of violence committed by gang members acting on their own do not represent gang violence and also do not occur because they are members of a gang. These acts are related to gangs only in the sense that the individuals involved have defiant individualist character traits (gang motive crimes versus gang member crimes). Violence results from the connections between the emotions of fear, ambition, frustration, testing of skills and the encounters during which such emotions are apparent."

Police department and county sheriff's annual crimes statistics routinely show that gang-motivated crimes are a very small portion of overall crime (gang statistics show that approximately 20 percent of all aggravated shootings are generally gang related; therefore, approximately 80 percent of all shootings (gang member and nongang member-based) were non-gang related).

Thus, real gang members most often commit crimes that have no nexus to P.C. 186, with the majority of non-P.C. 186 crimes committed by actual gang members and have nothing to do with the direction of, association with, or for the benefit of any gang.

Criminal Sophistication of Street Gangs and Members

On April 20, 2005, Chris Swecker, assistant director, Criminal Investigative Division, Federal Bureau of Investigation, issued a statement before the subcommittee on the Western Hemisphere House International Relations Committee, whereby he summed up criminal street gang sophistication by stating:

> ... the gang is still a loosely structured street gang; however, its threat is based on its violence and its potential to grow, not only geographically, but *in its organization and sophistication*. There is some evidence of an *increased level of sophistication* and some indications of a *hierarchy of leadership*. This is based in part on reports of *multiclique meetings* in which gang members pay a fee to attend, coordinate their activities, exchange information regarding law enforcement actions and efforts, and issue punishment and/or sanctions for infractions of the *gang's code*. Cliques throughout the country often follow the lead of the Los Angeles-based cliques, and there are reports of Los Angeles-based members traveling throughout the United States for the purpose of recruiting new members, establishing new cliques, and taking over existing Latino gangs, and instilling discipline through violence and intimidation. ...

Similarly, Jankowski's (1990) study of gang members in three large cities included data that *gangs can be sophisticated*, which requires leadership, strategic planning, and time-lined tactics in areas such as:

Services: The most common are protection, demolition of property (usually arson), and prostitution. The most common form of protection involves extortion. Gangs also provide services to punish others, such as loan sharks may hire gangs for collections. Murder for hire is a more sophisticated violent service and other similar homicides. The El Rukins (Blood gang i.e., Black P Stones) gang is another example, as they were hired by Libyans to act as terrorists in the United States and abroad.

Other forms of sophistication in violence suggest planning in committing murders of rivals with intelligence gathering, surveillance, lookouts, using GPS, Twitter, and other deployed tactics, according to a survey of 500 LA gang members by Estevane and Khatibloo (2013).

Leaving the Gang

The criminal street gang myth—blood in, blood out, by death or death in prison—is a myth. Nothing could be farther from the truth. Deck and Van Winkle (1996) found the typical gang member is active for a year or less. Esbensen and colleagues (2001) surveyed more than 5,000 people and detailed that the large majority of members quit after a brief stay in the gang, noting gang membership is "… a rather fleeting experience for the most of these youth. Half of the male gang members reported being in a gang for one year or less, and only 7 percent reported being a gang member for more than four years. Two-thirds of the females were in a gang for less than one year, with almost all or none reporting membership for over four years."

Jesuit priest Father Greg Boyle, who founded Homeboy Industries, a program that specializes in the rehabilitation of gang members (usually *veteranos* in leadership from "the life of gangs") works with those same gang members who want and do leave the gang lifestyle. Father Boyle observes gang members leave gangs and do stay gang free on many occasions.

Gang Labeling

Winfree, Esbensen, and Taylor (2001) call for help in focusing on behavior rather than gang membership. "Given the permeability of gang membership, policies linking legal action to an individual's perceived status may erroneously criminalize that individual. As such, we suggest that legislation targeting gang status should be discouraged in favor of legislation that focuses on actual behavior."

Research suggests that gang control policies that fix the gang label on youths do the opposite of getting them out of gangs as soon as possible; they keep former gang members or even worse, fringe "wannabe" gang bangers from acquiring work or social skills they need in order to survive in mainstream society during the most formative and critical time in their lives from 17 to 25 years of age.

Some gang policies deter youths from leaving the gang by ensuring that they will be treated as pariahs no matter what they do, or tragically push fringe associations into full-blown gang membership where none previously existed.

Sociogang Evaluation/Qualitative Investigative Field Work

As a defense gang expert, field interviews may be conducted and testified to at trial as an expert witness exception to hearsay as the basis of the expert opinion rather than for the truth of the hearsay. These field interviews may outline a "day in the life of an alleged client," showing a day-to-day lifestyle—work, church, spouse, kids, family, sports, education, etc., all of which would be inconsistent with the demanding aspects of being a gang member.

All loyalty, time, effort, and work goes directly to the gang and the gang's ongoing criminal activities as a gang member, with any contrary evidence utilized to support the reasonable conclusion that a person is not doing acts to benefit a gang if that same person is living a lawful life as a law-obeying citizen.

Factual Summary and Issue(s)

The client is alleged to be a gang member or to have committed a criminal act for the benefit of, in association with, or at the direction of a criminal street gang, which he strongly denies.

Arguments will be made that the Mexican Mafia is not a criminal street gang and is more than its origins as a prison gang; the Mexican Mafia, much like La Costa Nostra (The Italian Mafia), are a transnational group of crime organizations.

The client is alleged to have committed a crime in furtherance of a criminal street gang under P.C. 186, as well as other charges. The focus of this evaluation is the P.C. 186 charge:

1. Can the alleged acts be motivated by personal reasons rather than gang-related?

    There are no facts that the crime at the bar was gang motivated, other than the opinion of the police gang expert. Therefore, it is equally plausible that this alleged crime could have been fueled by personal reasons. There are some facts in dispute that the alleged victim was a sexual predator and that his murder could have been a personal revenge killing. The state has not met the burden of proof.

2. Do gang members and nongang members commit acts, criminal acts, which are for personal benefit and not for the benefit of a gang?

   As stated earlier, approximately 80 percent of all crimes committed are *not* gang-related. Gang members commit the majority of their crimes for personal benefit. There are no facts presented in this case that alleged acts were committed for, on behalf, in association with, or to benefit a gang.

3. Do the facts surrounding the alleged crimes suggest crimes of opportunity or a sophisticated, orchestrated, criminally driven endeavor of a committed strategic criminal lifestyle?

   This alleged crime presents as an immediate crime of opportunity with little or no indicia of planning or sophistication, without any clear facts as to gang benefit. No gang cries out loud before or during the crime, no follow-up gang graffiti, no witnesses that there was fear in the community were present as evidence in this case.

Gang Expert Opinion

Legal Standard: Beyond a Reasonable Doubt

Unfortunately, in the pantheon of excessive prosecutorial modern gang enhancement filings, this case, however, factually fascinating, trots out the same tired dogged attempts to "dirty up a defendant with past alleged gang associations" while leashing that past associations onto an unrelated current matter that has no real gang indicia or, at best, dual explanations of personal conduct or gang conduct. P.C. 186 is a specific intent crime requiring that there is proof, other than a police expert, that the alleged acts were committed for the benefit of, at the direction of, or in association with a specific criminal street gang.

Based upon my review of this case, as stated above, it is my opinion that there exists doubt that the client allegedly committed the acts at the direction of, in association with, or for the benefit of a gang in the instant matter.

Thank you,

(Signature)
Gregorio 'Greg' Estevane, P.I.:J.D.

DP Mitigation/Gang Investigator/CJ Professor
ASTIS Consulting

GE/im: enclosures

References

Estevane, G. and M. Khatibloo. 2013.

Taylor, R.W., Fritsch, E.J., and Caeti, T.J. (2006). *Juvenile Justice: Policies, Programs, and Practices, Second Edition*. McGraw-Hill College. New York.

Sánchez-Jankowski, M. (1990). *Islands in the Street. Gangs and American Urban Society*. UC Press. Berkley, California.

Justice Policy Institute. 2007. *Gang Wars: The Failure of Enforcement Tactics and the Need for Effective Public Safety Strategies*. Washington, D.C., July.

Kent, D.R, Donaldson, S. I., Wyrick, P.A., and. Smith, P.J. (200). "Evaluating criminal justice programs designed to reduce crime by targeting repeat gang offenders." Paper. Claremont Graduate University. Claremont, California.

McCorkle, R. and Miethe, T. (2002). *Panic: The Social Construction of the Street Gang Problem*. Prenctice Hall. Upper Saddle River, NJ.

Sheldon, R. G., S. K. Tracy, and W. B. Brown. 2004. *Youth Gangs in American Society*. Belmont, CA: Thomson Wadsworth.

Evensen, F.A., Winfree, L.T.. He, Jr., N.. and Taylor, T.J. (2001). Youth gangs and defintional issues: When is a gang, a gang, and why does it matter? *Crime and Delinquency*, 47(1):105–130.

Ziedenberg. 2005.

Evolution of Gangs from History to Today

Predictions and Recommendations for the Future

12

JOHNNIE (LAST NAME ANONYMOUS DUE
TO EMPLOYMENT RESTRICTIONS)

Contents

Introduction

Today's worldwide society, particularly in the United States, is faced with a threat the public, and even most law enforcement personnel, are not totally aware of. The menace is the growing evolution from "gangs to terrorist." Prior to discussing this development in detail and analyzing the trends, we need to understand their foundations. The US Department of Defense Dictionary of Military Terms defines terrorism as: *The calculated use of unlawful violence or threat of unlawful violence to inculcate fear; intended to coerce or to intimidate governments or societies in the pursuit of goals that are generally political, religious, or ideological.* The FBI defines terrorism as: *The unlawful use of force or violence against persons or property to intimidate or coerce a government, the civilian population, or any segment thereof, in furtherance of political or social objectives.* Obviously, both definitions focus on a common goal: political objectives. According to an online dictionary, *A gang is defined as a group of people, through the organization, formation, and establishment of an assemblage, share a common identity. In current usage it typically denotes a criminal organization or, else, a criminal affiliation.*

How did everything get started? Overall, gang members generally come from broken homes or dysfunctional families. Teenagers who became parents and have kids beyond their control, dropping out or getting kicked out of school for various reasons, and unemployment are also some of the main grounds why many individuals join gangs. The bottom line refrain mentioned several times previously in this book is: *Joining the gang is like starting a new family.* Organized street gangs take good care of and constantly reinforce each other. Getting recognized in the society, in the world, and recognition and receiving emotional support from gang members is another main motivation.

In the early 1960s, Black P. Stone Nation became one of the most notorious Chicago-based gangs. The leader of this gang was Jeff Fort. The gang started with only a few members, but due to its greed and demand for power and respect, Black P. Stone started to merge with other gangs having the same ideologies, spreading throughout all of Chicago, especially the south side of the city. The most critical part was when the group decided to collaborate with Muammar Gaddafi of Libya and planned to commit terrorist acts within the United States in the mid-1980s.

The collaboration between Jeff Fort's Black P. Stone Nation, and Libyan terrorist groups was considered to be the first nexus between gangs and terrorists on American soil. Fortunately, the plan for terrorist acts was unfolded and thwarted by US law enforcement.

The world famous dirty bomber, Abdullah al-Muhajir or Muhajir Abdullah, also known as Jose Padilla, is also another prime example of how gang members in the United States had ties to al-Qaeda. Jose Padilla worked his way up the ranks, from an ordinary street gang member in Chicago to be one of the key players with significant ties to al-Qaeda.

Born and raised in Brooklyn, New York, Padilla relocated to Chicago. He was a troubled kid and, not surprisingly, decided to join a street gang: the Maniac Latin Disciples. As a gang member, he constantly committed petty crimes, and was arrested by local authorities numerous times. He was in and out of police stations as often as a frequent flyer uses the passenger lounge.[1]

One of the common procedures for a Latino gang member is to have several aliases with the intention to throw authorities off track when they conduct records or background checks. In this case, Padilla used and maintained aliases such as Jose Rivera, Jose Ortiz, Jose Ibrahim Padilla, and Jose Hernandez. The world recognizes him today as Jose Padilla, The Dirty Bomber.

In 1990, Padilla converted to Islam during one of his times in prison. His religious instructor was Adham Amin Hassoun. Both were good friends and known to attend Masjid Al-Iman mosque in Fort Lauderdale, Florida. Whether Padilla was aware or not, Hassoun was once accused by law enforcement of consorting with radical Islamic fundamentalists, including the world notorious al-Qaeda. In 2002, Hassoun was arrested by the US Department of Homeland Security for overstaying his visa. Hassoun's case was built up, "dots were connected," and he was charged with weapons offenses, perjury, and similar other charges.

Padilla moved on with his life and married Shamia, an Egyptian immigrant. They had two sons, believed now to be somewhere in the Middle East. Supported by terrorist funding, Padilla became a frequent traveler, especially between 2001 and 2002 when he travelled to Afghanistan and Pakistan. It was reported that Padilla was trained to a professional level in employment and construction of radiologic weapons also as known as "dirty bombs." Fortunately, he was arrested before he had a chance to commit terrorist acts on American soil. This American-born individual evolved from a regular street gang member to be one of the world's famous international terrorist with focus on imposing death to fellow Americans.

Padilla's case is a wake-up call for everyone in the United States. We all learn that a homegrown terrorist is an extremely dangerous entity and can be extremely difficult to detect. They are categorized as "sleeper cells." They are already here, but we still don't know when or where they are going to commit terrorist acts. We need to be more proactive than reactive. In other words, we need to be ahead of the threat and help prevent terrorist acts by having good intelligence. According to the transcripts of US Court of Appeals for Padilla's case:

In 2002, Padilla's detention as an "enemy combatant" (pursuant to the president's order) was based on the following reasons:

1. Padilla was "closely associated with Al-Qaeda, a designation for loosely knit insurgent groups sharing common ideals and tactics, with which the United States is at war."
2. Padilla engaged in "war-like acts, including conduct in preparation for acts of international terrorism."
3. Padilla had intelligence that could assist the United States in warding off future terrorist attacks.
4. Padilla was a continuing threat to American security.

Jeff Fort and Jose Padilla are only two examples of how regular gang members on American soil evolved into or collaborated with international terrorist organizations, such as al-Qaeda and a terrorist group based in Libya. One of the similarities is recruitment motivation. Both wanted to be accepted to the society, in this case, upgrading to terrorist organizations. They wanted to go global instead of domestic. Ultimately, their dream was to get the world's attention by taking advantage of free publicity in case their operation was successful.

Correctional and jail facilities are full of such individuals. Once inside any penal institution, most of these individuals will try to adapt to the environment, seek protection, social acceptance, and respect from others, thus entering the gateway to gang recruitment. This survival technique applies to any correction facility worldwide.

Gang members, like any criminal element, exploit *good practices* and thrive on manipulations. American citizens enjoy freedom of religion. Incarcerated gang members manipulate this freedom by holding meetings to propagate the gang's agenda. Gang members will minimally educate themselves in the Islamic religion and utilize religion as a cloak in the form of *prayer meetings*. This allows gangs to further their agenda, while being protected under Constitutional law.

Gang Members Successfully Enlisted and Signed Up with the US Armed Forces

Graffiti, gang signs, gang tattoos, etc., for some reason showed up in many places in the Middle East, especially around places where there was US military. How could that happen?

Prior to budget cuts within the US Department of Defense, enlisting or signing to join the US military was not difficult. However, in order to get a good job in the military all depends on the Armed Services Vocational Aptitude Battery (ASVAB) test score. The higher the score, the better job and training they will be offered starting from basic training or boot camp. However, US Army Reserves and National Guard units, compared to other branches within the US military, were the forces most activated to deploy to combat zones in the Middle East.

Early in the morning of October 13, 1992, Davis Dantrell, a 7-year-old boy, was shot and killed by sniper fire from an AR-15 rifle in a housing complex in Chicago. The shooter was arrested and reported to have served in the US Army and was found to be a gang member. The shooting on October 13 was a gang-related situation when Davis Dantrell was at the wrong place and the wrong time. The little boy was walking with his mother on their way to school when he was fatally hit by a stray bullet.

Anonymous survey questionnaires were designed and conducted to measure various aspects of the problem with gang members in military service. The results from the survey revealed that the US Coast Guard was shown to have the lowest estimated current or former gang member population, followed by the Air Force. The US Coast Guard is shown to have a mean estimated former or current gang membership of 6.3 percent, compared with 7.8 percent for the Air Force. It is of some interest that National Guard respondents gave their own outfit the highest mean average of former/current gang membership (mean = 25.6 percent).

Gangs in the Middle East and Ties to Terrorism

In January 2011, gangs in the city of Cairo, Egypt, took the opportunity during the "revolution" against President Mubarak to attack several jails across Egypt. Their main mission was to free hundreds of Muslim militants, other gang members, and several other inmates. Unfortunately, some of the escapees were terrorists that had been hunted worldwide. This perfect opportunity for the gangs arose when Cairo police abandoned and deserted their stations when everything was out of control. The Egyptian government set up curfews and activated the Egyptian army to patrol the streets. However, without the presence of the police force and with untrained military personnel in this kind of situation, the gang members had no fear and easily got away.

The escapees included at least nine senior members of a major gang. Looting and arson, typical standard operating procedures for the gangs, continued until dawn as the police officers totally disappeared from the streets of the capital and several major Egyptian cities. Gangs were also stopping innocent people on the streets and robbing them. Obviously, Cairo police lost the battle. The police in Egypt are well-known for brutality and solving crime in-house behind closed doors. Egyptian security officials reported to the news media, which later also became targets of the police, that army troops were hunting for the escaped prisoners. Only state television within Egypt was able to broadcast footage of what it said were dozens of prisoners recaptured by the Egyptian Army, squatting on dirt while soldiers kept watch over them. However, the main subjects still managed to get away with little or no trial. This is a serious concern for law enforcement worldwide.

This is considered to be one of the most recent examples of seeing the connections between how gang members have the potential to become terrorists and their job of helping terrorists escape from jail, especially from jails in the Middle East. It now resembles: *"Help me, help you."*

In this case, after the crisis in Cairo, it will be the ambient time for the gangs and terrorist to rendezvous and share ideas, tactics, trainings, and intelligence. It's perfect timing for the gangs to be recognized and assigned for worldwide missions. Gangs will be trained by terrorists in many areas, such as countersurveillance, counterintelligence, and how to find case-targeted locations without being detected.

Street gangs and terrorists working together become more symbiotic in their relations and in helping each other out. Street gangs in US and other major cities worldwide are utilizing the drug connections that international terrorist groups need. It's becoming more structured, drugs are easier to obtain for distribution overseas by the terrorists, and, therefore, satisfying the goals of both organizations, especially when there is a great worldwide demand and supply.

Terrorism in US Corrections[2]

Growth of Radical Islam in the US Correctional Systems

Research shows that social networks are very important in explaining how people are recruited into new movements and organizations. The left wing terrorists of the 1970s were connected, as much by the fact that they hung out in the same bar or that they came from the same university as by their ideology, meeting in small informal gatherings, weaving a network of like-minded individuals, discussing political or religious agendas, until they reached a point of intolerance and took decisive action, usually, with bombs and bullets.

Very similar agendas are being played out today with international jihad groups converting recruits to their fanatical religious beliefs. These religious converts are young people coming from local neighborhood gangs who have met, not in training camps in Afghanistan or Pakistan, but in prison. Prison cellblocks, prison classes, yards, recreation areas, and prison chapels are ripe recruiting grounds for conversion to radical religions and should be areas of concern to law enforcement. Those who know the most about the religious lives of prisoners—prison chaplains—agree that inmate conversions take place through friendship and kinship networks. This is especially so for nontraditional groups.

Further research by going into these prisons and interviewing chaplains, gang intelligence officers, and prisoners who have undergone conversion to either Islam or some other non-Judeo-Christian faith, is of importance. Most of the available limited research previously conducted on jailhouse conversion to Islam suggests it is a bona fide religious experience that contributes to prison stability, noting that one of the most famous jailhouse conversions in history was by Malcolm X, who went on to be a positive role model for many African Americans. However, Malcolm X was from a different era—before planes were hijacked and deliberately flown into buildings, and before the US became entangled in difficult wars in Iraq and Afghanistan. Carlos the Jackal, arguably the most famous terrorist of all for his exploits during the 1970s, converted to Islam at the age of 26, right before his most spectacular acts of terrorism, the taking of hostages of the OPEC oil ministers during their conference in 1975.

Prison chaplains agree that membership in a religious group does not necessarily equate with conversion. Individuals can be members of the same group in different ways and with varying degrees of commitment. Moreover, it is possible to participate in religious groups and rituals either with or without assuming a new way of life. Religious involvement among prisoners is a complex phenomenon, motivated by a host of social and psychological factors.

Social and Psychological Factors

1. *The Crisis Convert:* Some prisoners turn to religion for the same reason that many people do: to cope with personal crisis brought on by the loss of a loved one, divorce, illness, drug and alcohol addiction, or (and this is unique to prisoners) emotional trauma caused by the loss of liberty due to incarceration.

2. *The Protection-Seeking Convert:* Membership in a faith group may be motivated by an inmate's need for protection from theft and physical assault (the basis of "wheeling and dealing") through the establishment of a strong cultural identity within the prisoner subculture.

3. *The Searching Convert:* Men and women who come to prison with little or no religious background are suddenly thrown into an environment where religious options abound, and where an estimated one in three inmates participate in some form of religious program. Due to their inexperience with sacred texts, rituals, and the disciplinary practices of religion, some prisoners will stumble in their attempts to find a faith group.

   Some join a religion out of haste, some affiliate with a group out of peer group pressure, and still others become serial joiners, jumping from one religion to another. The searcher is similar to a notion of "conversion careers," a process whereby certain people on spiritual quests are able to assume and subsequently abandon a succession of convert roles.

4. *The Manipulating Convert:* Prisoners may "get religion" for manipulative purposes, such as the right to special diets, access to books, musical instruments, and religious gatherings (including contact with the opposite sex), or the privilege of wearing religious emblems, beads, beards, or various articles of clothing if one's religious beliefs require it. Also, some inmates may hope that prison and parole authorities will view their religious involvement as an attempt to become moral, prosocial, and law-abiding.

5. *The Free-World Recruited Convert:* Membership in a faith group may involve the influence of free-world religious leaders.

6. *Authentic Conversions:* Authentic conversions involve radical personal change—a deep religious experience, one in which the prisoner is "slain in the spirit" through reflection, study, and ritual. As a result, prisoners acknowledge their criminal histories. They become penitent and attempt to redirect the focus of their lives. Authentic conversions are, as the term implies, genuine transformations of the soul. They entail "the displacement of one universe of discourse by another or the ascendance of a formerly peripheral universe of discourse to the status of a primary authority." Authentic conversions are thought to occur more often in maximum security prisons, with their stringent control mechanisms, scarce resources and programs, and a greater number of serious felons, than in lower-custody institutions with fewer controls, more leisure time activities, and fewer violent offenders.

The so-called homegrown groups of young people, who could be organized in prisons, now pose a greater risk than the al-Qaeda organization currently based in Afghanistan and Pakistan. Those responsible for terrorist attacks on Jewish targets in Casablanca, Morocco, in 2003; the Madrid train bombing in 2004; and the London bus bombings of 2005 were all "homegrown." Each incident involved retaliation against American involvement in Iraq.

Typically, prisoners engage in intensive interaction with whose recruitment efforts involve prison visits, along with their distribution of newsletters and religious materials to prisoners, and the promise of after-care resources for them (jobs, housing, education, etc.).

In the United States, the yearly number of conversions to Islam in municipal, state, and federal correctional institutions is estimated at 30,000—perhaps as many as 40,000. Based on these estimates, some 175,000 American prisoners have converted to Islam since the 9/11 attacks.

Muslims comprise about 6 percent of the 173,000 prisoners incarcerated in the Federal Bureau of Prisons (not including inmates who belong to the Nation of Islam or Moorish Science Temple). Muslims make up about 18 percent of the 63,700 inmates in New York state prisons; 18 percent of the 41,000 state prisoners in Pennsylvania; and, in California, where religious affiliation is not tracked, officials estimate that there could be thousands of Muslim prisoners in the system.

Moreover, 9/11 has brought new scrutiny of Muslim prisoners in America. A 2005 ambitious nationwide investigation of chaplains, prison volunteers, correctional officials, inmates, and former inmates affirms that there are opposing views about Islam in prison today. One side of the debate takes the position that Islam offers prisoners a viable path to rehabilitation. There is considerable social-psychological evidence to confirm this position. Research shows that involvement in religion contributes to feelings of well-being, reduces stress, and increases general health.

Indeed, the majority of those interviewed, including administrators, insist there is no evidence of terrorist recruitment by Muslims in their prisons. This squares with other media reporting, including a 2005 investigation that shows that prison officials in New York, Pennsylvania, and Ohio—states with large Muslim inmate populations—have seen no signs of terrorist recruiting.

According to these reports, the typical prison convert to Islam is a poor, black American upset about racism, not Middle East politics; someone who became a Muslim to cope with the pains of imprisonment, not to fulfill a religious obligation to Islamic law, al-Qaeda, or other nonspecific terrorist organizations.

Although some prisoners become Muslim in name only, either to seek protection from gangs or to take advantage of dietary or meeting privileges, others undergo an authentic conversion that helps them interact with other inmates in a positive manner. Whatever the motivation for converting to the religion, Islam provides a self-imposed discipline on inmates which, in turn, gives prison authorities a convenient force to help them maintain order.

Islamism in prison is not without its problems, so goes the argument, but they pale in comparison to the dangers posed by such prison gangs as the Crips, the Gangster Disciples, Mara Salvatrucha (MS-13), and the notorious Aryan Brotherhood.

The opposing side of the argument claims that Islamic prisoners represent a clear and present danger to the United States. Central to this concern is the fact al-Quaeda training manuals identify America's prison populationas candidates for conversion. This concern can be traced to radically conservative Wahhabiism in Saudi Arabia spending billions of dollars promoting Wahhabi Islam (a narrow, strict, puritanical form of Sunni Islam upon which the ideology of al-Qaeda is based). It is claimed that the Saudis have supplied "money that has been spent on funding leading terrorist and other extremist organizations that disseminate hatred in 'education centers,' charities, mosques, and even prisons—including many here in the United States." Other experts contend that nearly 10,000 copies of the Wahhabi Quran have been distributed to American prisoners. Alarmists were quick to charge that Saudi-trained imams had been "granted an exclusive franchise for Muslim religious instruction" at prisons.

A key factor in the spread of Wahhabi Islam is a shortage of "suitable" qualified modern or more liberal Muslim clerics available to work in prisons, combined with an inability on the part of correctional authorities to differentiate radical Islam from more moderate streams of the religion.

The real goal here is the conversion of large numbers of African-American prisoners to Wahhabism and its radical Islamist agenda. By converting to Islam, the prisoner is expressing his enmity toward the American society in which he lives and by which he believes himself to have been grossly maltreated. In short, analysts believe that the African-American Muslim prisoner movement is being hijacked by "puritanical" religious factions in Saudi Arabia. When released, these African-American offenders will support terrorist goals, "murdering their own countrymen in a kind of 'payback' for perceived injustices done to them by 'white America.'

The FBI believes prisons are fertile ground for extremists. Inmates may be drawn to an extreme form of Islam because it may help justify their *violent* tendencies. These people represent a heightened threat because of their criminal histories, their propensity for *violence*, and their contacts with fellow criminals. Complicating this threat is the wholly contradictory fact that radical inmates, wishing to avoid attention, act as *model prisoners*, leading prison officials to focus on violent prisoners while overlooking radicalization.

Melanics and the Muslim Boys indicate that some mutating Islamic groups are adopting gang techniques of intimidation to exert control over the institutions in which they are incarcerated. Melanics, who were influenced by the legal battles fought by Nation of Islam in the 1960s, used their own brand of Islam to wage a holy war against other prisoners, culminating in the 1999 riot at the Chippewa Correctional Facility in Kincheloe, Michigan. The Melanics killed one guard and one prisoner in the riot, injuring dozens of inmates. More than anything, the Melanics represent a mutating form of prison Islam similar to other recent cases, both foreign and domestic in nature. In early 2006, a gang known as the Muslim Boys began terrorizing other inmates at London's Belmarsh prison with beatings and stabbings.

Other forms of prison Islam have had a broader agenda. A great example is Kevin James and Peter Martinez. In 2003, James and Martinez, both incarcerated at the California State Prison/Sacramento, recruited more than a dozen fellow prisoners into a group called the JIS (Jamiyyat Ul-Islam Is-Saheed, roughly translated as the Assembly of Authentic Islam). Instead of trying to take over the prison, though, JIS launched a conspiracy to "kill infidels" in a guerilla war against the United States. Their targets included National Guard recruiting stations, synagogues, and the Israeli Consulate in Los Angeles; the group planned to carry out the attacks on September 11, 2005.

FBI Director Robert Mueller told reporters that the attacks "were well on their way" to being carried out, thereby underscoring the threat of "homegrown extremists" in prisons across the country. As a result, FBI agents nationwide were ordered to conduct risk assessments of prisoners who may have become radicalized and could commit extremist violence upon their release. "We are working with prison officials and academic leaders across the country," said the FBI director a year later, "to identify these potential recruiting venues."

Among those recruited was a 25-year-old inmate named Levar Washington. Following his release from prison in November 2004, Washington was arrested for a gas station holdup (one of more than a dozen robberies committed by JIS to fund the attacks). Whatever the findings of research into prison conversions to Islam, it is believed that good, old-fashioned police work and recognizing that a simple robbery may be more than meets the investigator's eye remains the best way to fight terrorism.

Brief History of Terrorist Recruitment in Prisons

- John William King, convicted ringleader in the 1998 truck-dragging murder of James Byrd, Jr. in Jasper, Texas, converted to Odinism at the Beto I Unit of the Texas Prison System in 1995. King's conversion occurred in conjunction with his swearing of allegiance to the North Carolina-based Ku Klux Klan faction, the Confederate Knights of America.
- Jose Padilla, a former member of the Chicago street gang the Maniac Latin Kings, was arrested in 2002 for plotting to attack the United States with a radioactive "dirty bomb." Padilla converted to Islam following a stint in South Florida's Broward County jail in 1992, where he had been influenced by a free-world imam.
- Richard Reid, the al-Qaeda "shoe bomber" who attempted to blow up an American Airlines flight between Paris and Miami in late 2001, converted to Islam in a British young offenders' institution while doing time for a string of muggings during the mid-1990s. Officials suspect he was radicalized by an imam who preached at the prison.
- Youseff Fikri, mastermind of the 2003 suicide bombings in Casablanca, was a former prisoner in Morocco. Upon his release, Fikri came under the influence of a radical imam of the al-Qaeda-affiliated Moroccan Combat Group and began a series of "Islamic" executions, leading to the Casablanca attacks.
- Jamal "el Chino" Ahmidan (1969–2004), the brains behind the 2004 Madrid train bombings, embraced the jihadist principles of radical Islam while serving time for immigration fraud in a Spanish detention center in 2002.
- Muktar Ibrahim, a British citizen born into a secular family in Eritrea, was the leader of the July 21 cell that attempted to bomb the London underground in a follow-on to the 7/7 attacks of 2005. Ibrahim converted to Islam in a British young offenders' institution while serving time for a series of muggings in the late 1990s.

- Abu Musab al-Zarqawi (1966–2006), of al-Qaeda in Iraq, did not convert to Islam in prison, but according to the terrorist's biographer, "… it was in prison that his magnetism and strength appeared in a new light." Prior to his incarceration at Jordan's high-security Suwaqah prison for terrorist-related offenses in 1996, Zarqawi's "reputation was that of a hoodlum with vague religious leaning." Zarqawi thrived under the harsh conditions of the desert prison, where he memorized large portions of the Koran, and developed the body of a fighter and the proselytizing techniques of a zealot. This allowed Zarqawi to recruit a band of ordinary criminals, drug addicts, and Islamists that would later prove vital to his terrorist campaign in Iraq. So enamored was Zarqawi of prison life that, when his release date came, he successfully petitioned the warden to allow him to remain in prison, where he continued his recruiting activities. Rather than undergoing a conversion, Zarqawi's experience resembles what has been referred to as a religious *regeneration,* or the enthusiastic adoption of a belief system (in this case, Wahhabism) that had not been taken seriously before, or that had been abandoned out of skepticism or indifference.
- The saga of Aqil Collins (aka Ansar Aqil) indicates that prison conversions to Islam may have important implications for national security. Collins, a blonde-haired, blue-eyed American from Phoenix, Arizona, converted to Islam in the early 1990s while doing time in a California boot camp for stealing cars and joyriding. Inspired by his religious transformation, Collins went to Afghanistan in 1994 to train in guerrilla warfare tactics at a camp alongside some future leaders of al-Qaeda, including one of the men who would be accused of kidnapping and beheading *The Wall Street Journal* reporter Daniel Pearl.

    Later, Collins fought alongside the mujahidin in Chechnya, where he lost his leg to a Claymore mine. On his way out of Chechnya in 1996, Collins entered the United States embassy in nearby Azerbaijan to volunteer for service in the CIA. The agency turned him down, but not before advising Collins to seek employment with the FBI, which he successfully did upon his return to the States in 1997. In 1998, while in London, Collins (now a one-legged jihadist turned FBI informant on radical Muslim groups) met a young Arab man with ties to Osama bin Laden's inner circle. However, when Collins presented this information to his FBI handlers and volunteered to infiltrate al-Qaeda and kill bin Laden, he was denied the assignment on the grounds that Collins could be "a loose cannon."

Recommendations and Some Final Thoughts

Hiring Institutional Chaplains in Overcrowded Maximum Security Prisons

Recent cuts in funding for religious services have created opportunities for Islamic prisoners to operate on their own, independent of chaplaincy oversight seeking to ensure moderation and tolerance. This has created the space for Islamic extremists to assert themselves as independent imams. Especially worrisome are those charismatic prisoners who espouse jihadist/Salafist teachings. Those inexperienced with sacred texts and rituals seek a personal path to reform and, therefore, gravitate toward religious guidance. For those who gravitate toward Islam, this guidance may be offered by family members or fellow inmates. Guidance also should be offered by qualified Muslim chaplains. However, there is a critical shortage of Muslim chaplains in state maximum security prisons. It is recommended that state maximum security correctional institutions seek full-time Muslim chaplains.

Hiring Muslim-Americans to Work in Prisons

Although Islam is the fastest-growing religion among prisoners in America, the number of Muslims in the correctional workforce has not kept pace. This imbalance perpetuates the outsider status of Muslim inmates, thereby fortifying the conditions that support and sustain the growth of prison Islam. Muslim-American guards, counselors, and especially wardens would bring important cultural and political capital to the correctional arena, which could be used to legitimize moderating voices of religious authority for Muslim inmates. It is recommended that correctional agencies encourage Muslim-American entry into the state prison workforce through diversity recruitment at job fairs, as well as offering such financial incentives as scholarships and tuition payments for college graduates.

There is near universal consensus among staff involved in religious programming that great benefit could result from the establishment of a central office coordinator for chaplaincy service in the prison system. Such an office could provide institutional program support, computerized recordkeeping on inmate religious affiliation, uniform policymaking on religious volunteers and inmate religious leaders, oversight on trends in prisoner radicalization, and enhanced intelligence sharing between institutional chaplains and the Office of Correctional Safety.

It is recommended that a central office chaplaincy service staffed with subject matter experts on Judaism and Christianity, Native American faiths,

Islam, Eastern religions, and the pagan faith groups (Wicca and Odinism), etc., be created.

There is an emergence of a particularly corrupt form of penal subculture borne of prison overcrowding, gang ascendancy, and global Islamic extremism lodged in powerful grievances over US imperialism. Some members of terrorist groups have been able to breach the security safeguards of community reentry programs due to outdated recordkeeping procedures. Prisoner radicalization is a dynamic process.

The training of staff on this process need not involve lengthy academic discussions of history and inmate subcultures. Rather, it is best handled through daily briefings on current gang recruiting activity and shifting power dynamics among prisoners. It is recommended that prison staffs receive daily roll call training on prisoner radicalization and potential terrorist recruitment.

These include attempts made by street gangs to form alliances with prison gangs; gang criminal activity, including attempts to own a stable of "clean" (nongang) inmates and staff members for the purpose of smuggling contraband; gang attempts to recruit mercenaries from the general prison population; gang attempts to compromise horticulture programs (the prime source for constructing IEDs (improvised explosive devices)); common forms of gang communication (statements, graffiti, calls-to-arms, "outside" and "inside" tattoos, etc.); the arrival of high-profile gang members or terrorist kingpins to institutions; the cultivation of informants within gangs; exploiting gang rivalries; and planning for the unexpected—an actual terrorist event.

Recommendation

It is recommended that the Department of Homeland Security and other federal, state law enforcement, and correctional agencies continue researching prisoner radicalization and terrorist recruitment and to support research on various facets of prison organizational culture that leads to extremism behind bars. Such a research agenda may provide answers to such fundamental questions as:

- What does prisoner radicalization actually mean?
- What specific criminal thinking skills are involved in plotting a terrorist attack?
- Do radical prisoners have these skills?
- What role will overcrowding continue to play in radicalizing prisoners?
- How will radicalization be affected by the current trend toward eliminating state prison chaplain systems?

- What effect will the ongoing war in Iraq and Afghanistan have on radicalization?
- Is it possible to create radicalization "safety zones" within correctional settings?

References

1. Online at http://www.officer.com/web/online/On-the-Street/Americas-Terrorist-Gateway/21$52494.
2. The following information is taken from various unclassified government reports and assorted websites under *The Growth of Radical Islam in the U.S. Correctional Systems.*

"Presumed Guilty" or "Dirtying Up the Defendant"

13

Criminal Gang Enhancement Prosecutions in California and Police/ Prosecution Misconduct

GREGORIO ESTEVANE

Contents

Introduction

The dominate theme of this chapter, "Presumed Guilty," applies to many cases where the government may have doubt of the defendant's "active" gang status and still moves toward a jury trial, asking for conviction of "gang enhancement" by a jury. It is this type of ultra aggressiveness or "misconduct" by prosecutors that drives the questionable presumption of guilt in the juror's minds during trial.

In addition, governmental prosecutorial misconduct often filters down to their police agents who are encouraged to sometimes lie as expert witnesses in trials to get convictions. Though this is currently not quantifiable as to if it happens seldom, sometimes, more than you think, or often, the point is that it happens in courts across California and the rest of the United States all too often and is most likely on the rise.

This type of misconduct, especially in gang enhancement trials where it is much easier to "dirty up the defendant"[1] (who is presumed innocent until proven guilty) with piled-on testimony of the historic horrors of the alleged gang onto the defendant, is cancerous to a just and fair American criminal justice system, a system that cherishes the presumption of innocence.

A new gang enhancement statute, California Penal Code section 186.22, seemed like a great idea in 1988/1989 when the murder rates climbed to more than 1,000 murders a year in Los Angeles, with many other California cities suffering from horrific accelerating murder rates that seemed to be gang-driven. After all, who has any sympathy for some "gangster" infesting our cities with death and destruction of all our values?

No one seemed to have a problem at that time with a "get tough on crime agenda," as the police, prosecutors, judges, and correctional systems, with full media and public support, worked to stop the malignant horror of gang-related death and blood on the streets.

Today, with contemporary murder rates historically low, numbering under 300 murders per year, with only approximately half of those murder convictions gang related, no one seems to still care, at least yet, that criminal gang enhancement trials have rocketed sky high hundreds of percentage points each year at an ever-increasing annual cost of more than $1 billion a year and ever-rising annual costs to the state of California taxpayers, for gang-related prosecutions. This in a new era of never-before seen statistically low crime rates, why is this? Yet after 25 years of ever-increasing convictions for gang-related crimes, why is it that the number of gangs and gang members has drastically increased since 1988/1989?

Questions and topics that arise and are addressed in this chapter include:

What is a gang?
What is gang criminal activity?
Approximately how many gang members are there?
Do gangs commit most crimes, including drug crimes?
Trail gang experts
How does case law work in gang cases?
Do gang cases increase misconduct of police and prosecutors?
Are we as taxpayers getting our money's worth, or is this a government-
    created crisis to increase funding, and other gang-related issues?

Academia, think tanks, not-for-profits, governmental officials, and others are beginning to seriously question the state, county, and local prosecutors' unquenchable financial thirst for more money, for more gang enhancement prosecutions with questionable filings that include teenage girls talking on three-way calls, speeding tickets, selling drugs, taggers, and others. Thus, effectively filling our jails and court rooms with increasing gang prosecutions with never-ending spending requests for the government's expanding "war on gangs." Many people, groups, and organizations are beginning to seriously question our government's increased expansion of this war onto our children, who may be delinquent, unruly, or otherwise nongang related, into increased gang-related convictions while ballooning the size and costs of these police and prosecutorial government agencies.

What Are Gang Enhancement Crimes?

In 1988, the California State Legislature confronted this "state of crisis" by enacting emergency legislation entitled the Street Terrorism Enforcement and Prevention Act (STEP Act). The STEP Act was codified in section 186.22 of the California Penal Code. As part of its findings, the legislature determined that nearly 600 gangs existed in California and that gang-related murders were on the rise. In 1986, Los Angeles County alone accounted for 328 such murders, and that number increased 80 percent by the following year.

With the "eradication of criminal [gang] activity as its end goal, the STEP Act did two things: (1) Subsection (a) created a substantive crime for "active participation in any criminal street gang," and (2) Subsection (b) imposed greater punishment for crimes committed "for the benefit" of a criminal street gang.

Subsection (a) creates a substantive offense and provides for the punishment of up to three years for anyone "actively participat[ing]" in a criminal street gang as either a felony or misdemeanor.

The STEP Act has been the subject of several constitutional challenges.

Constitutionality

California courts, in the face of challenges that the STEP Act's gang enhancements are unconstitutional, have consistently held that the very language of the act ensures constitutionality.

The act has been criticized as infringing on a person's First Amendment Constitutional right to the freedom of association. It has been argued that the overbroad and vague term "criminal street gang" results in the unlawful punishment of one's association with a group whose members may have committed criminal offenses.

In response, courts have instead found that "it is not the association with other individuals alone which section 186.22 addresses, but the association with others for the purpose of promoting, furthering, or assisting them in the commission of crime." The STEP Act "regulates conduct, not speech or association, and there is no right of association to engage in criminal conduct."

> *People v. Gamez*, 286 Cal. Rptr. 894, 975–76 (Ct. App. 1991); In re: Alberto R., 1 Cal. Rptr. 2d 348, 357 (Ct. App. 1991) (the STEP Act was not unconstitutionally vague because it included the California legislature's affirmation of the right of Freedom of Association and its intention not to interfere with that right, as well as limiting language regarding the proscribed criminal activity); *People v. Gardeley*, 927 P.2d 713, 724 (Cal. 1997) (The STEP Act does not violate due process because its "requirements … are sufficiently explicit to inform those who are subject to it what constitutes a criminal street gang for purposes of the act.").

Criminal Street Gang in Academic Studies

Perhaps the least settled issue in gang research is the age-old question: "What is a gang?"

It seems that the majority of academic authorities can agree on only one point in this regard: that there is no agreement, neither among the criminologists who study gangs nor among the police who police them. The picture becomes no clearer when we narrow the issue by asking: "What is a youth gang?" or "What is a street gang?" In an essay on gang research published in *Crime and Justice,* John Hagedorn says that the definitional debate about gangs has been "long and rancorous" (Hagedorn, 1998). He proposes that, in thinking about what gangs are, a good place to start is with the godfather of gang research, Frederic Thrasher, who pointed out that "ganging" is a normal peer activity for adolescents within a continuum of behaviors that range "from conventional to wild." In *American Street Gangs,* a popular college textbook, Tim Delaney poses a set of questions drawn from current media depictions to illustrate the problem of defining gangs:

> In fact, there is no single definition, although every definition includes some mention of the word, group. For example, is a group of young people hanging out together a gang? What if this group is hanging outside a convenience store talking loud and acting proud? What if this group creates a name for itself, starts identifying members with specific clothing, and uses secret hand signals and handshakes and intimidating nicknames such as "killer" and "assassin"? But, the group just described could actually be a sports team! Add to this description the commission of a number of deviant acts and fraternities and sororities would also fit this profile (Delaney, 2005).

For many influential experts (such as Malcolm Klein and Irving Spergel), criminal activity is intrinsic to the definition, but equally influential experts (such as James Short) think otherwise.

In his *Crime and Justice* essay, Hagedorn (1998) says he prefers Joan Moore's definition:

> Gangs are unsupervised peer groups who are socialized by the streets rather than by conventional institutions. They define themselves as a gang or "set" or some such term, and have the capacity to reproduce themselves, usually within a neighborhood.

More recently, Hagedorn, (<year>) who believes that gangs are reproducing themselves across a world that is increasingly urbanized, has adopted a more global, "postindustrial" characterization of what gangs are. "Gangs are organizations of the street composed of either (1) the socially excluded or (2) alienated, demoralized, or bigoted elements of a dominant racial, ethnic, or religious group."

While most gangs begin as unsupervised adolescent peer groups and remain so, some institutionalize in barrios, favelas, ghettoes, and prisons. Often, these institutionalized gangs become business enterprises within the informal economy, and a few are linked to international criminal cartels. Others institutionalize as violent supporters of dominant groups and may devolve from political or conventional organizations. Most gangs are characterized by a racialized or ethno-religious identity as well as being influenced by global culture. Gangs have variable ties to conventional institutions and, in given conditions, assume social, economic, political, cultural, religious, or military roles.

> The California Penal Code §186.22 (e)(f) defines a "criminal street gang" as "any ongoing organization, association, or group of three or more persons, whether formal or informal, having as one of its primary activities the commission of one or more of the criminal acts enumerated in paragraphs (1) to (25), inclusive, of subdivision (e), having a common name or common identifying sign or symbol, and whose members individually or collectively engage in or have engaged in a pattern of criminal gang activity."

At the opposite end of the continuum, legal definitions intended to prohibit gang activity focus almost entirely on intentional criminal activity and are typically spare in defining distinct elements of association.

After many years of fielding squadrons of specialized "gang" units to combat criminal gangs and compiling lists of hundreds of thousands of people in an effort to identify and target gang members and their associates for harsh treatment in the criminal justice system, American law enforcement agencies have not been able to agree upon a common definition.

Perhaps the least of the problems posed by this failure is that accurate tracking of gang-related crime statistics is difficult, if not impossible. Given the lack of consensus about how and when groups of people do or do not constitute a gang, classification of gangs by type is understandably a fuzzy area. Delaney (2005) says that while there are many types of gangs, his textbook is focused on "street gangs," and he includes only brief discussions of some "nonstreet gangs": motorcycle gangs, organized crime, the Ku Klux Klan, skinheads, and prison gangs.

Malcolm Klein (1995) similarly asserts that prison gangs, skinheads, "stoners," and motorcycle gangs are not street gangs. Klein says that skinhead groups do not qualify as street gangs because they are usually inside, and, when they go out, they are "looking for a target, not just lounging around." And bikers are usually focused on their motorcycles, out cruising or selling drugs. He says both types of gangs are narrowly focused in their criminality, "always planning something," while street gangs are more aimless and casual about the trouble they get into.

He doesn't explain why "heavy metal–influenced stoners," "punks," "satanic cults," and "terrorist gangs" don't qualify. And he dismisses "low riders" and kids who hang out on street corners without comment.

Brenda Coughlin and Sudhir Venkatesh say that while the popular image of gangs is synonymous with African-American and Latino youths in poor urban neighborhoods, this may be "an artifact of definitional boundaries" (Coughlin and Venkatesh, 2003). They maintain that evidence of ethnic diversity among street gangs, as well as the existence of delinquent white groups not conventionally considered to be gangs (fraternities, motorcycle and "biker" outfits, militias, skinheads, or the Ku Klux Klan) need more research attention. Studies based on self-reports as well as localized ethnographic research have documented that white and black gangs are *both* present in urban areas, and that white gangs *also* are involved in serious violence. Yet people of color predominate in law enforcement estimates of gang membership, and most of those arrested for gang offenses are African-American and Latino.

Criminal Street Gangs in the Law: The STEP Act

Gang enhancements under the STEP Act require that the alleged crime be *"committed for the benefit of, at the direction of, or in association with any criminal street gang"* (emphasis added). Penal Code section 186.22(f) defines a "criminal street gang" as "any ongoing organization, association, or group of three or more persons, whether formal or informal, having as one of its primary activities the commission of one or more of the criminal acts enumerated [therein], having a common name or common identifying sign or symbol, and whose members individually or collectively engage in or have engaged in a pattern of criminal gang activity."

Primary Activities

In determining the meaning of "primary activities," the California Supreme Court has looked to the plain language of the STEP Act, holding that the term implied that "one or more of the statutorily enumerated crimes be one of the group's "chief" or "principal" occupations." Therefore, the occasional commission of the enumerated offense will not constitute a "primary activity" within the meaning of the STEP Act.

As an example, the California Supreme Court quoted the Court of Appeal in *People v. Gamez (supra)*, where the defendant challenged the STEP Act on the grounds that it was so overbroad that it punished one's association with an organization whose members have committed crimes, and argued that members of groups, such as the Los Angeles Police Department or Humboldt County environmental activists, would fall within its ambit.

In response, the *Gamez* court cited the statute's language, stating that the STEP Act requires that "one of the primary activities of the group or association itself be the commission of crime" in order to fall within the meaning of a "criminal street gang," therefore, the STEP Act does not punish "association with a group of individuals who, in a separate capacity, may commit crimes."

In *People v. Sengpadychith*, 27 P.3d at 744, the Court agreed with the Court of Appeal's holding in *People v. Galvan* that the trier of fact may consider prior conduct to establish the "primary activities" required for a gang enhancement, as well as evidence of conduct that occurred at the time of the present charged offense. The court stated that the STEP Act's language did not prohibit the consideration of the present offense and that evidence of both past and present conduct is relevant in determining a group's "primary activities."

Pattern of Criminal Activities

Section 186.22 (e) defines a "pattern of criminal gang activity" as the "commission of, attempted commission of, conspiracy to commit, or solicitation of, sustained juvenile petition for, or conviction of two or more of the offenses [enumerated therein] ... committed on separate occasions, or by two or more persons. ..."

The offenses used to demonstrate a gang's pattern of criminal gang activity must occur within the specified time frame and are called "predicate acts." The *Gamez* court held that predicate acts must have been "gang-related" because "[t]o allow otherwise would be to punish [a] defendant for the unrelated actions of people with whom he associated." However, the California Supreme Court disagreed with this holding and instead held that while the predicate acts do not have to be gang-related, they do have to have been committed by gang members.

In interpreting the definition of "pattern of gang activity," the court has looked to the phrase "on separate occasions, or by two or more persons." The court has read it as allowing the prosecution to choose between showing either that the "two or more" predicate acts were committed on "separate occasions," or by evidence that "two or more" predicate acts were committed "by two or more persons" on the same occasion.

However, when one person is charged with a crime and another person is charged with aiding and abetting in that crime, this is not sufficient to show a pattern of criminal gang activity.

This is because aider and abettor liability stems from the commission of a single crime (the perpetrators) as opposed to the commission of two separate crimes on the same occasion.

Lastly, the pattern of gang activity can be proved through the current offense (if it is one of the enumerated offenses identified in the statute) and one other offense committed on another occasion by a fellow gang member.

So, is the dangerous gang's actual primary activities crime-related, or are their primary activities noncriminal: looking to party, looking for sex, looking for drugs, etc.? Probably not, as even 500 members whose supposed primary activity would be a crime spree, which is not supported by any facts from the police expert. The police expert will have nothing more to say than the gang's primary activities are criminal without any statistical proof.

Studies have routinely shown that most members in a gang are in the gang for approximately only one year. Of course, there are veteran and life-long members, but they are the exception. The majority of gang members get into a gang to party, get girls, get high on drugs, get protection, get mythical brotherly love—none of which is the same as the primary activity of committing crime.

Reliable data on the extent of gang crime do not exist. David Curry, Richard Ball, and Scott Decker produced estimates of total gang membership and gang crime for 1993—a peak moment for juvenile crime in the United States—by tabulating data from law enforcement surveys and using statistical estimates for jurisdictions that failed to provide information in the surveys (Curry, Ball, and Decker, 1996). Their method produced a "conservative" estimate of roughly 380,000 gang members and 440,000 gang crimes, and a "reasonable" estimate of 560,000 members and 580,000 crimes.

These gang crime numbers must be taken with fistfuls of salt. Even if all of the assumptions guiding the statistical estimates were accurate, Weisel and Shelley (2004) argue persuasively that there are serious problems with the reliability of the underlying data. Nevertheless, the numbers provide a point of departure for examining gang members' contributions to the total incidence of crime.

The Federal Bureau of Investigation's Uniform Crime Reporting (UCR) program recorded more than 14 million serious (Part I) violent and property crimes in 1993. If a range of 440,000 to 560,000 accurately captured the number of serious property and violent crimes committed by gang members in 1993, then gang members would have been responsible for 3.1 percent to 4.1 percent of serious crime in the United States. This estimate could be low if police departments recorded in their gang statistics only the most serious and violent offenses; crimes that receive more attention and resources. However, the estimate could be high if law enforcement agencies' gang crime reports counted less serious offenses (simple assault, disorderly conduct) or drug offenses that are not included in the overall index crime total.

The gulf between the estimate of gang delinquency obtained from youth survey data (20 percent to 25 percent) and the estimate of gang crime obtained from law enforcement surveys (3 percent to 4 percent) demands some explanation. One explanation is that law enforcement agencies may underreport gang crime because many jurisdictions lack the capacity—or the political will—to carefully track the extent of gang involvement in criminal activity. Law enforcement underreporting may account for some of the gap, but the most compelling explanation is that gang activity peaks during early adolescence and drops sharply as youths approach adulthood.[2]

Definition of Gang Crime

Classically there are at least two definitions of gang crime:

- *Gang-member (member-based)* crime, where all or most crimes are committed by individuals who are believed to be members of or are criminally associated with a criminal street gang, are treated as gang-related crimes, regardless of the offense or the circumstances surrounding the crime-gang member-all crimes by gang members are gang crimes.
- *Gang-motivated (motive-based)* crimes that include only crimes that have been committed for the benefit of, at the direction of, or in criminal association with the gang or as part of a gang function, regardless if, in fact, the defendant is a gang member or not.

Typically many quasimodern thinking law enforcement/governmental agencies trend toward gang member-based filings with strategic methods at trial that outline a protracted discussion of the *past* terror of the gang; in contrast to whether the *present* alleged crime was truly gang motivated.

Whether or not a governmental prosecutorial top-down policy decision is made to drastically increase the number of gang enhancement prosecutions, for increased funding or political policy purposes, is generally addressed in academic and media publications.

However, the exhausting, ever-increasing budgetary implications of a taxpayer financed "government war on gangs" (increasing gang enhancements prosecutions, sometimes up a thousand fold in the face of drastically lower reported annual crime convictions) often leads to government agent expert testimony that blurs the distinction of *motive-based versus member-based* methodologies and only focuses on member-based methodologies. Thus, this increases the financial strains on an already overextended budgetary criminal justice system, which is not limited to the police, courts, prisons, and parallel participants in trials when alleging Penal Code section 186 charges. These filings increase exponentially in the face of drastic annual crime conviction statistics. Increasingly, these tactical filings of gang enhancements are becoming known as "dirtying up the defendant" in defense circles.

In 2001, California criminology experts Cheryl Maxson and Malcolm Klein examined police reports in the Sacramento-based *Cal Gang Data Base*, focusing on South Central Los Angeles, and found that a motive-based definition reduced by half the amount of gang homicides committed by gang members in Los Angeles County conviction rates.

Consider the following illustrative examples:

Gang member shoots and wounds another gang member for transgressions over insults to his mother. A gang member (who is angry that day) spontaneously assaults and kills a person for no apparent reason. Neither of the two examples would count as gang-motivated crimes under the gang-motive definition. In the first example, the motive had nothing to do with the gang and was rather an event of highly personal familiar revenge. In the second example, the crime was initiated spontaneously by an angry individual, who happened to be a gang member. Paradoxically, both of these crimes would unjustly count as gang crimes under the gang-related (member-based) definition of a gang crime at great government tax expenditure.

Therefore, gang-motivated (motive-based) methodologies can often give a clearer examination as to what is or is not a gang crime.

If gang-motivated methodologies were in place in a city such as Los Angeles, the gang capital of the world, what would be the fiscal impact on the police, prosecutors, judges, and correctional entities if the actual adjusted crime rate statistics (adjusted downward from the always higher statistical numbers based on gang member theories) were substantially lower each year than currently reported? Would that decrease the amount of taxpayer money needed and used each year (fighting this war on gangs), thus reducing the taxpayer money provided to the police, prosecutors, courts, and correctional facilities?

Gang and Nongang Violence

A review of the research on gang violence reveals an overall misconception about the rate of gang violence. According to Miethe and McCorkle (2002), between 1989 and 1995, defendants that were alleged to be gang members accounted for just 6 percent of violent crimes and 5 percent of drug charges in Las Vegas. Fritsch, Caeti, and Taylor (2003) found that Dallas gang-related offenses accounted for less than 10 percent of serious violent crime. And, in California, Kent et al. (2000) came to the same conclusion in studies of a gang task force in Westminster, California, that showed rates of gang violence at 7 to 8 of all crime.

This data is in stark contrast to the government prosecution blind frenzy that "… those hordes of gangs are enveloping our cities" and is consistent with the National Crime Victimization Survey (Ziedenberg, 2005) that shows that gang members are responsible for a small share, 6 percent, of the violent crime from 1998 to 2003. The sheer contrast in the drastic falling rates of reports of and convictions for crimes annually in unequal comparison to the growing number of gang members, the increase in newly forming criminal street gangs and gang activity (even with a multifold increase over the past several years in gang enhancement filings and convictions) call into question whether the government, in relationship to gang crimes, knows when a crime is truly gang-related, at great cost to the taxpayer.

The Federal Bureau of Investigation's (FBI) Uniform Crime Reporting (UCR) program recorded more than 14 million serious (Part 1) violent and property crimes in 1993 nationally from cities across the United States. Only 3.1 percent to 4.1 percent (440,000 to 560,000) of these 14 million crimes were attributed to gang members nationally.

Another factor to consider when assessing gang violence is whether the gang violence is actually for the gang. In *Youth Gangs in American Society*, Sheldon, Tracy, and Brown (2004) stated that "… acts of violence committed by gang members acting on their own do not represent gang violence and also do not occur because they are members of a gang. These acts are related to gangs only in the sense that the individuals involved have defiant individualist character traits (gang motive crimes versus gang member crimes). Violence results from the connections between the emotions of fear, ambition, frustration, testing of skills, and the encounters during which such emotions are apparent."

Police departments and county sheriff's annual crimes statistics routinely show that gang-motivated crimes are a smaller portion of overall crime and were nongang related. (Gang statistics show that a smaller percentage of all aggravated shootings or illegal gun possession, being less gang related, with approximately half of murder convictions being nongang related; thus, many, if not most, of crime conviction stats [gang member and nongang member based].)

Active gang members and gang associates more often commit crimes that have no nexus to P.C. 186, with such committed crimes having nothing to do with the direction by, association with, or for the benefit of any gang, thus calling into question the rational for the government vastly increasing tax-based spending on gang-enhancement prosecutions in the face of lowering crime rates.

Gangs Do Not Dominate or Drive the Drug Trade

National drug enforcement sources claim that gangs are "the primary retail distributors of drugs in the country." However, studies of several jurisdictions where gangs are active have concluded that gang members account for a relatively small share of drug sales, and that gangs do not generally seek to control drug markets. Investigations conducted in Los Angeles and nearby cities found that gang members accounted for one in four drug sale arrests.

The Los Angeles district attorney concluded that just one in seven gang members sold drugs on a monthly basis. St. Louis researchers describe gang involvement in drug sales as "poorly organized, episodic, nonmonopolistic [and] not a rationale for the gang's existence." A member of one of San Diego's best-organized gangs explains: "The gang don't organize nothing. It's like everybody is on they own. You are not trying to do nothing with nobody unless it's with your friend. You don't put your money with gangs."[3] Researchers found that law enforcement officials overestimate gang member involvement in drug distribution, and why is that? Could it be that that would reduce the amount of money law enforcement agencies received in taxpayers funding? Does that impact how law enforcement agencies skew statistics for increased funding?

Further, researchers Malcolm Klein and Cheryl Maxson found that law enforcement officials have an exaggerated perception of gang member involvement in drug distribution. In the mid-1980s, the two conducted research on cocaine sales in South Central Los Angeles, where they were told that "upward of 90 percent" or "almost all" sales were gang-related (Maxson, 1995). A review of police records, however, showed that the share of arrests attributable to gang members ranged from 9 percent in 1983 to 25 percent in 1985. Despite stereotypes that gang drug activity is associated with "high levels of violence" (NDIC, 2005), the researchers found that gang members were no more likely to carry firearms than nonmembers (Maxson, 1995).

Maxson replicated these findings six years later when she used police records to examine 1,563 cocaine sale incidents and 471 other drug sale incidents in Pasadena and Pomona, California. Gang members accounted for just over a quarter of cocaine sale arrests (26.7 percent) and one in nine non-cocaine sale arrests (11.5 percent). The proportions of cocaine sales attributable to gang members—21 percent in Pomona and 30 percent in Pasadena—were consistent with the last year of the Los Angeles data (25 percent) and well below law enforcement estimates, which ranged from 30 percent to 50 percent.

The proportion of noncocaine sale arrests attributed to gang members (one in nine) also failed to meet the expectations of law enforcement officials who reported that "gangs were prominent in the distribution of marijuana, heroin, and PCP, although less so than in the distribution of cocaine." Maxson further notes that these proportions may overstate the role of gangs in the drug trade because many gang members sell drugs independent of their gangs. "It should also be noted that these gang member arrestees might have been entrepreneurs and involvement of the gang might have been minimal."

Gang Members Account for a Relatively Small Share of Crime in Most Jurisdictions

There are a handful of jurisdictions, such as Los Angeles and Chicago, where gang members are believed to be responsible for a significant share of crime (Los Angeles homicide convictions are around 50 percent committed for the benefit of in association with, or at the direction of a gang). However, when analyzing crime conviction statistics in Los Angeles County, the role of gang member responsibility is substantially less than 50 percent of all other crimes other than murder convictions.

Available evidence indicates that gang members play a relatively small role in the national crime problem despite their propensity toward criminal activity. National estimates and local research findings suggest that gang members may be responsible for less than 1 in 10 homicides, less than 1 in 16 violent offenses, and fewer than 1 in 20 serious crimes (one of the eight crimes listed on Part 1 of the Uniform Crime Reports: rape, robbery, murder, aggravated assault, burglary, larceny, theft of a motor vehicle, and arson). Gangs themselves play an even smaller role, because much of the crime committed by gang members is self-directed and not committed for the gang's benefit.

Criminal Sophistication of Street Gangs and Members

On April 20, 2005, Chris Swecker, assistant director, Criminal Investigative Division of the FBI, issued a statement before the subcommittee on the

Western Hemisphere House International Relations Committee, whereby he summed up *Criminal Street Gang Sophistication* by stating:

> "... the gang (MS 13) is still a loosely structured street gang; however, its threat is based on its violence and its potential to grow, not only geographically, but in its organization and sophistication. There is some evidence of an increased level of sophistication and some indications of a hierarchy of leadership. This is based in part on reports of multiclique meetings in which gang members pay a fee to attend, coordinate their activities, exchange information regarding law enforcement actions and efforts, and issue punishment and/or sanctions for infractions of the gang's code. Cliques throughout the country often follow the lead of the Los Angeles-based cliques, and there are reports of Los Angeles-based members traveling throughout the United States for the purpose of recruiting new members, establishing new cliques, and taking over existing Latino gangs, and instilling discipline through violence and intimidation ..."

Similarly, Jankowski's (1990) study of gang members in three large cities included data that *gangs can be sophisticated*, which requires leadership, strategic planning, and time-lined tactics in areas such as:

Gang Services: The most common are protection, demolition of property (usually arson), and prostitution. The most common form of protection involves extortion. Gangs also provide services to punish others such as loan sharks may hire gangs for collections. Murder for hire is a more sophisticated violent service and other similar homicides. The El Rukins (Blood gang, i.e., Black P Stones) gang is another example as the gang was hired by Libyans to act as terrorists in the United States and abroad (conspiring to downing a commercial airline in the United States with a surface to air missile).

Other forms of sophistication in violence suggest planning in committing murders of rivals with intelligence gathered, surveillance, lookouts, GPS, Twitter, and other deployed tactics.[4]

Who Is a Gang Member?

One of the difficulties of the STEP Act in California is determining what constitutes a gang and who counts as a gang member. Gangs are comprised of members with varying involvement and commitment and, as such, have been aptly described as "inherently ambiguous." Thus, creating a bright line definition of a gang or gang member is a difficult and complicated task. In his book, *Gangs in Court*, Lewis Yablonsky describes two types of gang involvement: (1) active gang roles and (2) nonactive gang roles.

"The active gang roles consist of the shot callers (the OGs or Veteranos), the troops or foot soldiers (the Gs), and the interns (the Wannabes). The nonactive gang roles include gangster groupies (those who associate with gang members, but do not generally engage in criminal activity), residents of a gang-dominated neighborhood, and former gang members. Often, those assuming nonactive gang roles are mistaken as active gang members."

Additionally, the different types of initiation and varying levels of participation in a gang create difficulties in determining who is a gang member. Many gangs require members to be "jumped in," which generally requires the applicant to perform some act to prove his loyalty to the gang. While "jumping in" may require some overt act that is violent in nature, often a mere verbal acceptance may suffice.

Another complication is that gangs tend to be extremely territorial. They are often located in urban centers of socially and economically disadvantaged communities, and while gangs are not exclusively a minority problem, it is estimated that 80 percent of gang activity is committed by African-American and Hispanic gangs. Often, youths living in a neighborhood under the control of a particular gang will likely be associated with that gang, and many of their acquaintances and neighbors, and even friends, will be members of the local gang. People with childhood friends or acquaintances who later became gang members may cause them to be mistaken as gang members themselves. They may even dress like their gang member neighbors, even if they themselves are not gang members.

In an effort to curb criminal gang violence, the Los Angeles Police Department assigned particular law enforcement officers, often called "gang cops," to gang-ridden areas.

In patrolling the same concentrated area, gang cops become familiar with the players in that neighborhood. They can initiate informal stops without probable cause and work directly with gang prosecutors. To better identify and track gang members, California implemented the CalGang database in December of 1997. The database is comprised of information gathered from Field Interview cards (FI cards).

When law enforcement officers encounter a person who is either a known gang member or a suspected gang member, the officers complete an FI card. FI cards are not only issued for arrests, but also for routine stops by neighborhood gang cops without probable cause and may include detailed information, such as gang monikers or affiliations, the location of the stop, vehicles involved, schools attended, addresses, tattoos, style of dress, and identifications by informants or associates.

This information is included in the CalGang database and is often accompanied by a photograph of the individual. In 2000, the database contained entries on more than 250,000 individuals. Nearly 90 percent of FI cards are for minority youths, and, in 2000, approximately two-thirds of the Los Angeles County residents in the database were Latinos and one-third were African Americans. The information from the CalGang database is provided to local prosecutors and is often used to support gang enhancements.

Unreliability of the CalGang Database

A gang database was first compiled in Los Angeles by the Los Angeles County sheriff the same year that Mayor James Hahn sought his injunction against the Playboy Gangster Crips. The Los Angeles database was taken statewide a decade later when the California Department of Justice created CalGang, which tracks some 200 data points of personal information and gang-related information.

By 2003, Loren Siegel reported, 47 percent of African-American men in Los Angeles County between the ages of 21 and 24 had been logged into the Los Angeles County gang database, and more than a quarter-million Californians had been entered into the CalGang database by law enforcement personnel across the state (Siegel, 2003).

African-American and Latino communities bear the cost of failed gang enforcement initiatives. Young men of color are disproportionately identified as gang members and targeted for surveillance, arrest, and incarceration, while whites, who make up a significant share of gang members, rarely show up in accounts of gang enforcement efforts. The Los Angeles district attorney's office found that close to half of black males between the ages of 21 and 24 had been entered in the county's gang database, even though no one could credibly argue that all of these young men were current gang members. Communities of color suffer not only from the imposition of aggressive police tactics that can resemble martial law, but also from the failure of such tactics to pacify their neighborhoods.

A person can be entered in the CalGang database if a law enforcement officer determines that the person meets at least 2 of 10 criteria (Advancement Project, 2006):

1. Admits gang membership or association.
2. Is observed to associate on a regular basis with known gang members.
3. Has tattoos indicating gang membership.
4. Wears gang clothing, symbols, etc., to identify with a specific gang.
5. Is in a photograph with known gang members or using gang-related hand signs.
6. Is named on a gang document, hit list, or gang-related graffiti.
7. Is identified as a gang member by a reliable source.

8. Is arrested in the company of identified gang members or associates.
9. Corresponds with known gang members or writes or receives correspondence about gang activities.
10. Writes about gangs (graffiti) on walls, books, paper, etc.

Jesuit priest Father Greg Boyle, (adviser to the author of this evaluation) founded Homeboy Industries and created a program that specializes in the rehabilitation of gang members. Homeboy Industries works with those same gang members who want and *do* leave the gang lifestyle. Gang members leave gangs, and stay gang free on many occasions. Father Boyle observes what sets gang members apart from other youths: "... It is their misery. Such youth does not need to be recruited, much less forced, to join a gang. They are kids who hang around older gang members hoping to be noticed and invited into the circle" (Boyle, 2005).

Gang membership requires the consent of the gang, not the words or actions of prospects. Born into the gang is one method of entering the gang world, as in many parts of Los Angeles, gang members live next to and associate with nongang members. Putting in work for the gang is associated with an ongoing series of criminal acts, i.e., going to jail, going to prison. It usually requires an almost full-time work schedule, and still one may not be accepted into a gang until the gang or gang leaders deem that the person has done enough bad deeds to prove his actions will benefit a criminal enterprise. "Wanna-be gang members" associate with gangs; gang members and nongang members often mix together.

It is not illegal to be a gang member or associate with gang members. Wanna-be gang members are not the same as prospects; wanna-bes may have no chance of ever getting into the gang whether they are allowed to hang out or not with the gang members. These wanna-be members can do all sorts of actions or declare all sorts of things and have zero benefit from those actions and the gang couldn't care less. Father Boyle points out, "... They are waiting to get into that inner circle ..., but until that moment, they are not gang members and associating is not the same as benefiting a gang."

The Criminal Street Gang Myth

Nothing could be farther from the truth than the criminal street gang myth: "Blood in, blood out, by death or death in prison." Deck and Van Winkle (1996) found the typical gang member is active for a year or less. Esbensen and colleagues (Esbensen et al., 2001) surveyed more than 5,000 members and detailed the large majority quit after a brief stay in the gang, "... a rather fleeting experience for the most of these youth. Half of the male gang members reported being in a gang for one year or less, and only 7 percent reported being a gang member for more than four years. Two-thirds (66 percent) were in a gang for less than one year, with most reporting no membership for over four years."

Can Specific Intent Be Proved Up *Solely* by Gang Expert Opinion Testimony?

Specific criminal intent is required to be proven. In *People v. Ramon, supra,* 175 Cal. App. 4th 843, officers stopped the defendant, a conceded gang member, while he was driving a stolen vehicle within his gang's territory with a fellow gang member in the passenger seat (*Id.*, pp. 846–847). Officers found a loaded, unregistered firearm under the driver's seat (*Id.*, pp. 846–848). The People charged the defendant with receiving a stolen vehicle, possession of a firearm by a felon, possession of a firearm while an active gang member, and carrying a loaded firearm in public for which he was not a registered owner, as well as corresponding gang enhancements (*Id.*, p. 848). The prosecution gang expert gave a possible motive or reason for the defendant being in possession of the stolen vehicle and gun. He explained that the defendant and codefendant were in the heart of Colonia Bakers' gang territory (defendant's gang) and that the primary activities of the gang were, among other things, car theft, drug sales, burglaries, robberies, and extortion. The expert explained that possessing a stolen car and unregistered firearm would allow the gang to commit crimes for which it would be difficult to trace (*Id.*, pp. 847–848).

The court found the gang expert's opinion insufficient to establish the specific intent requirement, notwithstanding the defendant's conceded gang status, the presence of a fellow gang associate, and the location of the crime in their own gang territory:

> Here, the People gave a possible motive or reason for Ramon being in possession of the stolen vehicle and gun. The prosecution, however, was required to prove this fact beyond a reasonable doubt. While the People's expert's opinion certainly was one possibility, it was not the only possibility. And, as stated *ante*, a mere possibility is not sufficient to support a verdict. The analysis might be different if the expert's opinion had included "possessing stolen vehicles" as one of the activities of the gang. That did not occur and we will not speculate.
>
> Simply put, in order to sustain the People's position, we would have to hold as a matter of law that two gang members in possession of illegal or stolen property in gang territory are acting to promote a criminal street gang. Such a holding would convert section 186.22(b)(1) into a general intent crime. The statute does not allow that. (See §186.22(b)(1); *People v. Hill* (2006)142 Cal. App.4th 770, 774, 47 Cal. Rptr. 3d875.)

The remaining cases we have reviewed, those cited by the parties and as a result of our own research, have not revealed any situation where expert testimony about a possible reason for committing a crime was sufficient, by itself, to establish the crime was committed with the specific intent to promote, further, or assist in criminal conduct by gang members. We confirm that such testimony is not sufficient to support a section 186.22(b)(1) enhancement. (*Ramon, supra,* p. 853)

The Ninth Circuit Court Approach

In two separate cases, the Ninth Circuit found the evidence insufficient regarding the specific intent to promote, further, or assist in other criminal activity. The reasoning appeared to hinge on a finding that section 186.22(b) requires that a defendant harbor the specific intent to further, promote, or assist *other* criminal conduct, i.e., criminal conduct apart from the charged current offenses. The Ninth Circuit approach in these two rulings has been heavily criticized by California appellate courts, (*People v. Hill* (2006) 142 Cal.App.4th 770, 774; *People v. Romero* (2006) 140 Cal.App.4th 15, 19; *People v. Vasquez* (2009) 178 Cal.App.4th 347, 353–354), and more recently by the California Supreme Court in *People v. Albillar, supra,* 51 Cal.4th 47. *Albillar* specifically rejected the reasoning of the Ninth Circuit, holding that, under the statute, section 186.22(b) does not require a specific intent to further, promote, or assist conduct *distinct* from the charged offense.

In *Garcia v. Carey* (2005) 395 F. 3d 1099, Garcia was a member of the El Monte Flores gang. Its turf included much of the city of El Monte. A male victim entered a liquor store in the early morning hours. Garcia and two or three other people were in the store. When the victim said hello to Garcia, Garcia told him not to talk to him if he did not know him. Garcia then asked if the victim had any change. The victim replied, "No." Garcia said, "Let's see when you come out the door." One of Garcia's companions asked the victim where he was from. As the victim left the store, Garcia stood in front of him and said, "I'm Little Risky from E.M.F., you want to get jacked?" Garcia told his friends to watch for police and then took $14.85 out of the victim's pocket. One of Garcia's friends lifted his own shirt and grabbed what looked like the handle of a pistol. Garcia told another friend to take the victim's bicycle. The Ninth Circuit found this evidence insufficient as to specific intent:

Here, Detective Hernandez testified that Garcia was a member of the E.M.F. gang, that the robbery was committed on gang territory, and that the E.M.F. gang was "turf-oriented." Detective Hernandez did not offer any testimony, however, on what was meant by being "turf-oriented," what implications arose from a gang being "turf-oriented," or how the gang's "turf-oriented" nature could support the conclusion that this robbery was committed with the specific intent to promote, further, or assist other gang-related criminal activity. Without this evidentiary link, it is unreasonable to conclude that a rational jury could find that Garcia committed this robbery with the specific intent to facilitate other gang crimes. There was simply a total failure of proof of the requisite specific intent. The district court correctly granted habeas relief on the gang enhancement, and on the firearm enhancement that depended on it. (*Id.*, pp. 1104–1105)

Shortly thereafter, in *Briceno v. Scribner* (9th Cir. 2009) 555 F.3d 1069, the Ninth Circuit again held that the prosecution gang expert's testimony dealing with hypotheticals and generalities was insufficient to satisfy the specific intent element of 186.22(b). The court was not persuaded by the oft-repeated arguments that fair inferences can be made as to specific intent from the generic gang expert testimony. In *Briceno*, two Hard Times street gang members went on a "grinchly crime wave," committing at least four armed robberies within a matter of hours (*Id.*, p. 1072.) A gang expert testified that gangs gain respect and power through acts of violence. He then added, through a hypothetical question based on facts of the case, that the crimes "were committed for the benefit of, at the direction of, or in association with the criminal street gang Hard Times, and with intent to promote, further, and assist criminal conduct by members of the Hard Times gang" (*Id.*, p. 107.)

Briceno held that the gang expert's testimony did not, and could not, establish Briceno's specific intent in committing the robberies (*Id.*, p. 1097) The court noted that the expert's testimony

… dealt almost exclusively in "hypotheticals" and did not provide any direct or circumstantial evidence of Briceno's own intent (*Id.*) The court further stated: Even when asked whether he had "an opinion as to whether or not [the robberies] … were committed … with intent to promote, further, and assist criminal conduct by members of the Hard Times gang," he did not provide such an opinion. Instead, he responded in generalities, stating that such crimes "glorif[ied]" the gang and increased the status of the offenders. (The expert's) testimony might have helped to establish the first element of the gang enhancement, i.e., that the crime ultimately benefitted the gang in some way. But, it says nothing about Briceno's *specific intent* in committing the robberies (*Id.*).

Specific Intent to Promote, Further, or Assist in Any Criminal Conduct by Gang Members

The gang enhancement element requires that the defendant has acted with specific intent to promote, further, or assist in the criminal conduct of a criminal street gang member (although the defendant does not have to be a member of that gang).

In *Garcia v. Carey*, 395 F.3d 1099 (9th Cir. 2005), the Ninth Circuit held that the prosecution must present evidence as to this specific intent requirement in order to distinguish the instant crime as one furthering a criminal street gang member's criminal conduct from the mere commission of a crime. The defendant identified himself to the victim as an El Monte Flores (E.M.F.) gang member. He and his companions then allegedly stole the victim's money and bicycle.

Although the prosecution offered the testimony of an El Monte police detective who was familiar with E.M.F. and was able to testify about the general behavior and tendencies of its members, the prosecution did not offer any evidence as to the defendant's intent to further the criminal conduct of E.M.F. Thus, the evidence justifying the gang enhancement was constitutionally infirm, leading the Ninth Circuit to uphold the district court's grant of habeas relief to the defendant. While this seems to be the correct holding, as we will later see, this requirement is often glossed over in the face of highly prejudicial gang evidence.

Directed by, Benefiting, or Criminally Associated with a Criminal Street Gang

Subsection (b) sentencing enhancements requires one of the following to be proved, any or all of which are specific intent elements:

- For the benefit of a criminal street gang
- At the direction of a criminal street gang
- In (criminal) association with a criminal street gang

Subsection (b) (hereinafter, the "gang enhancement") creates sentencing enhancements for felonies committed "for the benefit of, at the direction of, or in association with any criminal street gang," by a defendant with "specific intent to promote, further, or assist in any criminal conduct by gang members."

Under the current law, an enhancement under this subsection results in an additional term of two years to life imprisonment, depending on the underlying felony, and will run consecutive to the punishment of that felony. This section is frequently filed in prosecutions. Since its enactment, the STEP Act's most significant amendments have increased the penalties under the gang enhancement. Originally, gang enhancements added an additional term of one, two, or three years to the sentence imposed for the underlying felony conviction, and, in 1994, the low term was increased to 16 months, instead of one year.

Legal Standard of Review

Section 186.22, subdivision (b)(1): The Enhancement. The street gang enhancement provides, in pertinent part, "… any person who is convicted of a *felony* committed for the benefit of, at the direction of, or in association with any criminal street gang, with the specific intent to promote, further, or assist in any criminal conduct by gang members, shall, upon conviction of that *felony*, in addition and consecutive to the punishment prescribed for the *felony* or attempted *felony* of which he or she has been convicted, be punished as follows …" (Pen. Code, §186.22, subd. (b)(1), emphasis added). Under the clear language of the statute, Penal Code section 186.22(b)(1) cannot be imposed unless a defendant is convicted of a felony.

To receive a gang enhancement, the defendant need not be a current and active member of a gang (in re: *Ramon T.* (1997) 57 Cal.App.4th 201). In addition to the criminal street gang components discussed in Section I above, there are two other essential elements that must be proved: (1) that the charged crimes were committed for the benefit of, at the direction of, or in association with the gang; *and* (2) that they were committed with the specific intent to promote, further, or assist in criminal conduct by gang members (CALJIC No. 17.24.2; CALCRIM 1401; *People v. Gardeley* (1996) 14 Cal.4th 605, 619; *People v. Louen* (1997) 17 Cal.4th 1, 11; In re: *Ramon T.* (1997) 57 Cal.App.4th 201, 207–208; *People v. Ortiz* (1997) 57 Cal.App.4th 480, 484-485). As to the benefit/direction/association element, the "typical close case is one in which one gang member, acting alone, commits a crime" (*People v. Morales* (2003) 112 Cal.App.4th 1176, 1198). However, *Morales* also recognized "it is conceivable that several gang members could commit a crime together, yet be on a frolic and detour unrelated to the gang" (*Id.*).

Benefit

Here is yet another in a long line of terrible, absurd gang enhancement cases. California Penal Code sec. 186.22(b), the gang enhancement provision, requires that "the crime has been committed for the benefit of the gang." However, the Court of Appeal says that the crime doesn't *actually* have to be for the benefit of the gang. It's enough that there was evidence that the crime was committed "in association with" the gang with the intent to assist criminal conduct.

The facts here pretty clearly show that the robbery was not for the benefit of the gang, but it was committed with another gang member and the defendant was a member of the gang, that's enough to show the "association" required (*People v. Martinez*, 2008 DJ DAR 668; DJ, 1/17/08; C/A4th).

No Benefit If Crime Committed by Gang Member Is Committed Alone

The California Supreme Court points out in its December 27, 2012, landmark decision, *People v. Rodriguez*, California Supreme Court, S187680 (Dec. 27, 2012):

> We are again called upon to construe Penal Code section 186.22(1) the California Street Terrorism Enforcement and Prevention Act (the STEP Act) (§ 186.20 et seq.), involving the activity of criminal street gangs.
>
> At issue here is section 186.22, subdivision (a) (section 186.22(a)): "Any person who actively participates in any criminal street gang with knowledge that its members engage in or have engaged in a pattern of criminal gang activity, and who *willfully promotes, furthers, or assists in any felonious criminal conduct by members of that gang*, shall be punished. ..." (emphasis added).
>
> We granted review to resolve a conflict in the Courts of Appeal. Under the language of the italicized phrase, does a gang member violate section 186.22(a) if he commits a felony, but acts alone?
>
> The Court of Appeal below concluded that he does not. We agree and affirm the judgment of the Court of Appeal.

Further statutory references are to the California Penal Code, unless otherwise noted. For convenience, we will sometimes refer to section 186.22(a) as the "gang participation" offense.

Section 186.22(a) and section 186.22(b)(1) strike at different things. The enhancement under section 186.22(b)(1) punishes gang-related conduct, i.e., felonies committed with the specific intent to benefit, further, or promote the gang (see *Gardeley, supra*, 14 Cal.4th at p. 622). However, "[n]ot every crime committed by gang members is related to a gang. (*Albillar, supra*, 51 Cal.4th at p. 60; *People v. Rodriguez*, California Supreme Court, S187680, Dec. 27, 2012).

Association

What Does 'In Association with Any Criminal Street Gang' Mean?

The California legislature did not provide a specific meaning of what the phrase "*in association with any criminal street gang*" means. However, prosecutors and some appellate courts have interpreted it as essentially including any situation where two or more gang members happen to commit a crime together. This interpretation creates serious constitutional questions, inasmuch as it collapses the specific intent prong (specific intent to promote/further/assist in criminal conduct by gang members) with the first section (that the crime be committed for the benefit of, or at the direction of, or in association with, i.e., the gang-related section). (See discussion, *infra*, this prong, part E, Constitutional Thought: Applying the Gang Enhancement Too Broadly.)

In *People v. Albillar, supra,* 51 Cal.4th 47, three defendants participated in the rape and penetration of a female acquaintance at their shared apartment. The defendants were all related (two were twin brothers), and they occasionally socialized with the victim. There was no evidence the defendant's gang was involved or even aware of the crimes until after they were committed. The evidence was that the gang (Southside Chiques) would not engage in sexual assaults and would disapprove. Justice Werdegar explained in her concurrence and dissent:

> The prosecutor avoided the problem by providing the jury with a meaning of the phrase "in association with" that did not require such evidence, explaining: "Association has a plain, common, ordinary meaning. Two or more gang members is an association. All three Defendants are active participants in the Southside Chiques. They were aware obviously by their living status, by their knowledge of each other, by their group tie that [each] one is a member of Southside Chiques. It's obvious that they know that the ... other two ... are also members of the Southside Chiques. They commit the crime in concert with each other, in association with each other. They combine; they pooled their strength, they combined their muscle, they counted on each other's loyalty to be there and back them up, and it's easier to divide labor that way and [successfully complete] the crime. They do this crime in close proximity to each other, and they're assisting each other in committing the crime." (*Albillar, supra,* concurring and dissenting opinion, at Westlaw, p. 19)

The majority in *Albillar* came close to echoing the prosecutor's view. Relying heavily on the gang expert, the majority noted that gang members who choose to commit crimes together do so for the following reasons: to increase the success of completing crime, to bolster each other's confidence, to train younger members, to establish loyalty, to have a fellow member witness the crime to enhance one's status, and to enable the participants to rely on intimidation. Examining the specific facts of the sexual assault, the majority noted that one defendant suppressed his own personal interest in having sex with the victim by yielding to the others when asked. They further noted that one defendant held the victim's legs down while the third defendant raped her, and that they blocked the door for each other and remained in the apartment while each one had his turn. Concluding, the majority stated:

> In short, defendants' conduct exceeded that which was necessary to establish that the offenses were committed in concert. Defendants not only actively assisted each other in committing these crimes, but their common gang membership ensured that they could rely on each other's cooperation in committing these crimes and that they would benefit from committing them together. They relied on the gang's internal code to ensure that none of them would cooperate with the police and on the gang's reputation to ensure that the victim did not contact the police.
>
> We, therefore, find substantial evidence that defendants came together *as gang members* to attack Amanda M. and, thus, that they committed these crimes in association with the gang (*Albillar, supra,* at Westlaw, p. 12).

Justice Werdegar, in her concurrence and dissenting opinion, disagreed with the prosecutors and majority's approach. She found that the prosecutor's explanation "allowed the jury to find that defendants, knowing of each other's gang membership and acting together—pooling their strength and assisting each other in the commission of the crimes—acted in association with *the gang*" (*Albillar, supra,* at Westlaw, p. 19). In so doing, Werdegar explained, "It collapsed the requirement of the second prong of section 186.22, subdivision (b), that each defendant act to promote, further, or assist in criminal conduct by gang members, a finding supported by the evidence—with the requirement of the first prong—that the defendants committed the crimes in association *with the gang,* a finding having no evidentiary support" (*Id.*).

According to Justice Werdegar, it makes no sense for the phrase "in association with any criminal street gang" to equate to "in association with *members* of a criminal street gang."

What the legislature intended by "in association with any criminal street gang" is unclear, but that it meant acting "in association with *members* of a criminal street gang" is unlikely. That the legislature distinguishes between the gang and members of the gang is shown by its use of both terms throughout section 186.22, including subdivision (b).

Indeed, as indicated above, interpreting "criminal street gang" in subdivision (b) to mean "*members* of a criminal street gang" creates a redundancy in the provision, as the second prong of section 186.22, subdivision (b) already requires that the crime have been committed "with the specific intent to promote, further, or assist in any criminal conduct *by gang members.*"

The majority provides a different definition of "in association with" a gang, explaining it means that, in committing the offenses, defendants relied on their "common gang membership and the apparatus of the gang"

(Maj. opn., ante, 119 Cal.Rptr.3 datp. 426,244P.3 datp.1071). Again, by focusing on gang members as associating *with one another,* rather than as associating *with the gang,* the majority's definition also threatens to render a portion of section 186.22, subdivision (b) redundant.

Finally, the majority's interpretation, whatever its merit, was not provided to the jury. Thus, in finding the enhancements true, the jury necessarily relied on the construction of the phrase provided by the prosecutor, a construction neither consistent with the statute nor endorsed by the majority. Hence, on this ground alone, the enhancement should be reversed.

Until the precise meaning of the phrase "in association with any criminal street gang" is settled on statutory and constitutional grounds, practitioners should continue to argue, as was done in *Albillar,* that simply committing a crime with other gang members, without any other evidentiary support, is insufficient to establish the "in association with" criterion. If it were otherwise, the benefit/direction/association element would be collapsed into the specific intent element, there would be redundancy in the statute, and mere membership would be punished.

Membership in a Gang Not Required, but What Is Proof of Gang Membership?

It Doesn't Take Much to Prove You Are a Member of a Gang
Evidence of tattoos on the robbery defendant's head, and admissions to police, were sufficient for the jury to find active membership in a gang. The fact that the robbery was committed with another gang member was sufficient to prove the robbery was committed "in association with" the gang (*People v. Martinez,* (C.A. 4th, 1/15/08, G038150) 08 C.D.O.S. 614).

There must be some competent evidence to support each and every element of the offense or the finding must fail. Though circumstantial evidence may be considered in making the determination, all inferences must be reasonable, and any inferences that derive from speculation, conjecture, or guesswork must be discarded. Police gang expert speculation alone that a crime was for gang benefit is insufficient to support the enhancements.

Penal Code section 186.22 (b) applies where a person commits a crime for the benefit of, at the direction of, or in association with a criminal street gang while that person must have the "specific criminal intent" to assist, further, or promote criminal conduct by gang members. The prosecution's only evidence on this point was the opinion testimony of their gang expert officer. The police gang expert testified that the defendant allegedly committed the crime for the benefit of the gang and that the client had the specific intent to further his criminal conduct, without any facts to base that opinion upon.

There were no facts presented as admissible evidence in this case or cause to believe that the client had specific intent to commit a crime for the benefit of, at the direction of, or in association with a criminal street gang.

Section 186.22 (b) criminalizes conduct, not mere association. Here, the prosecution presented the police gang expert's opinion testimony that the crime was committed for the benefit of a gang. The police gang expert's testified that there was a continuing battle over this area where the crime occurred between rival gangs. He opined that the defendant acted for this purpose of benefiting a gang, without any facts that were admitted into evidence at the preliminary hearing.

The prosecution also relied on the client's friendships with suspected gang members. Then attempting to make an absolute conclusion based upon the faulty premises that all actions of gang members are never personal in nature; the prosecution had no facts to bootstrap its illogical argument.

The second element of subdivision (b) of section 186.22 requires that defendant have "the specific intent to promote, further, or assist in any criminal conduct by gang members."

Evidence of Gang Membership Alone Is Insufficient

Gang membership alone does not show that a crime is committed for the benefit of, at the direction of, or in association with a criminal street gang. Gang enhancements require "some evidentiary support" other than merely the defendant's record of prior offenses and past gang activities or personal affiliations, for a finding that a specific crime was committed with specific intent for the benefit of, at the direction of, or in association with a criminal street gang.

Consequently, even if the court assumes that the client is an active gang member, that alone is insufficient to support the gang enhancement. Here, the prosecution argued that the crime would benefit the gang. The only evidence concerning the purpose of the alleged charges was the opinion testimony of the police gang expert. No evidence was presented to show that any particular gang was involved, nor was a particular identity mentioned, before, during, or after the incident; gang graffiti or that there was any bragging or acceptance of responsibility, community fear, or area forms of communication the "gang branding" after the incident that would benefit the gang's reputation. Further, the police gang expert admitted that not all crime is gang-related.

The Court of Appeal considered this precise question in the 2007 *People v. Albarran* case. In *Albarran*, a known gang member and an accomplice shot at a house during a private party hosted by a man from another gang. The prosecution relied solely on the expert testimony to prove gang benefit.

The expert testified that Albarran was a gang member, had gang tattoos, a gang moniker, and gang graffiti in his home. Though no gang names or signs were displayed during the incident, the gang expert "insisted that the shooters would gain respect within the gang, absent such evidence," and that "by word of mouth, word on the street, it was known the … gang was at the party."

In reversing the gang enhancement conviction, the Court of Appeal held, "[T]here was insufficient evidence to support the contention that this shooting was done with the intent to gain respect. [T]he motive for the underlying crimes, in particular the shooting … was not apparent from the circumstances of the crime."

Despite the expert's opinion that the crime was committed to gain respect, the court disagreed, holding "… this shooting presented no signs of gang members' efforts in that regard," there was no evidence that the shooters announced their presence or purpose, before, during, or after the shooting." The court also found it significant that "[t]here was no evidence presented that gang members had "bragged" about their involvement or created graffiti and took credit for it." In conclusion, the court ruled "[t]here is nothing inherent in the facts of the shooting to suggest any specific gang motive. In the final analysis, the only evidence to support the 'respect' motive is the fact of (defendant's) gang affiliation."

Usually the facts in your case are indistinguishable from *Albarran*. Usually there is no evidence that any of the participants announced their presence, gang name, gang graffiti, gang sign, or a gang purpose at any time. There is usually no suggestion that the gang members bragged to others or sought to take credit for the fight, or that the community even knew that there was an alleged crime that was gang-related. Like *Albarran*, there is no evidence to suggest that a client's actions were motivated by any specific intent of gang motive. Just as the expert's testimony in *Albarran* failed to prove a gang benefit, here, the expert's conclusionary statement that a crime committed, even in contested "turf" necessarily confers a gang benefit fails "to suggest any specific intent of gang motive."

It is truly a sad commentary on the judicial system that prosecutors, knowing the above law and facts that there are no facts to establish fear as a benefit, abuse their duty as prosecutors to seek the truth and instead "dirty up the defendant to win and chalk up the conviction count," even knowing that a cop expert is exaggerating or, at worst, lying and putting a citizen in prison who will never be the same again.

Just as the expert's testimony in *Albarran* failed to prove a gang benefit, the expert's conclusory statement that a crime committed, even in contested "turf," necessarily confers a gang benefit fails "to suggest any specific intent of gang motive."

Moreover, *In re Frank S.* held that expert opinion testimony on the issue of specific intent was improper. While the fact finder may rely on expert testimony about gang culture and habits to determine a gang allegation, the court cannot rely on expert opinion alone to show that "a specific individual possessed a specific intent." In *Frank S.*, a gang expert testified that Frank, who was charged with illegal weapons possession, was a gang member. Frank had identified himself as a gang member during intake, wore gang clothing, and admitted that he carried the knife to protect himself against other gang members.

The expert testified that the minor possessed the weapon to protect himself against rival gang members and to assault rival gangs, and those weapons help the gang members protect themselves if they should be assaulted. In reversing the gang allegation, the Court of Appeal found "no substantial evidence supporting the specific intent element."

The court expressly found that "[w]hile the evidence established that the minor has an affiliation with [the gang], membership alone does not prove a specific intent to use the knife to promote, further, or assist in criminal conduct of gang members." The recent *Ramon* case also supports the same conclusion. There, Ramon and another gang member were driving a stolen car and were in the possession of guns on gang turf when stopped. The Court of Appeal reversed the conviction.

Thus, the police gang expert opinion as to why the client was shooting without some indication that the targets were gang members is improper expert testimony. Indeed, the police gang expert does not even try to suggest these people are likely members. The police gang expert reliance on the client's alleged gang status is not enough to show gang benefit, as illustrated by *Albarran, Frank S.*, and *Ramon*.

The prosecution has the burden of proving beyond a reasonable doubt the elements of California Penal Code §186.22. Therefore, the prosecution has the burden of proving beyond a reasonable doubt that the client had "specific intent" to commit a felony, "for the benefit of, at the direction of, or in association with any criminal street gang, with the specific intent to promote, further, or assist in any criminal conduct by gang members. ..." (Penal Code § 186.22 (b)(1)).

People v. Gardelely, 59 Cal. Rptr. 2d 356, qualifies expert witnesses to testify at criminal street gang trials. Gardeley states the following, "Under Evidence. Code, ß 801, expert opinion testimony is admissible only if the subject matter of the testimony is 'sufficiently beyond common experience that the opinion of an expert would assist the trier of fact'" (Evid. Code, ß 801, subd. (a)). The subject matter of the culture and habits of criminal street gangs meets this criterion.

An expert generally may render opinion testimony on the basis of facts given in a hypothetical question that asks the expert to assume his/her truth. Such a hypothetical question must be rooted in facts shown by the evidence, however.

Expert testimony also may be premised on material that is not admitted into evidence, so long as it is material of a type that is reasonably relied upon by experts in the particular field in forming their opinions (Evid. Code, ß 801, subd. (b)). Of course, any material that forms the basis of an expert's opinion testimony must be reliable, because an expert's opinion is no better than the facts on which it is based. So long as this threshold requirement of reliability is satisfied, even matter that is ordinarily inadmissible can form the proper basis for an expert's opinion testimony. And because Evid. Code, ß 802 allows an expert witness to "state on direct examination the reasons for his opinion and the matter … upon which it is based," an expert witness whose opinion is based on such inadmissible matter can, when testifying, describe the material that forms the basis of the opinion.

Gang Experts Used by the Government versus Defense Gang Expert

Evidence Code section 720, subdivision (a), provides, in relevant part: "A person is qualified to testify as an expert if he has special knowledge, skill, experience, training, or education sufficient to qualify him as an expert on the subject to which his testimony relates." Expert testimony on criminal street gangs has been deemed appropriate for establishing most of the requirements of Penal Code section 186.22 (*People v. Hernandez* (2004) 33 Cal.4th 1040; *People v. Williams* (1997) 16 Cal.4th 153, 196; *People v. Gardeley* (1996) 14 Cal.4th 605, 617; *People v. Olguin* (1994) 31 Cal.App.4th 1355, 1370). Case law recognizes that police officers may testify as experts about the sociology, psychology, customs, and methods of operations of street gangs (*People v. Ferraez* (2003) 112 Cal.App.4th 925, 930; *People v. Gamez* (1991) 235 Cal. App.3d 957, 966; *People v. McDaniels* (1980) 107 Cal.App.3d 898, 905).

This includes testifying about the gang's composition and size, their primary activities, and an individual defendant's membership in or association with the gang (*People v. Killebrew* (2002) 103 Cal.App.4th 644, 657). The courts also have sanctioned gang expert testimony on "whether and how a crime was committed to benefit or promote a gang" (*Id.*).

In fact, the gang expert may testify to opinions that comment on the ultimate issues to be resolved by the trier of fact (*People v. Valdez* (1997) 58 Cal. App.4th 494, 508–510; *People v. Olguin* (1994) 31 Cal.App.4th 1355, 1370–1371). However, a gang expert is prohibited from testifying about whether an individual had specific knowledge or possessed a certain specific intent (*People v. Killebrew, supra*, 103 Cal.App.4th 644, 658).

In *Killebrew*, the defendant was convicted of conspiring to possess a handgun, even though he did not have a handgun in his possession. A police officer testified as an expert on gangs to establish not only "there must be some competent evidence to support each and every element of the offense; or the finding must fail. Though circumstantial evidence may be considered in making the determination, all inferences (a factually constructed bridge leading to the present charge) must be reasonable, and any inferences which derive from speculation, past conjecture, or guesswork must be discarded as an uncompleted bridge to nowhere."

Academic studies, field interviews of the day-to-day life of the defendant, as well as interviews of actual people with personal gang knowledge as it relates to the defendant's lack of activity for, with, or by a gang are beyond the pale of speculation, conjecture, or guesswork.

Trial Court Gang Experts Standard of Review

It is often said, "... any expert's opinion is only as good as truthfulness of the information on which it is based. ..." (*People v. Ramirez, supra*, 153 Cal. App.4th at p. 1427). *A gang expert is a kind of practical field anthropologist*, whose primary source material comes directly from real, live gang members. (See *People v. Olguin* (1994) 31 Cal.App.4th 1355, 1370 (*Olguin*) [noting there was sufficient foundation for gang expert's opinion]; see also *People v. Hill* (2011) 191 Cal.App.4th 1104, 1119 (*Hill*) [noting a gang expert spent 90 percent of his time investigating certain street gangs, including interviews of gang members, *community members*, as well as continually monitoring gang activity].) This field work necessarily involves much personal contact and listening to what gang members say (*Olguin, supra*, 31 Cal.App.4th at p. 1370).

Gang expert trial testimony throughout our legal literature, outlining what is proper, not proper, and necessary in the testimony of the gang expert at trial, has almost exclusively looked at the role of the prosecution's use of a governmental agent in trial, as a government gang expert, in light of the constitutional protections of an accused who is presumed innocent until proven guilty.

Little if any legal guidance, American Bar Association or other legal guidance, exists as to what is proper, not proper, and necessary in the preparation and testimony of a defense gang expert at trial, for an accused to be afforded a reasonable opportunity to defend himself or herself against unproven government gang allegations.

It is more than reasonable to affirm that the defense gang expert and police government gang expert are two sides of the same coin, though with different messages on either side with the same value. Government and defense gang experts should be held to the same standards in the general legal sense that the information on which the expert relies is true and accurate. However, due to the intrinsic differences in an adversarial trial setting, it would not be logical or fair that the governmental or defense gang expert uses the exact same sources of information or comes to the same conclusions in all cases. Whether guided by statute, case law, or other legal guidance, each government and defense gang expert either uses, evaluates, reviews, develops different sources of information that are interpreted and delivered in sworn testimony by the opposing experts in differing adversarial opinions in a trial setting.

Jury instructions, in harmony with case law, such as CALCRIM No. 332, the current standard form jury instruction on expert opinion testimony, instructs the jury that it "must decide whether *information on which the expert relied was true and accurate*," and it may "disregard any opinion" that it finds "unbelievable, unreasonable, or unsupported by the evidence." (See Pen. Code, § 1127b [*sua sponte* instructions required on expert testimony.)

An expert may state on direct examination the matters upon which he or she relied in forming his or her opinion, as long as the matter is reliable and the expert is not precluded by law from using such reasons or matters as a basis for the opinion (Evid. Code, §§ 801, 802; *Gardeley, supra,* 14 Cal.4th at p. 618 ["Of course, any material that forms the basis of an expert's opinion testimony must be reliable."]).

To be sure, "an expert's need to consider extrajudicial matters, and a jury's need for information that is sufficient to evaluate an expert opinion may conflict with an accused interests in avoiding substantive use of unreliable hearsay" (*Montiel, supra,* 5 Cal.4th at p. 919) when proffered by a governmental interest. However, that same client's interests, interestingly enough, may not be in conflict with a defense gang expert's opinion and may actually further the client's interests.

Personal contact (by the experts in the field talking to the community), however, often means a gang expert must rely disproportionately on out-of-court statements taken from others in the community, colleagues, reports, gang members, or other sources for his or her opinions (e.g., *Hill, supra,* 191 Cal.App.4th at pp. 1122-1123). However, the defense gang expert cannot *only* rely upon the government's discovery, court transcripts, or prosecutorial gang theories, and, in addition and in contrast, must rely also upon defense theories and developed information that is true and accurate to come to a complete and well-rounded reasoned opinion, otherwise a jury may "disregard any opinion" that it finds "unbelievable, unreasonable, or unsupported by the evidence."

Just as prosecution government experts rely on what they believe to be true and accurate information of reports, interviews of other officers, interviews of other gang members, interviews of community leaders, interviews of others, and other materials, so must the defense gang expert rely upon not just prosecution-generated materials but defense generated materials as well. Such things as reports, interviews of other defense-related people, interviews of other gang members, interviews of community leaders, interviews of others, and other materials are needed to come to a supportable defense expert opinion that is true and accurate at trial.

Each fact or opinion that is proffered by the government gang expert, as to the client's association, direction, benefit to a gang by the defendant's past actions, i.e., FI cards, tattoos, statements of witnesses, other documentation, and all opinions of a government gang expert at the preliminary hearing or grand jury or other government gang theories, requires the defense gang expert be prepared in providing alternate defense expert witness trial opinions to all the government's gang theories, by supportable defense evidence that can be ascertained, by the defense gang expert, as true and accurate.

Police officers as gang experts hopefully expend vast hours reviewing reports from many sources, interviewing gang members, interviewing others in the community to directly ascertain the truth and accuracy of this information prior to rendering government expert gang opinions at trial. With the flip side of the same coin, so must the defense gang expert expend vast time in defense evidence and, in an additional burden, the review and analysis of ongoing government evidence that can be ascertained by the defense gang expert as true and accurate. The gang expert has the expertise to render a proper expert opinion in this complete review much in the same way a medical doctor has the expertise to come to an expert medical opinion by personally reviewing all materials and people directly, for truth and accuracy, to come to a proper expert opinion.

A defense gang expert as well must rely upon personal observations of the materials or people to ascertain these materials are truthful and accurate as the basis in rendering a proper defense gang expert opinion at trial. The defense gang expert, in order to render a properly supported opinion, must, as the police gang expert, not only evaluate all government-provided discovery, but evaluate all defense-generated discovery or testimony as well, for truth and accuracy, to come to a properly reasoned defense gang expert opinion, by supportable evidence that can be ascertained, by the gang expert, as true and accurate.

Defense Gang Expert Witness versus Police Gang Expert Witness in Adversarial Trials

As a fundamental pillar of our uniquely honored American adversarial system, a defense attorney has an obligation to make every ethical effort to show the government has not overcome the just and high presumption of innocence. Failing to call a defense gang expert witness to rebut the testimony of a governmental gang expert witness would most likely be a failure to adequately represent his or her client.

A defense attorney has a duty to investigate whether an expert is necessary (*People v. Frierson* (1979) 25 Cal.3d 142, 162–164; see *Baylor v. Estelle* (9th Cir. 1996) 94 F.3d 1321, 1323–1324). An attorney has a duty to present an expert when an expert is necessary to present a defense (*Id.*). And, an attorney has a duty to properly prepare an expert witness. (See, e.g., *Hovey v. Ayers* (9th Cir. 2006) 458 F.3d 892, 925–928; see also *Forensis Group, Inc. v. Frantz, Townsend & Foldenauer* (2005) 130 Cal.App.4th 14, 33–35 [attorney has a duty to make sure the expert understands the governing legal principles, understand the details of the testimony and field of expertise, make sure the testimony is understandable, the declaration is complete, and the qualifications are properly presented]; but see *People v. Carter* (2003) 30 Cal.4th 1166, 1211–1212 [no IAC on balance when expert witness gave some damaging testimony].)

Defense gang experts, whether having gained their experience in the streets as a public defender, as private investigators, in the halls of academia, in research, as former gang members, as nonprofit gang interventionists, as news reporters specializing in the gang beat, as outreach centers like Homeboy Industries, as religious antigang outreach (churches of all faiths), as social workers, as defense investigators, and as other similarly situated defense gang experts, mostly do *not* utilize the same materials or people to evaluate the alleged gang enhancements charges as the police gang expert. They should not be evaluated on the basis of different materials or witnesses used by the police gang expert standard either in qualifying as an expert or in their substantive testimony and opinion of the alleged gang enhancement(s), as long as the materials or people relied upon by the defense gang expert are supportable evidence that can be ascertained by the gang expert as true and accurate.

Defense gang experts are focused on the behavior (lack of specific intent of the client in relationship to the alleged crimes), lack of *current* gang background, and lifestyle of the client, with those client behaviors and lifestyles as *not* being gang-related (at the exact time of the allegations), as well as other areas. This is in complete contrast to the "police gang expert," who opines that long past specifics of a particular gang, i.e., history, boundaries, graffiti, and the client's long past associations (if any), as the only possible explanation in the universe of multiple explanations to the present gang enhancement allegations.

The defense expert witness opinion is often multifold: (1) does the alleged crime not fit a gang crime with the crime more closely resembling crime motivated by personal benefit (not gang benefit); (2) whether the client's specific intent in committing the crime may be personally motivated—not in association with, at the direction of, or for the benefit of a gang—regardless if the client is a gang member or not; and (3) was the government agent's expert courtroom testimony (prior hearings or at trial) devoid of any "competent evidence to factual support all of the alleged corpus delecti elements" of the present alleged crime? Often police experts rely on the conjectured inferences or other nonsupported opinions, such as the "gang history of the gang," the client's past, or other nonconnected (to the actual charges) conjectured inferences rather than evidence where one could reasonably infer the client's *mens rea* or *actus reus* at the time of the current alleged offense to specifically support the allegations presently at bar.

It, therefore, is not helpful to the jury, in a proper defense of the gang enhancement allegations, to attempt to render a defense gang expert as using different and often more reliable source materials to that of the police gang expert when the methodologies and basis of the opposing expert gang opinions are diametrically opposed, in an adversarial trial testimonial setting, and utilize fundamentally different analysis and processes.

Additionally, methods and techniques differentiate police gang experts from defense gang experts' opinions in determining if the alleged crime could be articulated as personally motivated (not gang motivated, thus not qualifying as directed by, associated with, or benefitting a gang), regardless if the client is an actual gang member or not.

For example, two paroled, face gang tattooed, active gang OG members, in the CalGang database, who are actively committing gang and other crimes daily, have a personal argument over one's girlfriend having sex with the other gang member, leading to one gang member killing the other. Though the surviving perpetrator would most likely be in danger of a murder charge(s), it is highly improbable (with the competent testimony of a gang defense expert at trial) a jury would render a guilty finding if a P.C. 186 gang enhancement also was alleged; as the hypothetical crime was purely personal in nature, regardless if the defendant was an active gang member or not.

Specifically, as to the corpus delicti of P.C. 186, the government only needs to convince a jury that one of the three elements (no direction, noncriminal association, and no benefit to a gang) presents itself through "facts" beyond a reasonable doubt. In the above example, there is no *direction by a gang*, as the killing is one of the most raging personal acts—personal revenge— that was self (nongang) directed. Doubly failing is the "profound *lack of any criminal association*." The final unnecessarily expensive government bridge to nowhere, in the above hypothetical, glaringly shows that *no gang benefits* occur from a lone wolf of an unplanned, contemporaneous, horrific killing out of personal jealousy, even though the alleged murder was at the jealous hands of a hardened active gang member.

Gang members and those who are not gang members, but associate with gang members (Webster's dictionary definition of association, not specific criminal intent association) more often than not commit crimes that are *personally motivated* and have *nothing* to do with being directed by, associating with, or benefiting any gang.[5]

The Government's View of Police Gang Experts

A 2009 University of California Hastings College of the Law article in the *Hastings Race and Poverty Law Journal* (7 Hastings Race & Poverty L.J. 111) illustrates the power that prosecutors' gang experts have in gang trials.

> Prosecutors often call gang experts to testify for two purposes: (1) to give testimony involving statutory gang allegations under the STEP Act, and (2) to give testimony involving some other material issue which may be in dispute such as identity, motive, bias, or knowledge. The police officer gang expert has considerable evidentiary power. While testifying, the police officer gang expert will often justify his or her opinion *by making universalizing assertions about the nature of gang culture that transcend the gang at issue.*

While California Penal Code sections 186.22(a), (b), and (d) are not identical, each of the provisions have certain required elements in common. Described most broadly, they each require proof of the existence of a "criminal street gang" and proof the offense in question was gang-related. The "gang-related" requirement takes two forms, depending on whether the prosecution is attempting to prove specific criminal intent in the substantive offense (section 186.22(a)) or attempting to prove the sentence enhancement or alternate penalty (sections 186.22(b) and (c)).

For the substantive offense, gang expert testimony is used to prove that there was a pattern of gang activity by the members of the gang, that the defendant had knowledge of that pattern, and that he or she "with specific criminal intent, articulated by facts, willfully promotes, furthers, or assists in felonious conduct by members of the gang." Further, there must be a showing that the defendant was an active participant.

In order to satisfy the gang-related element, specific criminal intent articulated by facts, for the enhancement and alternate penalty, the prosecution gang police expert must prove that an offense has been committed "for the benefit of, at the direction of, or in association with a criminal street gang."

In sum, police gang experts will often testify to one or more of four elements when testifying in a case where the defendant is charged with an offense under the STEP Act:

1. Existence of a criminal street gang
2. Commission of the crime for the benefit of, at the direction of, or in association with the gang
3. Commission of the crime to promote, further, or assist the gang
4. Active participation of the defendant in the gang

However, most police experts only opine that the alleged crime was for the benefit of, at the direction of, or in association with a gang, without any specific facts, such as a gang shout out, gang signs, graffiti, instilling fear into the community or other gang; in essence "communication" the gang intention, thus most police gang experts fail to articulate specific criminal intent with facts.

> ... What is the proper subject matter for the expert? The simple answer is, all the juicy stuff. The expert is the witness who will identify the defendant as a gang member. From the witness stand, the expert can establish the defendant's gang affiliation in several ways, including the defendant's admission of membership to the expert, the defendant's tattoos, and his consistent association with other gang members. The expert can also relate the defendant's gang's rivalries in the community, as well as the gang's history and structure. The meaning of tattoos as more than identifiers of gang membership is proper subject matter for a gang expert, as well as the interpretation of graffiti, gang slang, and gang monikers. The expert may also explain the gang's criminal tactics, culture, and habits. Remember, the expert is giving opinions. There are no "wrong" answers. The hypothetical question is a powerful tool that prosecutors can and should use to their advantage. It should be viewed as a free bite at the apple—an opportunity to set out the facts of the case the way the prosecutor wants the jury to see them. Therefore, because the prosecutor will recite the facts most productive to his or her case, the hypothetical question should be viewed as a mini closing argument. Because of the persuasive power of the hypothetical question, the gang expert should be called to the stand as close to the end of the prosecutor's case as possible. The more often the jury hears the evidence couched in the prosecutor's terms, the more persuasive it will be. Coupling the hypothetical with the closing arguments means that the jury will hear the prosecutor's version of the facts three times versus the defense attorney's single argument.
>
> Otherwise inadmissible evidence—hearsay, for instance—can be the proper basis for an expert's opinion. For example, experts can base their opinions on the defendant's statements, other gangsters' statements, the review of graffiti or photographs of graffiti, conversations with other police officers, the review of prior police reports, and centralized computer database records. However, anything upon which the gang expert relies is subject to discovery. Gang intelligence files, therefore, may become discoverable if the expert does not track the original source of the information contained in the case file or database. If internal intelligence files are turned over to the defense, ongoing investigations could very well be compromised. Advise the expert to follow up on information uncovered in gang intelligence files to independently corroborate the facts so that only the original source information is discoverable.[6]

In other words, dirty up the defendant as much as possible.

Why is this important? Because jurors often do not understand that there are severe problems with police gang units, especially in Los Angeles. One only has to think of the Rampart scandal with the Los Angeles Police Department so corruptly exposed and dramatized in the movie *Training Day* with Denzel Washington. Or the ongoing scandals with the Los Angeles Sheriff's Department in the county jail system and many more examples.

Keeping in mind that with tens of thousands of criminal charges filed each year, with the majority of cases being settled at approximately 95 percent or more each year, only a small, single-digit number of gang cases actually go to trial. So, is it possible that 100 percent of trial cases have guilty defendants that will be convicted? No, of course not. Juries have, in a slightly higher percentage of gang P.C. 198.22 trials, found defendant's either not guilty or have had a hung jury on the gang allegations. That means that jurors in a higher percentage of cases can find the governments and police expert gang testimony not credible enough for conviction.

Police Misconduct

Los Angeles Police CRASH (Community Resources Against Street Hoodlums) Program

The intensity of the LAPD's war on street gangs and its propensity for corruption were laid bare in the late 1990s when investigations of police misconduct exposed the operations of the CRASH (Community Resources Against Street Hoodlums) program. According to former California State Representative Tom Hayden, CRASH had evolved from TRASH—Los Angeles' first anti-gang police unit—established under a federal grant in 1977. T stood for *total,* and the goal was total suppression of gangs. The investigation became known as the Los Angeles Police Ramparts scandal.

In 1998, a CRASH officer working out of the Rampart police precinct house, Rafael Perez, was charged with theft of 8 pounds of cocaine from a police locker. Facing a long prison term, Perez broke the code of silence and revealed the inner workings of the antigang squad. Operating jointly with federal agents in the FBI and the Bureau of Alcohol, Tobacco, Firearms, and Explosives, CRASH officers in the Rampart district conducted gang sweeps in 1997 and 1998 that resulted in Immigration and Naturalization Service (INS) deportation of 160 people.

Some INS officials in Los Angeles were appalled at the tactics being used. INS documents handed over to a *Los Angeles Times* reporter revealed complaints by INS officers that CRASH was waging war against "a whole race of people." Perez testified that potential witnesses to police misconduct were being handed over to the INS for deportation.

Perez talked of framing cases against some 100 people, and implicated scores of other officers. Perez admitted that he and his partner had shot one Pico-Union gang member in the head and then planted drugs and guns near his fallen body. The brain-damaged victim, released from prison after Perez's testimony, had been sentenced to 23 years in prison for his "crime." Tainted cases were dismissed against 99 other defendants.

A *Los Angeles Times* article published in 2000 characterized the Rampart CRASH unit as hosting a secret fraternity of more than 30 officers and sergeants with "an organized criminal subculture." Officers were awarded plaques that celebrated incidents in which they had wounded or killed people (Glover and Lait, 2000).

Los Angeles Police Ramparts Division Scandal

Based mainly on statements of the admitted corrupt officer (Pérez), initially more than 70 police officers either assigned to or associated with the Rampart CRASH unit were implicated in some form of misconduct, making it one of the most widespread cases of documented police misconduct in U.S. history. The convicted offenses include unprovoked shootings, unprovoked beatings, planting of false evidence, framing of suspects, stealing and dealing narcotics, bank robbery, perjury, and the covering up of evidence of these activities. Of those officers, enough evidence was found to bring 58 before an internal administrative board. However, of the officers named by Pérez, only 24 were actually found to have committed any wrongdoing, with 12 given suspensions of various lengths, 7 forced to resign or retire, and 5 fired. As a result of the probe into falsified evidence and police perjury, 106 prior criminal convictions were overturned. The Rampart Scandal resulted in more than 140 civil lawsuits against the city of Los Angeles, costing the city an estimated $125 million in settlements. As of 2013, the full extent of Rampart corruption is not known, with several rape, murder, and robbery investigations involving Rampart officers remaining unsolved.

... In 2000, Prof. Erwin Chemerinsky described it as the worst abuse of civil rights by police in the history of the United States. He also characterized it as typical of "police states and most repressive regimes. ... The Blue Ribbon Review Panel Report (2006) concluded that the investigation was deliberately restricted to prevent it from exposing the full scope of the corruption, which was much wider than represented in any of the available reports ... and that LA County justice system could not investigate itself, prosecute itself, and adjudicate itself. It recommended an "outside investigation." It was the biggest corruption investigation in the history of the United States with 200 investigators assigned to it for two years. ...

The investigation and prosecution were under the charge of California Department of Justice, Los Angeles County District Attorney, with the end result of prosecution at the LA Superior Court. ... The trial was derailed, and, with that, an end came to the prosecutions of the Rampart scandal culprits, and also an end to any attempt to release the thousands of victims. ...

California Court of Appeals [Justice] Hastings said it was clear to him that since the result of the alleged conspiracy [by Rampart police officers] was the filing of criminal charges against suspected gang members, an instruction explaining what conduct might have justified those charges was necessary. He was mystified, he said, by the fact none was given.[7]

Following are random comments collected by Human Rights Alert (nongovernmental organization) about the justice system of Los Angeles County, California, with specific reference to the "Ramparts Scandal." Quotes from the past decade:[8]

- "Los Angeles County got the best courts that money could buy." KNBC (October 16, 2008)
- "Innocent people remain in prison." LAPD Blue Ribbon Review Panel Report (2006)
- Los Angeles Superior Courts must be "examine[d for] its role in accepting pleas from innocent defendants and failing to detect police perjury or the conviction of the innocent." LAPD Blue Ribbon Review Panel Report (2006)
- "... Law enforcement, prosecutors and judges, inexorably chose containment. It is not that individuals or entities conspired to cover up corruption, it is that, when a window on its true extent opened, they simply closed it." LAPD Blue Ribbon Review Panel Report (2006)
- "The response by police to the Blue Ribbon Panel report was of interest in that it failed to ever mention past, present, or future investigation into the Rampart scandal abuses that were the reason the Panel was instituted, and were the subject of its report. Obviously, the LA Superior Court and the DA office, the two other parts of the justice system that the Blue Panel Report recommends must be investigated relative to the integrity of the system, have not produced any response that we know of. ..." LAPD Blue Ribbon Review Panel Report (2006)
- The justice system of Los Angeles shows tolerance "of a subcult of criminality in the ranks." LAPD Blue Ribbon Review Panel Report (2006)
- Los Angeles County is "the epicenter of the epidemic of real estate and mortgage fraud." FBI (2004)
- "... Judges tried and sentenced a staggering number of people for crimes they did not commit." Professors David Burcham (Dean) and Katherine Fisk, Loyola Law School, Los Angeles (2000)
- "This is conduct associated with the most repressive dictators and police states ... and judges must share responsibility when innocent people are convicted." Prof. Erwin Chemerinsky (Dean), University of California, Irvine Law School (2000)

Prosecutor's Misconduct

In our adversarial judicial system, the overriding assumption is "innocent until proven guilty beyond a reasonable doubt," with the burden of proof being on the prosecution. The unfortunate dominate theme, however, by prosecutors is "presumed guilty" in the cases they themselves have reasonable doubt of the defendant's "nonactive" gang status (yet they can't help themselves and are pushed to up the body count on convictions annually). Nonetheless, in effect, due to society's "get tough on crime" policy, it is the prosecutors and their "misconduct" and borderline "misconduct" that drives major ethical problems into the illegal presumption of guilt. In addition, the government's prosecutorial misconduct filters down (almost training and ordering their government witnesses—the police) to their police agents who are encouraged to sometimes lie as expert witnesses in trials to get convictions. Prosecutorial misconduct is the heart of the argument.

There is no doubt via the "innocence assumption" that 100 percent of all people charged with crimes, especially gang enhancement cases, are not guilty of the crimes charged, with juries in agreement that the government is wrong in some cases. However, you would not think so if you ever attended or were involved in real gang prosecutions. It is as if the prosecutors believe or want us to believe that 100 percent of the time the government is 100 percent always correct; something all of the rest of us know to be absurd.

Pressures on prosecutors to win cases is never an excuse for misconduct; however, data show that prosecutors in California are experiencing higher and higher numbers of misconduct as shown in the few following examples, selected from hundreds of similar cases in point:

In re Bacigalupo; 2012 DJ DAR 11861; DJ, 8/28/12; Cal. Supreme Court
The California Supreme Court reversed a death verdict on the basis of a *Brady* (373 U.S. 83) violation at the penalty phase. The defendant claimed that he killed because the Columbian Mafia had threatened to kill the defendant and his entire family if he didn't. The prosecution had evidence that supported this claim, but failed to turn it over. The DA actually argued at the penalty phase that there was no evidence to support the duress claims of the defendant.[9]

February 12, 2010—San Diego Police Misconduct: Court of Appeal Orders "Brady" Discovery From Police Personnel File In Lying Cop Case
The defendant was convicted of murder, and a key witness testified against him. The police detective told the defense that the witness wasn't a paid informant. Some years later, the defense stumbled across information that showed that the witness was, in fact, a paid informant. The defense now files a habeas petition. The defense seeks *Brady v. Maryland* (373 U.S. 83) discovery

of complaints in the detective's personnel file that the detective claimed that informants weren't paid when, in fact, they were. This is an interesting case because the C/A finds no basis for *Pitchess* (11 C3d 531) discovery, but does order review of the detective's personnel file on *Brady* grounds, correctly finding that prior complaints about the detective lying about informants being paid would impeach the detective's testimony at any habeas hearing. This is the first possible published case where the court finds a discovery duty under *Brady*, but not *Pitchess*.[10]

Prosecutor's Four-Year Suspension For Misconduct Upheld

A former deputy district attorney abused his office and violated the due process rights of several criminal defendants.

[The attorney] "disregarded prosecutorial accountability in favor of winning cases," the three-judge panel upheld the recommendation of [the] hearing judge and also urged that [the attorney]be given five years of probation.

"Although our system of administering justice is adversarial in nature and prosecutors must be zealous advocates in prosecuting their cases, it cannot be at the cost of justice," wrote Judge Catherine Purcell, who was joined in the decision by Judges JoAnn Remke and Judith Epstein.

[He] lost sight of this goal," Purcell continued, " … and, in doing so, he disregarded the foundation from which any prosecutor's authority flows. The first, best, and most effective shield against injustice for an individual accused … must be found … in the integrity of the prosecutor."

The allegations stemmed from four cases and charged:

- [He] obtained a dental examination of a minor accused of sexual assault in violation of a court order. He was attempting to try the youth, who claimed to be 13, as an adult. A juvenile court judge suppressed the evidence obtained in the examination.
- In a murder case, [he] intentionally withheld a defendant's statement favorable to co-defendants. As a result, the judge dismissed a 25-year gun enhancement against one of the co-defendants.
- He made an improper closing argument in a sexually violent predator (SVP) case, which an appellate court described as "deceptive and reprehensible." The court reversed a judgment committing the man as an SVP.
- He intentionally withheld a witness's statement that was favorable to the defense in a 2003 habeas corpus proceeding involving a sexual assault.

[The attorney's] misconduct escalated over time and constituted "a calculated scheme to hide evidence favorable to the defense." In the same case, [he] obtained five search warrants despite the judge's doubts about his tactics. Indeed, when [he] asked the judge what to do if he needed a warrant in an emergency, the judge testified, "I looked him right in the eye and I said, "… just don't do it.'" Five days later, [the attorney] obtained a search warrant in another state without notifying the judge.

The review panel found the [attorney] committed several acts of moral turpitude, and did not obey a court order or follow the law.[11]

June 3, 2009—California criminal defense: San Francisco may pay $4.5 million to wrongfully convicted man. It's payback time for prosecutors who break the law. San Francisco citizens will pay for prosecutorial misconduct.[12]

San Francisco officials have tentatively agreed to pay $4.5 million to a man who spent nearly 14 years in prison before a judge reversed his murder conviction, finding that city authorities had withheld evidence his attorneys said could have cleared him. [The man] was freed in 2003 after a federal judge overturned his conviction for the August 1989 killing. ... He had been serving a prison term of 25 years to life.

Another judge freed [the man's] co-defendant, who was serving 27 years to life. A Superior Court judge subsequently declared both men "factually innocent." They then sued in federal court, saying the city had violated their civil rights.

Attorneys for [the two men] have long argued that prosecutors and the two police investigators kept possibly exculpatory evidence from the defense at the time of trial and afterward.

Defendant's defense team said the evidence included a post-trial confession of another man and the earlier statement by a woman who indicated that the man may have been involved in Shannon's killing.

In freeing [the man], [the] U.S. District Judge concluded not only that authorities had withheld key evidence from the defense, but also that the prosecution's case was weak to begin with.

"No physical evidence was presented at trial tying [him to the] shooting," she said. "The prosecution's entire case was dependent upon the testimony of ... two young girls whose eyewitness identifications of [the defendant] were questionable."

The Police View on Gangs That Often Seep through in Criminal Trials

The objectives of a gang control effort depend on whether the problem is defined as gang violence, gang crime, or the gangs' very existence. Law enforcement officials often take the public position that gangs must be eradicated. In the words of Captain Ray Peavy, who heads the Los Angeles sheriff's homicide bureau, "Everyone says, 'What are we going to do about the gang problem?' It's the same thing you do about cockroaches or insects; you get someone in there to do whatever they can do to get rid of those creatures" (Garvey and McGreevy, 2007).

Why Law Enforcement Agencies Form Gang Units

The proliferation of specialized gang units has been justified as a natural response by police officials to the spread of gangs and growing public concerns over gang crime. The argument for such units is that they permit officers to develop the technical skills and expertise needed to diagnose local gang problems and to assist the rest of the agency and the community to address them. However, the idea that the formation of a gang unit is "a result of *rational considerations* on the part of police agencies" that face "*real* gang problems" has been challenged by several researchers (Katz and Webb, 2003a).

Marjorie Zatz examined the establishment of a gang unit in Phoenix and determined that police officials had invented a serious gang problem in order to secure federal resources (cited in Katz and Webb, 2003a). Richard McCorkle and Terrance Miethe found that the formation of a gang unit in the Las Vegas Police Department was driven by a search for resources and scandals within the department rather than an emerging gang crime problem (cited in Katz and Webb, 2003a).

Law enforcement officials fomented a "moral panic" by linking "national reports of a growing problem to local concerns of increasing crime in order to divert public attention away from problems within the police department and to justify an infusion of additional resources into the department." Gang panics are not always generated by law enforcement. Carol Archbold and Michael Meyer document a particularly disturbing example of how a handful of troubling incidents can snowball into a full-scale moral panic (cited in Katz and Webb, 2003b). The researchers found that the public fear generated by a series of youth homicides in a small Midwestern city led police to begin designating local minority youths as gang members. Fear continued to rise as the number of documented "gang members" grew. The situation eventually "spun out of control, resulting in community panic, even though there was no actual evidence of any gang-related activity in the city."

Charles Katz, Edward Maguire, and Dennis Roncek examined factors that influenced the establishment of police gang units in about 300 large US cities (cited in Katz and Webb, 2003b). The researchers found no relationship between the formation of a gang unit and "the size of a community gang or crime problem." Instead, they found that gang units were most likely to be formed in cities with larger Hispanic populations, and among police departments that received funding for gang control efforts. The authors "reasoned that police organizations might be creating units when the community feels threatened by a minority group."

This finding was strengthened in subsequent research by Katz and Webb examining police responses to gangs in four Southwestern cities: Albuquerque, New Mexico; Inglewood, California; Las Vegas; and Phoenix (2003b). The authors concluded that the creation of gang units was largely a reaction to "political, public, and media pressure" rather than a response to an objective problem *or* a strategy for securing additional resources or controlling marginalized populations.

The isolation of gang units from host agencies and their tendency to form tight-knit subcultures—not entirely unlike those of gangs—also contributes to a disturbingly high incidence of corruption and other misconduct. The Los Angeles Police Department's Rampart scandal is the most famous example of a gang unit gone bad. Katz and Webb cite several other places where police gang units have drawn attention for aggressive tactics and misconduct, including Las Vegas, where two gang unit officers participated in a drive-by shooting of alleged gang members; Chicago, where gang unit officers worked with local gangs to import cocaine from Miami; and Houston, where gang task force officers were found to routinely engage in unauthorized use of confidential informants, warrantless searches, and firing weapons at unarmed citizens. They also concluded that at least some of the gang units "might have been created prior to receiving external funding for the purposes of justifying the need for more resources."

Police Lying in Gang Cases

In this era of mass incarceration, the police shouldn't be trusted any more than any other witness, perhaps less so. That may sound harsh, but numerous law enforcement officials have put the matter more bluntly. Peter Keane, a former San Francisco police commissioner, wrote an article in *The San Francisco Chronicle* decrying a police culture that treats lying as the norm: "Police officer perjury in court to justify illegal dope searches is commonplace. One of the dirty little not-so-secret secrets of the criminal justice system are undercover narcotics officers intentionally lying under oath. It is a perversion of the American justice system that strikes directly at the rule of law. Yet, it is the routine way of doing business in courtrooms everywhere in America."

The New York City Police Department is not exempt from this critique. In 2011, hundreds of drug cases were dismissed after several police officers were accused of mishandling evidence. That year, Justice Gustin L. Reichbach of the State Supreme Court in Brooklyn condemned a widespread culture of lying and corruption in the department's drug enforcement units. "I thought I was not naïve," he said when announcing a guilty verdict involving a police detective who had planted crack cocaine on a pair of suspects. "But even this court was shocked, not only by the seeming pervasive scope of misconduct, but even more distressingly by the seeming casualness by which such conduct is employed."

The word *testilying* and its meaning have been publicized by defense attorney Alan Dershowitz, notably in a 1994 *The New York Times* article, "Accomplices to Perjury," in which he said: "As I read about the disbelief expressed by some prosecutors ... I thought of Claude Rains' classic response, in the 1940s movie, *Casablanca,* on being told there was gambling in Rick's place: 'I'm shocked–shocked.' For anyone who has practiced criminal law in the state or federal courts, the disclosures about rampant police perjury cannot possibly come as a surprise. 'Testilying,' as the police call it, has long been an open secret. ..."[13]

Former federal judge and law professor Irving Younger once described "police perjury as commonplace."[14] Before his death in 1988, Younger had distinguished himself as an outstanding lawyer, jurist, and law teacher.[15] Younger asserted that while police perjury is commonplace, "judicial recognition of the fact is extremely rare." He explained further in a hearing on a motion to suppress evidence under *Mapp v. Ohio* 367 U.S. 643 (1961), "... for example, the policeman testifies to his version of the circumstances of the search and seizure, invariably reflecting perfect legality. The defendant testifies to his version, invariably reflecting egregious illegality. The judge must choose between the two versions, and, not surprisingly, he habitually accepts the policeman's word. The difficulty arises when one stands back from the particular case and looks at a series of cases. It then becomes apparent that policemen are committing perjury at least in some of them, and perhaps in many of them.[16]

Based on this sudden and systematic change in police testimony, Younger concluded that police had begun to lie during hearings and to create stories that would meet constitutional requirements and, correspondingly, avoid suppression of drug evidence. A study conducted by students at Columbia Law School that was published in 1968 suggested that Younger was correct. The students evaluated the evidentiary grounds for arrest and disposition of misdemeanor narcotics cases in New York City before and after *Mapp*[17] ... finding that the most common form of police corruption in the New York City criminal justice system was probably "police falsification," especially in connection with arrests for possession of "narcotics and guns" and that falsification was so common, it had spawned the name "testilying."[18]

In 1992, after noting "very little empirically grounded information on the [exclusionary] rule's application and effects[,]" Myron W. Orfield, Jr., published the results of a study of the Chicago criminal justice system, which went well beyond an acknowledgment of police perjury. After interviewing a sampling of judges, prosecutors, and defense lawyers, he announced that "structured interviews with judges, prosecutors, and public defenders in the

Chicago criminal court system" and in which "respondents outlined a pattern of pervasive police perjury intended to avoid the requirements of the Fourth Amendment" ... judges in Chicago often knowingly credit police perjury and distort the meaning of the law to prevent the suppression of evidence and assure conviction. ... His research revealed that a sampling of judges, public defenders, and prosecutors estimated that "police commit perjury between 20 and 50 percent of the time they testify on Fourth Amendment issues."

In his book, *The Best Defense*, Alan Dershowitz identified 13 "key rules" of our justice system, including "Rule IV: Almost all police lie about whether they violated the Constitution in order to convict guilty defendants. Rule V: All prosecutors, judges, and defense attorneys are aware of Rule IV. ... Rule VIII: Most trial judges pretend to believe police officers who they know are lying. Rule IX: All appellate judges are aware of Rule VIII, yet many pretend to believe the trial judges who pretend to believe the lying police officers. Rule X: Most judges disbelieve defendants about whether their constitutional rights have been violated, even if they are telling the truth."[19]

Using various research methods and evaluating data from jurisdictions beyond New York, other legal scholars came to the same, reasoned conclusion as did Younger, the Columbia law students, and the Mollen Commission— police officers lie, even under oath, especially during suppression hearings. Based on extensive and personal observation research in a city of about 400,000 people, Jerome H. Skolnick, explaining that, when the police see case law "as a hindrance to the primary task of apprehending criminals, they usually attempt to construct the appearance of compliance rather than allow the offender to escape apprehension."[20] He concluded that police sometimes fabricate probable cause when they think that search and seizure laws are too restrictive.

> By the very nature of the offense, numbers on the extent of police perjury are impossible to come by. According to conservative U.S. 9th Circuit Court of Appeals Judge Alex Kozinski, police perjury and prosecutorial misconduct to gain convictions is "an open secret long shared by prosecutors, defense attorneys, and judges."
>
> University of Florida law professor Christopher Slobogin conducted an exhaustive survey of the literature on police perjury. His findings were shocking: "Whether it is conjecture by individual observers, a survey of criminal attorneys, or a more sophisticated study, the existing literature demonstrates a widespread belief that testilying is a frequent occurrence." In one survey cited by Slobogin, defense attorneys, prosecutors, and judges estimated that police perjury occurs in between 20 and 50 percent of Fourth Amendment suppression hearings, which result when defense attorneys attempt to argue that police had no probable cause to stop or search a suspect.
>
> Veteran police observer Jerome Skolnick called police perjury of this sort "systematic." Even prosecutors, or at least former prosecutors, Slobogin

noted, use terms like "routine," "commonplace," and "prevalent" to describe the scope of the practice. "Few knowledgeable persons are willing to say that police perjury about investigative matters is sporadic or rare, except perhaps the police," Slobogin concluded, "and even many of them believe it is common enough to merit a label all its own."

The Mollen Commission,[21] established in New York City in the early 1990s in the wake of police scandals there, reached a similar conclusion. "Officers reported a litany of manufactured tales," its report noted. "For example, when officers unlawfully stop and search a vehicle because they believe it contains drugs or guns, officers will falsely claim in police reports and under oath that the car ran a red light (or committed some other traffic violation) and that they subsequently saw contraband in the car in plain view. To conceal an unlawful search of an individual who officers believe is carrying drugs or a gun, they will falsely assert that they saw a bulge in the person's pocket or saw drugs and money changing hands. To justify unlawfully entering an apartment where officers believe narcotics or cash can be found, they pretend to have information from an unidentified civilian informant or claim they saw the drugs in plain view after responding to the premises on a radio run. To arrest people they suspect are guilty of dealing drugs, they falsely assert that the defendants had drugs in their possession when, in fact, the drugs were found elsewhere where the officers had no lawful right to be."[22]

The LAPD is said to call the practice "joining the liars' club." In a 1996 article in the *Los Angeles Times* (Has the Drug War Created an Officer Liars' Club?), Joseph D. McNamara, then chief of police of San Jose, said, "Not many people took defense attorney Alan M. Dershowitz seriously when he charged that Los Angeles cops are taught to lie at the birth of their careers at the Police Academy. But, as someone who spent 35 years wearing a police uniform, I've come to believe that hundreds of thousands of law enforcement officers commit felony perjury every year testifying about drug arrests." He noted that "within the last few years, police departments in Los Angeles, Boston, New Orleans, San Francisco, Denver, New York, and other large cities have suffered scandals involving police personnel lying under oath about drug evidence." Police officers who have been dishonest are sometimes referred to as "Brady cops." Because of the Brady ruling, prosecutors are required to notify defendants and their attorneys whenever a law enforcement official involved in their case has a sustained record for knowingly lying in an official capacity.[23]

In an article published in *Criminal Justice Ethics*, [24] the author states:

… The point here is not whether to deplore the police violations of the Fourth Amendment or the lying of police in the testimonial context, rather, it is to understand how police who engage in it themselves come to justify it, so that moral prescriptions might be given a better chance of being persuasive to police who do not find them compelling in practice. The policeman lies because lying becomes a routine way of managing legal impediments, whether to protect fellow officers or to compensate for what he views as limitations the courts have placed on his capacity to deal with criminals. He lies because he is skeptical of a system that suppresses truth in the interest of the criminal.

Moreover, the law permits the policeman to lie at the investigative stage, when he is not entirely convinced that the suspect is a criminal, but forbids lying about *procedures* at the testimonial stage, when the policeman is certain of the guilt of the accused.

Thus, the policeman characteristically measures the short-term disutility of the act of suppressing evidence, not the long-term utility of due process of law for protecting and enhancing the dignity of the citizen who is being investigated by the state. ..."

In an article dated September 18, 2011, Jack Leonard, *Los Angeles Times*, reported:

… Panelists' (jurors) concerns over what they see as "fabrications" spur an internal affairs investigation into law enforcement actions and testimony in a Compton weapons case. When Compton jurors recently deliberated the fate of a man charged with possessing a concealed firearm, they thought the evidence was overwhelming—not that the man was guilty, but that the Los Angeles County sheriff's deputies who testified against him had lied.

Jurors said a video of the arrest and inconsistent testimony from deputies left them no choice earlier this month but to vote for acquittal. The five jurors who spoke to *The Times* said authorities should investigate the (Los Angeles) deputies from the sheriff's antigang unit who were involved in the case. ..."[25]

A February 2013 article or an online site for the California Criminal Defense Lawyers discussed the recent existence of a "clique" or "rogue group"[26] (Editor's Note: euphemisms for "gang.").

… They wore distinctive clothing, had similar tattoos, and celebrated shootings. But the members of this gang weren't standing on a street corner, they were jumping out of cop cars. They were members of the L.A. County Sheriff's Department's "elite" gang enforcement team. By all accounts, the group was a gang. But media sources are being cautious to call them that, instead using words like "clique" or "rogue group."

They called themselves the "Jump Out Boys." Their inclusion in the gang meant they got a tattoo—a skull wearing a bandana and holding a gun. In true gang form, the tattoo had various playing cards behind it and smoke would be added to the gun when the gang member celebrated a shooting.

Yes, the gang would change their tattoo when they shot a civilian. The Jump Out Boys were reportedly "discovered" when they made a pamphlet describing their "group." But, as the secretive nature of police forces are well-documented, there is a good chance that many in the force knew about the gang before its "discovery" became official.

The L.A. County Sheriff's Department alone has a "long history" of secret groups. Officials say they are now working to root out those cliques that serve to tarnish the department's image. Investigators say they found no criminal behavior involved in the Jump Out Boys. The investigators, incidentally, also were employed by the sheriff's office. Seven members have been informed that their firing is imminent. Obviously, the department couldn't keep them on staff after the discovery of their involvement went public. ...

"We get called a gang within the badge? It's unfair," said one member. "People want to say you have a tattoo. So do fraternities. Go to Yale. Are they a gang?... Boy Scouts have patches and they have mission statements, and so do we."

Boy Scouts, Yale students, and fraternities, however, don't carry firearms as part of their daily routine. Nor do they have the power of a police officer. And he may have overlooked the fact that they don't celebrate shooting at people.

"We do not glorify shootings," he went on. "What we do is commend and honor the shootings. I have to remember them because it can happen any time, any day. I don't want to forget them because I'm glad I'm alive."

When Cops Lie: A Report from Los Angeles

Cops lie. Under oath, on the witness stand. "I saw him reach for a gun." "I found the drugs in his pocket." But, what happens when juries refuse to believe their testimony? Do cops ever get in trouble for fabricating evidence or lying under oath? Do they ever get charged with perjury?

The *Los Angeles Times* in a page one story today named three L.A. sheriff's deputies who jurors, in a case in Compton, California, said had told "one lie after another" under oath. They said authorities should investigate the three.

The case involved a 19-year-old man arrested at a party at a house in South Los Angeles. Deputies testified at a preliminary hearing that when they arrived at the party, they saw the man run and then toss a loaded revolver on the roof of a garage. They said they ordered him to stop, and that he walked back to them and they then arrested him.

The defendant pleaded innocent and at his trial shouted, "Fingerprint the gun!" The gun was never fingerprinted.

Defense attorneys found that another guest at the party had videotaped the events, and that the video did not show the defendant running or throwing anything on the roof. The video showed him standing still when the deputies arrived and arrested him. The jury concluded the deputies had lied under oath. And the *LA Times* posted the video on its website.

Are the three deputies who backed up each others' testimony going to be prosecuted for perjury? Award-winning investigative reporter Jack Leonard of *The Times* reported that the sheriff's captain told him that "the deputies made errors that will be addressed with additional training," but that "their actions were not criminal." In the meantime, one of the three has been promoted to

detective. The defendant, meanwhile, spent more than a month in jail await-
ing trial, at which he was found not guilty.[27*]

In yet another report of Los Angeles police lying, two current and one
former Los Angeles police officers are on trial for perjury. They are accused
of lying in a 2008 drug investigation.[28]

> What prosecutors saw in a surveillance video won freedom for accused gang
> member Guillermo Alarcon and instead led to felony charges against three
> LAPD officers.
>
> It all started in 2006. Officers say they saw Alarcon with something in his
> hand and they chased him. They say Alarcon tossed the object—a box with
> cocaine—that they found immediately. They swore on the police report and
> in Alarcon's trial that they were telling the truth. Then came the stunning
> disclosure from Alarcon's public defender: There had been four cameras on
> the property and one even recorded audio. The tape appeared to reveal mul-
> tiple inconsistencies with the officers' account and raised questions about
> who really dropped the drugs. In July 2008, public defender Victor Acevedo
> described to *Eyewitness News* what statements were heard on the tape. "One of
> the officers turns around and just blatantly tells the other officer, 'Hey, be cre-
> ative in your writing.' To top that off, you have other officers actually respond-
> ing, 'Hey, don't worry, we've done this before,'" said Acevedo. Former Officer
> Evan Samuel faces five charges, Richard Amio faces three, and Manuel Ortiz
> faces two.

Testilying

Los Angeles Times writers Fredrick N. Tulsky, Ted Rohrlich, and John
Johnson, write:

> How often police testify falsely or withhold evidence is impossible to know.
> Every day in court, witnesses and police accuse each other of lying about what
> police were told during their investigations. But seldom is there independent
> evidence to disprove the police version. In each case that was reviewed, there
> were lingering questions about whether the alleged police misconduct resulted
> from an intentional act or an innocent mistake.
>
> For people who are victims of such conduct, "it doesn't matter that the
> officers say it was an innocent mistake," said Georgetown University law
> professor Abbe Smith. "It is a terrible thing to come into court and watch an
> officer testify falsely, and watch everyone else believe the testimony."
>
> Police are authorized to lie during investigations in pursuit of the truth. Police
> can lie during undercover operations. They can use ruses to find out where people

* Wiener, Jon. *When Cops Lie: A Report From Los Angeles*: on September 19, 2011 http://
www.thenation.com/blog/163479/when-cops-lie-report-los-angeles# Retrieved 03/10/13.

live so they can get search warrants. At homicide school, a reporter watched as officers were taught to bluff suspects into confessing by pretending to have evidence when they did not. They were taught to use falsely labeled notebooks, supposedly containing reams of evidence. Detectives put this kind of advice into practice.

With more recent "gang enhancement statutes," such as P.C. 186.22, we are starting to see a troubling increase in police "testilying" from the LAPD Rampart scandal to the Los County Sheriff's gang-like activities in county jails and other areas.

The question to be answered in the near future is: If testilying is a crime of perjury, conspiracy to obstruct justice (and other possible crimes), how deep does the "aiding and abetting" run in allowing these crimes to continue, does it flow from government prosecutors and should they too be charged with crimes if they knowingly allow this perjury, and what of the judicial branch and their duty to not turn a "blind judicial eye" to this testilying?

At the heart of abuses in gang enhancement trials is not only the harsh and probable unintended consequences of the STEP Act, enacted in 1988 (over 30 years ago), in netting and convicting persons that were not intended by the Act, but the creation of a government testilying culture, on many cases, that want higher conviction rates at nearly any cost to the very criminal justice system itself.[29]

Unfortunately, the historical evidence is in. Since *Mapp v. Ohio*, the police, prosecutors, and others have turned a blind eye, and not the "justice is blind" eye, on police and prosecutorial misconduct.

Most prior studies have focused on search and seizure, drug, and gun crimes as the main suspected areas of police "testilying." But with more recent gang enhancement statutes, such as P.C. 186.22, we are starting to see a troubling increase in police testilying, from the LAPD Rampart scandal to the Los County Sheriff's gang-like activities in county jails and other areas.

The question to be answered in the near future is: If testilying is a crime of perjury, conspiracy to obstruct justice, and other possible crimes, how deep does the aiding and abetting run in allowing these crimes to continue? Does it flow from government prosecutors, and should they, too, be charged with crimes if they knowingly allow this perjury? And what of the judicial branch and its duty to not turn a blind judicial eye to this testilying?

In his dissenting opinion on *Olmstead v. United States* (1928), US Supreme Court Justice Louis D. Brandeis, wrote in support of the rule of law:

Decency, security, and liberty alike demand that government officials shall be subject to the same rules of conduct that are commands to the citizen. In a government of laws, existence of the government will be imperiled if it fails to observe the law scrupulously. Our government is the potent, the omnipresent teacher. For good or ill, it teaches the whole people by its example. Crime is contagious. If the government becomes a lawbreaker, it breeds contempt for the law; it invites every man to become a law unto himself; it invites anarchy.

To declare that in the administration of the criminal law the end justifies the means—to declare that the government may commit crimes in order to secure the conviction of a private criminal—would bring terrible retribution. Against that pernicious doctrine this court should resolutely set its face.[30]

At the heart of abuses in gang enhancement trials is not only the harsh and probable unintended consequences of the STEP Act, enacted more than 30 years ago in 1988, in netting and convicting people that were not intended by the act, but the creation of a government testilying culture, on many cases, that want higher conviction rates at nearly any cost to the very criminal justice system itself.

Follow the Money: Why the Government Will Increase Gang Convictions as Crime Rates Decrease

Though an entire book could be dedicated in the future on the government's obsession with drastically increasing gang convictions at any costs, what are the costs or, better yet, what are the financial benefits to the government in increasing gang convictions?

With county government budgets being drastically cut throughout California, police, prosecution, and correctional, taxpayer-based entities can be counted on to seek more and more taxpayer money to expand their government agencies, and there is no better way than a war on gangs and all those associated with gangs. Even in the face of facts that show that crime convictions are substantially lower and, as previously shown, gang crime is not the dominant factor in overall crimes.

Studies vary as the costs associate with gang crime or the money sought by government agencies to wage the war on gangs, but most agree there are billions in taxpayers' money to be spent.

In a Stanford University paper published in 1999, these financial costs were explored:[31]

Narcotic Prevention: $295,000
Community Mobilization: $629,000
Gang Prevention: $986,946
Prosecution: $1,060,473
Probation: $1,107,214
Law Enforcement: $1,312,061
Education: $1,770,866

These are only some of the costs affecting the gang situation in California. By the year 2000, expenditures associated with the gang problem in California could possibly grow to several billion dollars. The conclusion of the report cited Father Boyle, who commented that out of the three ways to combat gangs, intervention is the least dealt with, but is equally important, if not more important than the other two tactics.

The Vera Institute of Justice has further estimated that, adjusting for inflation, we calculated that the approximate criminal justice government costs of gang violence that occurred in 2005 totaled $1,097,036,170. Vera adjusted for inflation using the West Region Consumer Price Index from the US Department of Labor's Bureau of Labor Statistics.

Funding Analysis Cluster Vera Institute of Justice for Los Angeles sampling:[32]

Los Angeles Police Department
LAPD Costs
2005 Citywide arrests: $159,106
Part 1 arrests: $29,292
2005 Part 1 gang arrests: 6,619
Total budget: $1,368,277,896
Cost per Part 1 arrest: $36,828
Total cost: $243,764,532

City Attorney
Gang Unit Budget: $3,115,992

Sheriff's Department Costs
Annual corrections budget: $843,553,021
Percentage of inmates from LA City: 39%
Cost of housing LA City inmates: $328,985,678
Percentage of gang-involved inmates: 70%
Cost of LA City gang-involved inmates: $230,289,975

Adult Probation Costs
Per capita cost (yearly): $1,533
Number of adults on probation: 63,000
Percentage from LA City: 31%
Number of probationers from LA City: 19,530
Percentage that are gang-involved: 3%
Number of gang-involved probationers: 586
Total cost: $898,338

Probation (Home) Costs
Number of probationers per year: 20,000
36 percent from LA City: 7,200
56 percent gang involved: 4,032
Per capita cost (annual): $5,252
Total cost: $21,176,064

Probation (Detention) Costs
Per capita cost (daily): $215
Average length of stay (days): 37
Per capita cost (based on average stay): $7,955
Detentions per year: 15,710
Total cost of detentions per year: $124,973,050
36 percent from LA City, 56 percent gang involved: $25,194,567

Superior Courts Costs
Number of annual nontraffic criminal cases: 307,307
Budget approximation for nontraffic criminal cases: $73,752,800
Cost per case: $240
Number of cases from LA City (39%): 119,850
Number of gang-related cases (23%): 27,566
Total: $6,615,840

CDCR (Prison) Costs
Per capita cost (yearly): $34,150
Total number of offenders: 170,475
33 percent from LA County: 56,257
39 percent from LA City: 21,940
70 percent gang involved: 15,358
Yearly cost of LA gang members: $524,475,700

The funding for all and more of the above is taxpayer, grants, forfeitures, and other areas.

The STEP Act Is Ineffective in the 'War On Gangs'[33]

In 1988, the California legislature enacted the STEP Act in order to "seek the eradication of criminal activity by street gangs" within the state of California. In the two decades since the Act was approved, it has been amended several times in order to more effectively combat gangs.

Recently, the state of California announced a renewed "war on gangs," and, in early 2007, Los Angeles County law enforcement began escalating gang crackdowns in order to eliminate gangs.

As part of the war on gangs, Los Angeles County prosecutors have become increasingly likely to seek the STEP Act's sentencing enhancements in order to elevate the prison terms of suspected gang offenders.

The City of Los Angeles has been so aggressive in attempting to combat gangs that it has spent over $1 billion on surveillance and policing, and the incarceration costs of its increased sentences for gang members over the past 20 years.

However, despite the aggressiveness on the part of law enforcement officials and prosecutors in using the STEP Act's sentence enhancements in order to combat gangs, the Act has not been a successful tool in the war on gangs.

Moreover, it has not been successful in combating crime more generally because its provisions have not contributed to the decrease of criminal activity in Los Angeles County or the State of California.

In the 20 years since the STEP Act was enacted in 1988, gang involvement in Los Angeles has skyrocketed. Today, there are at least six times as many gangs and twice the number of gang members in Southern California than in 1988.

Gang researchers estimate that there are approximately 700 active gangs in Los Angeles and anywhere from 40,000 to 200,000 gang members.

Also, according to FBI Director Robert Mueller, gang activity has particularly increased in Los Angeles in recent years, with Los Angeles Chief of Police William Bratton asserting gang activity increasing by almost 16 percent in 2006 alone (see http://www.fbi.gov/).

So, what did we get for our $1-billion-a-year bill as taxpayers—more gangs and more gang members?

And with those that have been incarcerated numbering in the tens of thousands, eventually to be released back into California society, how will the crime rates react with the release of tens of thousands of unrehabilitated convicted gang members?

Conclusion

The STEP Act, gang law enforcement specialists, gang prosecutors, the courts, and correctional facilities all have benefited from increased funding with the never-ending war on gangs. Even in the face of historic lowering crime rates and convictions, the government's insatiable appetite for more funding to expand the war on gangs nationally and internationally is never-ending.

Through prior research in academia, nonprofits/for profits, governmental agencies, and others whom I relied upon for this chapter, it is clear that gangs are increasing in size and numbers geographically, in the face of lowering crime rates. This can only lead one to postulate whether the governmental forces really know how or want to contain, reduce, or even end gang violence in California or the United States.

In an age of diminishing taxpayer money and resources, can we continue to spend billions of dollars when gangs are increasing in size and numbers annually? Or is it time to examine other models, such as those in New York state, which has spent even more money, but not in areas of enforcement, prosecution, and imprisonment (as we do here in California) exclusively, but rather in a wrap-around approach while driving down the gang crime, gang membership, and gang numbers.

Can we really prosecute and imprison our way out of this growing gang epidemic, or is it time to spread our taxpayer bets into other rehabilitative programs, such as New York and other states have successfully used in recent times?

To even begin in California with a more balanced approach of prevention, intervention, rehabilitation, and other methodologies (mixed with a more surgical use of our police, prosecutors, courts, and prisons), we must first understand what are gangs, who are really gang members or who are not, what are gang crimes or not, what are the facts about gang crime, how does the law need to evolve paying attention to police and prosecutorial misconduct, and limited, more effective use of taxpayer funding.

After all, do we really want a war on our children who are just on the fringes of this gang culture that is more closely resembling delinquency than gangs? Or do we want an all-out, military-like government and police assault on our communities of children and young adults, our young people in our families and neighbors, sweeping them all into the rarely forgiving criminal justice system when our law enforcement and criminal justice is only now, in California, learning what is and is not a gang associate or personal crime?

There is no doubt that approximately 150 murders a year in Los Angeles (that are gang-related) are always too much, but we have come a long way with a major decrease in gang murder convictions of more than 1,000 since 1988 when we enacted the STEP Act.

Additionally, no one doubts that there are not dangerous gangs, gang members, and gang associates that must be prosecuted and imprisoned, but in proportion to the real crime statistics that are related to gang crime rather than just playing into the fear game of gangs while disproportionately funding police, prosecution, courts, and corrections with limited taxpayer money at hand.

As a gang expert in courtroom testimony in gang-related trials for murder, death penalty, drug cartel, and a never-ending list of horrors, there is becoming an increasing concern from many corners of the criminal justice field that we are netting up way too many kids or young adults into prisons that may have well been better served by our system. Most of us are sure that the day these marginal kids and young adults leave the correctional system that we may have an increased gang problem of amplified gang crimes matched with the perfect gang storm of increasing gang numbers and gangs nationally.

It is time for another look at how we determine who is a gang member, associate, or wanna-be, and another look at whether these crimes are all gang related or more personal in nature.

With a deeper and more concentrated look at these gang enhancement-related issues, the courts will be in a better position to update, through new case rulings, how the STEP Act should modernly be interpreted, along with additional fiscally reapportioned wrap-around remedies to reach the solutions we all wish for: vastly decreased gang membership, association, and reduced gang crimes to the greater enjoyment of our civil society.

Endnotes

1. A conscious attempt by the prosecution (including police) to make a defendant's actual criminal involvement appear worse to a jury than it actually is.
2. Judith Greene and Kevin Pranis, A Justice Policy Institute Report (Washington, D.C.: Justice Policy Institute, July 2007).
3. *Gang Wars, The Failure of Enforcement Tactics and the Need for Effective Public Safety Strategies* (Washington, D.C.: The Justice Policy Institute, July 2007).
4. Gregori Estevane, November 2009 survey of 500 L.A. gang members (See Appendix C).
5. County of Los Angles Crime conviction statistics on annual crime convictions PC 186.
6. As stated by Alan Jackson, deputy district attorney, Los Angeles County District Attorney's office, *Prosecuting Gang Cases, What Local Prosecutors Need to Know* (Alexandria, VA: American Prosecutors Research Institute, April 2004). Online at www.ndaa-apri.org.
7. Human Rights Alert, NGO. Online at http://human-rights-alert.blogspot.com/ http://www.scribd.com/Human_Rights_Alert 2010. UPR: Human Rights Alert (Ngo)-The United States Human Rights Record–Allegations, Conclusions, Recommendations, April 8, 2010.
8. Ibid.
9. Online at http://www.californiacriminallawyerblog.com/california_cases/ (retrieved March 10, 2012).
10. *Pitchess v. Superior Court* 11 Cal.3d 531 (1974). Online at http://www.californiacriminallawyerblog.com/2010/02/san_diego_police_misconduct_co.html; *Eulloqui v. Superior Court* 2010 DJ DAR 1930; DJ, 2/7/10; C/A 2nd, Div. 1 (Retrieved March 10, 2012).
11. Online at http://www.californiacriminallawyerblog.com/2010/03/santa_clara_prosecutors_fourye.html (retrieved March 9, 2012).
12. Online at http://www.sfgate.com/cgi-bin/article.cgi?f=/c/a/2009/06/03/BATB17VOV1.DTL.
13. Alan Dershowitz, "Accomplices to Perjury," *The New York Times*, May 3, 1994, A1. Alan Dershowitz, "Testimony on Testilying," (Washington, D.C.: U.S. House of Representatives Judiciary Committee, December 1, 1998).

14. Melanie D. Wilson, *Judging Police Lies: An Empirical Perspective* (SelectedWorks™, January 2010). Online at http://works.bepress.com/cgi/viewcontent.cgi?article=1002&context=melanie_wilson.

15. Stephen Labaton, "Irving Younger, Lawyer, 55, Dies; Judge, Law Professor and Author," *The New York Times*, Obituary, March 15, 1988.

16. Irving Younger, *Constitutional Protection on Search and Seizure Dead?* Trial 41 (Aug./Sept. 1967). Younger, Constitutional Protection, supra note 4, at 41.

17. Effect of *Mapp v. Ohio* on Police Search-and-Seizure Practices in Narcotics Cases, 4 Colum., J. L. & Social Prob. 87 (1968). Online at heinonline.org/HOL/LandingPage?handle=hein.journals/collsp4div=9&id=&page=.

18. The Report of City of New York, Commission to Investigate Allegations of Police Corruption and the Anti-Corruption Procedures of the Police Department, (July 7 ,1994), at page 36, appearing in Myron W. Orfield, Jr., *Deterrence, Perjury, and the Heater Factor: An Exclusionary Rule in the Chicago Criminal Courts* from 63 U. Colo. L. Rev. 75, 75-76 (1992) (discussing the results of a study of police perjury in the Chicago justice system), *Effect of Mapp v. Ohio on Police Search-and-Seizure Practices in Narcotics Cases*, Colum. J. L. & Social Prob. 87 (1968) (in which Columbia law students discuss the results of a police perjury study they conducted), in Part II.A.; J. Skolnick, *Justice Without Trial*, at 215 (1967) (reporting the findings of a study finding police perjury based on observation evidence).

19. Alan M. Dershowitz, *The Best Defense* (New York: First Vintage Books edition, May 1983).

20. Jerome H. Skolnick, *Justice Without Trial*, supra ote 35, at 215.

21. Online at http://what-when-how.com/police-science/mollen-commission-police/.

22. *Tip of the Iceberg: Police Perjury Goes Far Beyond Tom Coleman*, 1/28/05. Online at http://stopthedrugwar.org/chronicle/372/iceberg.shtml.

23. Joseph D. McNamara, "Has the Drug War Created an Officer Liars' Club?" *The Los Angeles Times*, February 11, 1996; Lewis Kamb, and Eric Nalder, "Cops Who Lie Don't Always Lose Jobs." *Seattle Post-Intelligencer,* January 29, 2008.

24. Requests for permission to reprint multiple copies may be directed to cjejj@cunyvm.cuny.edu (vol. 1, no. 2, Summer/Fall 1982).

25. Jack Leonard, *Jurors question deputies' testimony.* Online at http://articles.latimes.com/2011/sep/18/local/la-me-sheriff-credibility-20110919.

26. MyCaliforniaDefenseLawyer.com. *LA County Secret Police Gang Exposed.* Online at http://www.mycaliforniadefenselawyer.com/2013/02/la-county-secret-police-gang-exposed/#more-1086.

27. Jon Wiener, *When Cops Lie: A Report From Los Angeles,* September 19, 2011. Online at http://www.thenation.com/blog/163479/when-cops-lie-report-los-angeles# (retrieved March 10, 2013).

28. Miriam Hernandez, In an ABC (KABC) news report, Monday, October 22, 2012. *3 LAPD officers on trial for perjury, conspiracy.* Online at http://abclocal.go.com/kabc/story?section=news/local/los_angeles&id=8856616.

29. Fredrick, N. Tulsky, Ted Rohrlich, and John Johnson, "When-Cops-Lie-Report-Los Angeles," Testilying in L.A. Online at http://www.cs.cmu.edu/~pshell/gammage/testimonies/testilying-la.html. (Editor's Note: This is merely a brief condensation of the entire article, which cites several more instances and examples of police "testilying."

30. *Pearson Criminal Justice Series* (New York: Pearson Custom Publishing, 2009).

31. Matt Friedrichs, *Gangs: Problems and Answers: Poverty & Prejudice: Gang Intervention and Rehabilitation*. Online at http://www.stanford.edu/class/e297c/poverty_prejudice/ganginterv/gangsproblems.htm.

32. According to the Vera Institute of Justice, Megan Golden, Jena Siegal, and Dall Forsythe. Online at http://www.vera.org/topics/policing http://councilcommittee.lacity.org/stellent/groups/boardcommissions/@councilcmte_contributor/documents/contributor_web_content/lacityp_019575.pdf.

33. Judith Green and Kevin Pranis, *Gang Wars: The Failure of Enforcement Tactics and the Need for Effective Public Safety Strategies* (Washington, D.C.: Justice Policy Institute Report, 2007).

References

Advancement Project. 2006. *Citywide gang activity reduction strategy: Phase I report.* Los Angeles. Online at www.advanceproj.com.

Boyle, Fr. Gregory. 2005. Remarks to National Juvenile Defender Summit. Los Angeles.

Curry, G. D., R. A. Ball, and S. H. Decker. 1996. Estimating the national scope of gang crime from law enforcement data. In *Gangs in America,* 2nd ed., ed. C. Ronald Huff. Thousand Oaks, CA: Sage.

Delaney, T. 2005. *American Street Gangs.* Upper Saddle River, NJ: Pearson/Prentice Hall.

Esbensen, F.-A., and L. T. Winfree, Jr. 2001. Race and gender differences between gang and nongang youths. In *The Modern Gang Reader,* 2nd ed., eds. J. Miller, C. L. Maxson, and M. W. Klein. Los Angeles: Roxbury.

Garvey, M. and P. McGreevy. 2007. L.A. mayor seeks federal aid to combat gangs. *Los Angeles Times,* January 4.

Glover, S. and M. Lait. 2000. Police in secret group broke law routinely, transcripts say. *Los Angeles Times,* February 10.

Hagedorn, J. M. 1998. Gang violence in the postindustrial era. In *Youth Violence,* eds. M. Tonry and M. H. Moore, in *Crime and justice: A review of research,* vol. 24, ed. M. Tonry. Chicago: University of Chicago Press.

Hayden, T. 2005. *Street Wars.* New York: New Press.

Katz, C. M., and V. J. Webb. 2003. *Police Response to Gangs: A Multi-Site Study.* Phoenix: National Institute of Justice, December.

Klein, M. W. 1995. *The American Street Gang: Its Nature, Prevalence and Control.* New York: Oxford University Press.

Maxson, C. L. 1995. *Street Gangs and Drug Sales in Two Suburban Cities.* Washington, D.C.: National Institute of Justice, July.

Maxson, C., and M. Klein. 2001. Defining gang homicide: An updated look at member and motive approaches. In *The Modern Gang Reader,* 2nd ed., eds. J. Miller, C. L. Maxson, and M. W. Klein. Los Angeles: Roxbury.

Shelden, R. B., S. K. Tracy, and W. B. Brown. 2004. *Youth Gangs in American Society,* 3rd ed. Belmont, CA: Wadsworth Thomson.

Siegel, L. 2003. Gangs and the law. In *Gangs and Society: Alternative Perspectives,* eds. L. Kontos, D. Brotherton, and L. Barrios. New York: Columbia University Press.

Weisel, D. Lamm, and T. O'Connor Shelley. 2004. *Specialized gang units: Form and function in community policing.* Research report submitted to US Department of Justice in October.

Ziedenberg, J. 2005. *Ganging Up on Communities? Putting Gang Crime In Context.* Washington, D.C.: Justice Policy Institute.

Further Readings

Advancement Project. 2007, January. *Citywide gang activity reduction strategy: Phase III report.* Los Angeles. Online at www.advanceproj.com.

Boyle, Fr. Gregory. 2011. *Tattoos on the Heart: The Power of Bondless Compassion.* New York: Free Press.

Bureau of Justice Assistance, Center for Program Evaluation. Undated. Online at http://www.ojp.usdoj.gov/BJA/evaluation/psi_gangs/gangs2.htm.

Butts, J. A., and J. Travis. 2002. *The Rise and Fall of American Youth Violence: 1980–2000.* Washington, D.C.: Urban Institute.

Bynum, T. S., and S. P. Varano. 2003. The anti-gang initiative in Detroit: An aggressive enforcement approach to gangs. In *Policing Gangs and Youth Violence,* ed. S. H. Decker. Belmont, CA: Wadsworth.

California Gang Node Advisory Committee. 2007 (revised September 27). Policy and procedures for the CALGANG ˚ system.

California Attorney General's Office. 2004. *Gang homicide in LA, 1981–2001.* Sacramento: State of California.

California Youth Justice Coalition. 2006. *Los Angeles Department of Homeland Boy Security, 1980–2005: Coordinating local, state and federal laws and law enforcement tactics to intensify the war on gangs.* Campaign document circulated in connection with a May city council hearing on gang injunctions.

City of Los Angeles Police Department. 2008. Crime and arrest statistics. Los Angeles, CA.

Curry, G. D. 2000. Self-reported gang involvement and officially recorded delinquency. *Criminology* 38 (4).

Curry, G. D., S. H. Decker, and A. Egley, Jr. 2002. Gang involvement and delinquency in a middle school population. *Justice Quarterly* 19 (2).

Davis, M. 2006. *City of Quartz* (new ed.). New York: Verso.

Decker, S. H., and J. L. Lauritsen. 1996. Breaking the bonds of membership: Leaving the gang. In *Gangs in America,* 2nd ed., ed. C. R. Huff. Thousand Oaks, CA: Sage.

Decker, S. H., and B. Van Winkle. 1996. *Life in a Gang: Family, Friends, and Violence.* New York: Cambridge University Press.

Decker, S. H., and G. D. Curry. 2003. Suppression without prevention, prevention without suppression: Gang intervention in St. Louis. In *Policing Gangs and Youth Violence,* ed. Scott H. Decker. Belmont, CA: Wadsworth.

Decker, S. H., T. Bynum, and D. Weisel. 2001. A tale of two cities: Gangs as organized crime groups. In *The Modern Gang Reader,* 2nd ed., eds. J. Miller, C. L. Maxson, and M. W. Klein. Los Angeles: Roxbury.

Egley, A., Jr., J. C. Howell, and A. K. Major. 2006. *National Youth Gang Survey: 1999–2001.* Washington, D.C.: Office of Juvenile Justice and Delinquency Prevention, July.

Egley, A., Jr., and C. E. Ritz. 2006. *Highlights of the 2004 National Youth Gang Survey.* OJJDP fact sheet. Washington, D.C.: Department of Justice Office of Justice Programs, April.

Esbensen, F.-A., L. T. Winfree, N. He, and T. Taylor. 2001. Youth gangs and definitional issues: When is a gang a gang and why does it matter? *Crime & Delinquency* 47 (January).

Fagan, J. 1990. Social processes of delinquency and drug use among urban gangs. In *Gangs in America,* 2nd ed., ed. C. R. Huff. Thousand Oaks, CA: Sage.

Fagan, J., and D. L. Wilkinson. 1998. Guns, youth violence and social identity. *Crime and Justice: An Annual Review of Research* 24. Chicago: University of Chicago Press.

Federal Bureau of Investigation. 2007. Documents online at http://www.fbi.gov/pressrel/speeches/mueller011807.htm; http://www.fbi.gov/page2/jan07/gangs011607.htm.

Federal Bureau of Investigation Uniform Crime Reporting Program. 2002. *Crime in the United States: 2001.* Washington, D.C.: Department of Justice.

Green, J. and K. Pranis. 2007. Gang wars: The failure of enforcement tactics and the need for effective public safety strategies. A Justice Policy Institute Report. Washington, D.C.: Justice Policy Institute.

Gutierrez, A. 2011. deputy public defender, County of Santa Clara, February.

Hagedorn, J. M. Online at http://www.uic.edu/cuppa/gci/bios/facultyfellows/johnhagedorn.htm.

Hagedorn, J. M. 2005. The global impact of gangs. *Journal of Contemporary Criminal Justice* 2 (May).

Hagedorn, J. M. n.d. *Institutionalized gangs and violence in Chicago.* Country Report for the United States, International Study on Children in Organized Armed Violence (COAV). Online at http://www.coav.org.br/.

Hagedorn, J. M., and B. Rauch. 2004. Variations in urban homicide: Chicago, New York City, and global urban policy. Paper presented at the City Futures conference, Chicago, July.

Hagedorn, J. M. 2009. *A World of Gangs, Armed Young Men and Gangsta Culture.* Minneapolis: University of Minnesota Press.

Howell, J. C., and S. H. Decker. 1999. The youth gangs, drugs, and violence connection. *Juvenile Justice Bulletin*(January). Washington, D.C.: Office of Justice Programs, January.

Howell, J. 2007. U.S. Menacing or mimicking? Realities of youth gangs. *Juvenile and Family Court Journal* 58 (2), Spring.

Jackson, A. 2004. *Prosecuting gang cases: What local prosecutors need to know.* Washington, D.C.: American Prosecutors Research Institute, April.

Klein, M. W., and C. L. Maxson. 2006. *Street Gang Patterns and Policies*. New York: Oxford University Press.

Maxson, C., K. Hennigan, and D. Sloane. 2003. For the sake of the neighborhood? Civil gang injunctions as a gang intervention tool in Southern California. In *Policing Gangs and Youth Violence*, ed. S. H. Decker. Belmont, CA: Wadsworth.

Maxson, C. L., K. M. Hennigan, and D. C. Sloane. 2005. It's getting crazy out there: Can a civil gang injunction change a community? *Criminology & Public Policy* 4 (August).

Maxson, C. L., K. J. Woods, and M. W. Klein. 1996. Street gang migration: How big a threat. *National Institute of Justice Journal* (February).

Mays, G. L., (ed) 1997. *Gangs and Gang Behaviour*. Belmont, CA: Wadsworth Publishing.

McGreevy, P. 2007a. L.A. gang prosecutions called overzealous. *Los Angeles Times*, March 29. McGreevy, P. 2007b. Mayor seeks record number of police officers. *Los Angeles Times*, March 30.

National Youth Gang Center. 2006. *National youth gang survey analysis*. Online at http://www.iir.com/nygc/nygsa/ (retrieved May 7, 2007).

Petersen, R. D. 2004. *Understanding Contemporary Gangs in America: An Interdisciplinary Approach*. Upper Saddle River, NJ: Prentice Hall.

Quick, L. 2014. Challenging expert testimony in gang cases. Online at www.sdap.org/downloads/research/criminal/laq14.pdf.

Schmalleger F. 2009. *Criminology Today: An Integrative Introduction*, 5th ed. Upper Saddle River, NJ: Prentice Hall.

Smalley, S. 2006. Hub police sweeps get slim results. *The Boston Globe*, November 26.

Snyder, H. N., and M. Sickmund. 1999. *Juvenile Offenders and Victims: 1999 National Report*. Washington, D.C.: U.S. Dept. of Justice, National Center for Juvenile Justice.

Snyder, H. N., and M. Sickmund. 2006. *Juvenile Offenders and Victims: 2006 National Report*. Washington, D.C.: U.S. Department of Justice, Office of Juvenile Justice and Delinquency Prevention.

Spergel, I. A., K. M. Wa, and R. V. Sosa. 2005a. Evaluation of the San Antonio comprehensive community-wide approach to gang prevention, intervention and suppression program. Research report submitted to U.S. Department of Justice in May.

Spergel, I. A., K. M. Wa, and R. V. Sosa. 2005b. Evaluation of the Bloomington-Normal comprehensive gang program. Research report submitted to U.S. Department of Justice in May.

Spergel, I. A., K. M. Wa, and R. V. Sosa. 2005c. Evaluation of the Tucson comprehensive community-wide approach to gang prevention, intervention and suppression program. Research report submitted to U.S. Department of Justice in May.

Spergel, I. A., K. M. Wa, and R. V. Sosa. 2005d. Evaluation of the Mesa Gang Intervention Program (MGIP). Research report submitted to U.S. Department of Justice in May.

Spergel, I. A., K. M. Wa, and R. V. Sosa. 2005e. Evaluation of the Riverside comprehensive community-wide approach to gang prevention, intervention and suppression program. Research report submitted to U.S. Department of Justice in July.

Spergel, I. A., K. M. Wa, and R. V. Sosa. 2006. The comprehensive, community-wide gang program model: Success and failure. In *Studying Youth Gangs,* eds. J. Short, Jr. and L. A. Hughes. Lanham, MD: AltaMira Press.

State of California, 2009. *Understatement of gang-related homicides 2005–2007.* Sacramento, CA: Department of Justice (DOJ), Office of Gang and Youth Violence Policy (OFYVP), March 24.

Sullivan, M. L. 2005. Maybe we shouldn't study "gangs": Does reification obscure youth violence? *Journal of Contemporary Criminal Justice* 21 (May).

Sullivan, M. 2006. Are "gang" studies dangerous? Youth violence, local context, and the problem of reification. In *Studying Youth Gangs,* eds. J. Short, Jr. and L. A. Hughes. Lanham, MD: AltaMira Press.

Thornberry, T. P. 2001a. Membership in youth gangs and involvement in serious and violent offending. In *The Modern Gang Reader,* 2nd ed., eds. J. Miller, C. L. Maxson, and M. W. Klein. Los Angeles: Roxbury.

Thornberry, T. P. 2001b. Risk factors for gang membership. In *The Modern Gang Reader,* 2nd ed., eds. J. Miller, C. L. Maxson, and M. W. Klein. Los Angeles: Roxbury.

Thornberry, T., D. Huizinga, and R. Loeber. 2004. The causes and correlates studies: Findings and policy implications. *Juvenile Justice Journal* 9 (September).

Thornberry, T., M. D. Krohn, A. J. Lizotte, C. A. Smith, and K. Tobin. 2003. *Gangs and Delinquency in Developmental Perspective.* Cambridge, MA: Cambridge University Press.

Uribe, S. (staff attorney) n.d. *Proving gang offenses and enhancements.* Report to the California Community Access Program. Online at www.capcentral.org/criminal/articles/docs/gangoffenceenhancement.pdf.

U.S. Department of Health and Human Services. 2001. *Youth violence: A report of the surgeon general.* Rockville, MD. Online at http://www.surgeongeneral.gov/library/youthviolence/chapter5/conc5.html#topper.

U.S. Department of Labor, Bureau of Labor Statistics. 2006. *Latest BLS employee turnover rates for year ending August, 2006.* Online at http://www.nobscot.com/survey/index.cfm.

Venkatesh, S. 2003. A note on the social theory and the American street gang. In *Gangs and Society: Alternative Perspectives,* eds. L. Kontos, D. Brotherton, and L. Barrios. New York: Columbia University Press.

Villaraigosa, A. R. (Mayor) 2007. City of Los Angeles gang reduction strategy. Presented April 18.

Wyrick, P. A., and J. C. Howell. 2004. Strategic risk-based response to youth gangs. *Juvenile Justice: Causes and Correlates: Findings and Implications* 9 (September).

Yablonsky. L. 2008. *Gangs in Court.* Tucson, AZ: Lawyers & Judges Publishing Company.

Yoshino, E. R. n.d. *California's Criminal Gang Enhancements: Lessons from Interviews with Practitioners.* Los Angeles: USC's Gould School of Law.

Zimring, F. E. 2007. *The Great American Crime Decline.* New York: Oxford University Press.

Epilogue: Impact of Gangs Prison Population to Parole and Recidivism

DENNIS ALVARADO

The problem of prison overcrowding resulted in a federal court intervention and forced the state of California to examine viable solutions to reduce prison populations. Otherwise, the court would release 40,000 inmates to offset significant civil rights violations.

Correctional research studies argue that the primary factor for prison overcrowding was linked to a high return to custody rates, created by three strikes provisions, inconsistent parole supervision, and lack of community support for parolees. The issue of overcrowding is so critical that California inmates had been transferred to private prisons within and outside of California to relive the pressure on the California Department of Corrections and Rehabilitation (CDCR) and lower costs. In 2010, the Department of Adult Operations (DAPO) had approximately 175,000 parolees on active supervision. The California legislature sought to remedy return-to-custody rates by reducing parole agent to parolee ratios and by hiring more parole agents. CDCR and DAPO promoted the concept of creating lower parole caseloads so that increased parole supervision could become more effective. The outcome of having more parole agents would improve the delivery of services in areas related to drug treatment programs, housing, education, family support, and counseling objectives. CDCR planned to hire hundreds of new parole agents to work on these issues, but was sidetracked because the 2010 fiscal budgets could not sustain this plan.

Parole supervision came under fire from offender advocates, victim rights groups, and antigovernment activists who argued that the DAPO has failed to meet the needs of incarcerated felons, protect the public, and control cost overruns. Critics have no problem in defining how DAPO failed to protect the community. They often point to failed supervision circumstances and question how a convicted sex offender, under supervision, maintained compliance standards while living with a kidnapped victim over an 18-year period and fathering two illegitimate children. They want to comprehend how a discharged parolee was able to kill two female high school students living in Southern California, when he should have been kept in custody for his previous crimes. Critics are not pleased with CDCR's multibillion dollar budget and failed correctional policies.

The supervision of convicted felons requires an intense ability to balance law enforcement needs while providing alternatives to aberrant behavior. Parole supervision is often diminished by government oversight, lack of adequate training, and public support. California parole agents are required to manage their assigned duties and meet operational demands no matter how difficult the task, which is often overwhelmed by bureaucratic indifference and disdain. Most parole caseloads include strategies that consider community intervention objectives, public safety concerns, crisis management, family counseling, and drug and sex offender treatment programs. However, the impact of statutory regulations and policy directives underscores the problem of governmental stakeholders who want efficiency, but fail to provide incentives and support to maintain adequate staffing, training, and integrity.

Parole supervision is not just the process that involves the supervision of violent street gang members, sex offenders, and mentally ill felons. Parole supervision is a difficult and unforgiving job. One mistake can last a lifetime, and most parole agents comprehend that they will be placed under a microscope if things go wrong.

The future of parole rests with the people of California, the legislature, and the courts. Public outrage exists regarding public employees who are often the targets for political reform. The excess in overtime abuse and double dipping has caused a reactionary response by a public that has been impacted by foreclosures, increased taxes, loss of income, and a failed economy. However, the real issue is how society expects to control when it does not support the effort to prevent criminal behavior or provide adequate rehabilitative programs. Parolees are products of their environments, poor schooling, drug abuse, gang mentality, consumerism, mental disorders, and poor socioeconomic status. They have gone through a systematic process of failure, where their families have given up, schools have kicked them out, probation marginalized them, and they found themselves on borrowed time. A significant number of parolees had lived the cycle of going to prison or coming out as part of an accepted ritual. The whole concept of protecting society and creating a change in a human life is so convoluted that the outcome for parole will only become a systematic process of computer programs and numbers crunching, as the pressure to fight for government dollars impacts which program gets support or which does not.

Drawing upon my experience with parole supervision, it seemed quite clear that many parole agents wanted to do a good job. However, there were some parole agents who did not comprehend their duties nor could they comprehend the community in which they were working. Often these agents relied on their experience and culture to marginalize and minimize the communities that they worked with, and they often made judgmental assessments of the parolees and their families. This could be readily observed in how they spoke to parolees and members of their families. Parolees who received this approach in supervision suffered the consequences and could not voice their concerns because they feared retaliation. Some parole agents were so afraid of working in ethnic minority neighborhoods that they would not even do regular home calls without having the police with them as a tool to demonstrate authority. Parolees and their families were treated as second-class citizens and victimized by a systematic process of indifference by parole agents who should not had been given the authority to supervise anyone. The CDCR made a mistake when it allowed managers to hire individuals who had opinions and behaviors linked to classism, racism, and intolerance for authority. It was one of the reasons why recidivism was so constant. The mission of parole was lost and the authoritarian approach won out. The final outcome required invention though the courts. Why would the US Supreme Court take up the case of so many victimized felons who argued successfully that their civil rights had been compromised? The issue of incarceration is that anyone can be sent to prison. No one is immune from justice, and any-one can be convicted of a crime. Regular people can make mistakes, and that should weigh heavy with parole agents and administers. It's the community that cares about how safe it is. It can only be safe when every effort is made to make people whole, as the root cause of indifference, poverty, classicism, and authorize are assessed and overcome.

Appendix A:
Gang Survey

Sex and Criminal Street Gangs

Gregorio Estevane and Mohamad Khatibloo

A questionnaire survey of nearly 100 questions was distributed to nearly 500 teenage males throughout Los Angeles County, of whom most where preidentified as having either been gang affiliated, on the streets or in custody, most of their lives in close proximity to gang members and gang member associates.

The respondents of the survey were anonymous, and no personal information was taken concerning their identities. All indicated knowledge of the Southern California gang lifestyle, whether from Latino, African-American, white, Asian, or other backgrounds.

The survey was conducted in person by a group of individuals supervised by Gregorio Estevane and Mohamad Khatibloo personally observing each person filling out his or her individual surveys.

The survey takers were allowed to make notes on the survey, maps, or any other comments.

Questions were created by Estevane, with the completed survey questions analyzed and produced into the following graphs by Khatibloo.

The survey has clear themes in question groupings related to gang size, numbers, sophistication, drugs, violence, types of violence, getting away with criminal acts, sex, identifiable or nonindefinable gang status, police and government interactions, technology of gangs, and other grouped themes.

Following is a sample of questions and graphed answers that relate to understudied sexual mores of criminal street gangs and is to be the continuing basis for further papers that tie in cutting-edge researchers and other experts in the field.

While we noticed that many chose not to answer all of the questions, the sampling of 500 survey respondents still allowed a look into the mysterious and forbidden world of criminal street gangs.

The Survey

A. Your Age ____

1. What neighborhood were you raised in?

2. What is the highest grade completed?
   7th   8th   9th   10th   11th

3. Do you live with both your mother and father?

4. Do you live with only one parent; which one?

5. How many people live in your household?

6. How many persons work in your household?

7. What is the total gross income of your household?

8. In what religion were you raised?

9. What main gang was in the area in which you were raised?

10. What are all the street boundaries of the gang?

11. What are the rival (enemy) gangs?

12. What are the names of other gangs that are friendly and cooperate?

13. How often do gangs work with other gangs?
    (Never   Sometimes   Often   Always)

14. Does the gang have a bank account?
    (Never   Sometimes   Often   Always)

15. Does the gang keep computer records/photos on the computer?
    (Never   Sometimes   Often   Always)

16. Does the gang use websites, Twitter, My Space, and other social e-sources?
    (Never   Sometimes   Often   Always)

17. Does the gang use GPS, MapQuest?
    (Never   Sometimes   Often   Always)

18. Is the gang involved in check fraud, identity theft, or other white collar crime?
    (Never   Sometimes   Often   Always)

19. How many gang members do you estimate are active in the gang in 2009?

1–25   25–50   75–100   100+   250+   500+   1000+   2000+

20. Does the gang have other cities they operate in or have chapters in?

Yes   No

What other cities?

21. Are you, or were you, a gang member? Yes No

22. How long do gang members usually stay in a gang?

6 mo.–1 y   +1 y   +2 y   +3 y   or more

23. How does a person get into the gang?

24. Can a person get out of the gang if they want? If so, how? Yes No

25. What are some reasons for leaving the gang?

26. How many gang members are men?

(None   Some   Most   All)

27. How many gang members are women?

(None   Some   Most   All)

28. What are the breakdown of age groups (how many for each age group)?

10–12   12–15   15–18   18–21   +21

29. How many different races are in the gang?

1   2   3   4   +5

30. How many of your family members are in the gang?

(None   Some   Most   All)

31. How times have you been arrested?

1   2   3   4   +5

32. How times have your family members been arrested?

1   2   3   4   +5

33. How many of your family members are in jail?

0   1   2   3   4   +5

34. Are any of your brothers, sisters, or family members in a gang?

1   2   3   4   +5

35. Any gays in the gang?
    (None   Some   Most   All)

36. How many on probation?
    (None   Some   Most   All)

37. How many on parole from prison?
    (None   Some   Most   All)

38. How many have never been caught for a crime?
    (None   Some   Most   All)

39. What are the top drugs that are used and sold in the gang?
    (Meth   Crack   Cocaine   Marijuana   LSD   Heroin)

40. How does the gang make money?
    (Drugs   Stealing   Robbery   Extortion (Taxes)   Prostitution)

41. Does the gang have a leader, subleaders, what is the structure?

42. Does the gang have rules or a constitution? Yes No

43. Are there written rules? Yes No

44. What are the rules that you know of?

45. What are the ways you can get into the gang?

46. Must you be jumped into a gang?
    (Never   Sometimes   Often   Always)

47. Can you be born into the gang?
    (Never   Sometimes   Often   Always)

48. Can you be jumped out of the gang?
    (Never   Sometimes   Often   Always)

49. Can you walk away from the gang?
    (Never   Sometimes   Often   Always)

50. Can people who associate with gangs be nongang members?
    (Never   Sometimes   Often   Always)

51. Can people who associate with gangs have the gang tattoo and not be
    a gang member?
    (Never   Sometimes   Often   Always)

52. Can "wanna be" gang members have gang tattoos?

(Never   Sometimes   Often   Always)

53. Are taggers automatically gang members if they tag the gang of their neighborhood?

(Never   Sometimes   Often   Always)

54. Are girls/women leaders and decision makers of gangs?

(Never   Sometimes   Often   Always)

55. What type of work do girls/women do for the benefit of the gang?

56. How many girls are just sexual objects in that gang?

(None   Some   Most   All)

57. How many different sex partners will one have while in the gang life style?

1   2   3   4   5   5+

58. How many members have a sexually transmitted disease(s) (STDs)?

(None   Some   Most   All)

59. How much unprotected sex?

(Never   Sometimes   Often   Always)

60. How much oral sex?

(Never   Sometimes   Often   Always)

61. How much group sex?

(Never   Sometimes   Often   Always)

62. Are women required to have sex to get into a gang?

(Never   Sometimes   Often   Always)

63. How much jail sex?

(Never   Sometimes   Often   Always)

64. Does the role of women/girls change once they have children?

(Never   Sometimes   Often   Always)

65. What happens if homosexual acts are uncovered of a gang member?

66. Are there gay and lesbian gangs?

(None   Some   Most   All)

67. What drugs are used and sold most?

Meth   Crack   Cocaine   Marijuana   LSD   Heroin

68. How much profit of the gang is made from drugs?
    (None   Some   Most   All)

69. How many drug addicts are in the gang?
    (None   Some   Most   All)

70. What drugs are used prior to going to shoot or jump someone?
    Meth   Crack   Cocaine   Marijuana   LSD   Heroin

71. What types of drugs are injected by these gang members?
    Meth   Crack   Cocaine   LSD   Heroin

72. Have many members do you know have died from drugs?
    (None   Some   Most   All)

73. Do women get beat more than men?
    (Never   Sometimes   Often   Always)

74. How many members have been internally killed for being snitches?
    (None   Some   Most   All)

75. How much violence in gangs are related to sexual conflicts of any kind?
    (None   Some   Most   All)

76. Are children of gang members verbally or violently abused?
    (None   Some   Most   All)

77. How many members have been killed by rivals?
    (None   Some   Most   All)

78. How many guns are in the gang?
    (None   Some   Most   All)

79. What types of guns and ammunition?

80. Are women used to lure and kill rival gang members?
    (Never   Sometimes   Often   Always)

81. Are intel and surveillance used prior to killing rivals?
    (Never   Sometimes   Often   Always)

82. Is there any thought about innocent bystanders being shot?
    (Never   Sometimes   Often   Always)

83. Is there an increased desire in using mayhem, hacking limbs, disfiguring rivals?

(Never	Sometimes	Often	Always)

84. How many times do gang members successfully get rid of the victim's body?

(Never	Sometimes	Often	Always)

85. What is the percentage of times gangs get away with murder? _%

86. Is there a gang injunction in your area? Yes No

87. Have innocent people been convicted of violating a gang injunction?

(Never	Sometimes	Often	Always)

88. Do the police know how to tell the difference from an associate, a wanna be, and real gang member?

(Never	Sometimes	Often	Always)

89. Are there incidents of police corruption that you know of, re: having sex with home girls, involved with drugs, taking bribes, or other?

(Never	Sometimes	Often	Always)

90. Circle the agencies that you believe are involved in corrupt incidents.

LAPD	Sheriffs	Probation	Parole	Federal	Local	Agency

91. Have you ever been stopped by police?

(Never	Sometimes	Often	Always)

92. Have the police ever filled out an FI (field information) card on you?

(Never	Sometimes	Often	Always)

93. Do gang members admit to the police they are gang members?

(Never	Sometimes	Often	Always)

94. Do all nicknames/monikers mean you are a gang member?

(Never	Sometimes	Often	Always)

95. What percentage of the time do you think police misidentify a gang member? __%

96. What percentage of the time do you think police correctly identify a gang member? __%

97. Are gang members not getting tattoos, growing their hair out, dressing like others?

    (None   Some   Most   All)

98. Are gang members protected in jails and prisons?

    (Never   Sometimes   Often   Always)

99. Do nongang members get protection in jails or prisons?

    (Never   Sometimes   Often   Always)

100. What is the percentage of nongang members that become gang members in jail? _%

101. What percentage of nongang member taggers become gang members when they go to jail? __%

102. Can prosecutors tell gang from nongang types?

    (Never   Sometimes   Often   Always)

103. Can defense attorneys tell gang from nongang types?

    (Never   Sometimes   Often   Always)

104. Can court gang experts tell gang from nongang types?

    (Never   Sometimes   Often   Always)

105. Can judges tell gang from nongang types?

    (Never   Sometimes   Often   Always)

106. Any comments?

Appendix B: Conclusions from Gang Information Survey

GREGORIO ESTEVANE
MOHAMAD A. KHATIBLOO

According to data secured through the exclusive survey drafted by Estevane and Khatibloo in Appendix A, the following conclusions can be drawn

- It can be realized that there is a near 25 percent chance that people can associate with a gang and not be a gang member.
- According to the survey and its results, it can be secured that 45 percent of taggers who deface/vandalize in gang neighborhoods have no affiliation with the local gang of the neighborhood.
- The survey shows that nearly 40 percent of gangs and gang members utilize some sort of computer for maintaining not only gang-related photographs, but also gang-related documentation.
- The survey further shows that nearly 60 percent of gang members utilize social networking sites, such as Facebook, as well as instant messaging resources, such as Twitter, for their daily communications.
- Our survey shows that 60 percent of reported respondents have admitted to either having had unprotected sex at least once while engaged in the gang, to a reported 25 percent who have advised they routinely have unprotected sex. As a result, nearly 50 percent of the reported respondents admit to having one form of a sexually transmitted disease.
- The survey shows that nearly 25 percent of nongang members have reported that nongang members have tattoos that show affiliation to a gang, yet they are not actual gang members. While nearly 23 percent have reported that those who want to associate themselves with a gang will get a gang-related tattoo while the gang desired will not consider them an affiliate. We also have learned that in only 21 percent of instances does having a gang-related nickname define gang membership. Proving that in nearly 75 percent of gang-type monikers, there is no gang affiliation.

- Nearly 50 percent of respondents have admitted that a person can be born into a gang and not have to complete initiation rituals. While if a gang member does want to leave the gang life, they can be jumped out at a rate of 40 percent.
- Our survey has shown that nearly 75 percent of women who want to join a gang or become affiliates with a gang are required to be "sexed" in, in order to be considered a gang member/affiliate.
- We also learned new information about the rising role of females in gang leadership, in that nearly 30 percent of our respondents admitted that they have encountered female leadership in their gang.
- We learned that the role of a woman in a gang changes at a near 60 percent ratio when she becomes pregnant and becomes a mother.
- Nearly 75 percent of respondents advised that women in a gang are primarily seen as sex objects only.
- Our survey uncovered that the rate of oral sex and group sex in gangs is nearly 50 percent of the time. While this is for outside of incarceration, we learned that gang members in prison are engaging in sexual activity with other males at a rate of nearly 50 percent.
- Nearly 45 percent of respondents admitted that while in the planning of eliminating rivals, intelligence gathering and surveillance techniques are employed to ensure accuracy and delivery of objective. We are seeing a 30 percent increase in desire to have the elimination of the rival be through some extreme violent act, such as hacking limbs, disfigurement, etc. We also have learned that in such rival gang eliminations there is only about a 20 percent chance of concern of innocent civilians being shot or injured. Further, our survey uncovered that gangs are nearly successful to a 70 percent ratio in being able to hide the bodies of their victims.
- Further, we learned that, along with the use of social networking sites, gang members use resources such as MapQuest and GPS devices at or near 65 percent of the time for their routine daily affairs and gang activity.
- Our respondents have advised that in only about 45 percent of the time can prosecutors, defense attorneys, and gang experts signify between gang and nongang types. This ties in well with the ability of police/law enforcement to be able to distinguish between gang and nongang types at a 3 to 1 ratio favoring the gang members.
- The survey also showed that at a rate of nearly 25 percent do taggers either become or consider joining a gang when they are incarcerated.
- Research here has determined that children of gang members are, in fact, either verbally or physically abused at a rate of 75 percent.
- Membership in the gang is not determined by the member, rather by the gang itself, as our survey showed that nearly 60 percent of

respondents admitted that leaving life in the gang is not possible, but in the same series of replies, we discovered that, if 40 percent of respondents were able to leave the gang life, nearly 30 percent do so for family reasons, such as children, "baby momma," etc.

- Our survey has revealed some very key and new information with regard to homosexual activity in the gang, such that nearly 33 percent of respondents advised that there is either homosexual activity in the gang or that a growing number of gang members may in fact be gay.
- Our research has uncovered that nearly 50 percent of gang-related violence is internally centered on sexual conflicts between the gang members.
- Respondents advised that nongang members can associate with gang members at a possible rate of 55 percent and still not be a gang member.
- Although our survey produced a ratio of only about 45 percent of high school graduates, we did learn that about 10 percent of admitted gang members have progressed beyond high school and have even reported attending college courses (5 percent). This ties well into the family structure of gang members in that nearly 85 percent advised that they do not/have not lived with both parents for a period of at least five to seven years. This clearly shows the relationship to the repeated cycle of violence and abuse most likely suffered at the hands of either single parents or other noninvolved caregivers in the gang member's life. Leading further into the increased rate of physical and verbal abuse implemented upon the children of gang members as we revealed in another part of our report.
- The survey also produced concrete data that showed gangs do indeed have a formal constitution or set of rules (75 percent), but that in only 15 percent of the time are these rules written and passed from one member to another.

Selected Questions for the Complete Survey Listed at the End Relating to 'Sex and Gangs'

In your gang, how many members are female?
Are the females in your gang leaders and decision-makers?
What type of work do girls/women do for the benefit of the gang?
How many girls are only sexual objects in that gang?
How many different sex partners will the women have while in the gang lifestyle?
How many members have a sexually transmitted disease(s) (STDs)?
Do they have unprotected sex?
How much oral sex do gang member have?

How much group sex do they participate in?
How often are women required to have sex to get into a gang?
How much jail sex do gang member participate in?
Does the role of women/girls change once they have children?
What happens if homosexual acts are uncovered of a gang member?
Are there gay and lesbian gangs?
How much violence in gangs are related to sexual conflicts?
Are children of gang members verbally or violently abused?
Are women used to lure and kill rival gang members?
Are there incidents of police corruption that you know of, re: having sex
with home girls, involved with drugs, taking bribes or other?

(From Gang Survey. ASTIS Consulting (2013))

Appendix C: California Street Terrorism Enforcement and Prevention Act

California Penal Code Sections 186.20–186.33

186.20
This chapter shall be known and may be cited as the California Street Terrorism Enforcement and Prevention Act.

186.21
The Legislature hereby finds and declares that it is the right of every person, regardless of race, color, creed, religion, national origin, gender, gender identity, gender expression, age, sexual orientation, or handicap, to be secure and protected from fear, intimidation, and physical harm caused by the activities of violent groups and individuals.

It is not the intent of this chapter to interfere with the exercise of the constitutionally protected rights of freedom of expression and association. The Legislature hereby recognizes the constitutional right of every citizen to harbor and express beliefs on any lawful subject whatsoever, to lawfully associate with others who share similar beliefs, to petition lawfully constituted authority for a redress of perceived grievances, and to participate in the electoral process.

The Legislature, however, further finds that the State of California is in a state of crisis, which has been caused by violent street gangs whose members threaten, terrorize, and commit a multitude of crimes against the peaceful citizens of their neighborhoods. These activities, both individually and collectively, present a clear and present danger to public order and safety and are not constitutionally protected. The Legislature finds that there are nearly 600 criminal street gangs operating in California, and that the number of gang-related murders is increasing. The Legislature also finds that in Los Angeles County alone there were 328 gang-related murders in 1986, and that gang homicides in 1987 have increased 80 percent over 1986. It is the intent of the Legislature in enacting this chapter to seek the eradication of criminal activity by street gangs by focusing upon patterns of criminal gang activity and upon the organized nature of street gangs, which together, are the chief source of terror created by street gangs. The Legislature further finds that an effective means of punishing and deterring the criminal activities of street gangs is through forfeiture of the profits, proceeds, and instrumentalities acquired, accumulated, or used by street gangs.

186.22

(a) Any person who actively participates in any criminal street gang with knowledge that its members engage in or have engaged in a pattern of criminal gang activity, and who willfully promotes, furthers, or assists in any felonious criminal conduct by members of that gang, shall be punished by imprisonment in a county jail for a period not to exceed one year, or by imprisonment in the state prison for 16 months, or two or three years.

(b) (1) Except as provided in paragraphs (4) and (5), any person who is convicted of a felony committed for the benefit of, at the direction of, or in association with any criminal street gang, with the specific intent to promote, further, or assist in any criminal conduct by gang members, shall, upon conviction of that felony, in addition and consecutive to the punishment prescribed for the felony or attempted felony of which he or she has been convicted, be punished as follows:

(A) Except as provided in subparagraphs (B) and (C), the person shall be punished by an additional term of two, three, or four years at the court's discretion.

(B) If the felony is a serious felony, as defined in subdivision (c) of Section 1192.7, the person shall be punished by an additional term of five years.

(C) If the felony is a violent felony, as defined in subdivision (c) of Section 667.5, the person shall be punished by an additional term of 10 years.

(2) If the underlying felony described in paragraph (1) is committed on the grounds of, or within 1,000 feet of, a public or private elementary, vocational, junior high, or high school, during hours in which the facility is open for classes or school-related programs or when minors are using the facility, that fact shall be a circumstance in aggravation of the crime in imposing a term under paragraph (1).

(3) The court shall select the sentence enhancement which, in the court's discretion, best serves the interests of justice and shall state the reasons for its choice on the record at the time of the sentencing in accordance with the provisions of subdivision (d) of Section 1170.1.

(4) Any person who is convicted of a felony enumerated in this paragraph committed for the benefit of, at the direction of, or in association with any criminal street gang, with the specific intent to promote, further, or assist in any criminal conduct by gang members, shall, upon conviction of that felony, be sentenced to an indeterminate term of life imprisonment with a minimum term of the indeterminate sentence calculated as the greater of:

(A) The term determined by the court pursuant to Section 1170 for the underlying conviction, including any enhancement applicable under Chapter 4.5 (commencing with Section 1170) of Title 7 of Part 2, or any period pre-scribed by Section 3046, if the felony is any of the offenses enumerated in subparagraph (B) or (C) of this paragraph.

(B) Imprisonment in the state prison for 15 years, if the felony is a home invasion robbery, in violation of subparagraph (A) of paragraph (1) of subdivision (a) of Section 213; car-jacking, as defined in Section 215; a felony violation of Section 246; or a violation of Section 12022.55.

(C) Imprisonment in the state prison for seven years, if the felony is extortion, as defined in Section 519, or threats to victims and witnesses, as defined in Section 136.1.

(5) Except as provided in paragraph (4), any person who violates this subdivision in the commission of a felony punishable by imprisonment in the state prison for life shall not be paroled until a minimum of 15 calendar years have been served.

(c) If the court grants probation or suspends the execution of sentence imposed upon the defendant for a violation of subdivision (a), or in cases involving a true finding of the enhancement enumerated in subdivision (b), the court shall require that the defendant serve a minimum of 180 days in a county jail as a condition thereof.

(d) Any person who is convicted of a public offense punishable as a felony or a misdemeanor, which is committed for the benefit of, at the direction of, or in association with any criminal street gang, with the specific intent to promote, further, or assist in any crimi-nal conduct by gang members, shall be punished by imprisonment in the county jail not to exceed one year, or by imprisonment in the state prison for one, two, or three years, provided that any person sentenced to imprisonment in the county jail shall be imprisoned for a period not to exceed one year, but not less than 180 days, and shall not be eligible for release upon completion of sentence, parole, or any other basis, until he or she has served 180 days. If the court grants probation or suspends the execution of sentence imposed upon the defendant, it shall require as a condition thereof that the defendant serve 180 days in a county jail.

(e) As used in this chapter, "pattern of criminal gang activity" means the commission of, attempted commission of, conspiracy to commit, or solicitation of, sustained juvenile petition for, or conviction of two or more of the following offenses, provided at least one of these offenses occurred after the effective date of this chapter and the last of those offenses occurred within three years after a prior offense, and the offenses were committed on separate occasions, or by two or more persons:

(1) Assault with a deadly weapon or by means of force likely to produce great bodily injury, as defined in Section 245.

(2) Robbery, as defined in Chapter 4 (commencing with Section 211) of Title 8 of Part 1.

(3) Unlawful homicide or manslaughter, as defined in Chapter 1(commencing with Section 187) of Title 8 of Part 1.

(4) The sale, possession for sale, transportation, manufacture, offer for sale, or offer to manufacture controlled substances as defined in Sections 11054, 11055, 11056, 11057, and 11058 of the Health and Safety Code.

(5) Shooting at an inhabited dwelling or occupied motor vehicle, as defined in Section 246.

(6) Discharging or permitting the discharge of a firearm from a motor vehicle, as defined in subdivisions (a) and (b) of Section 12034 until January 1, 2012, and, on or after that date, subdivisions (a) and (b) of Section 26100.

(7) Arson, as defined in Chapter 1 (commencing with Section 450) of Title 13.

(8) The intimidation of witnesses and victims, as defined in Section 136.1.

(9) Grand theft, as defined in subdivision (a) or (c) of Section 487.

(10) Grand theft of any firearm, vehicle, trailer, or vessel.

(11) Burglary, as defined in Section 459.

(12) Rape, as defined in Section 261.

(13) Looting, as defined in Section 463.

(14) Money laundering, as defined in Section 186.10.

(15) Kidnapping, as defined in Section 207.

(16) Mayhem, as defined in Section 203.

(17) Aggravated mayhem, as defined in Section 205.

(18) Torture, as defined in Section 206.

(19) Felony extortion, as defined in Sections 518 and 520.

(20) Felony vandalism, as defined in paragraph (1) of subdivision (b) of Section 594.

(21) Carjacking, as defined in Section 215.

(22) The sale, delivery, or transfer of a firearm, as defined in Section 12072 until January 1, 2012, and, on or after that date, Article 1 (commencing with Section 27500) of Chapter 4 of Division 6 of Title 4 of Part 6.

(23) Possession of a pistol, revolver, or other firearm capable of being concealed upon the person in violation of paragraph (1) of subdivision (a) of Section 12101 until January 1, 2012, and, on or after that date, Section 29610.

(24) Threats to commit crimes resulting in death or great bodily injury, as defined in Section 422.

(25) Theft and unlawful taking or driving of a vehicle, as defined in Section 10851 of the Vehicle Code.

(26) Felony theft of an access card or account information, as defined in Section 484e.

(27) Counterfeiting, designing, using, or attempting to use an access card, as defined in Section 484f.

(28) Felony fraudulent use of an access card or account information, as defined in Section 484g.

(29) Unlawful use of personal identifying information to obtain credit, goods, services, or medical information, as defined in Section 530.5.

(30) Wrongfully obtaining Department of Motor Vehicles documentation, as defined in Section 529.7.

(31) Prohibited possession of a firearm in violation of Section 12021 until January 1, 2012, and, on or after that date, Chapter 2 (commencing with Section 29800) of Division 9 of Title 4 of Part 6.

(32) Carrying a concealed firearm in violation of Section 12025 until January 1, 2012, and, on or after that date, Section 25400.

(33) Carrying a loaded firearm in violation of Section 12031 until January 1, 2012, and, on or after that date, Section 25850.

(f) As used in this chapter, "criminal street gang" means any ongoing organization, association, or group of three or more persons, whether formal or informal, having as one of its primary activities the commission of one or more of the criminal acts enumerated in paragraphs (1) to (25), inclusive, or (31) to (33), inclusive, of subdivision (e), having a common name or common identifying sign or symbol, and whose members individually or collectively engage in or have engaged in a pattern of criminal gang activity.

(g) Notwithstanding any other law, the court may strike the additional punishment for the enhancements provided in this section or refuse to impose the minimum jail sentence for misdemeanors in an unusual case where the interests of justice would best be served, if the court specifies on the record and enters into the minutes the circumstances indicating that the interests of justice would best be served by that disposition.

(h) Notwithstanding any other provision of law, for each person committed to the Division of Juvenile Facilities for a conviction pursuant to subdivision (a) or (b) of this section, the offense shall be deemed one for which the state shall pay the rate of 100 percent of the per capita institutional cost of the Division of Juvenile Facilities, pursuant to Section 912.5 of the Welfare and Institutions Code.

(i) In order to secure a conviction or sustain a juvenile petition, pursuant to subdivision (a), it is not necessary for the prosecution to prove that the person devotes all, or a substantial part, of his or her time or efforts to the criminal street gang, nor is it necessary to prove that the person is a member of the criminal street gang. Active participation in the criminal street gang is all that is required.

(j) A pattern of gang activity may be shown by the commission of one or more of the offenses enumerated in paragraphs (26) to (30), inclusive, of subdivision (e), and the commission of one or more of the offenses enumerated in paragraphs (1) to (25), inclusive, or (31) to (33), inclusive, of subdivision (e). A pattern of gang activity cannot be established solely by proof of commission of offenses enumerated in paragraphs (26) to (30), inclusive, of subdivision (e), alone.

(k) This section shall remain in effect only until January 1, 2014, and as of that date is repealed, unless a later enacted statute, that is enacted before January 1, 2014, deletes or extends that date.

186.22

(a) Any person who actively participates in any criminal street gang with knowledge that its members engage in or have engaged in a pattern of criminal gang activity, and who willfully promotes, furthers, or assists in any felonious criminal conduct by members of that gang, shall be punished by imprisonment in a county jail for a period not to exceed one year, or by imprisonment in the state prison for 16 months, or two or three years.

(b) (1) Except as provided in paragraphs (4) and (5), any person who is convicted of a felony committed for the benefit of, at the direction of, or in association with any criminal street gang, with the specific intent to promote, further, or assist in any criminal conduct by gang members, shall, upon conviction of that felony, in addition and consecutive to the punishment prescribed for the felony or attempted felony of which he or she has been convicted, be punished as follows:

   (A) Except as provided in subparagraphs (B) and (C), the person shall be punished by an additional term of two, three, or four years at the court's discretion.

   (B) If the felony is a serious felony, as defined in subdivision (c) of Section 1192.7, the person shall be punished by an additional term of five years.

   (C) If the felony is a violent felony, as defined in subdivision (c) of Section 667.5, the person shall be punished by an additional term of 10 years.

(2) If the underlying felony described in paragraph (1) is committed on the grounds of, or within 1,000 feet of, a public or private elementary, vocational, junior high, or high school, during hours in which the facility is open for classes or school-related programs or when minors are using the facility, that fact shall be a circumstance in aggravation of the crime in imposing a term under paragraph (1).

(3) The court shall order the imposition of the middle term of the sentence enhancement, unless there are circumstances in aggravation or mitigation. The court shall state the reasons for its choice of sentencing enhancements on the record at the time of the sentencing.

(4) Any person who is convicted of a felony enumerated in this paragraph committed for the benefit of, at the direction of, or in association with any criminal street gang, with the specific intent to promote, further, or assist in any criminal conduct by gang members, shall, upon conviction of that felony, be sentenced to an indeterminate term of life imprisonment with a minimum term of the indeterminate sentence calculated as the greater of:

   (A) The term determined by the court pursuant to Section 1170 for the underlying conviction, including any enhancement applicable under Chapter 4.5 (commencing with Section 1170) of Title 7 of Part 2, or any period prescribed by Section 3046, if the felony is any of the offenses enumerated in subparagraph (B) or (C) of this paragraph.

   (B) Imprisonment in the state prison for 15 years, if the felony is a home invasion robbery, in violation of subparagraph (A) of paragraph (1) of subdivision (a) of Section 213; carjacking, as defined in Section 215; a felony violation of Section 246; or a violation of Section 12022.55.

   (C) Imprisonment in the state prison for seven years, if the felony is extortion, as defined in Section 519; or threats to victims and witnesses, as defined in Section 136.1.

(5) Except as provided in paragraph (4), any person who violates this subdivision in the commission of a felony punishable by imprisonment in the state prison for life shall not be paroled until a minimum of 15 calendar years have been served.

(c) If the court grants probation or suspends the execution of sentence imposed upon the defendant for a violation of subdivision (a), or in cases involving a true finding of the enhancement enumerated in subdivision (b), the court shall require that the defendant serve a minimum of 180 days in a county jail as a condition thereof.

(d) Any person who is convicted of a public offense punishable as a felony or a misdemeanor, which is committed for the benefit of, at the direction of, or in association with any criminal street gang, with the specific intent to promote, further, or assist in any criminal conduct by gang members, shall be punished by imprisonment in the county jail not to exceed one year, or by imprisonment in the state prison for one, two, or three years, provided that any person sentenced to imprisonment in the county jail shall be imprisoned for a period not to exceed one year, but not less than 180 days, and shall not be eligible for release upon completion of sentence, parole, or any other basis, until he or she has served 180 days. If the court grants probation or suspends the execution of sentence imposed upon the defendant, it shall require as a condition thereof that the defendant serve 180 days in a county jail.

(e) As used in this chapter, "pattern of criminal gang activity" means the commission of, attempted commission of, conspiracy to commit, or solicitation of, sustained juvenile petition for, or conviction of two or more of the following offenses, provided at least one of these offenses occurred after the effective date of this chapter and the last of those offenses occurred within three years after a prior offense, and the offenses were committed on separate occasions, or by two or more persons:

(1) Assault with a deadly weapon or by means of force likely to produce great bodily injury, as defined in Section 245.

(2) Robbery, as defined in Chapter 4 (commencing with Section 211) of Title 8 of Part 1.

(3) Unlawful homicide or manslaughter, as defined in Chapter 1 (commencing with Section 187) of Title 8 of Part 1.

(4) The sale, possession for sale, transportation, manufacture, offer for sale, or offer to manufacture controlled substances as

defined in Sections 11054, 11055, 11056, 11057, and 11058 of the Health and Safety Code.

(5)   Shooting at an inhabited dwelling or occupied motor vehicle, as defined in Section 246.

(6)   Discharging or permitting the discharge of a firearm from a motor vehicle, as defined in subdivisions (a) and (b) of Section 12034 until January 1, 2012, and, on or after that date, subdivisions (a) and (b) of Section 26100.

(7)   Arson, as defined in Chapter 1 (commencing with Section 450) of Title 13.

(8)   The intimidation of witnesses and victims, as defined in Section 136.1.

(9)   Grand theft, as defined in subdivision (a) or (c) of Section 487.

(10)   Grand theft of any firearm, vehicle, trailer, or vessel.

(11)   Burglary, as defined in Section 459.

(12)   Rape, as defined in Section 261.

(13)   Looting, as defined in Section 463.

(14)   Money laundering, as defined in Section 186.10.

(15)   Kidnapping, as defined in Section 207.

(16)   Mayhem, as defined in Section 203.

(17)   Aggravated mayhem, as defined in Section 205.

(18)   Torture, as defined in Section 206.

(19)   Felony extortion, as defined in Sections 518 and 520.

(20)   Felony vandalism, as defined in paragraph (1) of subdivision (b) of Section 594.

(21)   Carjacking, as defined in Section 215.

(22)   The sale, delivery, or transfer of a firearm, as defined in Section 12072 until January 1, 2012, and, on or after that date, Article 1 (commencing with Section 27500) of Chapter 4 of Division 6 of Title 4 of Part 6.

(23)   Possession of a pistol, revolver, or other firearm capable of being concealed upon the person in violation of paragraph (1) of subdivision (a) of Section 12101 until January 1, 2012, and, on or after that date, Section 29610.

(24)   Threats to commit crimes resulting in death or great bodily injury, as defined in Section 422.

(25)   Theft and unlawful taking or driving of a vehicle, as defined in Section 10851 of the Vehicle Code.

(26)   Felony theft of an access card or account information, as defined in Section 484e.

(27)   Counterfeiting, designing, using, or attempting to use an access card, as defined in Section 484f.

(28) Felony fraudulent use of an access card or account information, as defined in Section 484g.

(29) Unlawful use of personal identifying information to obtain credit, goods, services, or medical information, as defined in Section 530.5.

(30) Wrongfully obtaining Department of Motor Vehicles documentation, as defined in Section 529.7.

(31) Prohibited possession of a firearm in violation of Section 12021 until January 1, 2012, and, on or after that date, Chapter 2 (commencing with Section 29800) of Division 9 of Title 4 of Part 6.

(32) Carrying a concealed firearm in violation of Section 12025 until January 1, 2012, and, on or after that date, Section 25400.

(33) Carrying a loaded firearm in violation of Section 12031 until January 1, 2012, and, on or after that date, Section 25850.

(f) As used in this chapter, "criminal street gang" means any ongoing organization, association, or group of three or more persons, whether formal or informal, having as one of its primary activities the commission of one or more of the criminal acts enumerated in paragraphs (1) to (25), inclusive, or (31) to (33), inclusive, of subdivision (e), having a common name or common identifying sign or symbol, and whose members individually or collectively engage in or have engaged in a pattern of criminal gang activity.

(g) Notwithstanding any other law, the court may strike the additional punishment for the enhancements provided in this section or refuse to impose the minimum jail sentence for misdemeanors in an unusual case where the interests of justice would best be served, if the court specifies on the record and enters into the minutes the circumstances indicating that the interests of justice would best be served by that disposition.

(h) Notwithstanding any other provision of law, for each person committed to the Division of Juvenile Facilities for a conviction pursuant to subdivision (a) or (b) of this section, the offense shall be deemed one for which the state shall pay the rate of 100 percent of the per capita institutional cost of the Division of Juvenile Facilities, pursuant to Section 912.5 of the Welfare and Institutions Code.

(i) In order to secure a conviction or sustain a juvenile petition, pursuant to subdivision (a), it is not necessary for the prosecution to prove that the person devotes all, or a substantial part, of his or her time or efforts to the criminal street gang, nor is it necessary to prove that the person is a member of the criminal street gang. Active participation in the criminal street gang is all that is required.

(j) A pattern of gang activity may be shown by the commission of one or more of the offenses enumerated in paragraphs (26) to (30), inclusive, of subdivision (e), and the commission of one or more of the offenses enumerated in paragraphs (1) to (25), inclusive, or (31) to (33), inclusive, of subdivision (e). A pattern of gang activity cannot be established solely by proof of commission of offenses enumerated in paragraphs (26) to (30), inclusive, of subdivision (e), alone.

(k) This section shall become operative on January 1, 2014.

186.22a

(a) Every building or place used by members of a criminal street gang for the purpose of the commission of the offenses listed in subdivision (e) of Section 186.22 or any offense involving dangerous or deadly weapons, burglary, or rape, and every building or place wherein or upon which that criminal conduct by gang members takes place, is a nuisance, which shall be enjoined, abated, and prevented, and for which damages may be recovered, whether it is a public or private nuisance.

(b) Any action for injunction or abatement filed pursuant to subdivision (a), including an action filed by the Attorney General, shall proceed according to the provisions of Article 3 (commencing with Section 11570) of Chapter 10 of Division 10 of the Health and Safety Code, except that all of the following shall apply:

  (1) The court shall not assess a civil penalty against any person unless that person knew or should have known of the unlawful acts.

  (2) No order of eviction or closure may be entered.

  (3) All injunctions issued shall be limited to those necessary to protect the health and safety of the residents or the public or those necessary to prevent further criminal activity.

  (4) Suit may not be filed until 30-day notice of the unlawful use or criminal conduct has been provided to the owner by mail, return receipt requested, postage prepaid, to the last known address.

(c) Whenever an injunction is issued pursuant to subdivision (a), or Section 3479 of the Civil Code, to abate gang activity constituting a nuisance, the Attorney General or any district attorney or any prosecuting city attorney may maintain an action for money damages on behalf of the community or neighborhood injured by that nuisance. Any money damages awarded shall be paid by or collected from assets of the criminal street gang or its members. Only members of the criminal street gang who created, maintained, or contributed to the creation or maintenance of the nuisance shall be personally liable for the payment of the damages awarded. In a civil action for damages brought pursuant to this subdivision, the Attorney General, district attorney, or city attorney may use, but is not limited to the use of, the testimony of experts to establish damages suffered by the community or neighborhood injured by the nuisance. The damages recovered pursuant to this subdivision shall be deposited into a separate segregated fund for payment to the governing body of the city or county in whose political subdivision the community or neighborhood is located, and that governing body shall use those assets solely for the benefit of the community or neighborhood that has been injured by the nuisance.

(d) No nonprofit or charitable organization, which is conducting its affairs with ordinary care or skill, and no governmental entity, shall be abated pursuant to subdivisions (a) and (b).

(e) Nothing in this chapter shall preclude any aggrieved person from seeking any other remedy provided by law.

(f) (1) Any firearm, ammunition, which may be used with the firearm, or any deadly or dangerous weapon, which is owned or possessed by a member of a criminal street gang for the purpose of the commission of any of the offenses listed in subdivision (e) of Section 186.22, or the commission of any burglary or rape, may be confiscated by any law enforcement agency or peace officer.

   (2) In those cases where a law enforcement agency believes that the return of the firearm, ammunition, or deadly weapon confiscated pursuant to this subdivision, is or will be used in criminal street gang activity or that the return of the item would be likely to result in endangering the safety of others, the law enforcement agency shall initiate a petition in the superior court to determine if the item confiscated should be returned or declared a nuisance.

   (3) No firearm, ammunition, or deadly weapon shall be sold or destroyed unless reasonable notice is given to its lawful owner if his or her identity and address can be reasonably ascertained. The law enforcement agency shall inform the lawful owner, at that person's last known address by registered mail, that he or she has 30 days from the date of receipt of the notice to respond to the court clerk to confirm his or her desire for a hearing and that the failure to respond shall result in a default order forfeiting the confiscated firearm, ammunition, or deadly weapon as a nuisance.

(4) If the person requests a hearing, the court clerk shall set a hearing no later than 30 days from receipt of that request. The court clerk shall notify the person, the law enforcement agency involved, and the district attorney of the date, time, and place of the hearing.

(5) At the hearing, the burden of proof is upon the law enforcement agency or peace officer to show by a preponderance of the evidence that the seized item is or will be used in criminal street gang activity or that return of the item would be likely to result in endangering the safety of others. All returns of firearms shall be subject to Chapter 2 (commencing with Section 33850) of Division 11 of Title 4 of Part 6.

(6) If the person does not request a hearing within 30 days of the notice or the lawful owner cannot be ascertained, the law enforcement agency may file a petition that the confiscated firearm, ammunition, or deadly weapon be declared a nuisance. If the items are declared to be a nuisance, the law enforcement agency shall dispose of the items as provided in Sections 18000 and 18005.

186.23

This chapter does not apply to employees engaged in concerted activities for their mutual aid and protection, or the activities of labor organizations or their members or agents.

186.24

If any part or provision of this chapter, or the application thereof to any person or circumstance, is held invalid, the remainder of the chapter, including the application of that part or provision to other persons or circumstances, shall not be affected thereby and shall continue in full force and effect. To this end, the provisions of this chapter are severable.

186.25

Nothing in this chapter shall prevent a local governing body from adopting and enforcing laws consistent with this chapter relating to gangs and gang violence. Where local laws duplicate or supplement this chapter, this chapter shall be construed as providing alternative remedies and not as preempting the field.

186.26

(a) Any person who solicits or recruits another to actively participate in a criminal street gang, as defined in subdivision (f) of Section 186.22, with the intent that the person solicited or recruited participate in a pattern of criminal street gang activity, as defined in subdivision (e) of Section 186.22, or with the intent that the person solicited or recruited promote, further, or assist in any felonious conduct by members of the criminal street gang, shall be punished by imprisonment in the state prison for 16 months, or two or three years.

(b) Any person who threatens another person with physical violence on two or more separate occasions within any 30-day period with the intent to coerce, induce, or solicit any person to actively participate in a criminal street gang, as defined in subdivision (f) of Section 186.22, shall be punished by imprisonment in the state prison for two, three, or four years.

(c) Any person who uses physical violence to coerce, induce, or solicit another person to actively participate in any criminal street gang, as defined in subdivision (f) of Section 186.22, or to prevent the person from leaving a criminal street gang, shall be punished by imprisonment in the state prison for three, four, or five years.

(d) If the person solicited, recruited, coerced, or threatened pursuant to subdivision (a), (b), or (c) is a minor, an additional term of three years shall be imposed in addition and consecutive to the penalty prescribed for a violation of any of these subdivisions.

(e) Nothing in this section shall be construed to limit prosecution under any other provision of law.

186.28

(a) Any person, corporation, or firm who shall knowingly supply, sell, or give possession or control of any firearm to another shall be punished by imprisonment pursuant to subdivision (h) of Section 1170, or in a county jail for a term not exceeding one year, or by a fine not exceeding one thousand dollars ($1,000), or by both that fine and imprisonment if all of the following apply:

(1) The person, corporation, or firm has actual knowledge that the person will use the firearm to commit a felony described in subdivision (e) of Section 186.22, while actively participating in any criminal street gang, as defined in subdivision (f) of Section 186.22, the members of which engage in a pattern of criminal activity, as defined in subdivision (e) of Section 186.22.

(2) The firearm is used to commit the felony.

(3) A conviction for the felony violation under subdivision (e) of Section 186.22 has first been obtained of the person to whom the firearm was supplied, sold, or given possession or control pursuant to this section.

(b) This section shall only be applicable where the person is not convicted as a principal to the felony offense committed by the person to whom the firearm was supplied, sold, or given possession or control pursuant to this section.

186.30

(a) Any person described in subdivision (b) shall register with the chief of police of the city in which he or she resides, or the sheriff of the county if he or she resides in an unincorporated area, within 10 days of release from custody or within 10 days of his or her arrival in any city, county, or city and county to reside there, whichever occurs first.

(b) Subdivision (a) shall apply to any person convicted in a criminal court or who has had a petition sustained in a juvenile court in this state for any of the following offenses:
   (1) Subdivision (a) of Section 186.22.
   (2) Any crime where the enhancement specified in subdivision (b) of Section 186.22 is found to be true.
   (3) Any crime that the court finds is gang related at the time of sentencing or disposition.

186.31

At the time of sentencing in adult court, or at the time of the dispositional hearing in the juvenile court, the court shall inform any person subject to Section 186.30 of his or her duty to register pursuant to that section. This advisement shall be noted in the court minute order. The court clerk shall send a copy of the minute order to the law enforcement agency with jurisdiction for the last known address of the person subject to registration under Section 186.30. The parole officer or the probation officer assigned to that person shall verify that he or she has complied with the registration requirements of Section 186.30.

186.32

(a) The registration required by Section 186.30 shall consist of the following:
   (1) Juvenile registration shall include the following:
      (A) The juvenile shall appear at the law enforcement agency with a parent or guardian.
      (B) The law enforcement agency shall serve the juvenile and the parent with a California Street Terrorism Enforcement

and Prevention Act notification, which shall include, where applicable, that the juvenile belongs to a gang whose members engage in or have engaged in a pattern of criminal gang activity as described in subdivision (e) of Section 186.22.

(D) A written statement signed by the juvenile, giving any information that may be required by the law enforcement agency, shall be submitted to the law enforcement agency.

(E) The fingerprints and current photograph of the juvenile shall be submitted to the law enforcement agency.

(2)   Adult registration shall include the following:

(A) The adult shall appear at the law enforcement agency.

(B) The law enforcement agency shall serve the adult with a California Street Terrorism Enforcement and Prevention Act notification, which shall include, where applicable, that the adult belongs to a gang whose members engage in or have engaged in a pattern of criminal gang activity as described in subdivision (e) of Section 186.22.

(C) A written statement, signed by the adult, giving any information that may be required by the law enforcement agency, shall be submitted to the law enforcement agency.

(D) The fingerprints and current photograph of the adult shall be submitted to the law enforcement agency.

(a) Within 10 days of changing his or her residence address, any person subject to Section 186.30 shall inform, in writing, the law enforcement agency with whom he or she last registered of his or her new address. If his or her new residence address is located within the jurisdiction of a law enforcement agency other than the agency where he or she last registered, he or she shall register with the new law enforcement agency, in writing, within 10 days of the change of residence.

(b) All registration requirements set forth in this article shall terminate five years after the last imposition of a registration requirement pursuant to Section 186.30.

(c) The statements, photographs and fingerprints required under this section shall not be open to inspection by any person other than a regularly employed peace or other law enforcement officer.

(d) Nothing in this section or Section 186.30 or 186.31 shall preclude a court in its discretion from imposing the registration requirements as set forth in those sections in a gang-related crime.

186.33

(a) Any person required to register pursuant to Section 186.30 who knowingly violates any of its provisions is guilty of a misdemeanor.

(b) (1) Any person who knowingly fails to register pursuant to Section 186.30 and is subsequently convicted of, or any person for whom a petition is subsequently sustained for a violation of, any of the offenses specified in Section 186.30, shall be punished by an additional term of imprisonment in the state prison for 16 months, or two or three years. The court shall select the sentence enhancement, which, in the court's discretion, best serves the interests of justice and shall state the reasons for its choice on the record at the time of sentencing in accordance with the provisions of subdivision (d) of Section 1170.1.

  (2) The existence of any fact bringing a person under this subdivision shall be alleged in the information, indictment, or petition, and be either admitted by the defendant or minor in open court, or found to be true or not true by the trier of fact.

(c) This section shall remain in effect only until January 1, 2014, and as of that date is repealed, unless a later enacted statute, that is enacted before January 1, 2014, deletes or extends that date.

186.33

(a) Any person required to register pursuant to Section 186.30 who knowingly violates any of its provisions is guilty of a misdemeanor.

(b) (1) Any person who knowingly fails to register pursuant to Section 186.30 and is subsequently convicted of, or any person for whom a petition is subsequently sustained for a violation of, any of the offenses specified in Section 186.30, shall be punished by an additional term of imprisonment in the state prison for 16 months, or two or three years. The court shall order imposition of the middle term unless there are circumstances in aggravation or mitigation. The court shall state its reasons for the enhancement choice on the record at the time of sentencing.

  (2) The existence of any fact bringing a person under this subdivision shall be alleged in the information, indictment, or petition, and be either admitted by the defendant or minor in open court, or found to be true or not true by the trier of fact.

(c) This section shall become operative on January 1, 2014.

Index

For Product Safety Concerns and Information please contact our EU
representative GPSR@taylorandfrancis.com Taylor & Francis Verlag GmbH,
Kaufingerstraße 24, 80331 München, Germany

Printed and bound by CPI Group (UK) Ltd, Croydon, CR0 4YY
01/05/2025
01858337-0004